U0512506

本书系国家社科基金重大项目
"军民融合战略下海上通道安全法治保障研究"
（18ZDA155）阶段性研究成果。

国际法与涉外法治文库

上海高水平高校（学科）建设项目资助
上海高水平地方高校创新团队"中国特色社会主义涉外法治体系研究"项目

沿海运输权法律问题研究

Current Issues of Maritime Cabotage Law

马得懿——著

上海人民出版社

目录
CONTENTS

绪　论

一

　　某种意义上，本专著的最终成稿属于典型的"教学相长"式科研成果。自从在华东政法大学任职以来，笔者长期从事涉海领域包括海商法和国际海洋法的教学和科研工作。在承担华东政法大学国际航运法方向研究生授课任务过程中，笔者有意识开设了若干涉海法律前沿专题。其中，沿海运输权法律问题被列为重要的专题之一。就沿海运输权法律问题而言，前人研究成果中的具有较大学术影响力的中文文献比较少。相对于中文文献而言，西方学者关于沿海运输权的研究（一般为英文文献）比较系统深入，形成了非常丰富的研究成果。其中，由阿尼坎·阿克潘（Aniekan Akpan）完成的 *Maritime Cabotage Law* 一书以庞大的体系探讨了沿海运输权的含义、理论来源、立法模式、形态以及各国的立法，是一部具有很大影响力的沿海运输权法律和政策问题的专著。在教学过程中，笔者高度重视该文献的重要学术价值，鼓励和引导研究生展开专题研讨，在授课中以读书会形式要求同学们以某一视角形成学术"读后感"。特别是华东政法大学 2021 级国际航运法研究方向的十多位研究生积极展开专题研究，尤其在搜集和检索沿海运输权判例基础上，同学们克服疫情带来的困扰，积极展开线上判例研习和研讨。其中，徐皓铖同学、李雨函同学、洪临瑞同学分别下载、搜集、梳理了保护主义沿海运输权、自由主义沿海运输权，以及灵活主义沿海运输权的相关立法和经典判例。何珊同学、韩孟琪同学、回珉同学、梁春谐同学、么炳乔同学以及王雨昕同学分别整理了关于各国实施沿海运输权的立法改革资料。韩轶同学、王文瑾同学以及赵诣同学分别从数据库下载并整理关于沿海运输权在各国的实施情况。同学们学术思想碰撞，形成很多富有创新性的观点或想法。这些教学中的学术活动为本研究成果的形成积累了丰富的学术素材。本书部分关涉沿海运输权的争端和判例，也来自该专著。某种角度上，本书中某些学术观点的形成和提炼是笔者与学生之间学术思想碰撞的结果。

长此以往，笔者对于沿海运输权法律问题的体会日益细腻和深入。同时，通过对阿尼坎·阿克潘所著的 *Maritime Cabotage Law* 一些观点，不再"惟命是从"，而日渐融入了自己的学术思考。诸如，制约沿海运输权的因素除了国家主权、发展观念以及经济竞争因素以外，是否还存在其他重要的因素制约沿海运输权的立法和政策的形成？沿海运输权的私法基础是什么？就中国的沿海运输权立法和政策而言，是否存在基于中国本土实践而催生具有中国本土色彩的沿海运输权呢？这些问题不断激发笔者的学术思考。非常幸运的是，2018年笔者作为首席专家的国家社科基金重大项目"军民融合战略下海上通道安全法治保障研究"获得立项，笔者将沿海运输权问题融入国家社科基金重大项目下的子课题的研究任务之中，使得前期笔者对于该问题的思考上升到更高的学术层面。故此，某种意义上，本书既是笔者教学活动中受益于"教学相长"的结晶，也是笔者承担国家社科基金重大项目的重要阶段性研究成果。

二

某种意义上看，沿海运输权属于历史悠久的海洋运输法律和政策。沿海运输权法律和政策问题，基于不同国家的实践，形成了多元沿海运输权的政策和立法。沿海运输权形成的根本渊源，在于拥有漫长和复杂海岸线的沿海国认识到一个强大的沿海运输对于国家安全保障的重要性，并且在长期的沿海运输实践中意识到沿海国对于该国沿海海域进行监管的必要性和重要性。故此，各个沿海国逐渐形成了具有一定差异性的沿海运输权的法律和政策，进而保障自己的国家利益。这导致各国采取某种特定形式的沿海运输制度以确保其沿海贸易的持续发展能力。①通过考察世界各沿海国家已确定沿海运输权的不同立法和监管制度，基本上可以界分为保护主义沿海运输权、自由主义沿海运输权以及灵活主义沿海运输权。②当然，每一种沿海运输权立法和政策的形成，都是各个国家的具体沿海运输国情决定的。事实上，并不存在最佳的沿海运输权制度。但是，就某一沿海国而言，该国实施何种沿海运输权政策与法律，则是该国基于本国利益最大化的一种选择和考量。这通常取决于该国沿海运输实际的特点和能力。一般地，诸多沿海国所实施的沿海运输权政策都是为了如何平衡和协调外国航运和国内航运的竞争利益而制定的。一国所实施的沿海运输权政策意味着该国主动引入外国航运业的竞争力量，进而以最佳的市场价格提供海运服务。然而，另外一些沿海国则以国家主权为借口或考量，则对于沿海运输权实施排斥外国航运业的政策，进而以高于全球市场的价格提供海运服务。③这就是所谓的沿海运输权立法的自由主义（温和派）和保护主义（严厉派）之争。

　　自由主义沿海运输权被认为是对自由市场竞争至关重要的政策，因为它消除了阻碍市场自由互动的障碍。当然，也有许多国家将沿海运输政策视为属于该国国内运输政策的组成部分，适用统一的法律与政策。这是一种比较保守的沿海运输权政策。对于这类国家来说，沿海运输权被赋予本国的船舶公司、船舶或者船员，施行比较严格的沿海运输权监管制度。一般地，实施保护主义的沿海运输权的沿海国不情愿与外国展开开放沿海运输权的谈判，认为沿海运输权构成国内运输业的有机组成部分，而与外国

---

① Aniekan Akpan, *Maritime Cabotage Law*, New York: Routledge 2019, p.2.

② W. Oyedemi(2012), "Cabotage Regulations and the Challenges of Outer Continental Shelf Development in the United States", *Houston Journal of International Law*, 34(3), 607—651.

③ K. Magee, "U.S. Cabotage Laws: Protective or Damaging? A Strategy to Improve Cruise Vessel Competitiveness and Traffic to U.S. Ports" *Monterey Institute of International Studies*, 2002.

无关。当然，一些国家开始审视和反思过于保守的沿海运输权政策带来的负面影响，而开始逐渐尝试趋于灵活和自由的沿海运输权政策。[①]作为连接国内贸易和国际贸易的领域，各个沿海国家日益意识到维持比较灵活的沿海运输权政策的优势。

海运业具有天然的垄断属性，对于一个国家而言具有多重意义。一国所奉行的沿海运输权政策，意味着该国在沿海运输业领域执行的法律和政策取向。无论沿海运输权政策是针对本国航运业而实施，还是针对外国航运业对本国的影响而实施，沿海运输权都将不可避免地对国内航运业和国际航运业产生很大的影响。因此，有学者认为，沿海运输权政策应该不仅是国内关注的问题，而且也是国际法范畴意义的重要问题。[②]

事实上，沿海运输权的适用范围不断扩大，必然促使不同的国家可能会根据其国内运输产业的需求，采取灵活多样的沿海运输权政策。以一国的造船业政策为例，不同国家对其所持有的政策存在不同，而一些国家在考量该国的沿海运输权政策时，通常将造船业因素纳入其中，而某些国家则相反。通常而言，一国的造船业可能被认为是海洋运输业的一部分，可能被认为是该国工业体系制造业的一部分，可能被认为是国家安全的国防能力的一部分。比如，美国认为造船业是其航运业和国防能力的一部分。然而，加拿大却将造船业视为其制造业的一部分。[③]此外，一些沿海国的沿海运输立法法关于沿海运输权予以改革和革新，这主要是基于本国沿海运输业具体情境而做出考量。诸如，这些国家的相关立法规定，用于执行沿海运输权的船舶必须在东道国建造，或者相关立法还要求船舶高级船员受

---

① J. Chuah(2013)，"Short Sea Shipping：The Blue Belt Package"，*Journal of International Maritime Law*，19(1)，256—258.

② G. Oduntan，"International Laws and the Discontented：Westernisation, the Development and the Underdevelopment of International Laws"，in A. Dhanda and A. Parashar(eds)，*Decolonisation of Legal Knowledge*，Taylor & Francis 2009.

③ J. Lalor，"Coasting Trade" *Cyclopaedia of Political Science*，*Political Economy*，*and of the Political History of the United States*(Maynard，Merrill，& Co. 1881).

雇应该优先考虑本国国民。①

在某些沿海国立法中，往往将诸如勘探、水文测量和其他地震测量活动等服务，也纳入该国的沿海运输权立法体系之中。这体现出沿海运输权立法法领域不断扩张的趋势，导致沿海运输权的内涵逐渐脱离了通常意义上的沿海运输权范畴。②故此，建立一个充分顾及国家主权、商业安全和经济发展概念的沿海运输权法律体系或者框架是有充分理由的。③如前所述，一个沿海国所采取的沿海运输政策通常是基于该国主权和经济发展状况而决定的，而沿海运输权的立法与政策，通常涵盖了船舶建造、船舶所有权、船舶登记以及船员雇佣等因素。为此，本书在考察主要航运国家沿海运输权立法与政策基础上，对主要沿海运输权模式给予分类。

作为一项重要的航运政策和法律工具，沿海国通过实施沿海运输权保护主义、自由主义和灵活主义的不同路径，来维持一个强大而可持续的沿海国沿海运输体制的运作。沿海运输权适用于诸如岛屿之间的运输、岛屿与大陆之间的运输、大陆国家沿海运输以及内河运输等领域，在特定国家如美国，还存在大湖水域的运输等。与此同时，沿海运输权的准入政策存在很大差异性。

学理上对沿海运输权立法与政策的解读，通常会在特定理论框架之下展开，诸如基于经济发展理论框架、国家主权理论框架。这些理论强调一个理想的沿海运输权制度应该能够为沿海国提供多样化的海洋经济发展机遇，进而可以确保持续提供促进国家经济发展的理论支撑。有证据表明，适当的沿海运输权立法和政策有助于沿海国国内航运服务市场的发展。然而，由于不同国家对其领海的控制程度存在很大差异，尤其是各国对于领

---

① W. Oyedemi(2012)，"Cabotage Regulations and the Challenges of Outer Continental Shelf Development in the United States"，*Houston Journal of International Law*，34(3)，607—651.

② J. Hoffmann(2001)，"Maritime Cabotage Services: Prospects and Challenges"，Bulletin on Trade Facilitation and Transport in Latin America and the Caribbean(FAL Bulletin)，183(11)，1—7.

③ J. Lewis(2013)，"Veiled Waters: Examining the Jones Act's Consumer Welfare Effect"，*Issues in Political Economy*，22(1)，77—107.

海的无害通过权的态度存在分歧，引发各国所实施的沿海运输权政策的监管也存在很大迥异。从国际海洋秩序的理论层面上审视，早在 17 世纪，荷兰人格劳秀斯积极倡导海洋自由论，与英国塞尔登所提出的闭海论展开针锋相对的辩论，这也昭示着无边无际的海洋不应该向所有人开放的思潮。然而，海上运输历来被认为是一种国际性的冒险活动，最理想的状态是减少对其干扰性监管。事实上，不同国家很可能采取相同的沿海运输权政策，但是，其动机和目的却不尽相同。以美国和巴西所实施的沿海运输政策为例，美国的沿海运输权政策秉承保护主义态度，其目的在于重视美国的国家安全和海事劳工利益的保护。而巴西的沿海运输权政策奉行保护主义，其目的在于促进国家经济发展的需要。故此，沿海运输权既没有正确的，也没有错误的，更没有一个放之四海而皆准的沿海运输权模式。但是，这并不意味着一个国家可以随心所欲设计该国的沿海运输权立法和政策。

三

如前文所述，沿海运输权是复杂的。因此，清楚地了解沿海运输权的体系和范畴等是非常必要的。之所以沿海运输权问题具有体系性，主要是沿海运输权与沿海国主权、主权权利、国家经济发展、国家安全以及自由化等问题互为关联。主权是一个基础性问题，失去国家主权作为基础，任何沿海国家都无法行使沿海运输权。主权在沿海运输权政策上的主要体现，是沿海国有权在不受第三国干扰的情况下，制定该国在领海内的所有海上活动，包括沿海运输权政策，这种绝对控制的例外是外国船舶享有无害通过权。①

除了具有主权属性的领海以外，每个沿海国家都有使用和探索被划分为毗连区和专属经济区的海洋权利。这些海域通常分别距离沿海国 24 海里和 200 海里。值得关注的是，主权权利并没有赋予沿海国这些海域的绝对

---

① Aniekan Akpan(2019)，*Maritime Cabotage Law*，New York：Routledge，pp.3—6.

控制权。相反，它们允许所有相邻的沿海国家共同使用和勘探该海域。与此同时，一个国家所采用的沿海运输权模式其本质在于促进国内经济水平的发展。当然，正如前述，许多国家都实施严格的沿海运输法，主要理由是沿海运输权对于国家安全的至关重要。事实上，传统沿海运输权蕴含着一个相当朴素的理念，即如果沿海国能够禁止外国船舶在本国沿海水域航行或者活动，那么，就可以避免外国对沿海国本国的国家安全构成威胁。实际上，这种早期的关于沿海运输权的理念具有一定的幼稚性。

　　一国所实施的沿海运输权的宽严模式，必然反映出是否属于保护主义，抑或是自由主义的模式。一国实施的沿海运输权，经常被从贸易保护主义和自由主义的角度看待。尽管沿海运输权具有更深层次的问题，其已经超越了贸易政策的范畴。然而，考虑到各国对沿海运输的不同立法和政策，沿海运输权的体系性和复杂性是显而易见的。例如，一个典型的沿海运输权的保护主义，其鲜明的特征是用于沿海贸易和服务的船舶必须在本国国内建造，船舶在本国登记并由本国国籍的公民所拥有，雇佣本国船员并在本国注册。这实质上是防止外国人在该国沿海水域从事海上活动。美国是实施这种保护主义的沿海运输权的代表国家。而典型的沿海运输权自由主义是允许国内外实体在沿海水域自由航行或竞争。南非和新西兰是实行沿海运输权自由主义的代表国家。然而，欧盟所实施的沿海运输权则具有鲜明的特色，其尚不属于典型的自由主义。这是因为，欧盟所实施的沿海运输权从区域角度运作的，而不是一个主权国家可以效仿的。①同时，欧盟所实施的沿海运输权政策只适用于欧盟成员国内部之间，而对于第三国而言，这没有内部成员国的"自由"。故此，可以说欧盟的沿海运输权在某种程度上对非成员国而言，属于一种"保护主义"。

四

　　建设上海国际航运中心是我国的重大国家战略。为了维护和巩固上海

---

　　① A. Akpan(2014)，"A Precarious Judicial Interpretation of the Scope of EU Maritime Cabotage Law"，*Journal of International Maritime Law*，20(6)，444—447.

国际航运中心的战略地位，我国交通运输部门和上海市人民政府不断探索和创新航运政策和举措。其中，开展集装箱货物运输的沿海捎带业务是这些创新举措之一，这是一项与沿海运输权的立法与政策息息相关的举措。航运政策创新是我国自由贸易试验区创新制度中的重要组成部分。目前，我国船舶悬挂方便旗盛行，根据法律大量中资非五星旗船舶不能从事沿海捎带业务，由此导致我国进出口货物选择在境外港口中转。根据《中国（上海）自由贸易试验区总体方案》，允许中资公司拥有或控股拥有的非五星旗船，先行先试外贸进出口集装箱在国内沿海港口和上海港之间的沿海捎带业务。此谓沿海捎带试点政策。中远集装箱运输有限公司"中远泗水轮"从上海港捎带货物驶往天津、青岛两港口。这是我国首次试行中资非五星红旗船沿海捎带业务。

实施沿海捎带试点政策是否会带来"政策红利"？实施沿海捎带试点政策，旨在吸引我国沿海港口货物回国中转，拓展上海国际航运中心的服务功能，有效降低海运物流成本，促进航运业节能减排。沿海捎带试点政策实施后，渴望达到"一石三鸟"的政策效应：提高货主商品的市场竞争力、提升航运公司的航线舱位利用率、增强港口的货物集聚能力。从政策角度来说，沿海捎带政策打开了中国沿海运输市场的封闭闸门，集装箱班轮运输的国内市场和国际市场是否合并，成为多方博弈的焦点。沿海捎带业务政策将造成国内港口集装箱运输量转移，甚至本港集装箱可能被转运到其他港口中转，从而对本港的干线航班发展产生不利影响。同时，直接冲击我国内贸航运企业和运输产业从业人员的就业。

沿海运输权政策的严与宽、管制抑或放开并不是一成不变的。一般而言，以1920年《琼斯法案》为代表的美国沿海运输权比较严格，而且鲜有修订。该法案体系比较复杂，从造船、船旗悬挂、船舶登记、船员雇佣以及税收等方面，限制外国船队运力介入美国的国内航运市场。由于与国内水路运输直接相关的经济活动对美国经济贡献很大，因此该法案在促进美国的就业、国家安全、贸易竞争力、船舶工业、军事保障和补救以及交通顺畅方面，发挥了积极的法律效应；而欧盟基于政治上的互信、地缘上特征相近等因素使然，形成了区域性的开放式沿海运输权。即便是美国《琼斯法案》，也因第一次世界大战的缘故而暂停实施。美国国会于 1914 年 8 月 8 日不得不由于战争的缘故而改变《琼斯法案》的实施。自 1935 年，《琼斯法案》一度在符合某些条件的前提下或者更加严格，或者适当开放。可见，一国通常会基于自身情况，实施更加严格或相对开放的沿海运输权政策。通过对我国《海商法》第 4 条的解读，不难推断出《海商法》下的沿海运输权应属于一种比较开放的形态。《中华人民共和国国际海运条例》第 28 条第 2 款显示，我国实施严格的沿海运输权政策。由于现代航运市场形态多元化趋势日益显著，各种商业合作频出，如何界定外国国际船舶运输经营者，是否属于"中资航运公司利用全资或控股拥有的非五星旗国际航行船舶"的经营者范畴，需进一步的解释和认定。20 世纪 90 年代，根据当时交通部发布的《关于同意国际班轮公司在我国沿海主要港口之间调运空集装箱的函》，允许国际班轮公司在我国沿海港口调拨空集装箱。这种业务即所谓的"捎带空箱"业务。"捎带空箱"业务为"捎带重箱"业务的开展奠定了基础和前提。开展"捎带重箱"业务，主要目的在于扭转我国外贸货物流失境外港口的局面，充分利用支线班轮的闲置运力优化航线布局，以实现降低干线班轮的营运成本，提升我国中转港口竞争力的目的。沿海捎带试点政策并非一个单纯的问题，它与船舶登记、国家安全以及国家间政治互信具有关联度。随着航运业的发展，航运公司之间的相互合作愈加普遍，同时，船舶大型化加剧航运公司联盟化趋势。因此，实施沿海捎带业务政策具有系统性，必须与船舶登记制度协调一致。作为一项古老而传统的航运政策，沿海运输权历来与国家的安全和政治理念夹杂在一起。欧盟沿海运输权的开放与欧盟政治和经济一体化发展同步，其内部开放沿海运输权是在经历 40 余年发展的基础上提出的。

　　沿海运输权政策的实施，彰显了国家安全理念和政治互信的高度融合与重视。目前，中日韩三国沿海运输权的开放程度不同，三国之间能否解决好政治互信、政策基础和国家安全问题，是制约沿海运输权能否开放的重要因素。本书认为，应谨慎看待沿海捎带试点政策，我国应对该政策进行国家立法的顶层设计。同时，在现阶段充分认识到沿海捎带业务绝非一个孤立的政策，它不仅涉及海商法典的完善，更关涉国际海运条例、船舶登记条例，以及水路运输管理条例等法律，是一个互相制约的体系。第一，沿海捎带政策涉及价值判断和抉择的问题。我国航运业软实力不足、软环境亟待优化、海员群体庞大、沿海运输和内河水域航运水平不高、与周边国家存在海洋争议。这些复杂因素决定了我国选择偏重管制的沿海运输权的合理性，符合我国的基本航运业国情。沿海捎带业务政策的试点实施，需要细化诸如船舶登记、中资航运公司的认定等问题。在强化管制色彩的沿海运输权同时，也要以沿海捎带业务等多种形式来丰富沿海运输权的模式和内涵，构建灵活、适度开放以及多元的沿海运输权模式。第二，不能简单机械地复制或模仿美国或欧盟的做法。作为一项传统航运政策，沿海运输权不是一成不变的，其法律内涵与外延因国情和历史阶段的不同而存有变迁。美国《琼斯法案》的变迁历史就是一个有力证明。近期，美国积极修订能源法案，以鼓励沿海运输和船舶所有人扩张船队规模，并且允许国内船舶公司利用美国建设资本基金（CCF），新建集装箱滚装船用于沿海和五大湖区的运输。欧盟是主张废除《琼斯法案》的重要力量，原因是欧洲国家的海运实力较强，他们希望更多国家和地区放开沿海运输权，进而从中获益。第三，积极调整我国的海运业结构，提高海运竞争力。我国拥有丰富的国内和国际航运资源，应该统筹配置各种类型的航运资源和力量。探索以提高远洋运输量带动海运服务贸易出口额增加的法律机制，积极优化与运力结构和货物贸易的运输需求相适应的体制和机制。第四，政策倾斜发展沿海运输体系。鼓励扩张从事沿海运输船队的规模，增加港口投资；基于环境保护和陆运成本增加的因素考量，认真探索沿海运输服务新模式和新手段。[1]

---

① 马得懿：《谨慎审视沿海捎带试点政策》，《中国社会科学报》2015 年 5 月 13 日。

第1章 沿海运输权的属性、演进与模式

第一节 沿海运输权的属性

一、沿海运输权含义的学理阐释

学者对于沿海运输权属性的理解并不完全一致。故此，各国的沿海运输权的理论与实践也是存在很大差异性。一般地，沿海运输权作为一种立法和航运政策，其被认为是一个主权国家将其沿海内两个或多个港口（地点）之间的全部或部分海上活动（运输或其他海上活动）授权本国商业机构的立法或者政策。通常而言，本国商业机构，意指是指本国海上运输实体或者与海上运输有关的实体，通常包括海员、岸上人员、船舶登记机构以及造船厂等基础设施机构。

然而，沿海运输权在各类海洋运输等商业活动中包含更广泛的含义。有学者认为，在这种情况下，它是指一个国家的两个港口在同一海岸线或不同海岸线之间的海上贸易，只要不同的海岸是作为统一的政治和地理单元国家的海岸。[①]事实上，不仅学者在研究文献中对于沿海运输权的阐释存在争议，而且各国实施沿海运输权的实践也是不同的。这主要是由于沿海运输权的立法和政策制定，主要取决于各国的沿海运输实际情况，以及本国的沿海运输利益因素。各国实施沿海运输权的实践表明，比较复杂的海

---

① L. Oppenheim(1908)，"The Meaning of Coasting-trade in Commercial Treaties"，*Law Quarterly Review*，4(1)，328—330.

岸线造成各国沿海运输具体情境不同。而某些国家诸如美国，不仅其东部海岸线和西部海岸线构成沿海运输，而且美国大陆与夏威夷等远离大陆的岛屿之间的运输，也构成沿海运输。[1]这导致沿海运输权的理论无法涵盖所有沿海运输权的实践。当然，学者的观点和国家的立法只是沿海运输实践的部分反映，其并非能涵盖沿海运输权的全貌。

无论如何，沿海运输权的适用不仅受制于国际法，而且也受制于现代贸易运输的发展，这导致沿海运输权的定义和范围不断得到演变。这也彰显出沿海运输权本身的复杂性和发展性。根据 1982 年《联合国海洋法公约》第 2 条，沿海国有权限制外国竞争者在本国海岸线之间港口进行沿海运输服务。但是，各个沿海国在理解该公约第 2 条的含义存在不同的解释，导致其含义具有不确定性。为此，早在 1921 年的巴塞罗那会议上，当时的国际联盟相关会议认为，一个主权国家应有权使用本国船舶将货物和乘客从一个港口运到另一个港口。而这项权利的行使条件是有关的两个港口处于同一个国家的主权之下。同样，1923 年在日内瓦制定的《国际海港制度公约》呼应了这一立场，认为沿海运输权的范围应限制在一国的两个港口之间的航行活动。[2]当然，这不是僵硬不变的。

沿海运输权的含义和范围因不同的沿海运输情境而不同。即便是有相关的国际法规则和相对成熟的国家实践，沿海国在解释其含义和范围，也是具有差别的。人们普遍认为，每个沿海国家都有权对邻近其海岸的一定范围海域拥有主权，一般称为领海。在国际法视阈下，一个沿海国距离海岸线一定范围的水域的法律地位是相对稳定和成熟的。然而，当沿海国根据本国需要而实施沿海运输权时，沿海运输权的立法目的变得复杂。[3]在许多沿海国，该国所实施的沿海运输权立法被应用于船舶建造、海洋运输公司设立、海洋经济发展、国家安全甚至海上移民等领域的活动。这催生了

---

① W. Preiser(1984), "History of The Law of Nations: Ancient Times To 1648", in R. Bernhardt(ed.), *Encyclopedia of Public International Law*, 7(1), pp.132—159.

② Article 9 of the Convention and Statute of the International Regime of Maritime Ports 1923.

③ C. Alexandrowicz, *An Introduction to the History of the Law of Nations in the East Indies*, Clarendon Press 1967.

沿海运输权的适用范围不断扩大。

在初略探讨沿海运输权含义的基础上，本书认为有必要对沿海运输权和海洋划界进行简略的区分。某些情况下，海洋划界而产生的问题会与沿海运输权构成一定的关联性。由于各国对于沿海海域的主权问题表现出相当的敏感，因此，在制定沿海运输权立法和政策时，对于沿海主权概念的适用也是相当谨慎。这是沿海运输权和海洋划界互为关联的主要原因。1982 年《联合国海洋法公约》作为"海洋宪章"，其承认沿海国对于领海、毗连区、专属经济区和大陆架具有主权或主权权利，虽然这些国际法体制具有很大的争议。[①]

许多海域涉及海洋划界争端，这导致世界上存在很多重叠海域，即因为海岸相邻或相向的海域为两个以上沿海国主张主权或主权权利。虽然沿海运输权与海洋划界分别属于两个不同类别或属性的问题，但是却也存在因为海洋划界争端而影响某个沿海国沿海运输权的立法和政策的实施。当然，这样的冲突比较鲜见。

二、沿海运输权的特征

很多因素构成沿海国实施沿海运输权的立法和政策的关键。其实，关于这一点被学者称之为沿海运输权的特征。沿海运输权的制度动机，主要侧重于作为一项规制沿海运输的立法或政策，其有别于其他海洋运输立法或政策而具有的属性。本书认为，可以通过不同的途径或手段来描述不同国家的沿海运输法的体制，进而探究其特征。绝大多数沿海国是通过满足实施沿海运输权的条件来展示该国所实施沿海运输权的特征，即从事运输的船舶必须建造于本国、船舶必须为本国的公民所拥有、必须仅雇佣或者主要雇佣本国船员以及船舶必须在本国注册和登记等。上述几个要素被学者称为是沿海运输权的特征，或者构成沿海运输权的基石。[②]然而，也有学

---

① 参见 1982 年《联合国海洋法公约》第 33 条和第 57 条。

② V. Okeke and E. Aniche(2012)，"An Evaluation of the Effectiveness of the Cabotage Act 2003 on Nigerian Maritime Administration"，*Sacha Journal of Policy and Strategic Studies*，2(1)，12—28.

者认为沿海运输权的基础是国家主权、经济发展和国家安全。①本书专注于沿海运输权特征的初步探讨，目标是为了阐述沿海运输权如何被各个国家展开立法和实施的。

事实上，每一个沿海国对于本国所实施的沿海运输权政策或立法存在差异的根本原因，取决于本国意识到沿海运输权的重要性程度。这实质上也是沿海运输权的重要特征的体现，也是导致沿海运输权的特征与许多因素有关联的根源。比如，以国家主权为例，如果一国在制定沿海运输权政策时，非常重视将国家主权因素融入沿海运输权体系之中，那么，该国的沿海运输权的特征必将凸显国家主权的色彩。因此，沿海国所实施的沿海运输权政策是属于保护主义、自由主义还是灵活主义，取决于对沿海运输中国家主权的考量程度。一般来说，沿海运输权的政策或立法通常通过对于以下四个基本条件来描述的：(1)船舶的建造、实质性的维修工作必须在沿海国的国内；(2)船舶必须在沿海国注册并获取相关文件，并悬挂沿海国旗帜；(3)船舶所有权全部或大部分必须为沿海国国民所有；(4)船舶必须全部或主要雇佣沿海国国籍的船员。上述几个沿海运输权的特征或者构成条件，属于沿海运输权的一般条件。②某些沿海国基于特殊目的，通常在实施沿海运输权政策时规定比较特殊的条件。诸如，从事沿海运输船舶应入级本国船级社；或者从事沿海运输船舶应在国内进行回收等。这种比较特殊的条件构成沿海运输权的"未来特征"。③沿海运输权的特征基本上反映出沿海国所实施的沿海运输权是保护主义抑或自由主义。总体而言，沿海运输权的特征基本是围绕着船舶建造和维修、船员雇佣、船舶所有权登记、船级社以及船舶回收等问题展开的。

美国和尼日利亚被认为是实施比较严格沿海运输权的国家。在尼日利亚，该国关于沿海运输权的立法和政策非常重视立法细节等问题。由于船

---

① J. Gabriel(2009)，"Revitalisation of the Shipbuilding Industry"，*Petrobas Magazine*，58(1)，5—10.

② J. Leahy and S. Pearson，"Rousseff's Dream of Brazilian Shipbuilding Titan in Deep Water"，*Financial Times*，Rio de Janeiro，25 January 2015.

③ Aniekan Akpan，*Maritime Cabotage Law*，London：Routledge，2019，p.251.

舶建造厂或者维修船坞存在合资或者外资控股的情景，导致在认定从事沿海运输的船舶一旦进入船坞维修，则会产生是否违反沿海运输权法律的问题。与此同时，沿海国法律鼓励从事沿海运输的船舶必须到本国船舶建造厂或者船坞进行维修，一定程度上促进了本国的就业机会并对沿海国的经济发展作出贡献。①因此，根据尼日利亚有关部门的统计，该国实施的沿海运输权立法确保了本国国内造船和船舶维修产业，为本国经济发展作出了不小的贡献。就美国的情况而言，根据美国商务部的一项研究，造船业在美国属于战略产业或领域。②因此，美国的 1920 年《琼斯法案》对美国国内造船业的生存至关重要。实践证明，沿海运输权立法下规制建造和修理船舶是否适用于从事沿海运输的船舶的政策产生非常明显的产业和经济效益。值得注意的是，亚洲部分国家包括韩国和日本等国家都没有具体将造船和船舶修理的要求纳入本国的沿海运输立法中。③

　　一般地，一国沿海运输权特征的形成往往与该国调整航运政策和战略有关。以中国为例，截至 2014 年，中国造船厂完成新型液化天然气运输船的建造实现历史新高，其目的是通过船舶建造产能的革新以逐步占领高技术船舶市场，进而提高中国的高技术造船能力，从而重组和保护中国造船行业。④但是，在将造船和修船的"特征"纳入一国的沿海运输立法和政策框架下时，还应考虑该国拥有技术专长的成本效益等因素。例如，2013 年在美国建造一艘 3 600 TEU 的船舶，成本约为 2.09 亿美元。相比之下，在亚洲国家造船厂，一艘同等的船舶的建造价格不到美国船厂的五分之一。⑤

---

①　National Shipbuilding and Procurement Strategy，"Results of the National Shipbuilding and Procurement Strategy"，Government of Canada，2011.

②　BXA，"U.S. Shipbuilding and Repair：National Security Assessment of the U.S. *Shipbuilding and Repair Industry*"，BXA，2001.

③　M. Brooks，"Maritime Cabotage：International Market Issues in the Liberalisation of Domestic Shipping"，in A. Chircop et al.(eds)，*The Regulation of International Shipping*：*International and Comparative Perspectives*，Martinus Nijhoff，2012，pp.293—324.

④　World Maritime News，"Chinese Shipyards Vying to Enter LNG Market"，*World Maritime News*，Shanghai，5 August 2014.

⑤　Drewry Maritime Research，"US Cabotage Protection gets more Expensive"，*Drew Maritime Research*，London，17 November 2013.

由于船舶建造的因素很复杂，导致部分沿海国在制定沿海运输权立法或政策时，将其排除在该国沿海运输权法律框架之外。在美国有越来越多的人士要求重新考虑在 1920 年《琼斯法案》中排除关于船舶在本国建造的要求。①在航空和陆路运输中，没有要求运输工具必须在运输国建造或修理的强制要求。有学者认为通过一国沿海运输权立法的实施，来促进本国的造船业或者修船业，这一点值得商榷。②制约沿海运输权立法和政策涵盖很多重要因素，其中之一，是船舶登记的因素。作为一项悠久的传统航运政策，船舶登记最初只是一种控制船舶是否能够在有关国家海域从事国内运输的手段。1958 年日内瓦海洋法条约体系也从立法角度强化了这一点。③船舶登记已经成为确立船舶所有权的一种方便的手段，同时也是对登记船舶行使行政和社会事项管理的重要依据。

沿海运输权立法或者政策具有的另一重要特征，即所有寻求从事一国沿海运输活动的船舶必须在该国进行船舶登记并悬挂该国国旗，使该国成为通常所说的"船旗国"。④因此，一个沿海国可以为从事沿海贸易运输的船舶经营者设立注册船舶所需满足的门槛，这属于一个主权国家的主权范围事项，而不必担心是否违反国际法。这一政策在一些沿海国被演绎为一项比较灵活的登记政策。比如，由于船舶在巴西建造而中止悬挂原国旗以悬挂巴西国旗的外国船舶，必须在巴西特别注册局（REB）获得登记才能够

---

① C. Papavizas and B. Gardner，"Coast Guard Rejects Industry Petition to Change Jones Act Vessel Rebuilding Regulations"，Winston & Strawn LLP，2012.

② W. Gray，2008 "Performance of Major US Shipyards in 20th/21st Century"，*Journal of Ship Production*，24(4)，202—213；W. Yost，2013 "Jonesing For a Taste of Competition：Why an Antiquated Maritime Law Needs Reform"，*Roger Williams University Law Review*，18(1)，52—77.

③ V. Okeke and E. Aniche，2012 "An Evaluation of the Effectiveness of the Cabotage Act 2003 on Nigerian Maritime Administration"，*Sacha Journal of Policy and Strategic Studies*，2(1)，12—28.

④ S. Sucharitkul，2006 "Liability and Responsibility of the State of Registration or the Flag State in Respect of Sea-Going Vessels，Aircraft and Spacecraft Registered by National Registration Authorities"，*American Journal of Comparative Law*，Vol.54，American Law in the 21st Century：U.S. National Reports to the XVII International Congress of Comparative Law(Fall)，409—442.

从事沿海运输。①另外，即使在欧盟成员国之间实施相对自由的沿海运输政策，然而，欲从事沿海运输活动也必须要求共同体船舶所有人将其船舶登记在一个成员国，并悬挂该成员国的国旗才能获得沿海运输权的资格。

除此以外，沿海运输权还与从事沿海运输的船舶所有权有关。通常而言，船舶所有权"特征"要求沿海运输船舶必须全部或实质上处于该国国民的所有权之下，通常要求该国公民必须持有船舶的全部或大部分股份，且对任何外国人无债务负担。②不仅如此，在一些沿海国的沿海运输权立法下，往往伴随着另一项要求，即从事沿海运输的任何这类个人或公司必须在该国建立并拥有其主要营业地点。在美国，1920 年《琼斯法案》要求所有在美国境内各点之间运输的商品只能由美国公民拥有的船舶来完成运输。③

与美国 1920 年《琼斯法案》相类似，2003 年施行的尼日利亚《海上运输法》规定，从事沿海运输船舶的所有权应由尼日利亚公民或尼日利亚公司完全拥有。此外，从事沿海运输船舶的所有股份必须由尼日利亚公民持有，无任何外国人债务负担。④在菲律宾，从事沿海贸易运输的船舶必须至少有 75% 的资本属于菲律宾公民。对于从事沿海贸易运输的公司，总经理或常务董事应由菲律宾公民担任。⑤与上述立法例相比较，日本沿海运输权立法和政策在这方面更加严格。从事日本沿海贸易运输的船舶必须满足更为繁琐的关于船舶所有权的立法上强制性规定。比如，在日本从事沿海

---

① S. Ajiye(2013)，"Nigerian Cabotage：Its Policy, Prospects and Challenges"，*Journal of Economics and Sustainable Development*，4(14)，11—17.

② M. Brooks，"Maritime Cabotage：International Market Issues in the Liberalisation of Domestic Shipping"，in A. Chircop et al.(eds)，*The Regulation of International Shipping：International and Comparative Perspectives*，Martinus Nijhoff，2012，pp.293—324.

③ 参见美国 1920 年《琼斯法案》。

④ V. Okeke and E. Aniche(2012)，"An Evaluation of the Effectiveness of the Cabotage Act 2003 on Nigerian Maritime Administration"，*Sacha Journal of Policy and Strategic Studies*，2(1)，12—28.

⑤ W. Yost(2013)，"Jonesing for a Taste of Competition：Why an Antiquated Maritime Law Needs Reform"，*Roger Williams University Law Review*，18(1)，52—77.

运输的船舶必须属于日本国家机关、日本国民以及根据日本法律设立的公司，该公司法人代表和三分之二以上的高级职员必须是日本国民。如果设立公司属于外国公司，公司法人代表必须由日本国民担任。①

即便是在沿海运输权立法上采取了广受欢迎的自由方式，但在有关沿海运输船舶的所有权方面，欧盟也实施比较严格的立法。欧盟理事会条例第 3577/92 号条例第 2(2)(b)条和第 2(2)(c)条，分别对第二类和第三类船舶所有人提出了立法要求，即根据欧盟关于沿海运输的法律，在紧急情况下，授权欧盟成员国可以对船舶进行"有效控制"。这种"有效控制"的立法目的，是促进本国从事沿海运输的船舶所有权"特征"能够有效促进经济增长和投资。②总而言之，沿海运输权的特征具有复杂的理论和实践背景，一国的相关立法模式与该国对于沿海运输权的制度价值或者功能认知息息相关。一个充满活力的国内沿海运输船队对于吸引更多的投资进入国内贸易运输领域是至关重要的，而前文所论及的沿海运输权的特征，必将构成衡量沿海运输权立法和政策是否具有活力的重要因素。

在理解沿海运输权"特征"方面，船员的雇佣"特征"是不得不考虑的重要因素。当然，在沿海运输权视角下探讨船员问题，与前述沿海运输权下的船舶所有权具有一定内在关联度。有学者认为，船员条件构成沿海运输权的特征属于一个富有争议的问题，其远远超出了沿海运输权"特征"的问题。美国 1920 年《琼斯法案》下，从事沿海运输的船舶至少75％的船员必须是美国公民。这项规定的直接影响是增加了船舶的运营成本。这是因为雇佣美国船员的劳动力成本较高，而雇佣发展中国家船员的劳动力成本较低。在印度尼西亚，所有沿海运输活动必须由在印度尼西亚登记的船舶来执行，配备的船员必须是印度尼西亚人。这一要求的例外情况是，有证据表明没有合格的印度尼西亚船员能够胜任空缺职位。日本沿海运输立法也规定，从事日本沿海贸易运输的船舶必须确保三分之二以上

---

① 参见 1899 年《日本船舶法》第 1 条。

② K. Li and J. Wonham(1999)，"New Developments in Ship Registration"，*International Journal of Marine and Coastal Law*，14(1)，137—146.

的配备船员是日本国民。尼日利亚沿海运输立法实施更为严格的规定，该法要求本国沿海运输船舶所配备的船员必须 100% 是尼日利亚人。欧盟的海上运输政策经常被认为是有效的自由主义海上运输方式的表现。然而，欧盟沿海运输权自由主义的做法只适用于欧盟内部的成员国。欧盟理事会条例 3577/92 引入保护主义因素有两种情况，第一种情况是执行大陆沿海运输船舶是小于 650 总吨的船舶，而第二种情况是从事岛屿沿海运输的情况。在这两种情况下，与船舶配备船员有关的所有事项均由东道国本国负责，该国通常规定全体船员来自东道国的国民。①

就沿海运输的目的而言，船员条件一般要求从事沿海运输船舶的船员全部或基本满足沿海运输国的国籍要求。而这也与沿海运输权立法动机有关。例如，巴西沿海运输法的一个关键目标是在国内沿海运输领域创造就业机会。因此，从事巴西沿海运输的外国船员只允许工作 30 天。一艘在巴西沿海水域连续作业超过 90 天的外国船舶，船上必须至少有五分之一的巴西雇员。在海上连续作业超过 180 天的船舶，三分之一的船员必须是巴西人。此外，悬挂巴西国旗的船舶的船长、轮机工程师以及三分之二的船员必须是巴西国民。②

除了前文探讨的制约沿海运输权的立法和政策若干因素以外，也可能存在其他制约沿海运输权立法和政策的重要因素，或者是潜在的重要因素。这些潜在的因素通常与船级社对从事沿海运输船舶的检验，以及从事沿海运输船舶的回收问题相关联。通常而言，船级社承担着对从事海洋运输船舶的资质评估。船级社有义务评估注册的船舶是否符合船旗国相关法律规定的安全要求，船级社通过定期进行船舶法定检验等方式来完成其使命。

就从事沿海运输船舶的回收要求而言，也构成晚近以来沿海国在沿海

---

① R. Coles and E. Watt，Ship Registration: Law and Practice，2nd edn，Taylor & Francis 2013.

② B. Baker(2012)，"Flags of Convenience and the Gulf Oil Spill: Problems and Proposed Solutions"，*Houston Journal of International Law*，34(3)，697—715.

运输权立法上重要考虑的因素。①事实上，沿海运输权立法下的船舶回收问题，构成与环境保护、劳动力就业、福利保障以及其他相关产业相关联的复杂问题。船舶回收是指对已达到使用寿命的退役船舶进行拆解的过程。船舶的船龄、货运市场和买卖市场是船舶回收市场的主要决定因素。此外，对废钢的经济需求、劳动力市场以及宽松的健康和安全法规，在许多亚洲国家创造了一个相对开放的船舶回收市场。沿海运输权立法和政策之所以将船舶回收纳入立法的视野，可能是由于造船用的钢材往往质量优良，而钢铁工业是经济发展的重要指标。②近年来，一些国家的经济繁荣导致这些国家对钢铁的需求大幅增加。根据有关统计，全世界回收的船舶吨位中，约有98%来自一些亚洲国家的船舶回收场。这些经济体都有一个共同的潜在因素，那就是拥有巨大的废钢需求市场。③当然，船舶回收中的拆船对安全和环境造成的危险是制约是否将其纳入沿海运输权立法和政策的重要因素。学者对于该问题一直存在这样那样的争论。有学者指出，船舶建造同样也是对安全和环境造成损害的重要因素。在这一点上，沿海运输权立法和政策对于船舶建造和船舶回收应该持有相同的立法态度。④

第二节　沿海运输权的演进

一、沿海运输权的起源与发展

沿海运输权的起源并不明确。一般地，学者认为它似乎来源于西班牙或

---

① J. Mansell, Flag State Responsibility: Historical Development and Contemporary Issues, Springer, 2009.

② A. Akpan, "*The Ship Recycling Industry: Hope or Despair?*" John Moores University, 2005.

③ C. Broadbent, "*Life Cycle Assessment in the Global Steel Industry*", World Steel Association, 2013.

④ N. Mikelis, "*Ship Recycling Markets and the Impact of the Hong Kong Convention*", International Maritime Organization, 2013.

法国的海洋文化。一般理解是，它来源于法语动词"caboter"，而"caboter"一词源自西班牙语的"cabotaje"，意思是一直遵循沿着海岸线顺时针方向航行。然而，这种狭义的含义在实践中从未被真正采用。一些国家根本不满足于将海上勘探和航行限制在沿海地区。事实上，一些海洋大国诸如美国、英国和葡萄牙等国将沿海运输权扩大到宗主国和其殖民地之间的海上贸易运输。因此，在 1898 年至 1899 年间，美国将其与菲律宾、夏威夷群岛和波多黎各岛之间的贸易也视为沿海运输权的范畴。[①]这意味着，即使是殖民地的对外贸易，也是由悬挂美国国旗的船舶展开的。当然，目前此种沿海运输权已经不多见，因为世界范围内殖民地不再存在。

地中海沿海国包括埃及、迦太基、罗德岛、腓尼基和罗马等海上强国曾对海洋进行冒险和探索，对其邻近水域非常重视行使控制权。这种控制权的目的是限制敌对国家的船舶在其港口和海域进行贸易或从事其他海上活动。因此可以说，当时的沿海运输权很可能是处于政治和商业的需要，而不是一个立法和政策的问题。根据考证，已知最早的有关沿海运输权的立法文件是 1382 年理查德二世统治时期通过的，它规定除了国王的船舶，任何人不得在英格兰王国的任何港口进口或出口商品。[②]

在英格兰，理查德二世的继任者们也一直保持着类似的立法，有时甚至更加严格。爱德华四世（1461—1483）、亨利七世（1485—1509）和伊丽莎白一世（1558—1603）都试图保护英格兰实施的沿海运输权体系，并禁止外国船舶参与其沿海贸易运输。[③]在奥利弗克伦威尔于 1651 年颁布《航海法案》之前，英国在长达两个半世纪（1382—1650）的时间里一直推行严格的沿海运输权政策。该法案禁止第三方外国船舶在英国水域进行贸易，进出英国殖民地的贸易运输权只保留给英国籍船舶。[④]该立法旨在控制荷兰商船过度增强的影响力。1660 年的《航海法案》是在复辟之后制定的，当时英国、苏格兰和爱尔兰的君主国在理查德二世的领导下重新建

---

① 　Aniekan Akpan, *Maritime Cabotage Law*, New York：Routledge 2019, p.9.

②④ 　参见 1651 年《航海法案》相关规定。

③ 　参见《沿海贸易法案》（*Coasting Trade Bill*）相关规定。

立起来，借此他修正了先前的法案。由于地理范围的扩大和对船员要求的严格，该法案变得更加严格。《航海法案》规定任何货物都不得进口或出口到亚洲、非洲或美洲，除非由英国船长指挥且四分之三的水手为英国人的船舶。该法案同时规定不得使用任何外国船舶将货物从英国的一个港口运输到另一个港口。①1849 年，《航海法案》在英国被废除。然而，直到 1854 年，英国船员控制的英国船舶的沿海运输贸易仍然受到保护。此时跨越四个半世纪（1382—1854）的保护主义法案的最后残余最终被废除。

其他海洋大国在同一时期颁布了保护主义的沿海运输权法案。1670 年，法国与其殖民地之间的贸易只保留给法国船舶。这种保护主义的海事政策于 1740 年成为法律，当时法国皇家法令中规定了沿海运输权立法。该法律规定了两种类型的沿海运输，即大沿海运输和小沿海运输。②在法国，大沿海运输涉及法国地中海港口与法国海外领土港口之间的贸易运输和提供的海事服务。这里重要的一点是，这两个港口应该是在不同的海岸线上。波尔多和马赛之间的航行也被归类为大沿海运输，因为这两个点在不同的海岸线上。小沿海运输涉及同一海岸的两个或多个法国港口之间的贸易运输和提供海运服务。加莱和马赛之间的航行，都在同一海岸线上，被归类为小沿海运输。大约半个世纪后，法国沿海运输的保护主义程度进一步提高，导致 1791 年公布了对外国船舶的禁令。③

1789 年，美国国会对由外国船舶运输的货物征收额外的关税。此外，还对外国建造的和外国所有的船舶征收禁止性的关税。④在近一个世纪前的行动中，美国国会颁布了 1817 年的《航海法案》。根据该法案禁止外国船舶进入美国国内的商业活动和在美国沿海水域的竞争性活动。1886 年的

---

① 参见 1651 年《航海法案》相关规定。
② 参见 1886 年《旅客运输服务法》（*the Passengers Vessels Services Act*）第 8 节规定。
③ 参见 1817 年《美国航海法案》（*Act Concerning the Navigation of the United States*）第 4 节规定。
④ 参见 1789 年《美国进口关税法案》（*An Act for laying a Duty on Goods，Wares and Merchandises Imported into the United States*）相关规定。

《旅客运输服务法》进一步扩展了美国沿海运输法的适用范围，将客船纳入其中。1817 年和 1886 年的法案共同将海上货运和客运保留给由美国建造、注册、拥有和配备船员的船舶。目前，有几项保护主义沿海运输权法律涵盖了美国沿海水域的疏浚、拖船和海上运输等业务。①目前，1920 年《琼斯法案》是美国适用于沿海运输的重要立法。从本质上讲，1920 年《琼斯法案》是 1789 年法案的一种更严格的立法成果，也是领海的保护主义立法和政策的延续。受到美国立法的影响，1869 年加拿大颁布了第一部关于沿海运输权的法律，规定在加拿大水域的海上贸易运输只限于英国船舶。之所以英国船舶被授予一定的特权，是因为加拿大在当时是英国的殖民地。②随着 1931 年《英联邦商船协议》的签署，英联邦国家的船舶拥有与英国船舶相同的地位，因此可以参与加拿大的沿海贸易运输。

由于英联邦的原因，英国的沿海运输权立法比较复杂。保护主义沿海运输权立法在英国经历了几次重要变革。首先是在 1849 年废除了《航海法案》，后于 1854 年取消了对英国港口之间的沿海运输的限制。从这些立法变迁中可以看出，尽管英国政府在英国结束了保护主义的沿海运输制度，却乐于在世界各地的殖民地保留沿海运输权保护主义的政策。然而，加拿大严格的沿海贸易政策起源于英国崛起前，可以追溯到 1763 年的《巴黎和约》。该条约促成了英国对海洋和海上贸易的无可争议的掌控地位。③尽管 1867 年的《英属北美法案》赋予了加拿大议会在航海方面的权力，但加拿大的立法仍被要求与英国有关立法保持一致。这种情况一直持续到 1934 年《加拿大船舶法》的施行。

在沿海水域实施沿海运输权的法律和政策，不仅集中在英国和北美地区，而且在欧亚大陆国家，包括俄罗斯在内都是如此。1830 年俄罗斯首次

---

① 参见 1906 年《疏浚工程法案》和 1940 年《拖航法案》相关规定。

② J. Hodgson and M. Brooks, 2007 "Towards a North American Cabotage Regime: A Canadian Perspective", *Canadian Journal of Transportation*, 1(1), 19—35.

③ J. Karel(1897), "Consular Report: Reports from the consuls of the United States on the commerce, manufactures, etc., of their consular districts", Vol.LV, No.204.

尝试沿海运输局限于俄罗斯船舶，但实施效果不佳。因为当时的俄罗斯认为沿海运输并不重要，所以没有在外国竞争中保护本国贸易。后来俄罗斯强化了沿海运输权的立法，更加重视沿海运输权的政策并利用其幅员辽阔的地理优势，不断强化沿海运输权的立法和政策实施。1999 年《俄罗斯联邦商船法》对俄罗斯沿海运输权进行规制。①

可见，绝大多数沿海国通过立法将其沿海水域的海事活动保留给本国的船舶和船员。因此，任何违反这些法律的外国船舶及其船员会受到如罚款、扣押货物、没收船舶和监禁船员等不同程度的惩罚。②然而，经过多年的发展，欧洲的一些国家同意放宽沿海运输权。欧盟理事会（EEC）第3577/92 号条例实现自由主义沿海运输权的形成。该条例在欧盟（当时被称为欧洲共同体）的主持下于 1993 年 1 月生效。欧盟理事会第 3577/92 号条例规定了欧盟成员国之间不受限制地提供海运服务的自由。③在这一条例出台前，欧洲的各个国家都有适合本国沿海运输的沿海运输权立法。北欧国家如丹麦、挪威，以及英国和荷兰，已经实施了自由的沿海运输权政策。而另一些欧陆国家包括希腊、西班牙和意大利在内，则奉行保护主义的沿海运输政策。④

二、国际法视阈下沿海运输权的演变

一般来说，由于沿海水域的贸易、航行和其他海事活动具有战略意义，沿海国家对其沿海水域实施保护性的立法和政策。几个世纪以来，许多从事沿海运输贸易的沿海国家都实施了保护主义沿海运输权法律。然而，现在要维持这种保护主义的做法已经值得进一步商榷。这是因为更多的国家

---

① 参见 1999 年《俄罗斯联邦商船法》第 4 条规定。

② B. Fassbender and A. Peters, "Introduction: Towards A Global History of International Law", in B. Fassbender and A. Peters(eds), *The Oxford Handbook of the History of International Law*, Oxford University Press 2012, pp.3—24.

③ 参见 1992 年欧盟理事会第 3577/92 条例。

④ W. Preiser(1984), "History of The Law of Nations: Ancient Times To 1648", in R. Bernhardt(ed.), *Encyclopedia of Public International Law*, 7(1), pp.132—159.

愿意在贸易和服务领域尝试自由政策，传统航运强国之间的激烈竞争似乎已经与以前不同了，而且海洋国家对于沿海运输权的认识今昔非比。

沿海运输权立法和国际法的演变规律属于不同领域。然而，这两个领域的法律发展过程中具有交汇点。对沿海运输法和国际法形成时期的评估将揭示当时许多国家面临的挑战。人们普遍认为，沿海运输权法和国际法并不是在同一时期开始的。然而，国家之间的贸易似乎是这两个法律领域发展的共同前提。万民法（ius gentium）通常被称为具有国际法意义的法律，颁布于公元 212 年，该法是基于地中海贸易实践中的商法而形成的。一些早期的贸易国家实施了与海洋有关的法规并延伸到沿海运输领域。这与国际法形成了鲜明对比，后者直到 19 世纪中叶才真正开始在各国之间逐渐被确认。[①]

虽然国际法在两次世界大战后逐渐被全球所接受，但沿海运输权立法却难以形成具有影响力的国际规则。这种情况不仅在国际层面上如此，甚至可能在国家层面上也令人惊讶地存在着。在国际法层面上，接受沿海运输权的困难主要是由于国际沿海运输框架议程缺乏明确性。除此以外，国家层面上的分歧可归因于许多国家的海运利益集团渴望施行本国的沿海运输法，并将其利益作为最重要的参照。例如，东道国船舶所有人会倡导保护主义的沿海运输权政策，这样他们就可以在没有外国船舶所有人竞争的情况下从事沿海运输服务。东道国造船厂亦是如此。然而，东道国托运人利益集团则倾向于寻求一项自由主义的沿海运输政策，允许外国船舶所有人参与本国的沿海运输领域。[②]

有证据表明，早在 1382 年英国就存在关于沿海运输的成文立法。17 世纪见证了海洋运输法和国际法领域的若干重大事件。诸如 1648 年《威斯特伐利亚和约》（*The Peace of Westphalia*）的签署，1651 年《航海条例》

[①]　H. Koh（1997），"Why Do Nations Obey International Law?"，Yale Law School Legal Scholarship Repository Faculty Scholarship Series，Paper 2101，1—62.

[②]　J. Hodgsonand M. Brooks（2007），"Towards a North American Cabotage Regime：A Canadian Perspective"，*Canadian Journal of Transportation*，1(1)，19—35.

(*Navigation Laws*)的制定以及被誉为"现代国际法之父"的荷兰人雨果·格劳秀斯(Hugo Grotius)的重要学术贡献,都是这两个领域法律发展的亮点。格劳秀斯关于国际法和海洋自由的著作因在这两个法律领域的演变中发挥的重要作用而备受赞誉。然而,许多学者认为,即使在那个时代,格劳秀斯关于国际法原则的假设也并非具有完全的开创性。显而易见,他的贡献和哲学思想深受阿尔贝里科斯·真提利斯(Alberico Gentili)1598 年《战争法》(*De Jure Belli*)的影响。①从中世纪的法律过渡到"国际法"(*Law of Nations*)的国际法律框架具有复杂的过程和动因。事实上,多边协议体系是中世纪国家间建立关系的普遍机制,该机制至今仍在大量领域包括海洋运输领域内被采用。然而,中世纪法律制度下多边协议的一个弱点是,协议各方可能会在最轻微的挑衅下退出多边协议,一国可以轻易地撤销承诺而不会受到任何影响。这就亟须一个具有约束力的国际监管框架,迫使国家更好地遵守承诺。②

17 世纪国际法发展的中心主题是"主权"问题。起初,该问题仅限于欧洲各国,但很快就蔓延到全球其他地区。17 世纪沿海运输的中心主题是关于海洋自由的辩论。这场辩论的核心问题是领海是否应该供所有人自由使用还是可以归国家所有。18 世纪国际法的中心主题是主权国家加快国家利益优先化的速度。此外,西方大国通过更好地利用外交和谈判共同努力构建和平关系。③18 世纪的沿海运输权立法围绕着主权国家在多大程度上对领海行使沿海运输管辖权展开了辩论。西方列强殖民地国家的减少以及民族主义和独立国家的崛起是 19 世纪国际法的中心主题。④主权国家继续

① G. Edmond(1995), "The Freedom of Histories: Reassessing Grotius on the Sea", *University of Wollongong Australia Law Text Culture*, 2(9), 179—217.

② L. Casey, and D. Rivkin, "Making Law: The United Nations' Role in Formulating and Enforcing International Law", in B. Schaefer(ed.), *Conundrum: The Limits of the United Nations and the Search for Alternatives*, Rowman & Littlefield 2009, pp.31—56.

③ I. Kant, *Perpetual Peace: A Philosophical Sketch*. Translated by W. Hastie 1891, Clark 1795.

④ G. Underhill, "Global Governance and Political Economy: Public, Private and Political Authority in the Twenty-first Century", in J.Clarke and G. Edwards(eds), *Global Governance in the Twenty-first Century*, Palgrave Macmillan 2004, pp.112—138.

寻求伙伴关系，同时建立国际关系以管理国家间冲突风险。英国于 1849 年废除了《航海法案》，1854 年废除了保护主义的沿海运输权法。①这一点意义重大，因为英国当时是海上的主导力量之一。人们普遍认为，英国作为一个岛国结束了其沿海运输权保护主义政策，因为担心世界其他国家随着经济实力的增强可能会以类似的保护主义政策对英国进行报复。②

20 世纪初叶以来，国家主权问题、全球治理、技术进步以及经济水平等发生重大变化。世界的中心主题是对和平前所未有的渴望，以及各国为尽可能避免冲突所做出的努力。20 世纪的沿海运输权立法曾经尝试构建促进沿海运输业所迫切需要的国际法框架，然而这种尝试并未成功。事实上，沿海运输权的国际法框架通常也与自由贸易议程相联系。在乌拉圭回合(Uruguay Round)谈判、多哈回合(Doha Round)谈判和其他世界贸易组织高级别多边协议体制下，各国试图就海洋运输服务的国际协调找到共同点，但都没有成功。③在此基础上，在乌拉圭回合和多哈回合谈判中都未能推进关于协调国际海运的讨论，应被视为错失了机会。此外，令人遗憾的是，有关国际论坛仍然回避或很少关注关于沿海运输权的国际立法问题，这进一步导致缺乏沿海运输权的国际法体制的形成。就一些发展中国家而言，其政府普遍认为其海事部门对国内外投资者来说是有吸引力的投资机会。④因此，这些国家可能会考虑采取保护主义的沿海运输政策，将其海上边界两点之间的所有海上活动保留给本国的商业机构，尽管人们普遍承认这类保护主义政策会阻碍海上运输的效率。

此外，这类政策还保护了效率低下的东道国沿海运输服务的提供商，从而增加了货物运输和消费品和服务的成本。晚近以来，发展中国家和工

---

① K. McKeever, *Researching Public International Law*, Columbia University 2006.

② A. Lorca, "Eurocentrism in the History of International Law", in B. Fassbender and A. Peters(eds), *The Oxford Handbook of the History of International Law*, Oxford University Press 2012, pp.1034—1057.

③ D. Desierto(2008), "Postcolonial International Law Discourses on Regional Developments in South and Southeast Asia", *International Journal of Legal Information*, 36(3), 387—431.

④ L. Oppenheim(1908), "The Meaning of Coasting: Trade in Commercial Treaties", *Law Quarterly Review*, 24(3), 328—334.

业化国家对国际法作用的认识发生了重大变化，它们的影响对国际法的正常运作至关重要。其结果是区域化已成为一个更加被接受的理念，国家之间更加有信心进行相互协作。然而，重要的是国际法继续以一种确保独立国家的主权得到保护的方式发挥作用。相比之下，21世纪以来各国沿海运输权已完全置于各国政府的监管自由裁量权之下，尽管国际法和跨国商业条约都承认沿海运输权。①此外，对沿海运输权立法的语境理解不再局限于贸易和航行。现在沿海运输权的立法和政策涵盖了属于主权国家公司、移民和劳工保障的领域。许多国家的沿海运输政策仍旧是一种政治工具，因此倾向于施行保护主义沿海运输政策。也就是说，沿海运输权法律正在逐步与国际合作法的原则接轨。许多国家通过双边和多边共识，找到了参与彼此沿海水域事务的途径。因此，许多国家逐渐放宽沿海运输业限制，这种倾向并不像前几个世纪那样令人感到不可思议。②例如，欧盟委员会对允许国际海运供应商在成员国港口之间移动或重新定位其船舶包括空集装箱在内的设备的想法持开放态度，前提是不涉及任何利润的获得。然而，即使不涉及收入，允许国际参与者参与一个国家的沿海运输，仍会带来深刻的挑战。

尽管如此，欧盟委员会的提议仍遭到欧盟船舶所有人的强烈反对。这表明，任何未能充分照顾国内运营商利益的提案都可能受到质疑。21世纪以来，更多的国家将接受区域沿海运输政策的理念。例如，欧盟沿海运输法允许成员国在欧盟范围内从事沿海运输。非洲联盟起草了一份沿海运输宪章，将开放区域沿海运输贸易和服务。亚洲、南美洲、北美和太平洋地区也考虑了区域沿海运输政策的实施。③然而，区域海上运输政策面临的挑

① S. Kumar and J. Hoffmann, "Globalization: The Maritime Nexus", in C. Grammenos (ed.), *Handbook of Maritime Economics and Business*, Informa 2002, pp.35—62.

② G. Mailer, "Europe, the American Crisis, and Scottish Evangelism: The Primacy of Foreign Policy in the Kirk?", in W. Mulligan and B. Simms(eds), *The Primacy of Foreign Policy in British History, 1660—2000: How Strategic Concerns Shaped Modern Britain*, Palgrave Macmillan 2010, pp.119—136.

③ C. Staker, "Jurisdiction. The Individual and the International Legal System", in M. Evans (ed.), *International Law*, 4th edn, Oxford University Press 2014, pp.309—335.

战是内部成员国的协调的挑战。这是因为地区经济较发达的国家可能会扭曲政策的范围和目标，使其偏向于对其有利的方向，而不利于发展中国家。许多海洋国家选择了妥协，接受了国际中继计划（International Relay Scheme）。因此，如果外国船舶在国际航程中抵达该国或在国际航程中离开该国，则可以从事该国的沿海运输贸易。[1]然而，在围绕保护主义沿海运输政策的众多问题中，该方案只关注一个问题，那就是高运费的问题。

在将国际法和沿海运输权立法的发展进行比较之后，可以清楚地看到这两个法律领域都有一些重要的中心主题，其中包括主权、发展、国家安全和国际合作等领域。虽然沿海运输权立法和国际法是在不同的框架下发展起来的，但二者往往融合在一起以规范国内海上运输活动和国际海洋运输活动。[2]国际法和沿海运输权立法在处理主权和领海问题时相互关联，国际海洋法事实上植根于国际公法原则。然而，沿海运输权立法属于一个国家的主权管辖范围，目前并没有剥夺该国根据国际法享有的主权权利的规定。

第三节　沿海运输权的模式[3]

一、沿海运输权的模式

简单地说，沿海运输法被视为一种沿海国的立法与政策的制度安排。虽然这在大多数国家中是常态，但也存在例外。一些国家的地理特征使得政府并不总是可能在本国内采用一种维持不变的沿海运输方式。这就是所谓的沿海运输权的模式。因此，对于某些国家来说，其中一些地区可能采

---

① 参见欧盟理事会第 3577/92 条例有关规定。

② T. Fulton，The Sovereignty of the Sea：An Historical Account of the Claims to England to the Dominion of the British Seas，And of the Evolution of the Territorial Waters：With Special Reference to the Right of Fishing And The Naval Salute（William Blackwood 1911）.

③ 关于沿海运输权的模式，学术存较大争论。本书在梳理前人相关研究文献基础上，提出本书的倾向。参见 Aniekan Akpan，*Maritime Cabotage Law*，London：Routledge，2019，p.80。

用自由主义的沿海运输制度，其他地区可能采用保护主义的沿海运输制度。事实上，在某些经济部门执行沿海运输权立法的变体所付出的财政和资源成本可能远远超过该国总体可能获得的经济效益。例如，纽约联邦储备银行 2012 年的一份报告揭示了 1920 年《琼斯法案》对岛屿和内河航运的影响。该报告最终得出结论：将一个 20 英尺的集装箱从美国东海岸运送至波多黎各岛，预估运费为 3 063 美元。同样的货物从美国东海岸运至附近的圣多明各，运费为 1 504 美元，而运至金斯敦的运费为 1 687 美元。同样，将 40 英尺的集装箱从洛杉矶运送至火奴鲁鲁需要花费 8 700 美元，而同样的货物从洛杉矶运至上海仅需 790 美元。①

　　根据各国实施沿海运输权的立法与实践，通常而言沿海运输权有三个主要的模式，即一般沿海运输权、大陆沿海运输权、岛屿沿海运输权。当然，沿海国家可以根据本国的海洋和地理特点，在该国实施上述任何一种或将三种变体组合。例如，欧盟放宽了对沿海运输权目标的限制，要求成员国确保其国家立法符合理事会第 3577/92 号条例。然而，隶属于希腊的一些岛屿距离土耳其较近，对希腊的国家安全构成严重威胁，这让希腊十分担心。因此，希腊主张允许其在这些岛屿地区继续实行保护主义沿海运输权政策，尽管其领海的其他部分已经实现自由化的沿海运输权政策。②一些国家或地区可能会选择在其特殊的海域实施比较特别的沿海运输权政策，而没有在其所有海域实施单一的沿海运输权政策。一般来说，在这种情况下，这种措施往往是由于避免影响岛屿与岛屿之间或者岛屿与大陆之间海洋运输差异性的需要。这是因为，一般情况下，从事沿海运输的船舶构成岛屿之间以及岛屿与大陆之间货物和乘客的唯一运输工具。③一般地，沿海运输权的执行通常是依赖公共服务合同作为依据。

　　公共服务合同是指确认主管部门与公共服务运营商之间协议的一项或

---

① 　B. Slattery，B. Riley and N. Loris(2014)，"Sink the Jones Act: Restoring America's Competitive Advantage in Maritime-Related Industries"，Backgrounder，No.2886，1—9.

② 　参见 2004 年 2 月 3 日《欧盟委员会致希腊正式通知函》。

③ 　参见欧盟理事会第 1370/2007 号指令有关规定。

多项具有法律约束力的文件。协议将公共运输服务的管理和运营委托给该公共服务运营商，并由其承担公共服务义务下的责任。主管部门可以选择提供服务或将这种服务委托给内部运营商。或者，它可以选择通过个别立法或监管法案来规范此类协议。①各国适用公共服务合同一般技巧是实施全面的保护主义法律，但往往对一些服务和部门给予例外的豁免。2008 年，印度尼西亚恢复实施保护主义的沿海运输权政策，但对石油和天然气运输给予豁免。同样，印度和马来西亚在过去也曾定期对其传统的保护主义沿海运输权给予豁免。②

　　在实施沿海运输权制度时，政府可能需要决定是否将某些部门或海事服务从国家沿海运输权立法的适用范围中豁免。这种豁免通常会引起许多不同利益相关者的强烈反对。人们通常会就一个根本问题进行争辩，即选择沿海运输权模式背后的驱动因素可能是什么？事实上，答案取决于政府如何理解和看待其沿海运输权立法和政策的目标。一方面，政府可能专注于推行有效的沿海运输权制度，以促进其海洋经济的发展。另一方面，政府可能会采取一种流行但无效的沿海运输权模式，从而导致其海洋部门的发展置于停滞不前的状态。尼日利亚的沿海运输权立法就是一个例证。尽管尼日利亚沿海运输权法案在最初施行时很受欢迎，但现在该法案发挥的能效不能适应该国的沿海运输实际情况，以至于破坏了尼日利亚海事部门曾经期望的经济发展目标。澳大利亚的情况虽然没有那么糟糕，但其与尼日利亚面临的困境相比并无两样，该国历届政府都倾向于采用不同的沿海运输法。③对于那些在澳大利亚沿海水域经营海运服务的公司来说，它们很难明白其沿海运输行为在短期、中期、长期内将适用哪种法律。不难理解，这种法律适用的不确定性将大大阻碍经济发展的进程。

　　一般地，沿海运输权具有一般沿海运输权、大陆沿海运输权以及岛屿沿海运输权三种模式。就沿海运输权的三种模式而言，一般沿海运输权是

---

① 参见欧盟理事会第 1370/2007 条例 2(e)有关规定。

② 参见欧盟理事会第 1370/2007 条例 2(i)有关规定。

③ 参见欧盟理事会第 1370/2007 条例 2(g)有关规定。

最容易受到国内运输网络中其他运输方式比如公路运输和铁路运输的竞争。欧盟的沿海运输权模式是一个典型的一般沿海运输权模式，它包含了不同沿海运输权变体。然而，一般的沿海运输权模式被排除在欧盟理事会条例 3577/92 条例范围之外，通常属于一般沿海运输权模式的服务，受欧盟理事会条例第 3921/91 号条例的约束。该条例规制非居民承运人在成员国境内的内河航道上的货物或乘客的运输。①岛屿沿海运输权是问题最多的一种沿海运输权模式，因为岛屿沿海运输权导致政府面临着与公共服务有关的敏感问题。大陆沿海运输权是引发较多争论的一种模式，即自由主义沿海运输权或保护主义沿海运输权的论争问题。

对于每一种不同模式的沿海运输权，沿海国通常根据所从事的海上活动的性质，考虑对本国人和非本国人的不同准入条件。这或许解释了为什么一个国家可以同时实施保护主义沿海运输权和自由主义沿海运输权的动机。通常而言，比较流行的沿海运输权模式，是在大陆地区采用自由主义沿海运输权，而在大陆与岛屿之间地区则实施保护主义沿海运输权的模式。②这一形式在欧盟是显而易见的，岛屿地区的海上运输规则比大陆地区的保护主义性更强。例如，保护主义沿海运输权模式下的船员雇佣要求和国家援助等财政政策是被欧盟成员国所支持和允许的，尽管自由主义沿海运输权模式是欧盟认可的基本沿海运输政策和立法。因此，沿海运输权模式在任何国家或地区的适用，在很大程度上取决于沿海运输权适用的变体。

二、一般沿海运输权

一般沿海运输权是指将一国沿海和内河航道的水上运输活动保留给东道国海事商业机构的权力或权利。这种沿海运输权最容易受到外国海运业机构或者国内公路和铁路等陆路运输方式的竞争。一方面，外国船舶经营

---

① 参见欧盟理事会第 3921/91 号条例的规定。

② B. Slattery, B. Riley and N. Loris(2014), "Sink the Jones Act: Restoring America's Competitive Advantage in Maritime-Related Industries", Backgrounder, No.2886, 1—9.

者总是试图尽可能地控制货物从头到尾的运输。另一方面，通过内河水道运输的大部分货物也可以通过其他运输方式运输。因此，由公路和铁路构成的陆上运输网络为内河航道运输提供了一个可行的替代方案。然而，在这一具体问题上，内河航道运输比其他国内运输方式更有优势。例如，荷兰内河航道的运输最大限度地减少了公路和铁路等地面运输，为减少温室气体的排放作出了巨大努力。①

在许多国家，中央和地方政府的监管权力之间存在重复和冲突，这也是一般沿海运输面临的重要挑战。尼日利亚是这种冲突的一个例证。拉各斯州政府于 2008 年成立了拉各斯州航道管理局，这在一定程度上与该国一般沿海运输权框架之下的监管机制相冲突。拉各斯州航道管理局有权管理在拉各斯州境内的水道、河流、小溪、湖泊、滩涂和潟湖内从事运输的任何类型的船舶。②然而，这一权力是与尼日利亚国家内河航道管理局的现有规定相冲突。除此之外，该局还管理低水位线以下的联邦内河航道内的运输活动。这些州一级政府机构既挑战了尼日利亚海事管理安全局的职能，也与其相冲突。根据 2003 年该国《沿海运输法案》的相关立法规定，该局是尼日利亚沿海运输的主要监管机构。③

因此，不同机构对监管权力的三重甚至多重划分令人困惑，因为经营者在内河航道上进行一般沿海运输时，并不清楚监管主体。这一点对于那些通过国家内河航道运输石油和天然气货物的运营商来说尤其重要。当尼日利亚的航运经营者被要求遵守监管时，就会出现进一步的混乱。例如，履行货物或乘客运输的合同义务意味着他们必须同时受到大陆沿海运输权和一般沿海运输权的规制。由于尼日利亚内河航运的立法权力属于国民议

---

① R. Petrova(1997), "Cabotage and the European Community Common Maritime Policy: Moving towards Free provision of Services in Maritime Transport", *Fordham International Law Journal*, 21(3), 1—76.

② A. Cafruny, "Flags of Convenience", in R. Jones(ed.), *Routledge Encyclopaedia of International Political Economy*, Routledge 2002.

③ R. Carlisle, *Sovereignty for Sale: The Origins and Evolution of the Panamanian and Liberian Flags of Convenience*, MD Naval Institute Press 1981.

会，而不是州议会，因此这种混乱情况会变得更加复杂。①美国也存在机构职能重叠和沿海航行监管机构不确定的问题，因为美国的航运经营者必须同时遵守州立法和联邦立法。在欧盟，并非所有成员国的内河航道运输服务都具有海事性质，符合欧盟理事会第3577/92号条例规定的可以归类为沿海运输服务。同时，这些运输服务也属于欧盟理事会第3921/91号条例规定的范围之内，该条例规定了非居民承运人在成员国内通过内河航道运输货物和乘客。②

一般沿海运输经营者所面临的混乱和不确定性意味着，主导这种沿海运输的支线服务运营商将面临违反州或联邦法律的重大风险，除非放宽国际货物支线服务的规定。这涉及在一般沿海运输规则下，授予沿海运输服务的外国供应商自由移动或重新定位其设备的自由。例如，使用他们自己的船舶在内陆航道中运输空载集装箱。此外，任何此类规则的放宽都必须以提供此类服务不会产生收入为前提条件。③

三、大陆沿海运输权

大陆沿海运输权是最著名的沿海运输权的变体，在大多数关于沿海运输权的争论中占主导地位。大陆沿海运输权的基本特征在于，在位于同一主权国家的大陆或主要领土的港口之间通过海上运送乘客或货物，而无需停靠岛屿上的港口。大陆沿海运输权的范围一般包括海港之间的海上活动，诸如港口之间的货物和旅客运输、转运以及船舶代理等。在欧盟，沿海服务似乎被归类为沿海运输的一种独特变体。然而，在许多国家，石油和天然气部门是大陆沿海运输的主要部分。这就解释了为什么在制定沿海运输权政策时通常以大陆沿海运输权为重点。从政策实施的角度来看，大

---

① 参见2007年尼日利亚《海运管理和安全机构法》相关规定。

② B. Parameswaran, *The Liberalization of Maritime Transport Services*, Springer 2004.

③ R. Carlisle, *Sovereignty for Sale：The Origins and Evolution of the Panamanian and Liberian Flags of Convenience*, MD Naval Institute Press 1981.

陆沿海运输权的立法很容易与岛屿沿海运输区分开来，因为后者需要政策的调整以适应其特殊性。①在欧盟，主要大陆沿海运输服务的提供者在一定程度上摆脱了欧盟岛屿沿海运输中存在的保护主义限制，例如对船员的要求。一般而言，许多国家的情况是，属于大陆沿海运输权的活动范围是沿海运输的三种变体中最广泛的一种。②

联合国贸易和发展会议（以下简称"贸发会议"）于 1974 年通过的《班轮公会行动守则公约》（以下简称《守则公约》）在不经意间为制定维持大陆沿海运输的原则作出了贡献。《守则公约》建立了 40∶40∶20 的多边协议，将货物运输的百分比分配给各方。根据这一安排，40％的货物分别分配给进口国和出口国的国家船队，其余 20％的货物开放给其他国家船队竞争。③《守则公约》的规定有几个漏洞即它们缺失一个详尽而复杂的监管机制来有效运作。贸发会议的《守则公约》往往与不相容的国家立法同时适用，从而产生冲突失去其效力。例如，菲律宾于 1982 年采用了贸发会议所制定的 40∶40∶20 的货运分配，但没有废除早先的政府法令，该法令将所有政府货物均保留给菲律宾的国家船队。在委内瑞拉，尽管其是贸发会议《守则公约》的签署国，但它也将运输货物的 50％都保留给国家船队。韩国将所有班轮货物的 100％都保留给韩国船队，而它仍然是《守则公约》的签署国。④

在《守则公约》出台前后，发展中国家对它们继续被排斥在欧洲和日本的闭门会议之外感到不满和沮丧。因此，它们非常盼望《守则公约》的出台。由欧洲和日本主导的闭门会议被用来影响和控制它们与发展中国家

---

①　参见欧盟理事会条例第 3577/92 号第 2(1)(a)规定。

②　A. Sefara(2014)，"Achieving Access to the Maritime Transport Services Market in the European Union：A Critical Discussion of Cabotage Services"，*Australian Journal of Maritime & Ocean Affairs*，6(2)，106—110.

③　L. Kanuk(1984)，"UNCTAD Code of Conduct for Liner Conferences：Trade Milestone or Millstone—Time Will Soon Tell，The Perspectives"，*Northwestern Journal of International Law & Business*，6(2)，357—372.

④　UNCTAD，"Guidelines towards the Application of the Convention on a Code of Conduct for Liner Conferences"，UNCTAD Secretariat，1986.

的贸易。闭门会议制度增强了对发展中国家的保护力度，妨碍了发展中国家的商船队运载本国相当份额的货物的努力。[1]必须强调的是，一个国家的商船规模在当时被视为国家主权和权力的重要象征。发展中国家所表达的关切是合理的。然而，它们的鼓动似乎更多的是对 20 世纪 70 年代国际航运业内日益严重的政治混乱的共同反应，而不是对国家发展政策的整合。例如，20 世纪 70 年代中期，连续两次石油危机导致海运贸易停滞不前，随后加剧了世界海运吨位盈余情况的恶化。[2]这迫使海上运输发生重大变化，特别是在欧洲，在涉及石油产品进出口链的世界其他地区也有体现。

因此，由于许多发展中国家采取了歧视性和其他保护主义的做法，大陆沿海运输权模式对于它们成为一个有吸引力的选择。这使它们能够通过其国家商业工具控制其大陆领土上的贸易和其他海上活动。[3]大陆沿海运输权模式，特别是在发展中国家，通过第二个国家船舶登记处来维持，这些登记处通常兼作开放登记处。开放登记处日益增长的影响力，对传统海洋国家的主导地位提出了强烈挑战，这些国家迄今为止一直在发展中国家的领海中主导着大陆沿海运输权。大陆沿海地区最广泛的活动主要是石油和天然气以及集装箱运输服务贸易。在许多沿海国家，本土承运人要求制定保护主义的大陆沿海运输权立法，允许他们在其领海内进行没有外国竞争的海上活动。在马来西亚、印度以及美国的大陆沿海贸易中，运输集装箱货物以及在某些情况下运输空集装箱是主要的海上活动。[4]然而，石油产品的转运才是印度尼西亚、美国和尼日利亚大陆沿海贸易的核心。

---

① L. Kanuk(1984)，"UNCTAD Code of Conduct for Liner Conferences: Trade Milestone or Millstone—Time Will Soon Tell, The Perspectives"，*Northwestern Journal of International Law & Business*，6(2)，357—372.

② J. Tapia Granados，"From the Oil Crisis to the Great Recession: Five Crisis of the World Economy"，University of Michigan，2013.

③ R. Petrova(1997)，"Cabotage and the European Community Common Maritime Policy: Moving towards Free provision of Services in Maritime Transport"，*Fordham International Law Journal*，21(3)，1—76.

④ A. Cafruny，"Flags of Convenience"，in R. Jones(ed.)，*Routledge Encyclopaedia of International Political Economy*，Routledge 2002.

四、岛屿沿海运输权

岛屿沿海运输权是三种沿海运输权模式中最复杂的一种模式。因为从地理位置上看，岛屿大多是独立的。在不影响沿海国主权的前提下，为远离大陆岛屿地区提供可持续的海洋运输服务是沿海国家面临的挑战，而这也正是沿海运输权的制度价值所在。一般地，岛屿沿海运输权是指在大陆和一个或多个岛屿的港口之间，或在同一国家岛屿的港口之间的海上货物运输。[①]可以说，岛屿具有比较特殊的地理政治地位，因而也往往需要特殊的立法和政策。岛屿的自然特征意味着这些地区的沿海运输权立法具有与其他沿海运输权变体不同的特征。因此，从政策制定和实施的角度来看，岛屿沿海运输权立法和政策更为复杂。一般来说，岛屿分散性这一特征影响了该地区提供的跨港口服务的质量。[②]

岛屿与大陆之间的地理特征导致两者之间的运输网络负担过重。故此，交通不便的后果之一是岛屿居民承担在岛屿上经营的价值高昂的消费品。这是由于进口多而出口少的交通流量不平衡造成的。岛屿的特殊性要求任何法律或政策框架必须既务实又灵活，以成功满足岛屿地区的不同特点。这可以解释为什么尽管欧盟实行了自由的区域性沿海运输权政策，但欧盟一些国家的岛屿地区的海事服务仍然实施保护主义沿海运输权体制。相比之下，亚洲及太平洋区域的岛屿沿海运输法并不像欧盟那样发达。与欧盟沿海运输权立法的框架相比，亚太及太平洋地区的沿海运输权立法和政策集中在一个狭窄的海事服务领域内。[③]这些岛屿面临诸多挑战，如远离全球主要市场，贸易量低，岛屿之间经济活动不平衡，港口之间缺乏稳定

---

① 参见欧盟理事会条例 3577/92 条例第 2(1)(c)的规定。

② M. Lekakou and T. Vitsounis(2011)，"Market Con-centration in Coastal Shipping and Limitations to Island's Accessibility"，*Research in Transportation Business & Management*，2(1)，74—82.

③ R. Petrova(1997)，"Cabotage and the European Community Common Maritime Policy：Moving towards Free provision of Services in Maritime Transport"，*Fordham International Law Journal*，21(3)，1—76.

和高效的运输服务以及昂贵的岛屿运输费用。

有学者建议在太平洋岛屿区域实施全面的区域性沿海运输权政策之前，通过在次区域地区试验沿海运输权的立法，可以最大限度地减少岛屿不利因素导致的负面影响。①对少数国家进行试验的战略选择可能特别有用。这是因为，那些本质上由岛屿组成、被海洋隔开但仍处于一个主权之下的国家，通常会受到缺乏公路和铁路运输网络中有关准入问题的困扰。此外，由于费用等因素的影响，航空运输的选择也很有限。因此，岛屿居民几乎别无选择，只能依靠内部水道作为货物和乘客维持经济的主要运输方式。②

由于岛屿沿海运输的多样性和复杂性，关于规范岛屿沿海运输权的最佳政策在国家层面引起了激烈的争论。在欧盟沿海运输权立法的框架之下，希腊、意大利、葡萄牙和西班牙的初衷是非常不愿意接受在其境内岛屿之间放宽沿海运输权政策。在欧盟委员会和欧洲联盟法院司法裁决的压力之下，这些国家才在其岛屿地区放开了沿海运输权。岛屿的独特性进一步表明，在制定国家沿海运输政策框架时，必须考虑海上运输特殊的问题。因此，试图制定一种单一的国家沿海运输权立法，以满足岛屿沿海运输的所有特点很可能是徒劳的。因为在解决岛屿地区的沿海运输困难时，任何框架性工作都必须充分地保证其务实性和灵活性。③

岛屿沿海运输权的显著特征要求相关沿海运输权立法要与之相吻合。为了满足这一点，它必须适当考虑到海运服务对巨大季节性变化的需求。这对于拥有一个以上岛屿的主权国家而言，沿海运输权在满足这些岛屿领土的需要以及确保其持续的社会经济一体化方面具有重要意义。④因此，允

---

① G. Lee，"Inter-Island Shipping Development in the ASEA Nand the Pacific Region"，in Korean Maritime Institute(ed.)，Seminaron the Development of an Integrated Transport and Logistics system in ASEAN countries and Pacific sub region(KMI 2012).

② CPMR Islands Commission，"Consultation on the 5th Maritime Cabotage Report"，CPMR，2009，p.1.

③ R. Greaves，*EC Transport Law*，Pearson Education 2010.

④ Article 2(e) and 2(i) respectively of Regulation(EC) No.1370/2007 of the European Parliament and of the Council，23 October 2007.

许外国运营商的竞争可能危及向岛屿提供定期的海运服务，这似乎成为了拥有岛屿领土国家的主要关切。市场力量如果不能充分为岛屿运输的航线提供服务，就会迫使政府进行干预以纠正这种违规行为。岛屿之间海上运输服务的风险，一方面与外国运营商长期承诺的不确定性有关，另一方面与外国运营商提供的服务的定价波动性有关。因此，为岛屿沿海运输找到适当的解决方案，许多国家逐渐探索依靠签署公共服务协议的途径来实现。

因此，拥有岛屿领土的沿海国在其管理岛屿沿海运输时的一个主要关切是他们是否可以通过公共服务合同来维持海运服务。在这种公共服务协议措施适用的情况下，它对服务提供商施加了一项义务，以确保海上运输服务的连续性和规律性，提升沿海运输的服务能力。然而，这也提出了一个备受争议的问题，即岛屿之间的沿海运输是否应完全属于公共服务的范畴？对于这个问题不能给出简单的回答，因为它需要对财务标准和所有重要事实进行交叉审查。此外，在试图回答这个问题时，人们应该了解自由市场在岛屿沿海运输背景下的优势，同时认清其缺点。①因此，许多政府选择通过施加公共服务义务或参与公共服务合同来管理岛屿沿海运输。这样做是为了保证在沿海运输的框架下进行持续的、畅通的、充足的运输和海事服务。②事实上，欧盟理事会第 3577/92 号条例的第 4 条支持了这一点。该条允许欧盟成员国在国内岛屿之间签订此类合同，但有一个前提，即合同应对所有欧盟运营商的待遇是非歧视性的。

应当指出，在欧盟内部提供海事服务的自由构成规则，而实行公共服务制度则可以被视为一种例外。因此，岛屿运输服务和相关海事服务并不

---

① A. Mikroulea，"Competition and Public Service in Greek Cabotage", in A. Antapassis, L. Athanassiou and E. Rosaeg(eds)，*Competition and Regulation in Shipping and Shipping Related Industries*，Martinus Nijhoff 2009，pp.185—206.

② 参见欧盟理事会条例第 3577/92 号第 4 条的规定。

自动构成欧盟内部的公共利益服务。[①]当然，也有一种担忧是一个国家可能在公共服务协议的幌子下实施保护主义的沿海运输权政策。这需要在探索岛屿沿海运输权的实践中，不断完善岛屿沿海运输权。

---

① A. Mikroulea, "Competition and Public Service in Greek Cabotage", in A. Antapassis, L. Athanassiou and E. Rosaeg(eds), *Competition and Regulation in Shipping and Shipping Related Industries*, Martinus Nijhoff 2009, p.218.

第 2 章　沿海运输权的私法理念与基础：公共承运人责任体系的演变

　　私法构成社会治理的公法规制的基础。沿海运输权的法律规制模式也深深地印上了相关私法体系和理念的痕迹。各国对于沿海运输权的立法模式和内容，一定程度上折射出普通法下公共承运人的责任体系的演变。本书在探究一系列中外相关判例的基础上，勾勒了一幅公共承运人责任体系的历史图景。不仅如此，本书在探究沿海运输权的私法理念与基础时，深入挖掘普通法和我国的相关司法实践的法理，进而提出相关论断。某种意义上，公共承运人责任体系内涵及其演变，构成了认知沿海运输权立法和实践的私法基础。

第一节　"瀛海诉马士基"案及其展开

　　普通法下的公共承运人（common carrier）在责任体系具有很强的沿海运输权的私法色彩和理念。相当多的中文文献将普通法下"common carrier"径直翻译为"公共承运人"。然而，通过对普通法下"common carrier"的历史渊源和发展脉络的体系性解读，"common carrier"具有多重的法律蕴意。不同的历史时期，"common carrier"在强制缔约义务和严格责任体系两个范畴上互有侧重而变动不居。在理解强制缔约义务的适用和公共运输的承担两个进路上，为界分普通承运人和公共承运人提供了历史的、经济的以及法理的动力。顾及中国《民法典》第 810 条的规定，进而可以将普通法下"common carrier"分别解析为普通承运人、公共承运人以及"从事公共运输的承运人"。考察《民法典》第 810 条的立法目的和背景，其实质是以基本上作为私法体系的合同法典来尝试规制国际航运市场秩序，这不仅映射出其立法技术的不足，而且一度造成人们对"common carrier"在不同法系和法律语境中的误读。在国际航运经济活动固有的特殊性背景下，解读"common carrier"这一具有跨国因素的法律概念，从立法技术、修法成本以及法律移植等基本范畴上看，我国《民法典》第 810 条具有重塑的可行性。

悠久的航运实践催生海商法领域诸多颇为独特的制度。其中，从事国际班轮运输的承运人是否承担强制缔约的义务，即是一个令人扑朔迷离的理论争议问题之一。厦门瀛海实业发展有限公司诉马士基(中国)航运有限公司国际海上货运代理经营权损害赔偿纠纷案(以下简称"瀛海诉马士基"案)将该争议推到高潮。虽然"瀛海诉马士基"案经过最高人民法院的再审程序而一锤定音，但是该案留给人们的反思与追问并未戛然而止。①各级法院的判决一波三折且耐人寻味。②该案产生的影响不可小觑，于 2014 年入选全国十大典型海事案例之一。该案明确了国际班轮运输是否属于"公共运输"并且填补了立法空白。从事国际班轮运输的承运人是英美法或者我国海商法理论上的"公共承运人"，而不是《民法典》第 810 条规定的"从事公共运输的承运人"。不仅如此，该案的再审有效规范了国际航运市场。③

---

① 2005 年 3 月马士基公司告知厦门外代停止向瀛海公司提供该公司的集装箱及集装箱铅封。瀛海公司遂以马士基公司等不接受其代理货主订舱托运造成其损失为由向厦门海事法院起诉，请求法院判令马士基公司向瀛海公司提供货运订舱和相关服务，并不得拒绝瀛海公司与马士基公司之间集装箱运输业务。参见《中华人民共和国最高人民法院案例公报》(2010)民提字第 213 号。

② 一审法院认为班轮公司不是公共承运人，不负有法定强制缔约义务，据此判决驳回瀛海公司的诉讼请求。二审法院认为，马士基公司属于公共承运人，其不接受瀛海公司运输请求，违反公共承运人的强制缔约义务。最高人民法院再审认为，公共运输是指为社会提供公用事业性服务并具有垄断地位的运输。国际班轮运输是服务于国际贸易的商事活动，不具有公益性和垄断性。故不属于《中华人民共和国合同法》第 289 条规定的公共运输。参见《中华人民共和国最高人民法院案例公报》(2010)民提字第 213 号。

③ 2014 年 9 月最高人民法院公布十大海事审判典型案例。参见 http://www.ccmt.org.cn/showws.php?id=5311，2016 年 2 月 21 日访问。

"瀛海诉马士基"案自始至终引发相关理论上的争议。有观点认为国际班轮公司构成我国法下"从事公共运输的承运人"，并且其强制缔约义务不能通过约定予以排除。①另一个流派观点认为，从事国际班轮运输的承运人，即便是属于英美法中"公共承运人"，也并不承担强制缔约义务，而只是追求营利性的专业承运人。②或许是受到最高人民法院判决的影响，从事国际班轮运输的承运人不承担强制缔约义务似乎已成定论。然而，由于普通法上 common carrier 的含义具有相当的复杂性，当其被引介或者移植到中国法体系之后，需要对其展开历史的、体系的甚至是经济上的解读，才有可能洞察其精准的含义及其变迁规律。从事国际班轮运输的承运人是否要承担强制缔约义务，并非一个"非此即彼"的简单问题。从事国际班轮运输的承运人是否属于"公共承运人"？英美法上的 common carrier 与"公共承运人"存在什么内在的关联？英美法上的 common carrier 的精确法律含义如何界定？只有破解上述困惑，才能给予 common carrier 一个理性的解读，进而可以有充分的理论依据重新审视"瀛海诉马士基"案。

事实上，"瀛海诉马士基"案的判决理由并不是完美无瑕和无懈可击的，某些判决理由甚至缺乏法理、历史与现实的支撑，其判决理由具有"蜻蜓点水"式浅尝辄止的倾向。而全方位、系统地研判从事国际班轮运输的承运人是否承担强制缔约义务及其法理何在，显然是一个具有理论价值的课题。笔者认为，只有对"common carrier"一词展开历史的、体系性的考察和探究，才能完成这一课题的破解。

第二节　普通法上 Common Carrier 法律蕴意的渊源与发展

一、什么是普通法上的 Common Carrier

几乎所有的中文文献都将英美法上的"common carrier"翻译为"公

---

① 参见陈亚：《国际班轮公司作为公共承运人的强制缔约义务》，《人民司法》2011 年第 14 期。

② 参见最高人民法院民事审判第四庭《最高人民法院海事海商审判综述》（2010 年至 2011 年），《武大国际法评论》第 15 卷第 2 期。

共承运人",并且引用普通法经典案例作为佐证以诠释其法律涵义。[1]在 Belfast Ropeword 一案中,common carrier 被描述为作为公职人员进行运输活动,没有区别地为公众提供承运服务。[2]英美法相当多的判例表明 common carrier 具有一个基本的特征即"公共性",其与"私人承运人"(private carrier)相对应。从历史维度看,伊丽莎白统治时期承运人和受寄人(bailee)是一个概念。[3]随着海上贸易的蓬勃发展,各地频繁的贸易往来和航运技术的发展也促进了海上运输法律的发展。英国的判例要求 common carrier 承担一定范围的强制义务,而没有把这些义务强加给私人承运人。[4]当时并没有权威的文献证明普通法下 common carrier 和私人承运人的严格界分。

自中世纪以降至 19 世纪中叶,丰富的海商判例揭示普通法上 common carrier 的基本含义是从责任体系的角度展开的,是法定义务与"除外责任"互为叠加而形成的体系。同时,common carrier 的基本含义的框定是通过与 private carrier 相对照来完成的。故此,早期的判例支持 common carrier 是通过缔约义务是否强制和责任体系是否严格两个范畴予以判定的观点。[5]这是当时的交易现状、市场规制情境以及法律和经济理论水平所使然。

二、"古代法的残余"

小奥利弗·温德尔·霍姆斯(Oliver Wendell Holmes Jr.)在名噪一时

---

① 具体可以参见杨良宜《提单及其付运单证》(中国政法大学出版社 2001 年版)、傅廷中《海商法论》(法律出版社 2017 年版)、吴焕宁《海商法学》(法律出版社 1996 年版)、小奥利弗·温德尔·霍姆斯(Oliver Wendell Holmes Jr)《普通法》(*The Common Law*),(冉昊、姚中秋译,中国政法大学出版社 2006 年版,第 164 页),以及韦经建、姚莹《公共运输领域中回归契约自由的尝试》,《中国海洋法学评论》2007 年第 1 期。

② See Clark v Gilbert(1835) 2 Bing. N.C.343.

③ See Nugent vs. Smith, 1 C.P.D.423, Cockburn, C.J., at p.428.

④ 这些义务基本有三个层面,即运输义务、严格责任以及收取规定的合理费用义务。通常 common carrier 义务是以英国普通法为基础,而不是罗马法。为了补偿 common carrier 因为此类义务而可能导致的损失,common carrier 通常具有对运输货物的留置权。参见 Clark v Gilbert(1835) 2 Bing. N.C.343。

⑤ Wm. H. Werth, "Contracts Limiting Carrier's Liability in Virginia," *The Virginia Law Register*, Vol.9, No.2(Jun., 1903), pp.73—85.

的《普通法》(*The Common Law*)中描述 common carrier 的角色时认为其属于"古代法的残余"。大量西文文献揭示 common carrier 的义务不过是一般受寄人的义务加上从事公共职业的义务。但是，该义务并没有被宣称为 common carrier 的专门义务，而是根据所涉当事人从事的职业的习惯法分别认定。①在 Coggs v. Bernard 案中，首席法官霍尔特(Holt)认为 common carrier 的责任适用于一切从事公共职业的且有报酬的受寄人。②同时期一系列的相关判例显示，如果某人从事公共职业，他就有义务在此职业所及的全部范围内为公众提供服务，如果他拒绝，可能被提起诉讼。③common carrier 通常用来指称诸多行业中某一具体的职业种类。

从文义角度解释 common carrier，普通法要求 common carrier 对所运送货物的损失承担绝对责任(absolute liability)，除非该损失由于托运人的过错、敌对国的行为或货物本身的缺陷造成的。从事旅客运输的 common carrier 仅仅承担过失责任。④英国法下一个人欲不承担 common carrier 的责任，那么他可以采用公告制度以宣告其不是 common carrier。⑤实践表明，普通法法院越来越倾向于接受此类公告，进而导致该公告具有契约性质。由此一来，common carrier 通常是根据具有契约性质的安排而形成的。历史上，英国的法律曾经明确排除了属于 common carrier 的范围，且common carrier 的范围很不确定。⑥

---

① See Edwin C. Goddard, "The Liability of the Common Carrier as Determined by recent Decisions of the United States Supreme Court," *Columbia Law Review*. Vol.15, No.5(May, 1915), pp.399—416.

② 小奥利弗·温德尔·霍姆斯(Oliver Wendell Holmes Jr)：《普通法》(*The Common Law*)，冉昊、姚中秋译，中国政法大学出版社 2006 年版，第 164 页。

③ See Hobbs v Southampton Steam Packet Co [1919] 2 K.B.135 at 145 per Atkin L., J, Upston v Slark(1827) 2 C. & P. 598.

④ 根据《元照英美法词典》的解释，合同承运人仅指与其认为合适的托运人订约并提供运输服务，而并非不加区分地为所有人提供服务的承运人。特约承运人(private carrier)是不以运输为主业，不公开招揽业务，只在其认为合适时有偿或者无偿地将旅客或者货物从一地运送到另一地的承运人。公共承运人(public carrier)是向公众提供运输服务的承运人。参见薛波主编《元照英美法词典》，法律出版社 2003 年版，第 260 页的相关解释。

⑤ Ropework Co Ltd v bushel, (1918) 1 K.B. 210 at 212 per Bailhache J.

⑥ See Halsbury, Vol.5(1), paras 526 et seq.

但是，相关文献却证明早期普通法下的承运人、旅社老板和铁匠这三种职业，通常具有 common carrier 的色彩。因为他们的职业比较公共，缺失固定的合同相对方。尔后，铁匠退出了这一范围；而旅社的地位也经历了数次变化。可见，公共运输的法律起源和发展历史一波三折。①从 common carrier 是否承担强制缔约义务角度审视，其所处的地位与私人承运人是迥异的，特别是从事海洋运输的 common carrier 更是利用契约自由这个神器而对提单条款随意取舍。在 Chartered Bank v. British Steam Navigation(1909) A.C.369 一案中，这一点得到淋漓尽致的表达。②common carrier 越来越多地利用契约自由把自己排除在公共承运人之外，这样就导致越来越多的私人承运人开始草拟标准条款，其目的在于为了防止自己被视为 common carrier。③这样私人承运人显著减少了自己被归于 common carrier 的风险，特别是在陆路交通运输领域。

由此观之，历史上无论是 common carrier 形成的初期，还是在其历史变迁进程中，其责任体系、责任基础、义务范畴以及是否负有缔约义务等，都不是墨守成规的，而且其深深受到不同行业领域特点、经济政策以及运输产业格局等多种因素的制约。common carrier 具有多重的法律内涵，不仅在不同的时期具有不同的法律责任体系，而且在是否具有"公共运输"的属性上也是漂泊不定的。④随着海洋运输和其他运输模式的不断发展，common carrier 的责任体系不断变迁着。普通法学者通常将 common carrier 被纳入"古代法的残余"的范畴，并认为其为"应该被废除"的制度。⑤

---

① Irwin S. Rosenbaum, "The Common Carrier-Public Utility Concept: A Legal-Industrial View," *The Journal of Land & Public Utility Economics*, Vol.7, No.2(May, 1931), p.160.

② 杨良宜：《提单及其付运单证》，中国政法大学出版社 2001 年版，第 398 页。

③ E. C. G, Limitation of the Amount of the Common Carrier's Liability: Hepburn Act, *Michigan Law Review*, Vol.9, No.3(Jan., 1911), pp.233—237.

④ See Electric Supply Stores v Gaywood(1909)100 L.T.885 at 856 per Pickford J. See also Benett v Peninsular and Oriental Steam-Boat Co(1848) 6 C.B.775 per Wilde C.J. and Digest of English Civil Law(4th ed., 1947), para.522.

⑤ Graham McBain, "Time to Abolish the Common Carrier," *Journal of Business and Law*, 2005, Sept., Sweet & Maxwell and Contributors.

三、揭开 common carrier 的历史面纱：消退与保留

1. common carrier 的本源

"Common"一词被赋予多重的内涵。法律意义上看，"common"和"public"表示相同的意思。要理解 common carrier 的法律渊源，首先要理解运输产业的发展和变迁背景。以历史上不同的运输模式变迁为线索展开考察，以深入理解 common carrier 的制度衍生规律，不失为一种路径选择。

就陆路运输（1066—1479）而言，尽管专业的有偿货物运输在英国的历史非常悠久，但是在诺尔曼征服英格兰之后，英格兰主要的货运方式还是驮马和货运马车。历史学家 J.F.威拉德（J.F. Willard）这样描绘了中世纪后期公路上的真实场景：

"行人，骑马的人，将驮篮挂在背上两侧或直接驮在背上的驮马，许许多多缓慢行驶的两轮货运马车以及偶尔驶过的一辆四轮货运马车。"①

在英格兰，那些以货物运输为专门职业的人最早被称为"carters"。②早期的专业承运人主要被雇佣运输皇家货物或者为富人阶层运输货物。当时的承运人最大的聚集区应该是在伦敦，从事煤、水和建筑材料的运输。"common carrrier"的概念第一次出现的时间并不明确，也没有关于它的成文法的基础。根据相关考证，1459 年，有证据显示一些合同引用了"common carrier"的概念。而在 1479 年，伦敦则首次成立了专供专业承运人进行货物运输或者旅客运输的站台。同年，伦敦的市议会的一项决议中提出"公共货运马车"（common caters）的服务。③因此，"公共"承运人的概念出现的时间至少可以追溯到 1479 年。

公路运输（1479—1911）的发展，使得 common carrier 的制度体系更加具体和丰富。在 1517 年，车夫们组成了一个同盟会，他们与市长约定可在

---

① Hey, Packmen, Carriers and Packhorse Roads, Landmark, Ashbourne, 2001, p.68.

② 即从事货物运输的马车夫。

③ Albert, *Turapick Road System in England 1663—1840*, Cambridge University Press, 1972, pp.68—70.

"约定的城市或者郊外以规定的价格提供运输";作为交换,这个同盟会的车夫们被授予了在伦敦市从事一切"公共运输"的独有权利。1529 年,普通法院的判决要求该同盟会的马车都要盖上印章,这是授权许可最初的形式。1564 年,出租马车在英格兰得到广泛的推广,而后发展成为一种公共运输工具。1694 年,从出租马车衍生出了公共马车,公共马车被用于从伦敦到英格兰其他各地的乘客运输。1829 年,一种出租承运车(hackney bus)被引进伦敦。1755 年的法案要求公共运输工具所有人把"公共运输工具"几个字漆在运输工具上。①

2. Common carrier 被赋予严格责任

Common carrier 就其运输的货物承担严格责任的具体起源时间并不明朗。②霍姆斯(Holmes)认为受托人对于返还托付的货物负有一种当然的高标准责任。然而,比尔(Beale)却认为这种说法并不可靠。③和比尔(Beale)持有相同观点的还有弗莱彻(Fletcher),他曾经就这一问题掌握更多的资料,并认为 common carrier 对于丢失货物所承担的责任,针对不同情境承运人所负责不同。④亨利八世时期的一个公告,表明 common carrier 在下列情况下是可以被指控承担责任的:"如果承运人自己选择有被抢劫危险的道路通行,或者夜晚行进,或者选择其他不便于行进的时间,然后被抢劫;或者承运人由于过度消耗马匹的体力而致使货物落水或发生其他类似的状况而造成货物受损。"⑤

然而在 Woodlife 案中,首席法官波帕姆(Popham)在附带意见中对承

---

① Gunn, Law of Inland Transport, Pitman, Londaon, 1932, p.88.

② Joseph H. Beale. Jr., "The Carrier's Liability: It's History," *Harvard Law Review*, Vol.11, No.3(Oct.25, 1897), p.161.

③ Edwin C. Goddard, "The Liability of the Common Carrier as Determined by Recent Decisions of the United Sates Supreme Court," *Columbia Law Review*, Vol.15, No.5(May, 1915), p.408.

④ 比如,就被抢劫和被盗的情境而言,承运人所承担责任不同。对于被盗情况而言,承运人似乎应当为此负责。而抢劫的情境,则属于承运人对此无能为力的情境,通常并不负有责任。依据 1285 年《温顿规约》(*Statute of Winton*),如果承运人被抢劫,那么他应当做出大声呼喊的行为。参见 Nugent v. Smith(1876) 1 C.P.D.428, per Cockburn, C.J.。

⑤ Selden Soc, Vol.91, p.261. See also Jones, pp.102—103.

运人赋予了严格责任。①即便如此，Common carrier 的责任体系及其理念，无时无刻地影响着国际贸易运输体制的发展，并且深深地融入承运人责任体系之中。以 1924 年海牙规则为肇端，海上货物运输公约下的承运人责任系统具有严格的责任体系。正是从此角度，海商法视角下的承运人是英美普通法上 common carrier 之变种，或被赋予严格的责任体系，或承担强制缔约的义务。②故此，通常人们认为，common carrier 制度是国际海上运输法律制度中的重要组成部分，不同类型的承运人将承担不同的法律责任。

普通法系下由于货物运输委托制度源于商人习惯，且成文法对此调整有限，基于普通法系的判例法，强制缔约被设为 common carrier 的一项默示义务，并对普通法下默示义务的发展具有较大影响。法律基于特别理由而承认强制缔约，最好表现为法律明确规定某类合同的当事人负有强制缔约的义务。如果因种种原因法律对此未设明文，但在特定场合若不缔约就意味着当事人故意侵害社会公共利益和社会公德，那么应当解释为有关当事人负有强制缔约的义务。③由此，渊源于英美普通法下的 common carrier 一直与"公共利益"或者"公共运输"具有千丝万缕的联系。

然而，不同国家法律对于"公共利益"或者"公共运输"的理解和规制亦不尽相同。因为这是一个相当复杂的法律与经济互动问题。由于公共企业在不同国家有不同的形式，在同一国家的不同历史阶段也会有不同的体现。公共企业所从事的经济活动具有特殊重要性，所以其需要具有某种权力以履行类似政府职能的经济活动。④英国普通法法院强加于 common

---

① John G. Haythe, "Limitation of Carrier's Common Law Liability in Bill of Lading," *The Virginia Law Register*, Vol.8, No.12(Apr., 1903), p.850.

② See The Democritos(1976), 2 Lloyd's Rep 149 at p.156.

③ 参见 ［德］迪特尔·梅迪库斯：《德国债法总论》，杜景林、卢谌译，法律出版社 2004 年版，第 73—75 页。

④ Lincoln F. Schaub and Nathan Isaacs, *The Law in Business Problems*, New York: Macmillan Co., 1922, pp.103—104.

carrier 的严格责任并不能满足实践的要求。1816 年，埃伦伯勒把它称作是"毁灭性的责任"。①旋即，Southcote 案判决便建立了 common carrier 的严格责任。common carrier 和他们的货主达成了特殊的契约来限制他们的责任，法院也赞成这种契约。

Common carrier 的严格责任问题是一个相对复杂的问题，其与社会经济状况、公共政策以及产业导向有关。始于 19 世纪初叶，法院前就开始权衡是否按照 common carrier 的标准来对待陆路承运人的问题。Common carrier 的严格责任是一种风险的例外，除外的风险包括天灾、国王敌人的行为、固有灾害以及货主的错误和欺骗。②早在 1830 年，《承运人法案》（*Act of Carrier*）有计划地补偿在运输过程中特殊的风险损失，确认了 common carrier 的权利。

四、Common carrier 法律蕴意的多重性

相关初步考察表明，作为英美普通法上的 common carrier 具有丰富和多重的法律蕴意。Common carrier 的法律蕴意不仅与历史有关，而且也受制于运输模式、国家的经济以及产业政策等多重因素。从这种意义上审视，common carrier 具有"公共承运人"（public carrier）的角色色彩；即便如此，由于国家的经济管制和运输模式的差异，导致 common carrier 在是否具有强制缔约义务、缔约的内容是否具有强制性以及责任体系方面也是变动不居的，common carrier 是否必然承担强制缔约义务并未形成定论。从历史的角度考察"common carrier"的确具有相当丰富和复杂的法律语义。

如此，顾及"瀛海诉马士基"案的判决及其理由，即便是作为国际班轮公司的马士基航运公司不负有强制缔约的义务，但是由于与作为英美普通法上的 common carrier 具有某种程度的历史关联度，在国际班轮公司是否属于我国《合同法》下的"从事公共运输的人"的问题上，则很难给出

---

① See Readhead v Midland Ry Co(1869) L.R. 4.Q.B.379 at 386 per Montague Smith J.

② John F. Wilson，*Carriage of Goods by Sea*，Pearson Education Limited，2010，pp.263—265.

一种十分清晰的判定。该案的判决结果或许是令人满意的，然而，其判决的法理阐释却存在不周全。故此，从这种角度看，法院在"瀛海诉马士基"案再审程序中的裁定并不是无懈可击的，至少在我国现行法的体例之下，具有逻辑上的不周全性，甚至是法律逻辑上的缺失和不足。这是由于脱胎于 common carrier 的承运人在缔约和责任体系两个范畴上所固有的复杂性使然。更何况，在中国几乎所有的文献将普通法上的 common carrier 径直翻译为"公共承运人"，这在一定程度上加剧了人们对 common carrier 具体和真正法律内涵的误读，或者产生一种以偏概全的认知。由此观之，笔者认为，将"common carrier"翻译为"普通承运人"，而不是"公共承运人"（public carrier），可以比较科学地精准界定 common carrier 的真正含义和历史发展脉络，且能够与"公共承运人"（public carrier）形成界分。倘若将普通法下的 common carrier 直接等同于"公共承运人"，鉴于"common carrier"具有丰富的、跨越历史和法系的涵义的考虑，如果不能从历史渊源角度审视"公共承运人"，其复杂多变的制度属性则可能与不同历史时期的制度相互混淆视听。"瀛海诉马士基"案的判决一波三折，某种程度上亦反映了这一点。

为了全面洞察 common carrier 的前世今生，笔者认为，从普通法上的 common carrier，发展到公共承运人，且顾及中国合同法典下的"从事公共运输的人"，应该深入研判"普通承运人"、"公共承运人"，以及"从事公共运输的人"的形成与发展的动因。

第三节　界分普通承运人和公共承运人的进路

从法律与经济的法理角度看，强制缔约和公共运输原本分别属于不同范畴或者领域，甚至是风马牛不相及。然而，在考察普通承运人和公共承运人语境下，这二者之间具有一定的内在关联性。在厘清和细化普通法上 common carrier 基础上，围绕"瀛海诉马士基"案班轮公司是否具有强制缔约义务问题的争论，便具有了切入点和理论支撑。以 common carrier 为原点，探索其衍生"普通承运人"和"公共承运人"的制度内因及其规律性，进而为体系性解读强制缔约义务和公共运输提供理论手段。从普通承运人到公共承运人，并不是一个简单的法律制度或者理论的变迁轨迹，其深层次的动因在于正确认知强制缔约义务的适用和公共运输的界定。

一、普通承运人与强制缔约义务的适用

普通法下提供公共服务的"公共承担者"（common carrier），要承担严格的缔约义务。[①]普通承运人承担严格的缔约义务，其重要表现之一就是强制缔约义务。但是，并没有足够的证据证明普通承运人承担强制缔约义务是一种常态，在英国早期的判例中，强制缔约义务表现得比较强烈。普通法判例表明，如果普通承运人没有充足的理由而拒绝运送他习惯上运送的货物，普通承运人将对他的行为负有责任。

强制缔约义务的适用标准是不断变化的，其受制于经济领域复杂的因素。在自由资本主义时期和垄断资本主义时期，其表现各异。这直接导致强制缔约制度的出现。公共资源领域的活动受到强制缔约的限制，海运中的班轮承运人也受到了这一原则的限制。[②]在国际班轮运输业这一有效竞争行业中，若使有关经营者负担强制缔约义务，应该以有关航线的班轮运输市场已经出现了经营者垄断市场或者滥用优势地位以致消费者缺乏替代性选择，或者选择过分不经济的情况为前提，由此有学者演绎出强制缔约的适用标准应该分别为公共性或公益性标准、垄断性标准以及限制性适用的强势地位标准。[③]学理上对于强制缔约义务的功能认识并不一致，强制缔约是对订约自由的限制，抑或是对契约内容的限制，并无定论。历史证明，早期的普通承运人兼具强制缔约义务和严格的责任体系，尔后发展到仅仅

---

① 朱岩：《强制缔约制度研究》，《清华法学》2011 年第 1 期。

② Scher Ka, Application of Mandatory rules in the Private International Law of Contracts, Frankfurt am Main：Peter Lang, 2010：21.

③ 彭阳：《国际班轮运输公司强制缔约义务否定论》，《中国海商法研究》2015 年第 2 期。

具备严格的责任体系而强制缔约义务渐次退出历史舞台的发展脉络。考察若干历史上的海洋运输国际公约的发展，亦彰显了类似的变迁规律。海洋运输在初期即具有此种表现，然而，随着海运的发展，强制缔约义务逐渐消退，而运输合同内容的强制则得以维系。①

然而，强制缔约制度从未迈出过经济领域，是微观经济领域中单个经济单位所承担的义务。强制缔约限制契约自由限于特定领域和行业，而非针对所有的经济主体。②市场秩序、竞争样态以及航运市场的复杂化导致了强制缔约义务必将与航运市场规制，诸如垄断与反垄断，反不正当竞争甚至是消费者权益的保护之间，皆具有不同性质的内在联系。在若干重要海运公约中，无论是 common carrier，还是私人承运人，基本上都遵循着契约自由，而不是承担强制缔约义务。由此，可以进一步推断出：单纯在法律视域内来考究强制缔约义务，欲对强制缔约义务展开深入的解读似乎是无能为力的。因为，社会经济的发展，导致强制缔约义务不仅仅是法律问题，而更是一个经济秩序和政策的问题。

从域外法看，各国强制缔约制度并不完全一致或相同。考察欧陆各国及亚洲部分国家相关法律，只有日本《铁路营业法》第 6 条、《海上运输法》第 9 条及第 65 条以及《仓库业法》第 5 条对运输和仓储业的垄断性作出了强制缔约义务。同时，强制缔约的适用条件各异，如德国的判断标准主要审查期是否属于垄断行业以及是否违反公序良俗，法国法包括垄断行业和服务行业，而日本是基于人们正常生活需要的考虑。③

按照如此逻辑推理，如果将普通法上 common carrier 以"普通承运人"的语义做出狭义界定的话，那么普通承运人基本上属于私法范畴的概念，历史上其不仅被赋予了强制缔约的私法义务，而且亦被普通法强加了

---

① 参见马得懿：《海上货物运输法强制性体制论》，中国社会科学出版社 2010 年版，第 16 页。

② 翟艳：《强制缔约制度与经济法的契合性解读》，《政治与法律》2013 年第 7 期。

③ 威廉姆森：《反托拉斯经济学——兼并、协约和策略行为》，经济科学出版社 1999 年版，第 209 页。

严格的责任体系。随着契约自由、公共利益以及产业政策的变迁，普通承运人所承载的强制缔约义务和严格的责任体制逐渐得到放松。特别是19世纪中叶以降，随着西方社会经济管制和市场秩序的监管力度得到强化，普通承运人的私法范畴上的严格责任得到进一步的深化和完善，而其早期所固有的强制缔约义务则日渐消退。因为，单凭私法范畴或者手段，已经无法满足被赋予浓厚经济秩序规制色彩的强制缔约义务的高标准。故此，普通承运人体系之下的强制缔约义务，似乎私法意义的缔约义务色彩比较浓厚，而其公法义务则相对淡薄。但是，考察普通法上 common carrier 的渊源，普通承运人具有一定的公法义务。

二、公共承运人与公共运输的承担：英国立法的佐证

在将 common carrier 解析出"普通承运人"之语义之后，common carrier 所固有的另一基本语义是"公共承运人"。普通承运人的"强制缔约义务"由于受到经济和产业政策的影响，不断侵染了承载公共性的历史担当，进而逐渐演化成为"公共运输"的主角色。根据前文的相关考察，此时普通法上的普通承运人逐渐具有"公共承运人"的地位，进而普通承运人具有"公共承运人"（public carrier）的正当性。相当多文献表明，普通法下 common carrier 被移植到或者引介到"公共"的领域，自然与"公共运输"、"公共产品"以及"公共利益"形成关联。这一点也是"瀛海诉马士基"案中的争议焦点和核心问题之一。

公共性在不同历史时期有不同的理论表达。[①]"公共运输"属于难以明确化的难题，并且并非一个全然的法律问题，具有浓郁的经济色彩。通常"公共运输"是指面向社会公众、为全社会提供运力的运输。各种合同法规范反映了多元化社会中主要的社会、经济以及制度上的力量比较。合同法的繁荣是法律制度对多元化的社会中存在的冲突的价值和利益所进行合理的、务实的妥协的产物。[②]国际海运业是否属于公共运输，以不同的标准

---

① 万俊人：《公共性的政治伦理理解》，《读书》2009 年第 12 期。
② 参见［美］罗伯特•A.希尔曼：《合同法的丰富性：当代合同法理论的分析与批判》，郑云端译，北京大学出版社 2005 年版，第 267 页。

来考察其结论可能存在很大的差异性，而且与特定的海运经济安全政策甚至是政治因素息息相关。一般地，公共承运人的存在是公共利益的需求。①历史上，运输业具有强烈的"排他性"，所有的运输产业都受反垄断法等法律体系的调整。然而，国际航运业有所例外，其自然垄断环节可以给予豁免。②根据前文分析，普通承运人在私法意义上强制缔约义务，也已经无法描述基于社会公共利益而产生的具体情境，因此，公共承运人的问世是历史的必然。然而，公共承运人的责任体系与缔约义务已经脱离了私法意义上的强制缔约义务，而逐步步入了公法意义的体制，故此，从此角度看，公共承运人对应的英文应该是"public carrier"，而不是"common carrier"。反之，在中国绝大多数研究文献将"common carrier"翻译为"公共承运人"，极易引发重大误解，属于一种败笔。

为了深入理解公共承运人与公共运输的承担之间的历史互动，本书考察了公共承运人与公共效用观念（the common carrier-public utility concept）在英国的历史发展。

从 15 世纪到 18 世纪初，随着城镇、贸易和皇族特权的上升，在英国商业立法呈现活跃局势。同一时期，曼彻斯特经济学院（Manchester school of economics）和亚当·斯密（Adam Smith）正在构建他们关于市场竞争秩序的理论。从殖民地时期到 19 世纪晚期，英国奉行的基本都是自由放任的经济发展模式，政府介入也仅仅是在社会治安管理的范畴上。19 世纪晚期，英国国内资产阶级和工人阶级的矛盾开始显现。铁路和类似行业的工人通常被认为是最为进步和最具反抗精神的。立法一方面是基于公共利益，即个人应该对公众承担的责任；另一方面是基于公共职能，即国家应该对个人承担的责任。立法发展非常迅速，很快涉及公共利益领域。③在 20 世纪初，出台了关于公共服务的有关规定，诸如交通行业、公共汽车和广播行

---

① Charles K. Burdick, "The Origin of the Peculiar Duties of Public Service Companies," Ⅱ *Columbia Law Review* pp.616—624.(November, 1911)

② 于立、吴绪亮：《运输产业中的反垄断与规制问题》，《中国工业经济》2008 年第 2 期。

③ See Public Opinion(New York: Harcourt Brace & Co., 1922), pp.89—91.

业等。

由于法院处理了很多与公共运输相关的案件，导致公共利益和公共职能的概念在法庭上广泛地被适用和推广。公共效用观念(public utility concept)的认知只能从法律的角度看，而不能从其他方面。公共承运人和公共观念的概念是法律思维的产物。法律在工业化时代被贴上"公共利益"的标签，衍生出一系列被规定了特殊的权利和义务的行业。这些特殊的权利和义务往往受于立法力量干预，而价格和服务则是首当其冲。[①]对此，可以分别从立法上、行政上以及法院本身探寻到内因。立法的过程就是社会不断思考的过程，立法的倾向就是不断影响公共利益的规则。如果没有法院利用宪法来限制行政机关，在英国很有可能会面对公共事业的产业立法的巨大泛滥。此外，其他的产业也将会不断地被吸纳进公共产业的概念中。[②]

在英国，法院是否采纳公共承运人和公共利益的概念要考量的因素很多。当然，其中政府的因素亦是衡量公共事业的另一重要力量。历史表明，在英国政府对公共承运人和公共事业的管理比其他的产业更加深入，但这些管理都是在合法干涉的情况下进行的。政府的管理也许是一种高效理想的管理模式。一个或几个因素都不能构成将承运人和公共事业与其他行业分开的理由。这些理由包括，诸如生产和分配里的垄断、社会依赖公共运输服务、事业规模、生产和分配上的特点以及收入分配和服务利润等。[③]由此观之，英国的立法理念决定公共承运人与公共运输的承担具有法律上的严谨性，而且其认定亦以立法为导向。

---

① Irwin S. Rosenbaum，"The Common Carrier-Public Utility Concept：A Legal-Industrial View"，*The Journal of Land & Public Utility Economics*，Vol.7，No.2(May，1931). pp.155—156.

② Irwin S. Rosenbaum and David E. Lilienthal，"Motor Carrier Regulation," *26 Columbia Law Review 954*，n.49 at 970(December，1926).

③ Irwin S. Rosenbaum，"The Common Carrier-Public Utility Concept：A Legal-Industrial View," *The Journal of Land & Public Utility Economics*，Vol.7，No.2(May，1931). p.167.

第四节　"从事公共运输的承运人"与国际航运秩序的规制

一、《民法典》第 810 条的立法背景与目的

纵然 "common carrier" 渊源于普通法，但是，无论是《海商法》第 4 章还是《民法典》第 810 条，都与 "common carrier" 具有某种 "一脉相承"。我国《海商法》第 4 章由于不同程度移植了 1924 年《海牙规则》、1968 年《维斯比规则》以及 1978 年《汉堡规则》，故此通常认为在中国存在 common carrier 的理论。而《民法典》第 810 条更是基于对航运市场垄断的隐忧而界定了 "从事公共运输的人"。某种意义上，"从事公共运输的人" 的表述来源于当时我国《合同法》第 289 条，具有中国本土的色彩。①从语义角度上看，其等同于 "公共承运人"。然而，当我们深究中国《合同法》第 289 条的立法背景，其绝非属于非此即彼那么简单。

我国《民法典》第 810 条的立法背景和立法动因是规范公共运输的市场秩序，是我国缺位《反垄断法》的情况下制订的针对具有市场支配地位的公共运输承运人的反垄断条款。在此意义看，我国合同法典下的 "从事公共运输的承运人" 是公共承运人（public carrier）在中国法语境下的立法表达。尽管《民法典》第 810 条规定从事公共运输的承运人的强制缔约义务，但没有定义何为 "公共运输"。强制缔约义务和价格管制是法律法规基于其公益性和垄断性而相应做出的规定。此为公法上的义务还是私法上的强制缔约义务尚存争议。由于国际航运市场发展千变万化，仅凭借《民法典》第 810 条所创设的 "从事公共运输的承运人" 来应对纷繁复杂的国际航运市场秩序，诸如航运竞争、航运垄断与反垄断、航运价格管制以及航运市场准入等系列问题的调控，显然是力所不及的。因为这是一个非常复杂的经济和法律问题，借助《民法典》第 810 条是无法完成这一立法使

---

① 我国《合同法》第 289 条所规定的 "从事公共运输的承运人不得拒载旅客，托运人的通常、合理的要求"，就是从事公共运输承运人所应履行的义务，即强制缔约义务。

命的。航运市场竞争和市场秩序囊括了诸多领域的问题，以航运价格为例，足以令法律疲于应对。因为，竞争的市场价格只是获得长期平衡（long-term equilibrium）的一个理性概念。它只是通过现实的市场制度进行分析，而从未完全实现过，即使假定这种市场价格是取决于竞争的。①

二、《民法典》第 810 条立法技术的考察

《民法典》第 810 条未必受到普通法或者海商法理论上 common carrier 的影响或者熏陶，而是受制于法律控制公共运输或者市场秩序的需要。我国《民法典》第 810 条来源于 1999 年的《合同法》289 条的规定，其间立法者并未对国际航运的发展趋向与市场竞争规则和态势有深入的理解和认识。同时，对于国际航运业的经济合作模式、航运产业政策以及相关先进的航运法律体系缺乏了解，导致立法者采用了相当简单的粗线条处理模式，即《民法典》第 810 条模式。此种立法模式，从立法技术上看，至少存在以下两点值得进一步商榷：其一，强制缔约义务置于基本上作为私法体系的合同法典之中是否合理。其二，仅仅以强制缔约义务来规范和调控航运市场竞争规则是否得体。前文考证普通法上 common carrier 的历史渊源及其变迁，我们很容易推论出我国《民法典》第 810 条立法技术存在瑕疵的结论。

就我国《民法典》第 810 条而言，虽然前文探讨了该条的立法背景与真意，但是"从事公共运输的人"的强制缔约义务究竟是私法意义上的义务，抑或是公法意义上的义务则显得无从界分。从法律逻辑上看，作为私法的合同法典下的"从事公共运输的人"，其应该属于私法范畴；然而，考究其立法目的，显然《民法典》第 810 条下"从事公共运输的人"的强制缔约义务，是以规范航运市场秩序为目的。故此，从立法技术和法律逻辑上看，我国 1999 年《合同法》和 1993 年《海商法》在吸收和反映"common carrier"的理念上具有不足。

由此，我们联系到"瀛海诉马士基"案的判决及其理由，之所以认为

---

① 参见（加拿大）Peter Benson：《合同法理论》（*The Theory of Contract Law*），易继明译，北京大学出版社 2004 年版，第 212 页。

该案法院的判决理由存在一定程度的可商榷性，具有说理上浅尝辄止的嫌疑，是因为判决中所提及的"公共承运人"或者"从事公共运输的承运人"直接由普通法上 common carrier 过渡而来，并没有从历史上、经济上以及航运产业政策上，综合考量 common carrier 所固有的复杂法律蕴意及其历史演变。

三、国际航运垄断的特殊性与"从事公共运输的承运人"

1. 航运业经济活动的特殊性

从经济学角度审视国际航运及其市场秩序，航运业经济活动具有一定的特殊性。1980 年以降，世界性海运规则的变迁和经营全球化趋势的发展，导致班轮公会退出历史舞台成为必然。国际班轮相继出现了"全球联盟"、"伟大联盟"以及"CKY 联盟"等不同形式的国际班轮联盟。近年来随着航运市场的持续低迷，国际班轮的市场日益复杂多变。[1]班轮联盟系统具有自组织性源于班轮公司的经济理性，由于这种经济理性，使得班轮企业能够对周围环境做出反应，以期到达最佳运输模式（参见表 2.1）。从国际班轮市场的供需来看，航运联盟虽然比单家班轮公司规模大，但仍然存

表 2.1　国际班轮运输的竞争模式比较[2]

	传统班轮运输竞争	联盟下的班轮运输竞争
竞争的形态	以单个企业为主	联盟系统内部
竞争的方式	对抗性竞争	协同与竞争共存
战略的基点	单个企业收益	联营系统盈利能力
整合的范围	企业内部资源与价值	联盟系统资源与价值协同
企业间交易费用	较大	较小
收益的来源	单个企业内部价值活动	联盟系统整体价值活动

---

① 陈继红、真虹等：《基于交易费用的航运组织制度演进机理》，《交通运输工程学报》2009
年第 9 期。

② 本表格有关数据是笔者根据论证目的的需要，从陈继红：《论集装箱班轮运输企业联盟的
管理协同机制》整理而成。参见《大连海事大学学报（社会科学版）》2012 年第 1 期。

在来自其他联盟的竞争,而且联盟内部之间的竞争并没有消除。①联盟的班轮企业之间存在多种特定关系。班轮联盟系统中的竞争关系是一种新型竞争,使班轮联盟企业之间的竞争方式更为灵活。②

早期观点认为,航运业属于"强自然垄断"行业,政府必须对其实行严格规制。但是技术进步可以降低固定成本,使得由于规模增大而带来的平均成本下降的趋势变得更加缓和,从而减弱了自然垄断的强度。因此,规制导致普遍存在的低效率现象,出现了"规制失灵"。③2006 年欧盟理事会通过废除班轮公会反垄断豁免权的决议,标志着航运联盟将取代班轮公会成为班轮运输间的主要合作形式。

因此,从国际航运垄断的特殊性角度看,从事班轮运输的承运人在特定情境下具有公共运输的属性,故此应该具有承担强制缔约义务的经济基础。从当今国际航运联营体或者航运联盟看,班轮联盟的复杂性彰显殆尽。其经济结构、产业政策导致其具有某种程度的"公益性"或者"公共性"。就单个班轮公司而言,其承担的社会公共属性并不强烈,然而班轮公司多以联营体或者联盟的形态来运营,这导致其具有某种程度的公共属性。尽管反垄断政策时时打着"公共利益"的招牌,但是它的出台与执行常常刻上了利益集团的烙印。④历史上,common carrier 承载了丰富的法律内涵。普通法曾经苛求 common carrier 承担强制缔约义务,通常属于一种私法范畴上的意义,但是一旦其具有"公共承运人"的法律意义时,法律便要求其摒弃承担强制缔约义务,而承载起规范航运市场秩序的历史使命。因为,"强制缔约义务"通常属于私法范畴,并不具有公法意义上的义务。而航运业天然具有极为复杂的经济形式,各类航运联盟不断推陈出新,其是否具有社会公共属性亦是令人扑朔迷离。

---

① 谢燮、王勇昌:《航运联盟的行业监管之道》,《中国港口》2014 年第 11 期。

② 参见陈继红:《论集装箱班轮运输企业联盟的管理协同机制》,《大连海事大学学报(社会科学版)》2012 年第 1 期。

③ 朱意秋、张琦:《我国集装箱班轮运输市场垄断程度研究》,《上海船舶运输科学研究所学报》2006 年第 2 期。

④ 参见吴玉岭:《遏制市场之恶——美国反垄断政策解读》,南京大学出版社 2007 年版,第 39 页。

2. 作为规范航运市场秩序的概念——"从事公共运输的承运人"之理性分析

前文向我们揭示了航运市场秩序的复杂性。当我们探寻一个富有理性的法律手段或者概念来应对国际航运市场秩序的规制时，本书受到 common carrier 的历史演变和公共效用观念的启迪，认为"从事公共运输的承运人"是一个合适的概念。因为其在规范航运市场秩序范畴上，具有与公共承运人(public carrier)相同或者类似的功能。关于这一点可以通过考察历史上的"公共"概念得到明证。

"公共"的判定可以依赖多种理论和标准，而垄断理论属于其一。垄断是阻碍公众利益的一个因素，所以防止垄断是国家调控的目标。这种分类是基于经济学而非法学的，而且普通法关于反垄断的原则一直存在。[1]在立法理论上，对市场行为的规范是立法主权基于公共政策考量做出的。中世纪的时候，教会限制经济发展，产生很多严格的规定。之后，国王为了增加税收开始促进商业贸易发展。最后，英国的商业力量逐渐强大，开启了自由贸易的时代。这种理论的支持者就批评了从法律上区分私有公司和公共事业。[2]政府本质理论认为，保护公共利益是政府固有的职能。政府没有行使该权力只是一种权宜之计。该权力的行使在市场主体、个人权利和公众利益保护之间寻求平衡。[3]以上理论都试图将经济学、社会学以及政治学的意义植入公共利益和公共观念的概念中。

"公共"这一词最早在普通法中是用来描述各个商业活动的布局特点。[4]当一个商业活动已经有了规律和布局时，就被称为"公共"。直到近些年，"公共"一词才被用于定义特定商业领域中负有更加严苛义务

---

[1]　Bruce Wyman, *Special Law Governing Public Service Corporations*, New York: Baker Voorhis & Co., 1921, Vol.1, p.6.

[2]　John B. Cheadle, "Government Control of Business," *20 Columbia Law Review* 438—550, 550—585, April, May, 1920.

[3]　Harleigh H. Hartman, *Fair Value* (New York: Houghton Mifflin Co., 1920), ch. i, pp.19—20.

[4]　Edward A. Adler, "Business Jurisprudence," *28 Harvard Law Review* 135 (December, 1914).

的领域。①如果一个商人对于任何人都提供服务的话，那么这些人的诉求也就形成了"公共诉求"。随着人类进入工业社会，几乎所有的商人都开始面向所有公众。法律所规定的公共运输侵权责任，后来演变为主张默示承诺(implied assumpsit)。②然而，由于积累的判例效力较强、公共运输对于公众的重要性以及特殊的责任规定对于商人非常有利等因素，导致人们对于公共承运人和公共效用观念的重视。把公共运输和公共效用的观念视为一个法律概念，能够奠定界分公共事业与私人企业的基础。最好的解决办法就是从和私人企业相对应的狭隘的"公共"概念中脱离出来。这种对公共运输和公共事业断裂性和不明确的解释，会导致在制定行业规范上的僵局。因为，现代生活的快速发展和世界经济变化需要更为合理的制度。我们必须坦率地承认，现在的公共运输和公共事业的概念不是基于充足的经济、行业、政治和社会现实，而是基于一种不稳定的偶然因素产生的。③

当我们将目光再次聚焦到我国《民法典》下"从事公共运输的承运人"之际，在考察"公共"历史性概念基础上，不难感受到该概念既具有继承common carrier这一古老概念的色彩，又具有超越和升华 common carrier 的属性，其基本上承载了公共承运人(public carrier)这一概念的功能。然而，令人遗憾的是，将"从事公共运输的承运人"置于基本作为私法体系的《民法典》框架下，既误解了"从事公共运输的承运人"在《民法典》中的立法目的，又一定程度上扭曲了 common carrier 的历史演变。

第五节　域外法的考察与完善中国相关法的方案

一、域外航运法体系的立法例与启迪

美国法没有重点区分公共承运人和私人承运人，而是以合同的方

---

① Charles K. Burdick，"The Origin of the Peculiar Duties of Public Service Companies," *II Columbia Law Review* 515—531，616—638，743—764(June，November，December，1911)．

② Lincoln F. Schaub and Nathan Isaacs，*The Law in Business Problems*(New York：Macmillan Co.，1922)，pp.101—104．

③ Irwin S. Rosenbaum，"The Common Carrier-Public Utility Concept：A Legal-Industrial View，"*The Journal of Land & Public Utility Economics*，Vol.7，No.2(May，1931)．p.168．

式——服务合同(service contract)来规制从事公共运输。根据美国《1984年航运法》及其修正案《1998年航运改革法》(OSRA，1998)，远洋公共承运人之间确定或调整运输费率、分配货载以及运力合作，在完成法定报备程序基础上，可以享有反托拉斯法的豁免。①美国具有健全的航运法律制度，美国航运秩序依赖其健全的航运法律体系来规制和保障。因此，公共承运人的强制缔约义务与责任体系没有在 19 世纪中叶以降的美国航运法律体系中得强化，因为其市场秩序依赖健全的单行航运法律体系得到保障。

　　以美国为代表的航运国家，在构建相对比较健全的航运法律体系以规制和保障航运市场竞争秩序的同时，特别强化了航运业反垄断制度的运行。美国《1916年航运法》首次确立了航运业在反垄断中的豁免制度。欧陆国家通过专门立法纷纷设立类似准则，亚洲的日本和韩国在海运运输法中也有相关规定。2010 年《美国航运法》取消班轮公会集体定价权，强化了承运人协议及服务合同的运用。1949 年以降，日本经过 4次修订相关法案，航运竞争法律体制日趋健全和严格。②上述立法例在应对复杂多变的国际航运市场秩序上，表现出很强的实用性和灵活性。立法者不应该指望通过一部合同法典即可以完成对航运市场秩序的规制，而应该积极探索应对国际航运市场的多变和复杂而展开有效的法律机制和模式。

二、完善中国相关法律的设计构想

　　比较法律经济学认为许多跨国因素的确影响了法律的演进和变迁。传统或文化因素仍可能被解释为真实世界中交易成本以及路径依赖模式，它们抵制法律向效率的进化。③前文解读 common carrier 这一具有跨国因素的

---

①　参见邹盈颖、丁莲芝、张敏：《国际班轮运输业反垄断豁免政策和立法之态势与启示》，《上海海事大学学报》2012 年第 2 期。

②　参见颜晨广、岳金卫：《国际航运市场反垄断豁免合理性研究》，《交通企业管理》2014 年第 1 期。

③　参见［美］乌戈马太：《比较法律经济学》，沈宗灵译，北京大学出版社 2005 年版，第120 页。

法律概念，为反思中国相关立法及其完善提供了思路和可能性。从立法技术、修法成本以及法律移植等基本范畴上看，我国《民法典》第810条具有重塑的必要性和可行性。其基本方案为：要么修改《民法典》第810条，并辅以必要的司法解释；要么彻底摒弃《民法典》第810条，而在合同法典中增设"服务合同"作为有名合同之一种；要么维系《民法典》第810条不变，而另行展开中国航运法的立法。

1. 完善《民法典》第810条

我国《民法典》第810条将"从事公共运输的承运人"和强制缔约义务相挂钩，这显然值得反思和商榷。公共承运人所担负的社会经济职能，并不必然和强制缔约产生关联。历史上，公共承运人具有强制缔约的义务，亦有缔约自由的权利。故此，两者并未形成法律上的"一一对应"的关系。就从事国际航运班轮运输的承运人而言，普通法下common carrier的历史变迁脉络也彰显了其与强制缔约义务的"藕断丝连"和"时断时续"的属性。更何况，在无法明确强制缔约属于私法义务还是公法义务的前提下，通常认为强制缔约属于作为私法体系的合同法范畴，因此，《民法典》第810条不仅在立法所依赖的法理上存在问题，而且从立法目的和立法背景来考察，其所规制市场秩序的立法目的并不能单单依赖缔约是否强制来完成。

不仅如此，从事国际班轮运输的承运人，由于国际航运市场秩序的复杂性决定其法律地位的变动不居。必要情境之下，不能断然否定从事国际航运班轮运输的承运人的强制缔约义务的发生。如此一来，笔者以为，为了立法的严谨起见，建议将《民法典》第810条予以修订，在"从事公共运输的承运人不得拒绝旅客、托运人通常、合理的运输要求"植入特定的适用条件，诸如"法律和法规规定的情景"；然而，由于"公共运输"和"法律法规规定的情景"认定的复杂性，在修订《民法典》第810条之际，还必须辅以相关的司法解释，以进一步完善之。更何况，如何界定"法律和法规规定的情景"是一个令人感到棘手的问题。

2. 摒弃《民法典》第 810 条

完善我国法下从事公共运输的承运人法律制度的另一方案是，完全摒弃《民法典》第 810 条，而在合同法典中增设"服务合同"为典型合同之一种。从立法资源和立法成本上看，此修改方案较之上一方案的立法代价大。本方案成败的关键因素在于如何论证我国法语境中的"航运服务合同"问题。

"航运服务合同"这一概念最先出现在美国 1984 年《航运法》。①从法典的性质可以看出其仅适用于班轮运输领域。②一般地，服务合同是指托运人与国际班轮运输承运人之间订立的除提单或海运单以外的书面合同。该合同下托运人承诺在一定期间内提供一定数量或一定比例的货物，承运人承诺以一定的运价提供运输服务。航运服务合同属于长期运输合同，属于基于自由协商订立的一种互惠性的安排。③不仅美国相关航运立法为立法者引入航运服务合同提供了某种立法借鉴，而且民事立法领域亦有相关经验可资考究。荷兰民法典开历史之先河，在服务合同中首次采用"类合同"的立法路径，在物与权利交易之外为服务合同设定总则性规定。日本和欧盟受其启迪，充分挖掘本国的立法资源和立法技术而不断完善服务合同的立法模式。我国曾经在《民法典》立法阶段设想创立服务合同，但是由于被一些学者认为服务合同缺乏典型性而最终缺位于我国合同法典中的 15 种典型合同之列。④晚近以来，典型合同具有在价值上注重人文关怀、新典型合同类型不断涌现、承认混合合同、合同规则日益复杂化和技术化以及合

---

①　1916 年美国施行《航运法》，1998 年美国国会通过了《航运改革法》。该法于 1999 年 5 月 1 日生效。

②　法案的第 3 条第 19 款规定："服务合同是指一个或多个托运人与一个远洋公共承运人之间，或两个或多个远洋公共承运人与其签订的除提单或货物收据以外的书面协议。一个或多个托运人承诺在一定的固定期限内提供一定批量或最低限量的货物，或保证承运人一定的运费收入；而远洋公共承运人承诺按照一定的费率或费率表收取运费，并就确定的服务水平，如舱位保证、运输期间、挂港顺序或类似的服务内容等作出承诺。"

③　See Edwin C. Goddard, Contract Limitations of the Common Carrier's Liability. *Michigan Law Review*. Vol.8, No.7(May, 1910).

④　曾祥生：《服务合同立法的比较研究》，《求索》2011 年第 12 期。

同法出现国际化和趋同化的发展趋向。①故此，摒弃《民法典》第 810 条之后的立法空白，可由在合同法典中补白服务合同这一典型合同来充实。

3. 在现有法律资源基础上启动航运法的立法

除了上述两种基本方案之外，笔者建议，在《中华人民共和国国际海运条例》的基础上，启动中国的航运法的立法工作。显然，作为规制航运市场和竞争秩序的基本法律，未来中国航运法承担了全面的调整和规范国际海运竞争和市场秩序的使命。在充分调研和论证的基础上，以《中华人民共和国国际海运条例》为基础，在充分考察和借鉴外国相关立法经验的基础上，全面启动中国的航运法的立法工作，以奠定和构建中国航运竞争法体系。

普通法体系内的法律实践者们天然地拥有广阔而自由的施展才华的空间，而法律的理论家则必然退居次要的地位，这种角色分配恰与以罗马法为渊源的大陆法系形成对照。②法律只有在涉及价值的立场框架中才可能被理解。法律的概念也只有在有意识地去实现法律理念的现实情况下才能够被确定。③本书以考察"瀛海诉马士基"案为突破口，以普通法上的 common carrier 为探究的原点，采用历史的、经济的以及比较的手段，考察了由 common carrier 到公共承运人，再到"从事公共运输的承运人"的立法进路和法理变迁，展示了普通承运人、公共承运人以及从事公共运输的承运人的历史演进、法理变迁以及经济基础的时空进化，基本上勾勒一幅关于 common carrier 的历史图景。顾及我国《民法典》第 810 条的立法技术、立法目的以及立法背景，笔者笃信，《民法典》第 810 条具有进一步完善或者修订的可行性和法理依据。

---

① 王利明：《典型合同立法的发展趋势》，《法制与社会发展》2014 年第 2 期。

② 参见［英］约翰·哈德森：《英国普通法的形成——从诺曼征服到大宪章时期英格兰的法律与社会》，刘四新译，商务印书馆 2006 年版，第 6 页。

③ ［德］G.拉德布鲁赫(Gustav Radbruch)：《法哲学》，王朴译，法律出版社 2005 年版，第 4 页。

第3章　制约沿海运输权立法与政策的主要因素

第一节　国家主权

根据国际法各国只能对 12 海里的海域主张主权，该海域构成国际法意义上的领海。[①]传统上，领海是国家拥有绝对主权的沿海水域的一部分。因此，沿海国可能对其他海域拥有主权权利而非主权意义上的海洋权利。国际法框架下被称为公海的那部分海域对所有人都是自由的，不受沿海国的管辖。许多海洋国家按照国际法在其领海 12 海里范围内行使其沿海运输权。然而，一些国家将沿海运输权从其领水基线延伸至 200 英里。早在 15 世纪和 16 世纪，关于沿海运输权的早期理论就关注一个国家是否拥有将海洋的任何部分划归其专属主权的权利。[②]该理论关注贸易运输问题诸如航行控制、市场准入、海关和税收制度等。早期，海洋主权的概念都体现在罗马法律体系中。[③]罗马法体系囊括了海洋是否应不受任何控制、是否应允许主权国家对其海洋行使控制权以及允许这种控制权波及距离沿海国基线多远的海域。

某种意义上，沿海运输权的保护主义、自由主义以及灵活主义，在很

---

① 参见 1982 年《联合国海洋法公约》第 2 条。

② S. Chester, "Grotius, Selden and 400 Years of Controversy", *Slaw Legal Magazine*, Toronto, 1 November 2009.

③ E. Gold, *Maritime Transport：The Evolution of International Marine Policy and Shipping Law*, D. C. Heath & Co. 1981.

大程度上映射出格劳修斯、约翰·塞尔登和宾克舒克提出的关于领海地位的理论和理念。荷兰法学家雨果·格劳修斯于 1609 年发表了《海洋自由》(*mare liberum*)一书，声称海洋无法被支配。他认为，海洋应可供所有投资的海洋权益自由使用。因此，如果一个国家不能声称拥有海洋，这意味着海洋不受该国主权的管辖。[①]从本质上说，自由海洋假定海洋是所有人的共同财产，任何国家都不应拥有对海洋的所有权。为了回应格劳修斯的立场，英国法学家约翰·塞尔登于 1635 年出版了《闭海论》一书。约翰·塞尔登反对海洋自由的原则，提出某些海域可以在一个国家的专属管辖权下主张。约翰·塞尔登认为，根据自然法和国际法海洋实际上与土地一样可以被占用。[②]此外，约翰·塞尔登认为外国船舶进入另一国家领水的机会应被视为享有的一种特权。

然而，另一位荷兰法学家宾刻舒克(Cornelius Bynkershoek)于 1702 年提出了与其他法学家不同的折中方案，认为一个沿海国家应该有权对其能够有效控制和保护的大部分海域拥有主权。宾刻舒克提出了公海自由和沿海国家领海主权的理论。一方面，他反对约翰·塞尔登的闭海论，认为主权必须从海岸线向外延伸到武器力量的极限。这就是所谓的大炮射程论。另一方面，他不同意格劳秀斯海洋自由学说，认为海洋的某些部分应该受到沿海国主权的控制。然而，在大多数国家追求其海上商业目标的时候，宾刻舒克的理论确实满足了各种政治、商业和战略需要。[③]此外，这在自由或封闭领海的政治秩序中也发挥了关键作用。宾刻舒克的观点促成了领海3 海里观点，该规则在 1982 年《联合国海洋法公约》之前一直普遍存在。

---

① H. Grotius, "Mare Liberum: The Freedom of the Seas or The Right Which Belongs to The Dutch To Take Part in the East Indian Trade", translated by R. Magoffin, in J. Scott(ed.), *Classics of International Law*, Oxford University Press 1916.

② G. Edmond(1995), "The Freedom of Histories: Reassessing Grotius on the Sea", *University of Wollongong Australia Law Text Culture*, 2(9), 179—217.

③ T. Fulton, The Sovereignty of the Sea: An Historical Account of the Claims to England to the Dominion of the British Seas, And of the Evolution of the Territorial Waters: With Special Reference to the Right of Fishing And The Naval Salute, William Blackwood 1911.

此外，根据 1982 年《联合国海洋法公约》规定，沿海国有资格主张 12 海里领海、24 海里毗连区、200 海里专属经济区和大陆架区。[1]然而，这些海洋权利并非排他性的，因为其他沿海邻国对这些区域拥有同样的海洋权利。[2]

目前，不同沿海运输权的学说争论，与 16 世纪海洋自由或者闭海论的争论具有学理上的和相通性和关联度。有学者认为，关于海洋自由的论点并不是因为任何一方优先考虑国际社会的利益。相反，该论点产生于各国基于保护本国财富来源的考虑而形成的偏见或者愿望。[3]例如，闭海论政策对英国有利，因为英国在世界范围内拥有大量的殖民地利益。因此，英国信奉领土主权的观念。而海洋自由论则对荷兰人更具吸引力，因此，荷兰人采取务实的方法而奉行海上贸易自由的商业哲学，以促进和维持荷兰的商业利益的拓展。在 1854 年之前的三个多世纪里，英国一直支持封闭海政策，并废除了保护主义政策，成为开放沿海运输权政策的主要支持者。有学者认为英国实际上并没有采取自由主义政策，相反，保护主义的沿海运输权政策是为了保护英国的国家利益。这一背后的驱动力是英国对其他主权国家的报复行为的恐惧，这些主权国家更希望采取保护主义的沿海运输政策。[4]"自由之海"和"封闭之海"的争论，在历史上可能集中在主权和海上贸易霸权上。然而，目前围绕选择沿海运输权政策的辩论更多地集中在经济发展和主权基础上。

一些重要的国际组织也关注沿海运输权立法和政策问题。作为重要

---

① B. Fassbender and A. Peters, "Introduction: Towards A Global History of International Law", in B. Fassbender and A. Peters(eds), *The Oxford Handbook of the History of International Law*, Oxford University Press 2012, pp.3—24.

② D. Harris, Cases and Materials on International Law, 7th edn, Thomson Reuters 2010.

③ G. Mailer, "Europe, the American Crisis, and Scottish Evangelism: The Primacy of Foreign Policy in the Kirk?", in W. Mulligan and B. Simms(eds), *The Primacy of Foreign Policy in British History, 1660—2000: How Strategic Concerns Shaped Modern Britain*, Palgrave Macmillan 2010, pp.119—136.

④ A. Lorca, "Eurocentrism in the History of International Law", in B. Fassbender and A. Peters(eds), *The Oxford Handbook of the History of International Law*, Oxford University Press 2012, pp.1034—1057.

的国际组织，世界贸易组织（WTO）的目标之一是促进无缝全球运输系统的形成。然而，虽然在一些运输部门的自由化方面取得了进展，但世界贸易组织在处理沿海运输权政策方面没有取得任何进展。在《服务贸易总协定》框架下，没有能够将沿海运输权议题纳入其框架之内。这引起了自由化程度的进一步发展的问题。从根本上讲，沿海运输权的政策理念与保护主义相一致，与世界贸易组织的自由化政策和原则相矛盾。①因此，尽管沿海运输权的困局依然存在，但海洋国家仍然可以自由制定更复杂和保护主义的沿海运输权政策。这挑战了世界贸易组织的自由化。此外，乌拉圭回合和多哈回合错失的机会，表明了世界贸易组织在寻求沿海运输权政策上的国际协调方面所面临的挑战。世界贸易组织成员在乌拉圭回合上关于协调沿海运输权的讨论没有达成共识。②这显然是很遗憾的。

1987 年，经济合作与发展组织（以下简称"经合组织"）通过了"成员国航运政策共同原则"倡议，以便寻求促进统一的航运政策和自由竞争。尽管这是一项不具约束力的政策，但经合组织成员国同意不在这一框架下采取任何限制竞争准入的新措施，其目标是促进开放的航运政策的形成，鼓励经合组织成员国之间的贸易和投资。根据经合组织关于航运政策共同原则的报告，该组织承认经合组织和非经合组织成员国都广泛实行沿海运输权体制。③

许多海运国家，无论是经合组织成员国还是非成员国，都认识到海运政策在促进其经济发展方面的重要性。美国认为 1920 年《琼斯法案》既是一个主权问题，也是一个航运问题。因此，有必要维持一支由本国国民为贸易和国防目的配备人员的本土商船队。同样，在尼日利亚实施沿海运输

---

① L. Weiss（2005），"Global Governance，National Strategies：How Industrialized States Make Room to Move Under the WTO"，*Review of International Political Economy*，12(5)，723—749.

② K. Kennedy，"GATT 1994"，in P. Macrory，A. Appleton and M. Plummer（eds），*The World Trade Organization：Legal，Economic and Political Analysis*，vol. 1，Springer 2007，pp.91—182.

③ W. Hubner，"Regulatory Issues in International Maritime Transport"，OECD，2001.

权立法的理由也是基于经济发展的目的。[①]关于保护主义沿海运输权政策的总体有效性，属于一个备受争议的课题。这表明，沿海运输权在自由化进程中可能会遭遇很多因素的阻碍。

第二节　经济发展

从经济发展这个视角看，沿海运输权政策对一个国家经济发展的促进作用比较显著。[②]经济发展在这里是指国内经济因实施了沿海运输权的政策或法律而出现的增长。在这种情况下，沿海运输权必然构成其他经济部门发展机会的主要刺激因素。困扰沿海运输权立法与政策的基础很多，其中，沿海国对于国家经济发展的维系是重要基础之一。当然，实践表明，各国无法确定一成不变的沿海运输权立法和政策。尽管如此，一般的做法是，主权国家根据促进国家经济发展的需要来选择沿海运输权的立法和政策。如果要考虑这一点，那么应该以评估经济发展作为确立沿海运输权立法和政策的衡量标准。[③]如果人们认同经济发展作为衡量沿海运输权立法和政策的基础，那么，发展主权理论提供了一种恰当的理论构造来衡量经济发展对沿海运输权模式的制约。而这一理论的重要性体现于它提供了一种达成对沿海运输权不同模式的统一认识的途径。这是因为，这一理论侧重于关于沿海运输权立法和政策对东道国的经济发展所产生的实际影响。

经济发展理论的重要内容之一是它体现了"可持续发展"的理念。因此，经济发展提出了一个重要问题，即主权国家对其所采用的沿海运输权模式的选择是否确实产生了该国所期望的经济发展，以及这种规则模式所

---

① M. Igbokwe, "Advocacy Paper for the Promulgation of a Nigerian Maritime Cabotage Law: Present and Potential Problems of Cabotage and Recommended Solutions" Presented on the Public Hearing of the Nigerian Cabotage Bill, at the House Committee on Transport, National Assembly complex, Abuja in April 2001.

② G. Rees and C. Smith, *Economic Development*, 2nd edn, Macmillan Press 1998.

③ D. Weil, *Economic Growth*, 3rd edn, Prentice Hall 2013.

取得的经济发展是否是可持续的。一般来说，可持续发展背后的理念意味着一种促进要实现的发展战略。[1]因此，在制定沿海运输权立法和政策时，国家自身利益的实现至关重要，是首要考虑的因素。经济发展理论认为，更现实和务实的模式才是更重要的。因此，如果主权国家的经济发展是制定沿海运输权政策的首要目标，则国家必须证明法律存在实现其预期目标的基础。此外，主权国家制定特定沿海运输权立法和政策模式的历史、政治和经济背景处于核心地位，一个国家的沿海运输权立法和政策的制定过程可能具有深刻的政治性和经济利益，从而掩盖了沿海运输权立法本身。[2] 2003年《尼日利亚沿海航行法》第3条规定，除由尼日利亚公民全资拥有和配备船员、在尼日利亚建造并根据尼日利亚法律注册的船舶外，其余船舶不得在其国内水域从事海上运输活动。通常而言，采取保护主义沿海运输权模式必然是该国对于沿海运输视为重要战略的结果。然而，当我们认真评估这项法律规定可以达到预期的效果时，其缺陷是很明显的。的确，尼日利亚造船业尚未达到能够大规模建造远洋船舶的水平。因此，就尼日利亚而言，沿海运输权立法缺乏实用主义功能，因为它无法实现其所预期的经济效果。[3]

许多主权国家都拥有某种形式的资源，无论是自然资源还是人力资源，并试图以此来发展他们的国民经济。实现这一目标的方式将对实现何种经济发展以及实现这一目标需要多长时间产生重大影响。在很多情况下，关于如何推动国民经济的向前发展需要制定短期、中期和长期计划。这当然取决于设计发展经济的初始状态。因此，发展中国家的经济发展规划将不同于发达国家。发展中国家的经济发展目标是激发经济增长，而发达国家则是维持经济发展和探索新机遇。此外，任何此类国家的经济发展

---

① D. Goulet, The Cruel Choice: A New Concept on the Theory of Development, Atheneum 1971.

② M. Hendrickson(2007), "Trade Liberalisation, Trade Performance and Competitiveness in the Caribbean", in N. Duncan et al.(eds), *Caribbean Development Report*, 1(1), 222—254.

③ S. Knowles and A. Garces-Ozanne(2003), "Government Intervention and Economic Performance in East Asia", *Economic Development and Cultural Change*, 51(2), 451—477.

计划需要考虑是否追求保护主义、自由主义或灵活的政策以促进其目标。而沿海运输权的立法和政策，在促进沿海国的国内造船产业、优化本国公民占有船舶所有权、构建有竞争力的船舶登记制度以及促进船员就业等方面发挥其制度功能。事实上，根据长期对美国1920年《琼斯法案》的跟踪考察，美国通过保护主义的沿海运输权立法和政策表明，美国计划继续遵循这种发展模式。多年来，美国通过充分利用其政治、社会和经济系统维持对1920年《琼斯法案》的支持，并已经取得了成功。①

因此，如果一个主权国家已将其沿海运输权政策视为经济发展的催化剂，其发展模式应体现一种务实的做法。例如，如果一国没有能力建造船舶，或者如果通过在其他国家建造船舶可以节省成本，则立法规定在国内沿海航行的船舶必须在国内建造是不理智的。同样，如果一国没有足够的适格的本国海员，规定船舶必须只雇用本国海员，必将是阻碍该国的经济发展。此外，任何此类国家经济发展规划都应针对长期经济发展的战略计划和明确的应急计划。以英国为例，英国沿海运输权就有应对欧盟成员国的欧盟理事会第3577/92号条例的应急计划和立法。②

因此，任何国家的经济发展规划都应该包含一个全面的经济发展战略。此外，它应注重于利用可支配资源促进经济的可持续发展的最佳方式。一个经典的保护主义沿海运输权模式下，经济发展理论通常适用于该国应拥有强大而充满活力的国内造船业、存在有能力拥有船舶的本国个人或公司、本国船舶登记可以为本土船舶所有人提供适当的制度优势以及认可的海员职业能力培训计划。③如果满足上述要求，保护主义沿海运输权政策将是促进经济发展的适当方法。因此，在不满足上述要求的情况下，如

---

①　D. Coulter, "Globalization of Maritime Commerce: The Rise of Hub Ports", in S. Tangredi (ed.), *Globalization and Maritime Power*, National Defence University 2009, pp.133—142.

②　M. Aoki et al.(1997), "Beyond The East Asian Miracle: Introducing the Market Enhancing View: The Role of Government in East Asian Economic Development", *Comparative Institutional Analysis*, 1(1), 1—37.

③　J. Powell, "Protectionist Paradise?", in E. Hudgins(ed.), *Freedom to Trade: Refuting the New Protectionism*, Cato Institute 1997, pp.57—68.

何通过保护主义沿海运输权政策来触发和维持一个国家的国民经济发展尚不清楚。在尼日利亚，船舶必须在国内造船厂建造的要求不切实际，因为尼日利亚国内造船业还没有能力建造商业规模的船舶。因此，经济发展理论认为，如果重新考虑在国内水域使用的船舶必须在国内造船厂建造的这一法律规定，将有利于经济发展。①

一般来说，自由主义沿海运输权政策允许外国实体在主权国家的沿海水域开展海上活动，但这并不一定意味着完全没有限制。因此，一项自由的沿海运输权政策是在可能的情况下将优先考虑本国公民，而不是全面禁止外国实体进入主权国家的沿海水域。南非和新西兰是两个采用自由主义沿海运输权模式的国家。欧盟的沿海运输权模式通常被称为自由主义沿海运输权模式的范本。然而，欧盟采用的自由主义的沿海运输权模式的优惠政策只是赋予其成员国。因此，第三方国家不能期望从欧盟沿海运输权政策框架中受益。自由主义沿海运输权模式的主要缺点是可能带来阻碍国内企业成长和发展的意外后果。因此，在采用自由主义沿海运输权模式情况下，经济发展理论通常适用于政策和法律框架应在支持国内航运企业和鼓励外国航运实体进入本国海上运输领域之间寻找到平衡，或者是构建一个机制来监测自由主义沿海运输权模式是否促进经济发展以符合国家利益。②自由主义沿海运输权模式的成功实施与外国参与本国沿海运输对国家经济发展的贡献程度有一定的关系。所以，经济发展理论将评估允许外国航运实体进入本国海洋运输领域是否有效促进国家经济发展，或是否阻碍本国产能和企业的发展。③

灵活主义沿海运输权模式旨在可以在保护主义沿海运输权和自由主义沿海运输权之间交替转换。这种转换可能是周期性的，并且通常取决于沿

---

① R. Matison，"Economic Growths False Paradigm"，*The Market Oracle*，27 January 2014.

② H. Singer(1970)，"Dualism Revisited：A New Approach to the Problems of Dual Societies in Developing Countries"，*Journal of Development Studies*，7(1)，60—61.

③ M. Syrquin，"Patterns of Structural Change"，in H. Chenery and T. Srinivasan(eds)，*Handbook of Development Economics*，vol.1，Elsevier 1989，pp.205—273.

海国的经济状况。灵活主义沿海运输权模式的主要优势在于它为沿海国提供了调整政策以适应其当前情况的机会。然而，这种模式的问题在于国内外航运实体的不确定性。尽管宽松的做法可能有利于外国航运实体，但是他们只可能进行短期投资，因为他们知道政策可能会改变。同样，保护主义沿海运输权模式可能无法为本国航运实体提供足够的安全性以鼓励他们进行长期投资。当然，在考察制约沿海运输权模式的基础因素中，主权的因素不可忽视。主权国家根据选定的沿海运输权政策所触发的经济可持续发展进程方面的作用，可以概括为根据经济发展理论制定适当的沿海运输权立法和政策、制定适当的法律和社会框架来指导政府政策、建立健全的监测和审查机制以帮助定期评估政府政策对经济的影响以及创造有利环境，进而促进经济蓬勃发展。[①]总而言之，为了在选择的沿海运输权模式的基础上促进航运经济可持续发展，政府应采取务实和灵活的沿海运输权机制和目标来追求海洋经济的发展。

　　经济发展框架必须充分顾及选择沿海运输权所涉及的各种利益，这些利益包括本国船舶所有人、外国船舶所有人、造船厂、本国海员、本国贸易商以及其他辅助沿海运输服务的提供商等。因此，沿海运输权理论框架是根据一种或多种利益的评估而形成的。[②]保护本国船舶所有人和本国船员利益需要而塑造了美国式沿海运输权政策框架，而保护本国贸易商利益而逐渐造就了马来西亚式沿海运输权政策模式。不仅如此，沿海国家可以自由决定其沿海运输权法律和政策的范围和严格程度，这也显示了沿海运输权立法和政策的灵活性。这一点在许多国家得到了证明。沿海运输权立法和政策可以在公司法、移民法、海关法和劳动法等领域得到推行。基于经济发展理论的沿海运输权的政策在促进一国的涉海经济发展上具有重要的制度价值。

---

　　① W. Bonefeld(2012)，"Freedom and the Strong State: On German Ordoliberalism", *New Political Economy*，17(5)，633—656.

　　② L. Taylor(1997)，"The Revival of the Liberal creed: The IMF and the World Bank in a Globalized Economy", *World Development*，25(2)，145—152.

当 1382 年英国理查德二世(Richard II)颁布了最早的沿海运输权法时，并没有设想它会成为促进经济发展的法律机制。当然，关于这一点的学术争论很大。沿海运输权立法和政策的实施具有涉外因素色彩，因为这是由与海运和服务相关的国际性因素导致的。尽管如此，沿海运输权的法律功能主要为本国航运业的利益服务的。[①]应当指出的是，没有足够证据证明这样的观点，即解除对沿海运输权管制政策的国家有失去主权的危险，或其国家安全受到威胁。正如南非和新西兰的实践提供了充分的证据，证明自由主义沿海运输权政策既不是国家经济发展的障碍，也不是国家安全漏洞。同样，欧洲联盟在其成员国之间实施了一项实质上自由化的沿海运输权制度，没有任何明显的不利影响。[②]

第三节　经济竞争

经济竞争法的核心是利用国内外的资源促进本国或本地区的经济发展。人们可以将经济发展视为最终产品的衡量标准，经济竞争法视为实现该目标的方法和手段。接受竞争法作为实现经济发展路径的国家数量显著增加。这种方法背后的理由是，自由和自由市场政策能够使竞争力量不受限制地相互作用，并激发出竞争活力，从而在有利的商业和市场环境中实现经济资源的最佳配置、最佳的市场价格和高质量的商品和服务。[③]然而，这不应被视为竞争法必然是促进经济发展的基础。此外，虽然竞争法可能有助于维持工业化国家的经济增长，但没有证据表明它是发展中经济体经济发展的主要催化剂。沿海国家在沿海运输权立法中采用的保护主义沿海

---

① B. Gurtner(2010)，"The Financial and Economic Crisis and Developing Countries"，*International Development Policy*，1(1)，189—213.

② T. Bartik(1990)，"The Market Failure Approach to Regional Economic Development Policy"，*Economic Development Quarterly*，40(4)，361—370.

③ L. Ioannis, A. Mateus and A. Raslan，"Is There Tension Between Development Economics and Competition?"，in D. Sokol, T. Cheng and L. Ioannis(eds)，*Competition Law and Development*，Stanford University Press 2013，pp.35—51.

运输权、自由主义沿海运输权和灵活主义沿海运输权等不同模式中，其中自由主义沿海运输权模式属于最迎合竞争法的理念。从沿海运输的角度看，自由主义沿海运输权旨在通过邀请所有感兴趣的参与者在平等的条件下进行竞争，以最佳的价格提供最高质量的服务。然而，国内航运企业与外国航运企业相比往往缺乏资源，无法与之在同一水平上进行竞争。国内航运企业可能会由此将这一公开邀请视为对其生存的威胁。因此，促进海洋经济发展的想法在很大程度上取决于适当的政府监管、影响和干预。

为适应竞争法理念而设计的有效制度需要全面评估该国现有资源和该国实施经济发展驱动的竞争法律框架的能力。这种评估将有助于了解国民经济的优势、劣势、机会和威胁的现状。事实上，竞争法体系与主权国家成功实施这种政策的能力之间的差距，构成了发展中国家在传统国际竞争法体系基础上实现经济发展所面临的更广泛挑战的一部分。[1]因此，无法保证自由主义沿海运输权在一个国家能够有效实施，而在另一个国家也会必然产生同样的效果。因此，不同国家将根据其国情去实施不同的沿海运输权。

经济发展的一个重要范式是鼓励竞争的经济繁荣。虽然竞争法在促进经济发展方面发挥着重要作用，但是根据不同主权国家的特殊情况，竞争法对经济发展的贡献存在着不同的情景。因此，不同模式沿海运输权政策的实施所产生的竞争法效果也是不同的。现代竞争法将 1890 年《谢尔曼反垄断法》（*Sherman Antitrust Act*）作为其起源，通过该法案禁止某些被视为反竞争的商业活动。[2]在 Spectrum Sports 股份有限公司诉 McQuillan 案中，美国最高法院裁定，1890 年《谢尔曼反垄断法》的目的不是保护组织免受市场机制的影响，而是保护公众免受市场失灵的影响。[3]因此，该法案

---

[1]　D. Gerber，"Economic Development and Global Competition Law Convergence"，in D. Sokol，T. Cheng and L. Ioannis(eds)，*Competition Law and Development*，Stanford University Press 2013，pp.13—34.

[2]　M. Furse，*Competition Law of the EC and UK*，6th edn，Oxford University Press 2008.

[3]　V. Power，*EU Shipping Law*，3rd edn，Informa 2015.

的目的是保护竞争，而不是像人们普遍认为的那样保护竞争者。相比之下，《欧盟竞争法》倾向于保护竞争对手不受市场竞争的影响。《欧盟竞争法》第 101 条至第 109 条适用于卡特尔、市场支配地位、兼并和国家援助的管制。适用于海运服务的《欧盟竞争法》由第 1/2003 号条例以及相关的第 1419/2006 号条例组成，后者于 2008 年废除了第 4056/86 号条例，因为它被认为损害了委员会的公平竞争政策。①竞争法的理念不是由 1890 年《谢尔曼反垄断法》带来的现象。事实上竞争法是从宪法性法律中借来的，早在该法颁布之前就已经以有组织的方式实施。

　　竞争法的目标和方法可能因管辖权而异。这意味着不可能总是给竞争法下一个标准的定义，也不可能总是确切地描述竞争法在不同法域的适用范围。竞争法在美国被称为"反托拉斯法"，而在俄罗斯等国法域则被称为"反垄断法"，这表明它们的目标和监管范围是不同的。因此，竞争法是最好通过理解其目的来界定其适用的范围和立法动机。竞争法的主要目的是防止或纠正自由市场体系失灵的情况。因此，市场经济中的公平竞争是竞争法的一个重要目标。然而，这种公平竞争是否直接导致经济发展是令人难以理解的。这是与沿海运输权立法和政策具有共同的特点，因为同一个问题的核心在于自由主义沿海运输权和保护主义沿海运输权究竟何者更能成为经济发展的最佳催化剂。②在实行自由海运政策的国家，海运法与竞争法的关系是明显的。这是因为这两个领域的法律有着相同的目标，即放松航运市场准入管制，避免政府补贴和国有资产私有化。这假设公平和有效的竞争为商业企业提供了一个平台，以争取提高在生产和提供海上运输服务的成本方面的效率。因此，竞争法应满足的三个要素可以表述如下：第一，应禁止限制或压制一国内航运企业之间的自由贸易和竞争的协定或做法。第二，必须防止因一家公司主导市场而导致的恐吓或滥用行

---

① M. Furse, *Competition Law of the EC and UK*, 6th edn, Oxford University Press 2008.

② A. Bhattacharjea, "Who Needs Antitrust? Or, Is Developing-Country Antitrust Different? A Historical Comparative Analysis", in D. Sokol, T. Cheng and L. Ioannis(eds), *Competition Law and Development*, Stanford University Press 2013, pp.52—65.

为，或可能导致这种主导地位的反竞争做法。第三，必须对大企业的并购进行监管，这包括一些可能威胁到一个国家竞争进程的合资企业。[1]美国《谢尔曼反垄断法》关注的是垄断组织的活动，该法案的目的是确定他们的行为，如合资或合并，是否会通过提高价格和降低产量来造成市场的不公平。[2]而《欧盟竞争法》的重点是监测主要参与者，以确定他们是否考虑合并或合资，以防止其他参与者进入市场。

　　美国和欧盟在这个问题上的出发点是不同的。欧洲普遍表示强烈希望在国际层面上规范竞争政策。然而，这一想法在美国却引起了相当大的反对，尽管这种立场似乎有所软化。这种新立场的一个例子是国际竞争政策咨询委员会(ICPAC)发布的报告承认美国反垄断案件在国际层面有增加的趋势。因此，美国倾向于支持欧盟立场表明有必要在国际层面建立一个基本的竞争监管框架。[3]然而，这一发展不应忽视的事实是，美国 1890 年《谢尔曼反垄断法》和《欧盟竞争法》唤起了一些非常相关的考虑：第一，发展中国家除了采用美国的 1890 年《谢尔曼反垄断法》或《欧盟的竞争法》之外，似乎别无选择。这样做的挑战在于，这些发展中国家往往缺乏能力成功地实施这两种复杂的竞争法体系。第二，关于发展中国家是否应该选择一条与工业化国家所规划的不同方向的道路。这是由于发展中国家普遍存在的诸如专业知识匮乏、市场迟缓、金融资本稀缺和市场准入紧张等问题所决定的。这些共同的问题可以解决这些发展中国家的特殊缺陷。[4]

　　竞争法的焦点是市场。竞争法假定市场经济中总会存在竞争，经济发

---

　　① 　M. Taylor, *International Competition Law: A New Dimension for the WTO?*, 2nd edn, Cambridge University Press 2006.

　　② 　R. Cass(2009), "Competition in Antitrust Regulation: Law beyond Limits", *Journal of Competition Law & Economics*, 6(1), 119—152.

　　③ 　T. Arthur, "Competition Law and Development: Lessons from the U.S. Experience", in D. Sokol, T. Cheng and L. Ioannis(eds), *Competition Law and Development*, Stanford University Press 2013, pp.66—78.

　　④ 　J. Jackson(2003), "Sovereignty—Modern: A New Approach to an Outdated Concept", *American Journal of International Law*, 97(1), 782—802.

展与宏观经济密切相关，这涉及管理国家、区域和全球经济的表现和结构。①然而，在竞争法与经济发展之间有一个关键问题值得认真考虑。如果我们承认不同的国家处于不同的经济发展阶段，那么我们就应该怀疑竞争法设计框架的变化在多大程度上是必要的，甚至是可取的。竞争执法的选择取决于一系列因素，包括社会、经济和政治环境。因此，各国应调整其国内竞争法框架和执法机构，以适应其国家结构。有学者认为竞争法在国家或区域的沿海运输权立法框架中发挥重要作用。这是因为，无论选择何种沿海运输权的立法和政策，一个国家都将不可避免地选择鼓励或阻碍其海洋经济中的竞争进程。因此，为了有效地促进海洋经济的发展，竞争法应辅之以支持海洋经济发展的相容政策。②因此，竞争法对一个国家海洋经济发展的影响取决于这种关系在多大程度上刺激海洋经济所预期的发展目标。

管理不善的竞争可能是破坏性的，特别是在市场竞争机会有限的情况下。一些市场参与者变得非常强大，以至于威胁到竞争的过程。除非采取措施规范这些参与者的行为，否则这两种情况都可能使经济发展陷于停顿。③因此，有关经济学家认为，管理一个国家的宏观经济需要执行适当的竞争法。自由主义沿海运输权在促进海洋经济增长、竞争法的制度价值和海洋经济可持续发展之间的作用至关重要。竞争法的一个基本原则是经济效率与发展的平衡。这表明，在许多领域促进经济效率是竞争政策的明确目标。因此，竞争法与经济发展之间的联系涉及两个问题。第一个问题是竞争法有效实施是如何对经济发展作出积极贡献的。第二个问题涉及执行有缺陷的竞争法框架可能产生的消极后果。因此，只有从"动态效率"的角度来看待经济发展，才能真正理解竞争和发展之间的关系。④这使得人们

---

① M. Stucke(2013)，"Is competition always good?"，*Journal of Antitrust Enforcement*，1(1)，162—197.

② S. Phang(2009)，"Competition Law and the International Transport Sectors"，*Competition Law Review*，5(2)，193—213.

③ B. Paasman(1999)，"Multilateral Rules on Competition Policy: An Overview of the Debate"，*ECLAC—SERIE Comercio Internacional*，2(4)，1—55.

④ J. Podolny(1993)，"A Status-based Model of Market Competition"，*American Journal of Sociology*，98(4)，829—872.

可以将精力集中在一个国家的短期和长期经济目标的可持续平衡上。

尽管沿海运输权立法和竞争法领域的问题具有全球影响，但它们都没有形成国际体制。此外，控制市场运作的要素市场和机构对于增强竞争法对一个国家最优经济发展的影响至关重要。这是因为，为了国家经济的革新发展战略，产业间的竞争会促进生产力的提高。①然而，对于竞争是经济发展的关键这一命题，有一个普遍接受的例外。在保护新兴产业方面，竞争通常被认为是不可取的。在这种情况下，保护主义是可以得到原谅的唯一理由。这种对保护主义的默许与鼓励经济发展的目标息息相关。实现这一目标的方法是使国内工业能够发展到一个水平，使其能够在不处于过分不利地位的情况下进行竞争。然而，长期保护国内企业不受竞争也确实会损害国家的经济发展。当贸易放松管制和私有化等自由政策被作为经济发展的手段时，如果没有有效的竞争法，这种自由化的预期利益可能会丧失。因此，在采取自由海运政策的国家，竞争是被鼓励的。自由主义政策的倡导者认为，在一个国家充分实施竞争法可以增强投资者信心以吸引外国投资。②如果一个国家的经济和市场得到了竞争政策的支持，就有可能从这种外国投资中受益。这是因为鼓励外国投资者通过投资资本和人力资源来支持能力建设，其总体目标是促进国家的经济发展。③此外，在基础设施发展和技术进步领域，竞争法与经济发展之间的联系是明显的。为了实现预期的发展，一些沿海国家必须明确选择奉行自由主义沿海运输权政策还是选择奉行保护主义沿海运输权政策。④在自由主义沿海运输政策下，经济

---

① R. Lucas(1988)，"On the Mechanics of Economic Development"，*Journal of Monetary Economics*，22(1)，3—42.

② M. Solow(1956)，"A Contribution to the Theory of Economic Growth"，*Quarterly Journal of Economics*，1(70)，65—94.

③ E. Brouwer et al.，"Market Structure，Innovation and Productivity：A Marriage with Chemistry"，in G. Gelauff et al.(eds)，*Fostering Productivity：Patterns，Determinants and Policy Implications*，Elsevier 2004，pp.199—212.

④ D. Sokol and A. Stephan，"Prioritizing Cartel Enforcement in Developing World Competition Agencies"，in D. Sokol，T. Cheng and L. Ioannis(eds)，*Competition Law and Development*，Stanford University Press 2013，pp.137—154.

发展和竞争之间是一种意识形态的融合。这是因为沿海运输权立法与竞争法都旨在通过促进各部门的增长来改善经济。因此，有一种理论观点认为，在没有健全的竞争法的情况下实施自由主义沿海运输权政策可能会引发另一种问题，诸如卡特尔化，进而阻碍经济发展。①

因此，竞争政策的有效执行需要高度的问责制和监督。此外，竞争规则的实施可以激励行业通过避免浪费来提高效率。这是因为竞争法通过鼓励创新、工业化和人力资源开发来改善经济监管和支持经济发展。②竞争法和竞争政策影响经济发展。当一个经济体的某一特定部门受到保护以鼓励其发展时，政府可能会进行干预以控制竞争。这往往伴随着政府以补贴、贷款和捐赠的形式提供的支持。在存在垄断经济体制的地方，鼓励自由市场和公平竞争将消除这种垄断。

另外，国家援助可以被定义为国家或地区政府通过提供某种形式的救济来增强市场竞争力量的过程。国家援助通常采取财政拨款、例外或放宽规则的形式，或通过减少国家援助受援国的正常财政义务的方式。正如前述，竞争适用于自由主义沿海运输权，国家援助在很大程度上是支持保护主义沿海运输权政策的一个重要组成部分。它通常会扭曲竞争，并试图让受益航运企业在竞争中占据优势。因此，国家援助被视为一种保护主义政策机制，因为它有可能在市场中引入不公平竞争。在欧盟，《欧盟竞争法》的竞争规则宣布成员国提供的国家援助与内部市场不相容。③然而，《欧盟竞争法》第 107(1)条所载的一般原则被第 107(2)条和第 107(3)条的规定所消减。这两条规定之间的区别是，虽然根据《欧盟竞争法》第 107 条第(2)款必须满足给予国家援助的目的，但根据第 107 条第(3)款则不要求这

---

① A. Fels and W. Ng，"Rethinking Competition Advocacy in Developing Countries"，in D. Sokol，T. Cheng and L. Ioannis(eds)，*Competition Law and Development*，Stanford University Press 2013，pp.182—198.

② R. Gilbert and S. Steven(1995)，"Incorporating Dynamic Efficiency Concerns in Merger Analysis: The Use of Innovation Markets"，*Antitrust Law Journal*，63(2)，569—602.

③ R. Gilbert(2006)，"Competition and Innovation"，*Journal of Industrial Organization Education*，1(1)，8，1—30.

种强制性。一般来说,《欧盟竞争法》第 107 条第 2 款是允许国家援助的,只是要求这种援助具有与内部市场相适应的三个特定目标之一。[1]在欧盟以外,国家援助通常以政府补贴的形式提供给本土船舶所有人,让他们在国内造船厂建造船舶,培训和雇佣本土海员,并在国内船舶注册机构登记船舶。此外,货物和旅客限额可以单独保留给提供沿海运输服务的国内承运人。

第四节　航运补贴[2]

航运补贴是 WTO 框架下的海运服务领域一个重要而又敏感的课题,也是制约一国采取沿海运输权模式的重要基础。在海运服务自由化的趋势下,很多海运国家为了不让自己国家的海运业丧失竞争力,依然纷纷在调整本国航运业的法律法规中制定相应的保护和扶持措施。此类保护和扶持措施在一国的航运业立法中往往体现在两个方面,一类是保护性立法,其主要表现形式是对国外竞争者的排除和限制;一类是扶持性立法,其最主要表现形式是对本国航运活动的补贴和扶持。扶持性立法成为当今各国航运立法中的核心内容,航运补贴扶持性立法的必然结果是航运补贴制度的形成。它对于维护本国海运业的发展和提升本国商船队的竞争实力起到显著的作用。目前,世界各国普遍采用的航运补贴的表现为直接补贴和间接补贴。

传统海运强国在本国的航运立法中制定有符合本国国情的详尽的航运补贴制度外,很多发展中国家和新型工业化国家如印度、韩国,新加坡等的航运立法中都有对于航运补贴的规定。但是,到目前为止,我国航运立法中对于航运补贴的规定却是少之又少,在我国现行的《中华人民共和国

---

　　① 　B. Rodger and A. MacCulloch, *Competition Law and Policy in the EC and UK*, 4th edn, Routledge-Cavendish 2009.

　　② 　本节内容是以本书作者和王幸子合作的学术论文《我国航运补贴的制度构架》(发表于《国际经贸探索》2011 年第 11 期)为基础而形成的。

国际海运条例》及其《实施细则》中对航运补贴的内容甚至鲜有提及，对于航运补贴的规定只在部分行政性法规或是地方性法规中有零散规定，为此，完善我国航运立法中的航运补贴制度对于促进我国海运服务竞争力的提高，维护我国政治经济的安全和利益具有重要价值。

一、航运补贴的理论基础考量与现实考察

（一）航运补贴的理论基础的简要梳理

从微观经济学的视角看，政府或者公共机构的补贴的动机是从海外公司向国内公司转移垄断租金。当引入产品垂直差异化因素后在进行价格竞争时，生产低质量产品的厂商的政府将会对其国内厂商的研发活动进行补贴，在进行数量竞争时，生产高质量产品的厂商的政府将会对其国内厂商的研发活动进行补贴。①当我们将眼光从微观经济学转向宏观的补贴制度视域之后，特别是在 WTO 框架下考虑航运补贴的理论之际，我们会意识到航运补贴的理论基础是丰富多彩而又不乏厚重性。

由于受到各种因素的制约，WTO 框架下并没有形成专门系统的航运补贴特别机制。但是，《补贴与反补贴措施协议》（即 SCM 协议）作为处理补贴与反补贴的最主要的国际法渊源，SCM 协议对补贴的界定成为衡量航运补贴的重要基础性依据。根据 SCM 可以认为在某一成员方的领土内由某政府或任何公共机构提供财政资助，或者在 GATT1994 年第 16 条所涉及的任何形式的收入或者价格支持都是可能构成航运补贴的②。据此，抛开微观经济学的禁锢而从制度的角度来看，航运补贴可以理解为一成员方政府或者任何公共机构提供的航运财政资助或者其他航运领域内的支持，并致使相关方获得利益。

各国的航运实践形成了各式各样的航运补贴理论，并不断得到充实和发展。航运补贴和反补贴理论流派具有一定程度的复杂性，可以从不同的

---

① 于谨凯、侯瑞青：《海洋运输业竞争力提升中的政府补贴机制研究》，《内蒙古财经学院学报》2009 年第 6 期。

② 尹立、张阿红：《WTO 框架下中国工业补贴方式改进之探讨》，《法学家》2008 年第 6 期。

角度对其予以阐释。从全球航运服务资源配置角度来看，航运补贴会使接收补贴者在国际航运中获得竞争优势，通过不公平竞争扭曲航运资源在全球的配置。从航运补贴提供方的角度看，根据 19 世纪 80 年代由詹姆斯·布兰德(James Brander)提出的战略贸易理论，政府选择航运补贴是基于航运在国民经济中的战略地位的考虑，从而增强本国在航运业中的战略竞争优势。从航运补贴受影响方的角度来看，存在两种截然不同的倾向。一种倾向认为航运补贴应该是有限度地实施，另一种倾向所谓"经济效益流派"(Economic Efficiency School)认为应该最大限度地限制扭曲航运自由的各种政策。而从航运补贴方与受影响方互相博弈的关系角度来审视，航运补贴和反补贴是共生的，全球福利和国内福利最大化的最有效战略就是让所有的国家避免成为第一个补贴者。①

由此观之，航运补贴机制具有很强的复杂性，这不仅仅是由补贴与反补贴的理论比较复杂所决定的，更是由于航运在世界经济格局的重要战略地位所决定的。航运补贴理论的发展脉络也是复杂的，即受制于经济学理论的变迁，更是与法律制度的发展密不可分。对于航运补贴的基本理论的简要梳理的重要价值在于，在深入考察我国航运补贴制度和我国航运现实的基础上，力求对我国的航运补贴予以反思和完善，形成具有生命力和可操作性的、符合我国航运利益的补贴机制。

(二) 航运市场与航运补贴制度之现实情境：以我国相关实践为考察对象

1. 我国航运市场发展概要

我国航运市场的海运市场是服务贸易领域开放程度最深、开放领域最广的一个行业。早在 2001 年加入世界贸易组织时我国就对海运服务贸易作出了较大程度的开放承诺。我国能够按照承诺实施最惠国待遇，对外国服务和服务提供者实行国民待遇，可以肯定地说，我国海运业已经进入全面开放阶段。根据我国交通运输部 2010 年 4 月 30 日发布的《2009 年公路水

---

① 林惠玲：《美国反补贴实体法律及实施问题研究》，上海人民出版社 2019 年版，第 86 页。

路交通运输行业发展统计公报》显示，截至 2009 年底，外商在华设立独资船务公司 40 家；独资船务公司设立分公司 186 家。外商在华设立外商独资集装箱运输服务公司 7 家，分公司 73 家。①

我国航运市场的发展现状存在以下特征：（1）新造船市场具备综合竞争优势。经过多年的发展，我国船舶工业已经形成了制造业体系完备、劳动力素质高、原材料配套强等综合竞争优势，船舶工业发展前景十分广阔。（2）航运基本市场缺乏国际竞争力。对于航运基本市场而言，我国航运公司不少，但普遍存在规模偏小、运力不足的情况。目前我国本土的航运企业除中远海运集团等大公司外，大多数航运企业规模较小。（3）航运市场中船队的科技含量较之国际先进水平尚有一定差距。中国虽然有不少海运企业已建立自己的电子商务及信息系统，部分研究机构也专门出具年度海运市场发展和预测报告，但这些信息往往仅限于在企业内部而未加入大型网络，或需支付高额费用才可使用。（4）立法偏差加重航运企业负担②。许多国家尤其是发达国家对航运业的立法中，各类补贴措施的规定对本国航运企业起到了积极的扶持和帮助作用，如造船补贴、营运补贴等直接性支持或/和造船贷款利率优惠，延长还款期等间接补贴措施。而我国于 1988 年取消货载保留后，又逐步取消了对本国船队的扶持和保护性措施，既没有造船补贴和营运补贴，也没有优惠造船贷款利率、税收与折旧等优惠。

2. 我国航运补贴制度一般情境

2010 年 6 月，国家为了加快船舶工业结构调整，增强自主开发能力，推动产业升级，促进我国船舶工业持续、健康、稳定发展，制定并颁布了《船舶工业调整和振兴规划》。作为船舶工业综合性应对措施的行动方案，该规划的规划期为 3 年，自 2009 年起至 2011 年止。规划对 3 年内的目标、主要任务和立法措施作出了说明和安排。本次船舶产业调整和振兴的主要

---

① 参见中国交通运输部发布的《2010 中国航运发展报告》。
② 郭艳、张蔚蔚：《中国航运企业发展现状及对策研究》，《中国水运》2007 年第 1 期。

任务分为九个方面，分别为稳定船舶企业生产、扩大船舶市场需求、发展海洋工程装备、支持大型船舶企业及其他骨干船舶企业兼并重组、提高船舶产业自主创新能力、积极发展修船业务、努力开拓国际市场以及加强船舶企业管理等。为此，在该规划中，特制定八种政策措施来实现上述任务，这些政策措施中与造船补贴相关的内容包括：①

从国家层面的立法而言，我国目前无船舶营运的相关补贴制度。按照我国 2008 年 1 月 1 日起正式实施的新《中华人民共和国企业所得税法》的规定，我国目前航运企业和造船企业同其他企业一样，按照 25% 的税率缴纳企业所得税。根据我国《中华人民共和国企业所得税法实施条例》第 60 条规定，我国船舶折旧期为 10 年。根据交通运输部与财政部、工业和信息化部、国家发改委联合出台的《促进老旧运输船舶和单壳油轮报废更新实施方案》，"在现有老旧运输船舶强制报废和单壳油轮限期淘汰的基础上，对于在 2011 年 12 月 31 日前已取得国内、国际运输经营资格的 1 000 总吨以上的中国籍老旧运输船舶和 600 载重吨以上的中国籍单壳油轮提前一定年限拆解，并在 2012 年 6 月 30 日前建成吨位不小于原报废船舶，并取得中国船级社的入级证书的新船，将由中央财政给予补贴。补贴标准将根据船舶类型、提前报废年限确定，最高为每总吨 1 500 元。"②

受 2008 年世界金融危机的影响，我国很多航运企业和造船企业的生产经营遭遇"寒冬"。很多以航运业作为经济支柱产业的省份为了帮助本省内的航运企业或造船企业渡过难关，出台了各种扶持或补贴措施来为航运企业或造船企业保驾护航。天津滨海新区政府在 2009 年 7 月出台《加快北方国际航运中心建设的若干意见》及《资金支持措施》，据此滨海新区将设立"加快北方国际航运中心建设专项资金"，"主要用于培育集装箱物流网络，增强保税港区和国际贸易与航运服务区对航运产业的聚集能力，提

---

① 参见 2010 年 6 月工业和信息化部出台的《船舶工业调整和振兴规划》。

② 参见我国交通运输部联合国家发改委等部门联合实施了《促进老旧船舶和单壳油轮提前报废更新实施方案》。

高现代航运服务水平，吸引航运人才教育资源聚集等"。①

二、航运补贴的应然性分析：WTO 框架下的补贴制度考察

由于航运业是一个开放的系统，它既包括船舶的建造和进出口，也包括对货物的运输等内容，即对航运业的补贴，一方面涉及货物贸易领域，一方面涉及服务贸易领域。而从适用范围上讲，WTO《补贴与反补贴措施协议》只适用于处理货物贸易的补贴，而关于服务贸易的补贴在《服务贸易总协定》中另有规定，以下将从这两个方面来对货物贸易领域的补贴和服务贸易领域的补贴进行研究。

（一）航运补贴的应然性之一：货物贸易领域的视角

目前，规制补贴和反补贴措施最具有影响力的国际规范是《补贴与反补贴措施协议》（*Agreement on Subsidies and Countervailing Measures*，以下简称 SCM 协议）。该协议是世界贸易组织《马拉喀什建立世界贸易组织协定》的附件之一，受到 WTO 各成员方的广泛接受并得到普遍适用。作为航运业重要组成部分的船舶制造业和船舶的进出口，对其的补贴常常被置于货物贸易领域受到 SCM 协议的调控。

1. WTO《补贴与反补贴措施协议》项下的补贴

SCM 协议将补贴分为禁止性的补贴、可诉补贴与不可诉补贴。禁止性补贴专指不允许成员方政府授予或维持的补贴。一旦成员方政府实施禁止性补贴，那么任何受其影响的其他成员方，都可以直接采取相应的反补贴措施。故禁止性补贴又被称为"红灯补贴"。SCM 协议明确规定出口补贴和进口替代补贴属于禁止性补贴。此外，为了便于确定禁止性补贴，SCM 协议在附件1中还以列举的方式阐明了禁止使用的出口补贴清单。可诉补贴是指在一定范围内允许实施，但如果其实施该补贴对其他成员方的经济贸易利益造成了损害，受到损害的成员方可就此采取反补贴措施的补贴。

---

① 更加详尽的信息，可以参照《滨海新区关于加快北方国际航运中心建设的若干意见》，http://www.bh.gov.cn/zwgk/system/2009/09/21/010034175.shtml。

故可诉补贴又被称为"黄灯补贴"。可诉补贴由于其存在的合理性而被世贸组织的规则允许其在满足一定条件时存在，而其存在的条件即为不得对其他成员方的经济贸易利益造成损害。对于如何认定是由于实施可诉补贴而对其他成员方利益造成的损害，SCM 协议中第 5 条和第 6 条对此作出了规定，大致可概括为：(1)对另一成员方的产业造成损害；(2)取消或者损害其他成员根据《1994 年关税与贸易总协定》直接或间接获得的利益；(3)严重损害其他成员的利益。不可诉补贴是指任何成员方在实施这类补贴的过程中，可以不受其他成员方的反对或申诉以及因此而采取反补贴措施的补贴，又被称为"绿灯补贴"。根据 SCM 协议第 8 条的规定，不可诉补贴措施包括非专向性补贴、对企业所进行的或者由与企业签订合同的高等教育机构所进行的研究活动给予的补贴、对落后地区提供的补贴以及环境保护补贴。

2. WTO《补贴与反补贴措施协议》对专向性补贴的认定

根据 SCM 协议，补贴是否具有专向性是直接关系到成员方进行补贴是否会引起其他成员方适用反补贴措施的一个关键因素，那么如何界定补贴的"专向性"，对此 SCM 协议的第 2 条提供了确定补贴是否具有"专向性"的原则。根据第 2 条的原则，对补贴的"专向性"的认定可以分为法律上的和事实上的"专向性"补贴。法律上的"专向性"补贴，是有关法律法规中的明确规定或执行有关法律、法规的主管机构的明确表示，补贴仅给予特定的企业或产业，则该补贴具有法律上的专向性。而事实上的"专向性"补贴则指尽管有关法律法规中规定所有企业都可以得到该补贴，但事实上只有某一个或几个企业或产业能得到该补贴或得到不成比例的大量补贴，则此类型的补贴具有事实上的"专向性"。从规则上讲，法律上的或事实上的"专向性"，只要两者居其一即构成"专向性"补贴。[1]

----

[1]　李国安：《WTO 服务贸易多边规则》，北京大学出版社 2007 年版，第 265 页。

（二）航运补贴的应然性之二：服务贸易领域的视角

1.《服务贸易总协定》中有关补贴的规定

《服务贸易总协定》（GATS)是《世界贸易组织协定》附件一所包含的三部分内容之一，是历史上第一个专门调整服务贸易的国际条约。服务贸易领域有关的补贴的内容，体现在 GATS 第 2 章《一般义务和原则》的补贴条款中。①该条款仅规定了解决补贴问题的方法和程序，并没有明确规定缔约方的义务。根据规定，缔约方将通过谈判制定一项有关服务贸易补贴的多边协定来避免因补贴而可能造成的服务贸易扭曲。但截至目前，国际社会尚未就此达成一项具有普遍适用效力的多边协定。②

2.航运补贴与海运自由化

海运服务业是服务贸易领域的一个关键部门，但由于其自身具有的政治因素和技术因素，使得有关海运服务的谈判从一开始就备受各种因素困扰而难以达成圆满共识，至今在国际社会仅形成了《关于海运服务谈判的部长决议》和《关于海运服务谈判的附件》两项文件。但是有关海运服务谈判的宗旨还是得到世界各国的普遍认可，即在 GATS 原则和框架下，逐步取消一切限制进入海运服务市场的各种措施，给予外国海运服务提供者国民待遇，最终实现海运服务全面自由化。③

最终实现海运服务全面自由化是世界各国的理想愿望，而要实现这个美好的愿望，则要求海运服务的各参加方，不仅要遵循 GATS 的一般义务，如最惠国待遇、透明度、发展中国家更多参与以及补贴等条款，还要遵循具体承诺义务如市场准入、国民待遇、附加承诺等条款。在实现海运服务全面自由化的过程中，要求各海运服务的参加方要尽力克服在海运服务过程中可能出现的"隐形壁垒"，将采用补贴和优惠本国承运人的有关做法、技术和安全标准等公开、公示。可见，航运补贴和海运自由化是手

---

① 一般义务是缔约方不需要承诺即须遵守的义务，与之相对应的是"具体承诺义务"。

② William K. Wilcox, GATT-Based Protectionism and the Definition of a Subsidy, *Boston University International Law Journal*，1998(6)：7—11.

③ 李国安：《WTO 服务贸易多边规则》，北京大学出版社 2007 年版，第 313 页。

段和目的的关系，海运自由化是世界各国发展航运服务的最终愿景，而航运补贴则是在实现该目的的过程中发展本国航运业所必须使用的手段。

(三) 航运补贴制度的应然性探讨

各国对于货物贸易领域的补贴措施并不是完全排斥，而是区分不同的补贴类型而区别对待，对于服务贸易领域的补贴，GATS 所秉持的态度是默许的，发展中国家给予本国服务提供者的补贴也是作为 GATS 有关国民待遇的例外而予以明文规定的。此外，从著名的欧韩造船补贴案的 WTO 裁决报告来看，专家组不仅进一步解释了相关条款特别是某些关键用语的含义，而且在一定程度上确定了某些造船补贴的合法性。那么既能够扶持本国航运业的发展同时又不会对国际航运发展产生扭曲作用，同时能够顺应国际服务贸易逐步自由化的趋势的航运补贴应具备哪些特征呢？

因为航运业是一个开放的系统，它既包括基本的航运运输业，也包括与航运基本运输业务相关的航运信息网络、船员劳务、船舶建造、航运资本等市场与业务。因此，对航运补贴的设定应同时满足 GATS 的有关规定和 SCM 协议的有关要求。也就是说，对航运补贴的设定应尽量规避禁止性补贴或可诉性补贴所具有的特征，如不能在法律或事实上视出口实绩为唯一条件或多种其他条件之一而给予的补贴，同时不能使用国产货物而非进口货物的情况为唯一条件或多种其他条件之一而给予补贴。[1]

对航运补贴措施的运用，最直接的目的是降低本国航运企业的生产经营成本，帮助和扶持本国航运企业提升国际竞争力，以便争取更多的国际航运市场份额。从长远来讲，这样本国的航运企业在面对国际航运市场实力雄厚的竞争者时才有可能有实力和能力排除或控制外国航运强者的不正当竞争或垄断，从而规范航运市场，为未来航运自由化打下基础。现代国际社会就像是一张纵横交错的网，国家与国家之间是彼此相互依存的关系，在经济往来的天平上，谁都无法永远只占据一边的位置。因此，一国在制定本国的政策措施时，不能以牺牲其他国家经济利益为代价，航运补

---

[1]　孙光圻：《国际海运政策》，大连海事大学出版社 1998 年版，第 232 页。

贴制度的设定同样如此。补贴措施如果设定不当，损害了其他国家经济利益，利益相对方很快就会启动相应的反补贴措施，甚至引发国家之间的贸易争端。

准确把握航运补贴措施的"度"，也是关系到航运补贴是否能顺利实现既定目标的一个关键因素。航运补贴，从补贴的领域到补贴力度再到补贴的形式的确定和实施，概括地讲就是为了提升本国航运业在国际航运市场的竞争力，但具体而言，不同的经济发展时期，运用补贴的既定目标或许稍有不同，如经济危机时期，补贴措施的实施主要是为了帮扶航运企业渡过难关；而经济繁荣时期，补贴措施的设定和实施则可能主要是为了提升航运业某方面的生产力。正所谓过犹不及，只有准确把握不同时期补贴设定的"度"，才能顺利实现既定目标。超过既定目标所需限度的补贴措施，则可能对贸易和航运产生双重的扭曲作用，进而引发世界其他国家的报复。

三、航运补贴制度的实然性分析：航运补贴制度比较简析

(一)各主要航运国家的航运补贴制度评析

1. 美国的航运补贴制度

美国早在 1936 年的《商船法》中就已规定了两项主要的财政直接补贴，即建造差额补贴和营运差额补贴。营运补贴计划虽已被《1996 年海上安全法》(*Maritime Security Act of 1996*)确立的《海上安全计划》(*Maritime Security Program*，MSP)所取代，而建造差额补贴计划也已于 1982 年终止，但二者在历史上曾发挥的作用和影响仍值得我们研究和借鉴。

建造差额补贴(Construction Differential Subsidy，简称 CDS)，是美国政府对美国航运企业在美国国内建造的船舶造价与在国外建造的船舶造价的差额给予一定比例的补贴。对该补贴的申请条件、补贴的额度以及申请补贴的范围，美国 1936 年《商船法》中都作出了明确的规定。美国的造船差额补贴，对美国航运业的发展的确起到了一定的推动作用，并在一定程度上刺激了美国船舶所有人在国内造船的积极性。

营运差额补贴（Operating Differential Subsidy，简称 ODS），是美国政府在一定条件下，根据同样条件航线营运条件，对那些悬挂美国旗、使用美国籍船员的航运公司，实行营运差额补贴，以使美国籍船舶同外国船的最低营运费用平衡。该项补贴是美国政府对美国航运业实行的一项非常重要的补贴类型。对该补贴的申请条件、补贴的额度、申请补贴的范围以及补贴的计算等，法律中也都作出了明确的规定。营运差额补贴对美国航运业的发展也确实起到了一定的推动作用，特别是对改善美国几家大班轮公司的经营状况起到了重要的作用。①但是，营运差额补贴在许多其他方面也显露出其不足之处。

美国国会于 1996 年颁布《海上安全法》，为美国籍船队建立了为期 10 年的"海上安全计划"以取代 ODS。依据该法案，对美国船舶经营人的补贴不再以美国籍船舶与外国籍船舶的运营成本差额为基础，而是对纳入"航运安全船队"的美国籍船舶以及船舶上的美国籍船员，每艘每年支付 210 万美元的航运安全补贴，为期 10 年。该计划原定在 2005 年 9 月 30 日终止。但根据《2003 年海运安全法》，美国海运管理局已批准在 2006 年至 2015 年期间，为 60 艘悬挂美国旗的船舶提供 17.3 亿美元的资金支持。

尽管在各个历史时期，美国政府对航运补贴的运用方式和程度不尽相同，但一直维持着对航运业强势的保护和扶持措施。而这些补贴措施即使本身存在一些政策设计上的缺陷，但不可否认的是，这些补贴措施都在一定程度上推动了美国航运业的发展和壮大。

2. 日本的航运补贴制度

日本整个国民经济对国际贸易和海外运输的依存度很大，因此，就日本近现代的航运发展史而言，日本政府对于本国航运业的发展基本上采取扶持色彩颇浓的保护主义政策。（1）造船补贴。各航运公司是以"计划造船"和"自有资金造船"两种方式来发展船队的。一般而言，在市场不景

---

①　于谨凯、侯瑞青：《海洋运输业竞争力提升中的政府补贴机制研究》，《内蒙古财经学院学报》2009 年第 6 期。

气时，以"计划造船"为主，而在市场繁荣时则除了"计划造船"外，也可发展部分自有资金造船。日本政府对执行"计划造船"的船舶给予低息贷款的支持。（2）拆船补贴。日本政府为鼓励企业汰旧换新，对所有从事远洋运输的船舶实施"远洋超龄船舶拆解补贴"。补贴额为拆解每总吨船舶 15—16 美元，1993 年该补贴提高到大约每总吨 22 美元。（国际航运管理人员培训教材编写委员会，2001）另外，为了早日实现用双壳体油船取代大批老龄单壳体油船以防止油船损伤造成海洋污染的目标，日本运输省海上交通局于 1995 年特别制订了促进"老龄油船拆解补贴措施"。（3）折旧与税收优惠。船公司可以按最大比例为 20.6％的固定比例法或按最多 15 年的单船固定数额法进行折旧，并允许在此两种方法之间进行转换。但在 1987 年 4 月至 1993 年 3 月间，为了减少船公司应税利润额，实行减税，日本政府实行了临时的特别折旧。①

3. 欧盟的航运补贴制度

欧盟航运补贴所呈现的一个特点是多数补贴措施是欧盟成员国根据本国航运发展情况实施的，而这些补贴措施又必须是经过欧盟委员会允许使用的。欧盟通过了给予海运业"国家援助"的新指南，以便为海运企业创造良好的税收环境。新指南豁免了"海员税"，制定了针对新型服务的援助规则，有利于欧盟船公司参与国际竞争。②2009 年 1 月 21 日，欧盟委员会通过了欧盟未来 10 年新交通运输政策，即"到 2018 年欧盟海运政策战略目标和建议"（简称"海运战略 2018"），该战略从具有竞争力的欧洲航运、人力因素、优质航运、国际合作、短途航运及研究和创新六个方面，提出了欧盟的战略目标和行动建议。

总之，尽管欧盟的航运政策和法律法规总体而言是偏向航运自由主义

---

① 具体做法是，每年可以提存船价的 15％作为折旧，提存不足额除延后一年外，还可以从以后 7 年的利润中扣除。对计算机化、自动化的 5 000 总吨以上专门远洋船舶，可以在第一个财政年度里，得到按船舶原值 18％折旧的特别许可；对 2 000 总吨以上的船舶可以在第一个财政年度里得到按船舶原价 12％进行折旧的特别折旧许可。

② 参见谢程《服务贸易补贴的特点和各国的做法》，中国服务贸易指南网，http://tradein-services.mofcom.gov.cn/c/2020-07-20/83463.shtml。

的，但欧盟多年来实施的一系列行之有效的造船补贴、买船补贴、税收优惠、营运补贴等措施既鼓励和促进了欧盟航运业的快速发展，又保护了欧盟航运业不受或少受国外同行的恶性竞争影响，并最终推动欧盟航运业成为当今海运市场当之无愧的"强者"。

4. 发展中国家及新兴工业化国家的航运补贴制度

一般而言，巴西政府用商业航运更新基金向本国所有人建造船舶提供贷款的方式取代向本国航运公司提供营运补贴。该项基金靠向进口货物征收运费税来维持，贷款大体上提供了船价的 70%，偿还期最大可以宽限 4 年。在税收方面，政策上巴西政府没有对航运公司和船厂进行减税，但是其同时也是不收取船舶建造税的。在船舶折旧方面，船舶所有人可以在不少于 5 年的时间内将一艘船折旧完毕。

基于航运业在韩国经济中扮演的重要角色，韩国政府推行了一系列法律法规，如《航运业促进法》《航运扶持法》等，对航运业实施扶持和保护，体现了"国货国运、国船国造、国船国修"的原则，使韩国造船业和航运业在当今国际航运市场都占有重要的一席之地。根据《航运促进法》第 14 条的规定，政府可以向从事国际班轮运输的航运企业提供营运补贴，以使这些企业为国家的外汇收入做出大的贡献。但从 1986 年以来，政府已停止提供营运补贴，并将该规定废止。韩国政府对于航运企业给予多方面的税率支持，例如对船用设备、材料和高科技进口实行减免关税；进口一年以上船龄的二手船只须缴纳 2.33% 的关税；因国内不能建造而进口的用于船舶建造或修理的原材料免交关税；所有进口船舶免交关税；当造船企业收入的一半以上为外币时，其折旧可以比正常情况增加 30%[①]。

（二）航运补贴制度的实然性分析

通过对各国航运补贴制度的梳理，可以看出，世界上大多数的航运国家都对本国的航运业实施过或正在施行类型多样的航运补贴。（见表 3.1）

---

① 蔡宏波：《WTO框架下战略性补贴政策的制约因素与应对策略》，《世界经济研究》2007年第 5 期。

表 3.1 各国航运补贴形态①

补贴类型 \ 国别	造船及利息补贴	营运补贴	进口船舶	船舶折旧	其他补贴
中国	造船利率过高，无任何直接补贴	无	进口税增值税共约27%	大多船舶折旧年限20年	无
美国	对企业在国内建造的船舶的造价与在外国建造的船舶造价之间的差额给予差额补贴	实施营运补贴，每艘船补贴额前5年每年达250万美元，后5年每年200万美元	进口船舶从事国际航运不纳税	采取余额递减法，折旧年限仅为5年，还采取年限总额法及双倍余额递减法折旧	资本建设金，资本准备金
英国	提供额度为船舶造价80%的贷款，利率7.5%还款期8.5年	设船舶建造调整基金对造船合同补贴，新船补贴最高为船价的9%	进口一年以上船龄的船只关税为船价2%—3%	余额递减法对船舶固定资本进行折旧，降低应税利润比例	免固定资产税、减免船员所得税社保费，增加回国、教育补助
日本	提供船价75%—90%的贷款，利率6.1%—8.6%还款期13年，利息补贴2.5%—3.5%，83年终止	对从事第三国运输的船公司给予利润3%—4.8%的补贴	进口船免征关税	远洋船舶折旧率18%，300总吨以上折旧率12%；油轮折旧为11—13年；其他船型15年	减轻远洋船舶登记许可税、光船租金不支所得税、远洋集装箱固定资产税特例征税
韩国	提供船价90%的贷款，利率8%，减少建造新船的定金，还款总量最长5年	对在国际运输中做出重大外汇贡献的船东给予补贴	1000总吨以下船舶的进口税19%		减免登记税、所得税、特征税等
德国	贷款额为船价的80%，利息率为8%，还款期12年	1996—1997年直接补贴达1亿马克。1999年采用吨税制	进口船从事国际航线运输免交任何税项	大型客船16年，其他12年	对船舶非赢利项目减税

① 本书作者根据各国有关航运补贴的法律、法规、指令等整理而成。

虽然航运自由化是发展的主流趋势，但面对激烈的国际竞争，各国在本国调控航运业的法律法规中，还是会或多或少地涉及航运补贴的内容。在面临特殊的经济时期，还会专门出台扶持和帮助航运业发展的法规。例如，美国海事管理局近期通过的"小型造船厂援助计划"和"联邦船舶融资计划"，目的就是帮助美国船厂面对全球造船业激烈竞争的挑战和改善美国舰船建造能力。同时，航运补贴的类型正在悄然发生变化。各国正逐步取消或已经取消一些传统的补贴类型，如造买船补贴、营运补贴等，而一些新型的，更具有隐蔽性的间接补贴措施正在被各国采用和实施。[1]

四、我国航运补贴制度之考察

我国航运市场的开放程度与我国航运业的实际发展状况并不相符合，我国航运市场的开放程度要快于我国航运业的发展，即我国目前的航运实力难以对抗大量涌入的拥有雄厚经济、技术、管理实力的外国航运竞争者。[2]因此，结合我国航运业发展的实际情况，借鉴国外航运补贴的典型措施，依托国际航运业未来发展的走向，进一步完善具有中国特色的航运补贴制度已显得确有必要。

（一）我国航运法规下航运补贴制度的原则之框定

首先，应服务于国家航运业的整体利益。作为航运业法规的重要内容的航运补贴制度的设立是为了扶持和帮助我国航运业的长远发展，因此，对于航运补贴的设立，在整个国家航运业内部不应造成"专向性"，而应服务于国家航运业的整体利益。其次，应保持透明度。航运补贴措施，应在其官方法律文本中明确规定补贴的范围、补贴的力度、补贴的期限以及补贴的方式等，并将官方文本置于公众可以随时查阅的地方。航运补贴设立的最终目的是扶持我国航运业的可持续发展，因此，航运补贴的设定就

---

① 孙光圻：《国际海运政策》，大连海事大学出版社 1998 年版，第 233 页。
② 井艳：《美国航运立法的研究与借鉴》，上海海事大学硕士学位论文，2008 年。

不应当妨碍公平竞争，应使国内航运企业在平等、公平和透明的机制下获得扶持和帮助。应在遵守不歧视和经济联系原则的前提下，呈递减趋势。根据目前国际经济贸易和航运业的发展趋势，贸易自由化和航运自由化是未来发展的主流，随着世界贸易和航运经济向更加国际化和更加发达的方向发展，以及世界贸易组织海运服务贸易新的谈判的展开和不断深入，各国会不断寻求分歧中的共荣，进而达成一项具有普遍适用效力的国际多边协定来取消各国的航运补贴和扶持措施。

（二）完善我国航运法规中航运补贴制度应达到的目标

1. 完善我国航运法规中航运补贴制度应达到的最终目标

航运补贴制度作为调控航运业发展的相关法律法规中一项重要的内容，其制定和设立的根本目的在于通过国家立法的形式将国家对航运业的支持和扶持态度固定下来，通过稳定、公开、可靠的国家补贴方式与航运市场调控作用相配合，最终达到建立在无国家补贴的情况下，我国航运船队依然具有雄厚的参与国际航运竞争的能力和实力，以及建立我国航运业的良性发展运行模式。

2. 完善我国航运法规中航运补贴制度应实现的具体目标

对于船舶工业的发展而言，加大国家对造船企业的扶持和补贴力度，提高国内船东在国内船厂投资造船的积极性，可以起到尽快拉动投资需求，带动多种关联产品和行业的经济增长，推动"国轮国造"的实现，进而对助力我国国民经济的增长起到积极的作用。例如以中远集团为例，作为三大主业之一的船舶修造业，已经成为中国船舶工业的第三支重要力量，在新造船、海洋工程制造方面，已经具备了相当的技术实力。国家能源，包括石油、铁矿石以及其他的战略性物资是关系到一国经济发展命脉的重要物资，对这些物资的进出口如果不能实现"国货国运"，也无法保证海上运输链的安全，更有可能将国家经济发展的重要领域交到他国手中而受制于人。为此，应从国家经济和国防安全的角度出发，坚持国家利益最大化原则，通过适度的补贴，扶持本国船队，实现"国货国运"以保证这些重要的战略物资的运输能够掌握和控制在我国企业手中，确保国家能源资源运输安全。

远洋运输业是涉及国家安全和国计民生的战略性行业，而海员职业是国际公认的特殊艰苦职业。当前，国内航运业对海员特别是高级海员的需求仍然十分旺盛，而且，我国在国际外派海员劳务市场的竞争实力还不够。为此，国家应出台和实施相应的海员从业补贴，以稳定壮大海员队伍，提高我国航运及海员劳务业的竞争力，扩大国际就业队伍。

（三）我国航运法下航运补贴制度之确定

1. 构建一套完整的补贴体系

（1）航运补贴力度的确定。在航运补贴制度的设计过程中，对于补贴力度的确定不能搞"一刀切"，国家航运主管部门应当要积极发挥桥梁沟通、协调的作用，根据不同航运公司的运力实力、不同的航线，在综合考虑船型、成本、收益等因素后，制定出适合某类航线或某类船型的补贴力度的幅度，然后由各个省内航运主管部门，依据本省航运业发展的情况，选择适当的幅度进行补贴，才能收到实际效果。

（2）航运补贴范围的确定。由于航运不仅包括进出我国港口的国际海上运输经营活动，还包括与国际海上运输相关的辅助性经营活动。因此，补贴的范围应做到全盘考虑，既有针对专门发展国际海上运输经营活动的各类补贴，同时也设置扶持和鼓励与海上运输相关的辅助性经营活动发展和提升的各类补贴。为了保证航运补贴能够用在实处，发挥实效，航运补贴制度的设计者应当在航运法规中合理选择补贴制度的发放者，并对发放对象作出充分的定义。

（3）构建政府补贴的监督机制。我国的航运法规中，应当对政府补贴的发放和使用构建合理的监督机制。第一，对政府补贴发放行为的监督。建立一套补贴发放的规范化流程和专业的资金流向通道，保证专款专用，使每一分补贴款都能及时地发放到受补贴的航运企业。第二，对接受补贴的航运企业的监督。加强对企业绩效的监督，加大对航运企业经营活动的评估，以此为依据对企业采取相应的补贴措施，并在补贴发放后对补贴的使用进行跟踪监督，以保证补贴款用到实处。

2. 在我国航运法规中创设符合世贸规则的新型的航运补贴类型

传统的航运补贴类型，已经不能满足现代航运业高速发展的要求，为了应对航运业发展过程中出现的新问题，应研究制定出相应的新型的符合世界贸易组织规则的航运补贴类型，总体而言，这些补贴类型应以奖励机制、税制、借贷优惠等间接补贴为主，对航运企业进行引导性的扶持。具体而言：（1）航运企业上市补贴。鉴于航运业和证券市场的特点，可以鼓励具备一定条件的航运企业通过资本市场进行融资。为此，国家可以推出相应的奖励机制，对于具备一定条件，实现成功上市的企业或具有一定条件，虽未能成功上市的，但具有上市潜力的航运企业给予上市补贴，对于航运企业进行前期上市准备的资金投入予以一定比例的补贴。（2）融资创新补贴。对于航运企业提出的新型的融资方式，如果既符合法律的规定，同时又具有一定的推广和普遍适用的意义，政府可以设立专项的奖励机制，用以奖励此种融资创新行为，鼓励企业开发和拓展融资途径。（3）航运企业业务创新补贴。该补贴的设立旨在鼓励我国的航运企业提高产品科技含量和核心竞争力、提升航运产业附加值、鼓励船舶更新换代、创新航运业务品种、提升航运服务水平、拓宽航运业务领域。（4）人员引进和培训基金。航运业不仅是一项资金密集型的产业，同时也是一项人员密集型产业，无论是航运运输基本市场，还是海运信息网络、船舶建造等航运辅助市场，都需要大批的具有专业素质的人才。同时，促进航运和海上职业形象，提高对就业机会的认识，促进航运业的劳动力流动；支持国际海事组织（IMO）和国际劳工组织（ILO）公平对待海员的工作；按照《2006 年海事劳工公约》的规定，更充分地利用各种技术手段、政策环境和资金支持全面保证海员职业安全和生命健康。（5）环境保护奖励基金。该基金用于争取限制或降低船舶温室气体的排放、用于促进实现我国船舶营运航线所在海域实现"良好环境状态"。

3. 提升我国航运法规中航运补贴制度的立法层级

我国有关航运补贴的规定散见于一些地方政府行政文件或国家部委出台的意见或规划中，而对我国航运业进行调控的法律法规《海商法》《海上交通安全法》《港口法》《国际海运条例》及其《实施细则》中，则很难觅其踪影。尤其是《国际海运条例》及其《实施细则》，它们是适用于调整进出中华人民共和国港口的国际海上运输经营活动以及与国际海上运输相关的辅助性经营活动，目的在于规范国际海上运输活动，保护公平竞争，维护国际海上运输市场秩序，保障国际海上运输各方当事人的合法权益的法规，但在其中也基本不曾提到任何有关对中国籍航运企业或船舶进行补贴的规定。此外，我国的《航运法》（草案）自 1996 年至 2004 年间，共起草了 11 稿，但终究因为条件不成熟而未能颁布实施。

为此，本书建议我国的立法机关应对我国的《国际海运条例》及其《实施细则》进行适当修改，增加有关航运补贴的内容，并在新制定的《航运法》中适度体现航运补贴的原则、目的等内容，并适时出台专门用于调整对航运业进行各类补贴和扶持的法律法规。

4. 增强航运补贴制度的信息化程度和实施动态的航运补贴政策

为了增强我国航运企业在面临国外航运反补贴措施的抗辩能力，应该在法律上明确我国中央和地方各级航运补贴措施的信息的权威性和法定性，同时构建航运补贴措施信息库。航运补贴信息化应该囊括如下范畴：(1)航运补贴政策措施的发布者；(2)航运补贴政策的有效期限；(3)航运补贴政策适用的航运领域；(4)航运补贴措施的优惠方案等。另外，基于航运服务的复杂性和战略性，法律上宜构建一种动态的航运补贴机制，这是由补贴和反补贴制度本身的特点和航运业的市场规律所决定的。

航运补贴是一个宏大的、难以言尽的话题。在 WTO 框架下，航运补贴的理论与实践的发展趋势充满着模糊性。可以预见，在世界各国理性追求本国利益最大化的前提下，世界航运市场将向一体化和竞争自由化的方向迈进，在这个过程中，航运补贴制度在各国的航运法规中一直是最重要的课题之一。尤其是对于像我国这样的发展中国家，无论经济实力还是航运实力较之其他发达国家还有一定的差距，故此，航运补贴制度是我国管理航运市场的不可或缺的机制之一。只要世界航运业竞争存在，强弱可分，那么就会有补贴制度存在的空间和意义。因此，在未来对世界经济和世界航运发展以及其他国家航运补贴制度进行跟踪研究，进而适时更新本国的航运补贴制度的内容，对不断发展和壮大本国航运业的整体实力，提升国际航运竞争力具有重要意义。

第4章　沿海运输权的实施路径

第一节　保护主义沿海运输权①：美国的实践

一、保护主义沿海运输权的典型模式：美国的立法与政策

沿海国基于本国各种因素和利益的考量，形成了实施沿海运输权的不同路径。一般地，保护主义沿海运输权涵盖了广泛的海上运输活动，并对从事海上运输贸易和服务的经营者提出了严格的要求。沿海国实施保护主义沿海运输权，通常衡量的因素包括：其一，船舶需有相关文件、已注册并悬挂东道国国旗，并且船舶主要营业地位于东道国。其二，船舶所有权人应当符合东道国国籍和原住民要求。其三，船员应符合东道国的国籍和原住民要求。其四，船舶应在东道国建造或者重新建造和修理。②在一些国家，保护主义沿海运输权的范围延伸到距离海岸线 200 海里以内的海上活动，其中包括专属经济区和大陆架。这种保护主义沿海运输权不仅涵盖了沿海海域内的海上运输，而且还包括其他各类海上服务活动，诸如地震测量活动、拖航、水文测量以及救助服务等。其中，美国实施的 1920 年《琼斯法案》为比较典型的实施保护主义沿海运输权的立法。

美国的保护主义沿海运输权立法是当初英国对美国实施殖民统治的遗

---

①　本节撰写中，华东政法大学 2021 级国际航运法方向硕士研究生在相关判例的收集和检索上，提供了很大协助。作者表示谢忱。

②　W. Oyedemi(2012)，"Cabotage Regulations and the Challenges of Outer Continental Shelf Development in the United States"，*Houston Journal of International Law*，34(3)，607—651.

产之一。从那时起，美国一直保持着可能是世界上最严厉的保护主义沿海运输权立法。1920 年《琼斯法案》是规范美国沿海运输权的重要法律，该法案在严格遵守船舶的建造、船旗国登记以及船员雇佣和船员管理等方面予以全面立法。当然，在紧急情况和自然灾害期间，该法案的实施会适度放松。1920 年《琼斯法案》的渊源可以追溯到 1789 年《关税法》。根据 1789 年《关税法》，美国对外国船舶运输的商品征收较高的关税，其立法目的在于鼓励美国航运经营人在美国国内船厂建造船、在美国国内注册、由美国船舶所有人拥有并雇用美国船员的船舶从事美国沿海运输。同年，美国立法明确了优先保护在美国建造、在美国注册并悬挂美国国旗航行且完全由美国公民拥有的船舶从事沿海运输。①尔后的 1817 年《美国航海法》第 4 条提高了对从事沿海运输船舶的监管标准，禁止外国船舶参与美国的沿海贸易。1886 年，美国国会通过颁布《防止走私法》，进一步对沿海运输的监管。根据更严格的法案，在美国北部边境的港口之间，通过外国船舶从外国港口转运的货物将被没收。同年，通过颁布 1886 年《旅客运输服务法》，美国沿海水域的保护主义政策已经超出了船载货物的范围，包括了乘客运输。该法将美国对货船的建造、船员雇佣、船舶所有权和船旗悬挂同样适用于客船。②然而，1886 年《防止走私法》和 1817 年的《美国航海法》都在 1892 年美国诉 250 桶钉案(United States v. 250 Kegs of Nails)中被规避了。③此案中法院认为，在美国港口之间通过外国港口进行的涉及转运的货物运输，无论货主的意图如何，都不属于美国海上货物运输法的范围。本案判决后，美国国会迅速采取行动，于 1893 年修订了 1817 年《美国航海法》，修正案禁止在美国的两个港口之间用外国船舶通过外国港口进行运输。④

---

① W. Marvin, The American Merchant Marine: Its History and Romance from 1620 to 1902, Charles Scribner 1902.

② J. Lewis(2013), "Veiled Waters: Examining the Jones Act's Consumer Welfare Effect", *Issues in Political Economy*, 22(1), 77—107.

③ Aniekan Akpan, *Maritime Cabotage Law*, London: Routledge, 2019, p.118.

④ 参见 1817 年《美国航海法案》第 4 节部分规定。

　　1920 年《琼斯法案》的初衷是为了在第一次世界大战后维持商船队的规模。因此，该法案被称为"沿海贸易法之母"。1920 年《商船法》第 27 条规定："任何商品都不得在美国境内各点之间直接或通过外国港口进行水运或水陆联运，否则将被没收，也不得在运输中的任何部分使用任何其他船舶，除非该船舶是根据美国法律建造并由美国公民担任船员，并由美国公民所拥有。"[①]这些要求适用于美国本土港口与阿拉斯加、夏威夷、波多黎各和关岛等非毗连州之间的所有海上活动。然而，根据"关岛豁免"规则，从事关岛的外围海洋的运输的船舶可以免于遵守 1920 年《琼斯法案》中强制性的美国"建造要求"。然而，这种豁免并没有特别的利益，因为从美国西海岸出发的西行贸易路线要经过檀香山。这实际上将从事关岛与美国州之间海洋运输的船舶建造要求联系在一起。美国严格的保护主义海上运输条例也涵盖了海上活动，诸如沿海客运、打捞、溢油、拖船和疏浚。此外，1930 年《关税法》第 446 条对悬挂美国国旗的船舶在外国进行修理的费用征收 50％的从价税，而且 1916 年《航运法》第 2 条规定只有美国公民才能成为沿海贸易船舶的所有者。[②]

　　从本质上讲，1920 年《琼斯法案》只是 1789 年《关税法》更严格的版本。由于在美国建造船舶的成本很高，以及在美国境内用符合沿海运输条件的船舶运输货物和乘客的成本很高，因此在废除或改革 1920 年《琼斯法案》上存在严重的争论。美国国际贸易委员会(ITC)在 1991 年进行的一项研究报告表明，1920 年《琼斯法案》是造成国内航运成本高的根本原因。该委员会提出，采用沿海船舶运输货物的成本远远高于其他的运输方式。1995 年至 1999 年，为废除 1920 年的《琼斯法案》进行了激励的论战，形成了两派对立的观点。[③]一方面，由国内托运人组成的"琼斯法案改

---

　　①　参见 1886 年《防止走私法》第 20 节部分规定。

　　②　J. Lewis(2013)，"Veiled Waters：Examining the Jones Act's Consumer Welfare Effect"，*Issues in Political Economy*，22(1)，77—107. The Jones Act Reform Coalition(JARC) was formed by Rob Quartel in 1995.

　　③　K. Magee，"U.S. Cabotage Laws：Protective or Damaging? A Strategy to Improve Cruise Vessel Competitiveness and Traffic to U.S. Ports"，Monterey Institute of International Studies，2002.

革联盟"（JARC），试图废除或大幅度改革 1920 年《琼斯法案》。另一方面，由海运业者组成的"美国海运伙伴关系"（AMP），则捍卫 1920 年《琼斯法案》的保护主义制度，反对任何此类改革。

1996 年，"琼斯法案改革联盟"的努力导致了美国国会通过了《航运竞争法》。美国《航运竞争法》寻求允许使用外国建造和悬挂外国国旗的船舶从事沿海运输。然而，这些船舶仍然必须由美国公民拥有、经营或租用，才能够有资格从事美国的沿海贸易运输。这一努力没有成功，因为"琼斯法案改革联盟"未能获得足够的支持。同时，另一项名为"开放美国水域法"的提案主张，1920 年《琼斯法案》阻碍了自由贸易并有利于工会而不利于美国广大消费者。然而，2010 年废除 1920 年《琼斯法案》的努力未获成功。因此，1920 年《琼斯法案》自生效以来，基本上没有变化。①

当然，1920 年《琼斯法案》也经过了若干次修正。诸如，1956 年的一项法案增加了对 1920 年《琼斯法案》的限制性条款，规定"在美国境外重建的船舶也将丧失以前因在美国境内建造或根据美国法律记录而获得的从事沿海贸易的任何合法权利"。②美国船舶所有人曾经试图通过在海外建造船舶的主要部件，然后将这些部件运输到美国的船厂安装，以实现规避 1920 年《琼斯法案》有关规定。然而，1960 年修正案对 1920 年《琼斯法案》第二条但书的修正堵住了这个漏洞。该修正案规定在国外建造船体或上层建筑的任何主要部件都将导致该船舶不符合沿海运输的要求。③

二、《琼斯法案》引发的争论及其实证分析④

1920 年《琼斯法案》的通过和实施得到了美国政府的巨大支持。因

---

① D. Hamilton and P. Schwartz, A Transatlantic Free Trade Area: A Boost to Economic Growth?, New Direction—The Foundation for European Reform 2012.

② W. Gray(2008), "Performance of Major US Shipyards in 20th/21st Century", *Journal of Ship Production*, 24(4), 202—213.

③ R. Pouch(1999), "The U.S. Merchant Marine and Maritime Industry in Review", *Proceedings Magazine*, 125(5), 1, 155.

④ 本书的实证分析对象来源于 Aniekan Akpan, *Maritime Cabotage Law*, London: Routledge 2019, pp.118—125.

此，贸易商和船舶所有人利用的每一个法律漏洞都被美国国会以立法的形式一丝不苟地堵住。1920 年《琼斯法案》中最有争议的一个方面是关于船舶建造或者船舶重建的要求。该规定引发了几个问题，并导致了一些争端。这些诉讼的争议焦点在于，为了节省造船成本，船舶所有人选择在外国船厂建造船舶的大部分部件，然后再运输到美国本土造船厂组装成船舶。这对船舶所有人来说是一种获利较丰的方式，同时确保船舶所有人仍然有资格进行美国沿海水域的贸易运输权利。1920 年《琼斯法案》在提供劳动力就业和创造国内收入方面发挥了重要作用。① 然而，批评者认为，在美国建造或者重建船舶比在亚洲国家做同样的事情要昂贵得多。这种成本差异导致的直接后果是，从事沿海贸易运输的船舶所有人被迫使用老旧船舶。这些老旧船舶的运营成本过高，更是对海洋环境造成了污染威胁。

1. 如何理解"沿海运输"

美国造船业委员会等诉美利坚合众国案（Shipbuilders Council of America et al. v United States of America et al）中一个石油钻井平台由于吃水太深，导致无法进入船坞进行修理。② 因此，该钻井平台在一个海岸点被装上一艘外国下潜式驳船进行运输并将钻井平台拖到另一个造船厂。石油钻井平台在那里进行了维修，同时仍然停在驳船的甲板上。修理完毕后，驳船回到了装载钻井平台的海岸点。驳船下潜后钻井平台被卸下。这一行动得到了海关总署的认可，因为它符合 1920 年《琼斯法案》的相关规定。法院认为，对石油钻井平台进行维修是出于航行的需要。因此，造船厂是这次航行的真正目的地，钻井平台在美国的两个海岸点之间雇佣外国船舶进行运输，从而违反了 1920 年《琼斯法案》的规定。这一裁决在上诉法院被技术性地推翻，因为原告对该裁决的质疑已经超过了时效。然而，

---

① Drewry Maritime Research，"US Cabotage Protection Gets More Expensive"，*Container Insight Weekly*，London，17 November 2.

② 868 F. 2d 452（DC Cir. 1989）. Decided March 3，1989 in the United States Court of Appeals，District of Columbia Circuit. Nos. 88-5095，88-5119.

上诉法院建议，根据 1920 年《琼斯法案》的规定，石油钻井平台不能被描述为"商品"。①本案引发了一个重要的问题，特别是在像美国实施保护主义沿海运输权的国家，是否有理由对发生在国内水域的所有海上活动适用1920 年《琼斯法案》，还是应该以海上活动的目的作为决定因素，这实质上属于如何认定"沿海运输"的问题。首先，该外国下潜式驳船带着国内货物在美国沿海水域的两个海岸点之间航行。其次，在修理厂花费的时间将使该作业超出"停泊服务"的传统定义。因此，不管钻井平台是否从驳船上卸下，修船厂在任何情况下都已成为一个目的地，有别于起运点。最后，根据 1920 年《琼斯法案》的规定，使用外国钻井平台无可争议地剥夺了符合条件的从事沿海运输服务的船舶以获得报酬的机会。钻井平台似乎没有对环境或人员安全构成足够的实际威胁。②

海关总署的裁决和上级法院似乎过于强调钻井平台在维修船厂没有从驳船上卸下的事实。然而，他们没有考虑到卸下钻井平台是否会使修理作业更具挑战性或完全无法进行。如果是这样，那么关于卸货的辩解是无效的。本案与阿尔皮纳和尼克拓尔思诉基奥贾港务局一案（Alpina and Nicko Tours v Chioggia Port Authority）的判决形成对比。该案中欧盟法院认为，所有在沿海水域提供的有偿海上运输服务都在欧盟理事会第 3577/92 号条例的适用范围内，无论它们是否在同一港口以相同的货物开始和结束。重要的是阿尔皮纳案再次强调了"港口"的定义，即任何临时或小规模的基础设施，作为海上运输货物的装卸终点。③

2."美国建造的船舶"的含义

海洋运输公司诉福勒案（Marine Carrier Corp. v. Fowler）提出了如何看待"美国建造的船舶"含义的问题。④本案涉及一艘通过连接其他船舶的几

---

① 19 Code of Federal regulation(C.F.R.) §4.80b(a).

② 参见 2006 年《墨西哥航海和海事贸易法》第 40 条。

③ Commission of the European Communities v Kingdom of Spain Case C-323/03(2006) ECR I-2161; 9 March 2006.

④ 429 F.2d 702(1970).

个部分(jumboize)而建造的名为观察者号的船舶是否适用于沿海运输权的争端。观察者号试图根据 1920 年《琼斯法案》的规定从事沿海贸易运输业务。观察者号最初来源于瓦佩罗号(Wapello)油轮,该轮 1953 年在美国船厂为巴拿马船舶所有人建造并注册。瓦佩罗号后来在日本船厂被拆开,它的前部被连接到一艘美国制造的油轮埃索—吉大港号(Esso Chittagong)的船尾,该油轮在利比里亚注册并被命名为圣海伦娜号(Santa Helena)。后来圣海伦娜号前半部分船身即先前的瓦佩罗号,在美国船厂与一艘美国建造和为美国公民所拥有的从事沿海运输的船舶托拉斯科号的船尾连接在一起。这种连接的结果就是本案中的观察者号。① 由于 1920 年《琼斯法案》对建造和所有权的要求,法院面临的问题是观察者号是否有资格从事沿海贸易运输。这个问题的产生是来自观察者号的前身之一圣海伦娜号是否有资格从事沿海贸易的争议。由于 1920 年《琼斯法案》增加了一些限制性条款,继而否定了瓦佩罗号在美国从事沿海运输的资格。这进一步导致观察者号的沿海运输权是否被承认的问题。

为此,该争论引发 1920 年《琼斯法案》的再次被修订。本案之后,1920 年《琼斯法案》有关规定被修订为:"任何总吨位超过 500 吨的船舶,如果因在美国境内建造或根据美国法律注册而获得从事沿海贸易的合法权利,但后来在美国领土或其属地以外重建,此后应有权从事沿海贸易。"② 本案引发的有趣而备受争议的问题是,观察者号的前部是瓦佩罗号的前部,占其总长度的 75%,而观察者号的船尾是托拉斯科号的船尾。托拉斯科号是在美国建造的、并且为美国人所拥有。本案被上诉人海洋运输公司辩称,由于该船在被出售和在外国登记之前从未被美国公民拥有,瓦佩罗号在任何时候都没有获得从事沿海贸易的合法权利。③

---

① 　R. McGeorge(1990), "United States Coastwise Trading Restrictions: A Comparison of Recent Customs Service Rulings with the Legislative Purpose of the Jones Act and the Demands of a Global Economy", *Northwestern Journal of International Law & Business*, 11(1), 62—86.

② 　Aniekan Akpan, *Maritime Cabotage Law*, London: Routledge, 2019, p.119.

③ 　Act of 17 February 1898. 30 Stat. 248.

法院通过裁定在美国建造的船舶获得了从事沿海贸易的有条件的权利，从而调和了本案在解释1920年《琼斯法案》措辞中看似矛盾之处的困惑。在作出这一裁决时，法院作出了一个重要的假设，即但书中的"合法权利"是指任何合法的权利，不管是有条件的还是无条件的。因此，法院接受了上诉人的解释，并得出结论认为圣海伦娜号已经获得了从事沿海贸易的合法权利。由于圣海伦娜号被卖到国外，她已经不可逆转地放弃了这一合法权利。因此，瓦佩罗号没有资格进行沿海贸易。在作出这一裁决时，法院参考了美国参议院和众议院的委员会报告。而这些报告的目的在于防止特殊情境下的船舶获得参与沿海运输的合法权利。这些特殊情境主要包括在美国建造或根据美国法律注册的船舶而后在国外被销售，在美国为外国人建造的船舶。①

3."国内两个港口之间海上运输"的解释

美国诉250桶铁钉案（United States v. 250 Kegs of Nails）成为如何理解"国内两个港口之间海上运输"的典型判例。②本案中一艘悬挂比利时国旗的船舶运输货物从纽约港到加利福尼亚。在此之前，该货物经过比利时安特卫普港的转船运输。在货物抵达加州后，海关以违反美国1920年《琼斯法案》为由对货主提起了没收之诉。同时，美国政府对外国船舶所有人和货物所有人提起了诉讼。该案中法院判决美国海关败诉。法官认为涉案船舶没有违反1817年美国《航海法》和1866年《反走私法》。法院的裁决主要基于这样一个事实，即这两个法案只涉及美国港口之间的国内沿海运输。因此，即使货物所有人的意图是在美国的两个港口之间运输货物，但在一个外国港口的停留和转运破坏了航程的连续性。这样导致该运输活动不属于两个法案的适用范围。③法院认为，根据适当的解释，"将货物从一

---

① The Shipbuilders Council of America, Inc. and Pasha Hawaii Transport Lines LLC. v. U.S. Coast Guard and Matson Navigation Company, Inc(2009). Case No.1:07cv1234. APA, 5 U.S.C. §§704.

② 52 F. 231(S.D. Cal. 1892), 61 F. 410(9th Cir. 1894).

③ 参见1817年《美国航海法案》相关规定。

个国内港口运到另一个港口"的普通含义只能是在一次连续的航行中运送货物。法院进一步推断，相关条款的措辞不可能合理地认为是在两个明显分离的航程中或在两艘不同的船舶中运送货物。在这一判决之后，美国国会迅速采取行动，于 1893 年修订了 1817 年美国《航海法》。该修正案禁止外国船舶在美国的两个港口之间通过一个外国港口进行的沿海运输。1898 年，该修正案被扩大到包括"这种航行的任何部分"。①

4. 1920 年《琼斯法案》下的"转运"的解释

美国海事协会诉布卢门撒尔（American Maritime Association v. Blumenthal）案中赫斯（Hess）公司使用一艘悬挂外国国旗的船舶将原油从阿拉斯加运到其在维尔京群岛的炼油厂。②然后，用一艘外国船舶将精炼产品运回美国。法院面临的问题是这种活动是否违反了 1920 年《琼斯法案》的规定。地区法院和巡回法院曾对原告作出裁决，认为提炼过程中产生了 11 种与离开阿拉斯加的原油明显不同的新产品。法院认为原始产品的这种变化程度是确凿的证据，证明炼油厂的产品是新的，与阿拉斯加原油货物不同。此外，由于这两批不同的货物是在两个不同的航次上运输的，这不能被视为"转运"，因此不存在违反 1920 年《琼斯法案》的情况。原告就该判决向上诉法院提出上诉，并辩称，无论原始原油产品经历了什么变化，被告的行为都违反了 1920 年《琼斯法案》意义上的"连续性"要求。他们争辩说，被告的主要的意图是利用一艘外国船舶在阿拉斯加和美国其他地方之间从事沿海运输。上诉人还争辩说原来的货物并没有发生重大变化，以至于失去了它的特性，因此而被称为不同的货物。③

关于"连续性"的识别很重要。因为后来美国国会修订了 1920 年《琼

---

① 　C. Grabow, "U.S. Maritime Sector Among the Jones Act's Biggest victims", CATO Institute, Washington, 28 June 2018.

② 　590 F. 2d 1156(1978). District of Columbia Circuit. See also: the decision of the District Court: 458 F. Supp. 849(1977).

③ 　458 F. Supp. 849(1977).

斯法案》，在美国诉 250 桶铁钉案的裁决后，禁止货物转运。关于"意图"问题，法院认为，托运人将货物送往最终目的地的"意图"并不重要，重要的是货物在商业过程中作为一个事实所经历的变化程度。关于产品改变的问题，法院认为，原始货物的性质已经发生了足够的改变，足以使它们成为新的产品，而不违反 1920 年《琼斯法案》的规定。这一判决的影响是，根据美国的海上运输法产品必须是新的，并与原来的产品有区别，而仅仅改变产品的等级是不够的。[①]

美国海事协会诉布卢门撒尔一案的判决现在已经得到了美国海关和边境保护局分别在 2014 年和 2015 年做出的两项裁决的支持。根据《反走私法》的规定，如果商品在中间港口或海岸点以外的地方被加工成"新的和不同的产品"，而后被运往该海岸点，则不需要海关的背书。该案裁决是关于在未变性的乙醇中加入传统的普通汽油混合原料（CBOB）和用于含氧化合物混合的重新配制的混合原料（RBOB），以生产变性的乙醇燃料等级。问题是这是否会产生一种新的和独特的产品，以满足《反走私法》的规定。海关和边境保护局（CBP）在 2014 年发布了 H254877 号裁决，指出未变性乙醇和变性乙醇只是同一原始产品的不同等级，没有明显的化学或结构差异。因此，在没有沿海运输权资格的船舶上运输不同等级的原产品，将违反《美国法典》第 46 章第 55 条的规定。[②]然而，针对类似的疑问，边境保护局在 2015 年发布了 H259293 号裁决，指出将烷基化物和重质芳烃混合以生产 87 辛烷值常规汽油和 93 辛烷值常规汽油将导致产生符合《反走私法》语境下的新的和独特的产品。因此不会违反《美国法典》第 46 章第 55 条的规定。由此，为了满足美国 1920 年《琼斯法案》的相关规定，无论原产品经过何种提炼或改制过程，都必须产生新的和独特的产品。

---

① 52 F. 231（S.D. Cal. 1892），61 F. 410（9th Cir. 1894）.

② R. Joshi，"WTO Review Fears Derail Proposed Jones Act Amendment"，Lloyd's List（London，28 October 2009）.

三、1920 年《琼斯法案》解读[①]

1920 年《琼斯法案》在美国被视为维持可靠的船队以应对紧急情况和国家安全问题的重要法律之一。在发生危机或威胁时，需要一支可靠的商船队来保障后勤方面的应急工作。因此，1920 年《琼斯法案》对于保护美国的利益和维持美国的造船工业基础是必要的。至此，国会的一项新法案提供了自 1936 年以来国会对 1920 年《琼斯法案》最有力的支持声明。"紧急危机和国家安全"的理由在过去可能有一些合理性。但是，现在的情况已经不一样了，因为这些观点都没有反映出美国实际的沿海运输方式。[②]因此，这些理由对美国的国家安全或其造船业的振兴没有任何影响。在美国建造的商业船舶数量的持续下降，清楚地表明了 1920 年《琼斯法案》的理论依据与美国海事部门的现实之间的脱节。根据美国交通部的统计，1955 年美国共建造了 1 072 艘符合 1920 年《琼斯法案》规定的商船。然而，到 2000 年国内建造的沿海船舶数量下降到 193 艘。到 2014 年全美国只有 90 艘商业船舶是根据 1920 年《琼斯法案》计划在造船厂里建造的。此外，美国国防部承认经常租赁外国船舶来执行海洋运输额外的任务。[③]

除此之外，在波斯湾战争期间军事海运司令部(MSC)将其超过五分之一的干货通过租赁外国船舶运输给美国武装部队。此外，海事局的预备役部队(RRF)在其船队的 46 艘船中有 30 艘在外国建造的船舶。预备役部队的建立是为了支持美国军队在世界范围内的快速部署，并对影响美国利益的其他紧急情况作出反应。这证明了 1920 年的《琼斯法案》对于紧急情况或处理国家安全问题是没有必要的。相反，该法的严格规定可能会使相关机构失去有效执行任务所需的资源。如果外国船舶在战时被用于美国的军

[①]　英文文献中更加翔实的关涉《琼斯法案》的评价和解读，请参阅 Aniekan Akpan，*Maritime Cabotage Law*，London：Routledge，2019，pp.112—118；125—129。

[②]　S. Galbraith，"Thinking Outside the Box on Coastal Shipping and Cabotage"，*Maritime Trade Intelligence*，Victoria，1 December 2014。

[③]　B. Edmonson(2011)，"Navy Official Calls for a Fleet of Dual-Use Marine Highway Ships"，*Journal of Commerce*，13 July。

事服务，将外国船舶用于商业用途会带来安全风险的说法是不符合逻辑的。因此，为了不存在的安全利益而使国民经济受到保护主义的1920年《琼斯法案》制度低效率的制约是不可靠的。①

美国国会的相关报告认为，公司税收的差异、对行业的过度监管、缺乏有力的竞争以及缺乏连贯的国家海事政策等因素都导致了美国商船运输业的衰落。这也能更好地解释这种情况继续保留1920年《琼斯法案》只允许悬挂美国国旗的船舶运输沿海货物，对本土托运人和船舶所有人来说越来越不利了。②一艘计划在2003年至2006年期间由美国船厂交付的2 890个标准箱的船舶，成本约为1.25亿美元。这比当时亚洲的市场价格高出四倍左右。③在美国建造任何类型船舶的高昂成本都凸显了美国正在实施的严格的沿海运输权政策具有负面影响。

坚持使用悬挂美国国旗的船舶来保护美国国内贸易的高昂代价表明，这有必要重新考虑。事实上，一些海运大国正逐步在其沿海运输部分引入一些自由措施。美国岩盐运输是典型的制约和影响1920年《琼斯法案》的领域。美国是最大的岩盐生产国之一。然而，对马里兰州和弗吉尼亚州来说，从智利进口大部分岩盐比从南路易斯安那港进口更便宜。2014年，新泽西州被阻止用外国船舶从缅因州运输岩盐以应对紧急灾难。这批货物离新泽西州只有400英里，外国船舶本来需要两天时间来运送这批货物。然而，花了大约一个月的时间才找到一艘符合1920年《琼斯法案》的船舶来运输货物。④在建立世贸组织的谈判中，人们一致认为应取消在《关税与贸易总协定》（GATT）中不符合规定的措施。这些措施包括1947年前与《关贸总协定》原则不一致的措施。然而，美国坚持认为1920年《琼斯法案》是神圣不可侵犯的，必须予以保留。1994年《关贸总协定》第3段记录了

---

① R. O'Rourke, "DOD Leases of Foreign-Built Ships: Background for Congress", *Congressional Research Service Report for Congress*, 7-5700-RS22454, Washington, 28 May 2010.

② J. Rodrigue et al., *The Geography of Transport Systems*, 3rd edn, Routledge 2013.

③ W. Gray(2008), "Performance of Major US Shipyards in 20th/21st Century", *Journal of Ship Production*, 24(4), 202—213.

④ J. Lewis(2013), "Veiled Waters: Examining the Jones Act's Consumer Welfare Effect", *Issues in Political Economy*, 22(1), 77—107.

这种特殊豁免。在世界贸易组织成立多年后，继续豁免保护主义的1920年《琼斯法案》是一个系统性的问题。[1]这并不是美国唯一一次拒绝将1920年《琼斯法案》纳入贸易协定的情况。尽管加拿大和墨西哥赞成在北美自由贸易协定的所有成员国中实行自由沿海货物运输政策，但美国还是特别要求将1920年《琼斯法案》从北美自由贸易协定的谈判中排除。事实上，在NAFTA成员国（美国、加拿大、墨西哥）就三国的区域性海上运输政策进行谈判的同时，1920年《琼斯法案》因"Byrnes-Tollefson"修正案而变得更为趋向保护主义。该修正案排除了加拿大造船厂为美国军舰提供维修的可能性。[2]

在美国，有人试图利用《为我们的劳动力和能源资源提供保障法》（POWER）来扩大1920年《琼斯法案》的范围，以涵盖海上可再生能源服务。《为我们的劳动力和能源资源提供保障法》收紧了现有立法中的一个漏洞，该漏洞允许外国船舶和工人安装和服务海上可再生能源。该法案规定，外大陆架（OCS）上的可再生能源资源的建设和服务应完全由美国海事工人来完成。外大陆架是指位于国家沿海水域向外三英里的所有水下土地。它还包括通航水域下的土地以外的地区，其中的底土和海床属于美国并受其管辖。这一区域由《外大陆架土地法》（OCSLA）管理。[3]该法将适用于领海基线200海里以内的美国联邦法律的范围扩大到外大陆架的底土和海床。《外大陆架土地法》还涵盖了为开发、生产或勘探石油而永久或临时附着在海床上的所有结构（不包括船舶）。因此，《为我们的劳动力和能源资源提供保障法》将扩大《外大陆架土地法》的范围，使之包括所有的近海能源活动，该法适用于近海天然气和石油生产。[4]因此，可再生能源

---

[1] C. Johnson（2014），"Advances in Marine Spatial Planning：Zoning Earth's Last Frontier"，*Journal of Environmental Law and Litigation*，29（1），191—246.

[2] A. Stoler，"The Current State of the WTO". Paper presented at Workshop on the EU，the US and the WTO，Institute for International Business，Economics and Law，California，28 February—1 March 2003.

[3] 参见美国《外大陆架土地法》有关规定。

[4] S. Kalen（2013），"Cruise Control and Speed Bumps：Energy Policy and Limits for Outer Continental Shelf Leasing"，*Environmental & Energy Law & Policy Journal*，7（2），155—189.

工人将被纳入 1920 年《琼斯法案》。由此，美国沿海的外大陆架水域的所有能源生产都需要由符合 1920 年《琼斯法案》的船队提供服务和运输，没有外国竞争。

第二节　自由主义沿海运输权：比较的视角

实施自由主义沿海运输权政策的海洋国家对于在沿海水域进行运输活动的经营者的管制性规定较少。通常情况下，所有船舶都可以在沿海国家自由从事沿海运输贸易和服务，而无论船舶的船旗国、船舶所有权、船舶建造地点或是船员的国籍为何。总的来说，采取自由主义沿海运输权政策的国家，意在通过鼓励竞争来促进本国海洋经济的发展。这是因为在任何情况下如果没有外国海运活动的存在，这些国家的沿海运输业务也将失去竞争的动力。与保护主义沿海运输权相反，没有证据表明实施自由主义沿海运输权政策的国家必然受到在其领海内进行海洋运输的外国船舶的威胁。相反，这些外国船舶的存在有助于提升其国内海运行业的竞争力和可持续发展。这是因为，允许外国船舶拥有从事沿海贸易的特权，剥夺了本国船舶所有人收取不合理运费的机会。此外，自由主义沿海运输权政策使本国船舶所有人接受公平竞争，激发本国航运服务水平的提升。

一、欧盟的自由主义沿海运输权

欧盟理事会第 3577/92 号条例对成员国之间以及成员国与第三国之间的海上运输实行自由服务原则。该条例的颁布意在建立一个单一的欧洲市场(即"内部市场")。建立内部市场是委员会在 1985 年白皮书讨论的中心议题，欧盟理事会第 3577/92 号条例最终实现了沿海运输自由化，并适用于整个欧洲经济区。欧盟的沿海航运框架被普遍认为是行之有效的自由主义沿海运输权的最佳例证。[①]欧盟理事会第 3577/92 号条例于 1993 年生效，

---

① European Commission, "Completing the Internal Market: White Paper for the Commission to the European Council", 1985.

其目的是允许欧盟的船舶所有人在欧盟成员国之间自由地提供海上运输服务。然而，从最严格的意义上讲，欧盟的自由主义沿海运输权不是绝对自由主义，这是因为自由主义沿海运输权政策只限于欧盟内部国家之间，并没有延伸到欧盟以外的国家。该条例不必然包括船员雇佣和财政要求，因为一些成员国仍然设置了一些必须达到的门槛。此外，该条例规定了保障措施。条例在序言的第三和第四部分描述了追求自由政策的目标，但尚未完全实现。这一点可以从欧盟内部围绕岛屿沿海运输的保护主义框架中得以解释。①欧盟理事会第 3577/92 号条例第 3(2) 条有效规定了有关岛屿沿海运输权自由化目标的例外。第 3(2) 条规定，东道国的法律适用于所有在岛屿之间提供沿海运输服务的船舶和船员相关之事项。这是对欧盟内部实施自由主义沿海运输权的财政和船员要求采取的类似保护主义沿海运输权的措施。第 3(3) 条规定当 650 总吨以上的载货船舶在进行岛屿沿海运输之前或之后进行国际航行时，船员的雇佣适用船旗国法。该条例第 1 条和第 3 条第 1 款对此进行了明确规定。②尽管规则因船舶登记而存在不同，但是与船员雇佣有关的规定统一适用于船旗国法律，这是一项传统的政策。欧盟的一些成员国对船员的国籍提出了严格的条件，要求所有船员必须来自欧盟国家。另一些成员国则不那么严格，仅仅要求担任船长、大副和轮机长职位的高级船员来自欧盟国家。

为了避免歪曲最敏感航线上的竞争，条例规定"东道主"成员国可以对从事岛屿沿海运输和从事其他种类沿海运输服务的小于 650 总吨的船舶适用本国的船员规则。然而，为了避免否定欧盟理事会第 3577/92 号条例的立法目的，凡是 650 总吨以上船舶从事往返本国与另一个国家的航行之后或之前，而执行岛屿沿海运输服务的载货船舶，可以适用于船旗国的法律。这就是所谓的连续的沿海运输权。这些规定提出了有关东道国权限范围的两个问题。第一个问题涉及东道国在雇佣船员要求方面的责任问题。

---

①　参见欧盟理事会第 3577/92 号条例第 1 条规定。

②　参见欧盟理事会第 3577/92 号条例第 3 条规定。

第二个问题是关于船旗国和东道国在连续的沿海运输权的主管当局的权力问题。关于第一个问题，在适用法律为东道国法律时，欧盟理事会条例没有具体确定东道国在有关船员的问题上有什么责任。基于条例明确的措辞提到"与人员配备相关的所有事项"，有观点认为东道国拥有无限的权力。[①]然而，欧盟委员会在这一问题上采取了更为保守的做法。关于第二个问题，欧盟委员会认为东道国的权力应该受到限制，以保护欧盟理事会第3577/92号条例所要达成的目标，即在欧盟内部自由地提供海上运输服务。因此，允许东道国将其船员配备要求强加于沿海运输服务的原则，背离了该条例的自由议程。[②]

欧盟委员会建议，东道国的权力应限于规定在执行岛屿沿海运输、小于650总吨以及欧盟成员国国民担任船员的船舶。[③]具体而言，这些船舶的船员必须全部由欧盟成员国的国民组成，同时，船上的船员必须拥有欧盟的社会保险。与此同时，在工作待遇方面，实行该国现行的最低工资规定。不仅如此，关于安全和培训的规则，成员国只能要求遵守欧盟或国际现行的规则包括《海员培训、发证和值班标准国际公约》（STCW）和《国际海上人命安全公约》（SOLAS）。此外，欧洲支线服务是否属于欧盟理事会第4055/86号条例的范围的问题，对此，该条例没有对船旗做出任何要求。换言之，在有船旗要求的情况下，此种服务是否应当被视为欧盟理事会第3577/92号条例规定的沿海运输服务，除法国和葡萄牙外，其他成员国通常将支线服务视为沿海运输服务，因为这些国家海上运输服务由悬挂欧盟旗帜的船舶进行。[④]然而，对所有推行开放沿海运输政策的成员国来说，自由地提供支线服务是免费的。

虽然欧盟关于沿海运输权的立法从1993年开始生效，但为了促进该法律得到全面的遵守，一些成员国被允许进行灵活变通实施该立法。希腊被

---

①　参见欧盟理事会第3577/92号条例第3(1)和3(2)条规定。

②　参见欧盟理事会第3577/92号条例第3(1)条规定。

③　参见欧盟理事会第3577/92号条例第9条规定。

④　参见欧盟理事会第3577/92号条例附录的规定。

允许延长遵守新规定的期限至 2004 年。虽然在 2002 年，希腊的沿海运输业已完全自由化。此外，希腊在 2010 年向在第三国登记的邮轮开放了航运市场，成功地使其沿海运输市场的自由化超出了欧盟委员会条例所要求的范围。然而，直到 2011 年，希腊才完全与欧盟的海上运输条例接轨。①这是因为欧盟理事会部长级会议第 3922/2011 号法律提出了一系列的修正案。而其他成员国直到 1999 年，才使岛屿沿海运输权自由化。在欧盟理事会第 3577/92 号条例生效之前，欧盟各成员国对沿海运输采取的做法各不相同。希腊、法国、西班牙和意大利实行保护主义沿海运输权，因此被要求修改立法以符合新的欧盟条例。然而，英国、荷兰和挪威在历史上实行的就是开放的沿海运输政策，因此不需要对其立法进行任何修改。②

欧盟理事会第 1370/2007 号条例的通过似乎引起了一些混乱。该条例第 1(2)条规定，它应适用于通过公路、铁路和其他轨道运输方式的公共旅客运输服务的国内和国际运输。然而，令人关注的是成员国可以在不影响欧盟理事会第 3577/92 号条例的情况下，将第 1370/2007 号条例第 1(2)条适用于内陆水路的公共旅客运输。这个问题源于一个事实，即"国家海域"一词在任何欧盟或国际法律文书中都没有明确的定义。因此，当第 1370/2007 号条例适用于欧盟内部的海上航行时，引起了与第 3577/92 号条例冲突问题。为此，欧盟委员会对这一担忧作出了如下回应：第 1370/2007 号条例并不自动适用于国家海域的公共旅客运输，除非成员国明确规定适用，而第 1370/2007 号条例仅适用于公路或铁路的公共旅客运输。然而，欧盟理事会第 3577/92 号条例所涵盖的大部分沿海运输服务是货物运输和旅客运输的结合。因此，第 1370/2007 号条例不能适用于只运载货物或旅客或者旅客和货物运输结合的沿海运输服务。第 1370/2007 号条例只有在不与欧盟理事会第 3577/92 号条例冲突的情况下，才可由成员国适用于本国的沿海旅客运输。如果这两部法律有冲突，应以欧盟理事会第 3577/92

---

① 参见欧盟理事会第 1370/2007 号条例的规定。

② B. Parameswaran，*The Liberalization of Maritime Transport Services*，Springer 2004，pp.348—350.

号条例为优先适用，而第 1370/2007 号条例仅仅作为一种补充。①

显而易见，在实施自由主义沿海运输权的欧盟沿海运输法律框架内，仍然存在着保护主义措施的因素。有学者提议扩大欧盟理事会第 3577/92 号条例的范围，以包括"成员国之间"的沿海运输服务，其意图在排除非欧盟国家的人提供共同体内的海上贸易或服务。因此，这显然阻碍欧盟内部在提供海运服务上全面的自由政策，是不小的挑战。例如，领水作为欧盟的外部边界，对海关管制来说是一个障碍。因此，在两个欧洲国家之间航行的船舶被法律视为已经离开了欧盟的海关领土。这样做的结果是，该船的货物在出发港和目的港都要接受海关的清关。这显然与欧盟理事会第 3577/92 号条例所设想的欧盟内部人员和货物自由流动的立法目的相互矛盾。②因此，真正的自由政策应当反映在提供海上运输服务的自由，即应当全面涵盖商业和运输环节。

二、欧盟实施自由主义沿海运输权引发的争端及其评析③

1. Alpina 案

原告瑞士公司（Alpina River Cruises GmbH）和德国公司（Nicko Tours GmbH）（以下简称 Alpina 和 Nicko Tours）。被告是意大利基础设施和运输部 Chioggia 港务局。本案争论的焦点问题是 Chioggia 港务局拒绝允许 Alpina 和 Nicko 旅游公司驾驶悬挂瑞士国旗的邮轮穿越意大利领海。Alpina GmbH 公司拥有涉案的邮轮（MS Bellissima），Nicko Tours 公司是该邮轮的目标用户。Alpina 和 Nicko Tours 安排了一个邮轮旅行，其行程包括从威尼斯出发，穿越威尼斯潟湖到 Chioggia 意大利，在 Chioggia 和 Porto Levante 意大利之间穿越领海，沿 Po 河（意大利）航行约 60 公里到

① J. Chuah(2013)，"Short Sea Shipping: The Blue Belt Package"，*Journal of International Maritime Law*，19(1)，256—258.

② European Commission，"Blue Belt: A Single Transport Area for Shipping" European Commission COM(2013) 510 final(Brussels，8 July 2013).

③ 关于欧盟实施自由主义沿海运输权引发争端的典型案例，选自 Aniekan Akpan，Maritime Cabotage Law，London: Routledge 2019，pp.186—210。

Polesella 镇(意大利),最后按相反的行程返回威尼斯。Alpina 和 Nicko Tours 请求授权穿越 Chioggia 和 Porto Levante 之间的领海的申请被 Chioggia 港口当局(Capitaneria di Porto di Chioggia)拒绝。①拒绝的理由是,根据意大利法律,沿海运输权只授权给悬挂欧盟成员国国旗的船舶。悬挂瑞士国旗的船舶不符合这一特定要求。Alpina 和 Nicko Tours 在威尼托地区行政法院对这一拒绝提出异议,但该案件被驳回。原告继续向意大利国务委员会(Consiglio di Stato)质疑这一拒绝。他们认为,根据理事会第 3577/92 号条例,沿海运输权只适用于涉及真正海上运输的服务。此外,他们还声称,除了在 Chioggia 和 Porto Levante 之间的领海内的短途航行外,预定的巡航并不涉及海上运输,而是在国内水域进行。这里需要注意的是,如果 Bellissima 号船体较小,就没有必要穿越 Chioggia 和 Porto Levante 港口之间的意大利领海,因为游船可以通过连接 Chioggia 和 Po 河的运河。②

欧盟理事会第 3577/92 号条例第 3(1)条中提到的"邮轮",以及同一条例中第 6(1)条因邮轮服务清楚地证明该条例涵盖邮轮运输。欧盟法院在其裁决中确认,欧盟的沿海运输条例只涉及其成员国境内具有海运性质的运输服务。因此,在成员国中不具有海洋性质的内河运输服务不在欧盟沿海运输条例的范围内。这类服务属于欧盟理事会第 3921/91 号条例,该条例规定了非居民承运人在成员国境内通过内陆水路运输货物或乘客。欧盟法院还认为,与 Alpina 和 Nicko Tours 的主张相反,有争议的邮轮并不具有主要的非海上运输性质。法院认为,除了 Chioggia 和 Porto Levante 之间的海域外,邮轮还必须在威尼斯潟湖和 Po 河口航行,这两个地方都是意大利国内海域的一部分。③

---

① Case C 17/13 [2014] Alpina River Cruises GmbH and Nicko Tours GmbH v. Ministero delle infrastrutture e dei trasporti—Capitaneria di Porto di Chioggia. Judgment of the court(Third Chamber) 27 March 2014.

② 参见 1942 年《意大利航运法典》第 224 条。

③ Commission of the European Communities v. Kingdom of Spain Case C-323/03, 2006, ECR I-2161; EU: C: 2006:159, paragraphs 25 to 27.9 March 2006.

虽然欧盟理事会第 3577/92 号条例并没有对"海"进行特别定义，但是欧盟法院根据该条例赋予了"海"更为宽泛的定义。有学者认为，这种更广泛的含义与 1982 年《联合国海洋法公约》框架下的"海洋"的通常定义截然不同。因此，根据欧盟理事会第 3577/92 号条例，"海"的范围超出了领海的界限，它包括领海基线向陆一侧的内部海洋水域。本案中所坚持的"海洋"之扩展定义意义重大。这是因为如果没有这种扩展定义，一艘较小的船舶就能够遵守条例，而不会引起是否适用沿海运输权法律的争议。① 对于较小的船舶可以选择在连接 Chioggia 和 Po 河的运河上航行。在此基础上，人们质疑一艘船舶应该在领海内航行多远才能赋予"海洋"性质。然而，法院没有考虑这个问题。此外欧盟法院提供了附带意见，表明由于第 2(1) 条所设想的服务种类是由"特别是"一词引入的，该条的规定不能被解释为详尽无遗。这是因为这种解释的结果将导致把具有沿海运输所有基本特征的运输服务排除在欧盟理事会第 3577/92 号条例的范围之外。② 因此，欧盟法院认为，欧盟理事会第 3577/92 号条例涵盖了在成员国海域提供的所有有偿邮轮服务。这与邮轮服务是否在同一港口以相同的乘客为起点和终点无关，尽管理事会第 3577/92 号条例的相关条款规定，海上运输必须发生在"同一成员国的两个或多个港口"之间。

该判例所引起的第一个困难，是关于沿海运输的"港口"的含义的争论。该争论的焦点在于港口是否为单一港口而不是多港口系统。第二个困难是关于"海洋"定义的争论。③ 通常而言，欧盟理事会第 3577/92 号条例范围内的"海上运输"的范围，已经赋予"海洋"的含义。对于如何理解"港口"而言，条例并没有对"港口"作出具体定义。然而，作为海上货

---

① Article 40 of The Navigation and Maritime Trade Law "NMTL" of Mexico(Article 40 Ley de Navegación y Comercio Marítimos)，which entered into force in 2006.

② Commission of the European Communities v. Kingdom of Spain Case C-323/03 ECR I-2161；9 March 2006.

③ C. Lopez(2013)，"Mexico：The Legal Treatment of Vessels and Offshore Installations under the Mexican Foreign Investment and Navigation Frameworks"，*Maritime and Transport Law News*，9(1).

物和旅客运输的装卸终端，它被定义为任何临时或小规模的基础设施。此外，在运输服务方面，欧盟理事会第 3577/92 号条例第 2(1)(a) 至 (c) 条明确规定，运输应该有一个不同于到达港的出发港。这一点意义重大，因为本案中的事实清楚地表明船舶计划在同一港口起讫，乘客亦相同。有学者认为，Alpina 案的判决明显违背了欧盟理事会第 3577/92 号条例第 2(1) 条的明确规定。一个更令人不安的问题是，船舶离开出发港的任何形式的航行活动，是否符合该条例的"不同港口"是值得关注的问题。此外，如果船舶只是运载其他类型的货物而不是乘客，那么到达同一出发港是否符合条例所设想的那种"海上运输"就值得商榷了。此外，欧盟法院关于第 2(1) 条的规定显然不应被视为详尽无遗的建议值得怀疑。[1]这是因为，即使可以说该条例并非详尽无遗，该概念也需要与国际上对海运业的一般理解保持一致。欧盟法院拒绝受制于条例的措辞，这有悖于人们对"海上运输"的普遍理解。欧盟理事会第 3577/92 号条例第 2(1) 条的明确措辞支持了这一理解。[2]此外，第 2(1) 条的措辞还提出了一些需要进一步解释的问题。首先，第 2(1) 条中使用的"between"一词不能具有任何其他语法和逻辑意义，除非同一成员国中始终存在两个或多个港口。其次，可以从商业货物的运输中进行类比。将商船从一个港口启航并携带相同货物返回同一港口等行为视为海上货物运输，没有商业、海事或逻辑意义。因此，这里海上运输的目的与通常商业上理解的海上运输大不相同。欧盟法院明确认为应该扩展解释这一概念。欧盟法院在解释欧盟理事会第 3577/92 号条例的规定时，所采取的不确定的解释方法引起了人们的关注。人们不禁要问，欧盟法院和成员国法院是否会像本案中所显示的那样，继续对欧盟理事会第 3577/92 号条例的条款进行广泛的解释。[3]

---

[1]　Case C-251/04 Commission v. Hellenic Republic EU：C：2007：5，paragraphs 28—32.

[2]　A. Akpan(2014)，"A Precarious Judicial Interpretation of the Scope of EU Maritime Cabotage Law"，*Journal of International Maritime Law*，20(6)，444—447.

[3]　Shipbuilders Council of America et al. v. United States of America et al. 868 F. 2d 452(DC Cir. 1989).

2. 法国案

欧盟委员会起诉法国案中，欧盟委员会认为法国没有在合理的时间内对其 1977 年《海关法》的一项规定进行修正。根据 1977 年法国《海关法》，只有悬挂法国国旗的船舶才有权参与法国的沿海运输活动。对此，法国解释说，它采取了行政措施以确保临时适用欧盟理事会第 3577/92 号条例。①欧盟法院认为，法国所采取的措施不足以解除欧盟委员会确保其国家法律符合欧盟法律的条约义务。欧盟法院认为，根据欧盟法律原则，如果一个成员国未能在合理的时间内修改与欧盟法律不一致的国家法律，则欧盟成员国便违反了欧盟条约义务。有学者认为，这是一个错误的不公平决定。②欧盟沿海运输法的本质是促进成员国之间提供海上运输服务的自由。因此，当一个欧盟成员国的船舶所有人被限制提供海上运输服务时，对该义务是否得到遵守将受到考验。故而，只要在任何时候来自另一成员国的合格船舶所有人能够在没有任何不必要的限制的情况下提供海运服务，那么该措施是临时性的还是永久性的都不重要。欧盟理事会第 3577/92 号条例规定了保障措施，允许成员国在内部运输市场受到严重干扰时暂停适用该条例，这进一步支持了上述立场。③

3. 希腊案

本案中欧盟委员会指控希腊违反了欧盟理事会第 3577/92 号条例的若干规定。而后双方试图通过诉前程序来解决这些问题，但没有成功。因此，委员会提起诉讼指控希腊违反了欧盟理事会第 3577/92 号条例的第 1、3 和 6 条。委员会对希腊未能履行义务的具体指控如下：（1）仅赋予希腊客船在希腊大陆港口之间载客的权利。此外，希腊岛屿之间超过 650 吨的客船进行旅游的权利也只赋予了希腊船舶。（2）要求二次登记或在国际登记

---

① Case C-160/99(2000) Commission v. France ECR I-6137.

② Van Gend en Loos v. Nederlandse Administratie der Belastingen(Case 26/62)；(1963) ECR 1；(1970) CMLR 1.

③ Article 5 of Council Regulation(EEC) No.3577/92. Spain used the safeguard measure in 1993 for two consecutive six-months periods.

处登记的船舶提供由船旗国主管当局签发的证书，声明该船舶有权在该成员国提供沿海运输服务。（3）Peloponnese 半岛是一个岛屿。（4）对共同体的油轮、货轮、客轮以及观光船舶，以及以沿海运输方式进行海上运输的共同体邮轮，适用其作为东道国有关人员配备条件的国家规则。同时，要求船舶所有人向商船监督部申请测量船舶总吨位，以使希腊当局能够计算出船员的组成。①

依据第欧盟委员会第 1115.65/2/98 号通告和第 1151.65/1/98 号通告，委员会在诉请中声称，希腊政府阻碍了提供海上运输服务的自由，从而阻碍了欧盟理事会第 3577/92 号条例的目标。希腊要求二次登记或在国际登记处登记的共同体船舶出示船旗国的证书，证明该船舶有资格在该船旗国从事沿海运输。这项请求的依据是欧盟理事会第 3577/92 号法规的第 1 条，该条规定将沿海运输权保留给以成员国为第一登记地登记的共同体船舶。此外，第 1 条还要求共同体船舶遵守在该成员国进行沿海航行的所有条件。这意味着仅仅登记船舶本身是不够的。相反，船舶必须在该成员国登记后取得在该成员国进行沿海运输的资格。这是因为在成员国"二次登记"和"国际登记"中，登记的船舶并不自动具备欧盟理事会第 3577/92 号条例规定的从事沿海运输的资格。欧盟委员会提出，确认哪些船舶有资格从事沿海运输的目标仍然可以通过限制性较低的措施来实现。②因此，它提出了以下替代方案，即共同体船舶所有人有义务提交一份由成员国授权二次登记船舶从事沿海运输服务的法律文件。

欧盟委员会辩称，根据欧盟理事会第 3577/92 号条例第 10 条，欧盟委员会每两年发布一次报告供成员国关注，这些报告有助于检视共同体船舶是否符合在船旗国开展沿海航行服务的法律要求。此外，欧盟委员会还声称，根据欧盟理事会第 3577/92 号条例第 9 条，它定期向成员国提供有关二次登记的国家立法修正案的信息。其中，包括两份报告之间的修正案，

---

① Case C-288/02(2004) Commission v. Greece ECR I-10071, Judgement of the Court(second Chambers)，21 October 2004.

② 参见 1973 年《希腊海事公法典》第 165 条。

前提是成员国将有关进展通知欧盟委员会。欧盟委员会认为其提议的措施没有船旗国提供证书以确认船舶有资格提供沿海运输服务的义务那么严格，希腊政府对此表示反对。①希腊政府认为，欧盟委员会建议将成员国授权船舶在其境内从事沿海运输服务的法律文件提交给东道国，这与所寻求的目标不相称。相反，希腊政府为这种建议会使问题复杂化，因为船旗国需要正式地翻译法律文件，以便东道国能对其进行解释。关于成员国之间的年度信息交流，被告认为这项提案充其量只能在相当长的和不可接受的延迟之后将所需信息传达给东道国。在某些情况下，这样的提议可能对共同体船舶所有人不利，因为共同体船舶所有人可能不知道修正案赋予了他们进行沿海航行的权利。根据欧盟理事会第 3577/92 号条例第 9 条，法律正案应当直接向欧盟委员会报告。然而委员会承认，其依赖于成员国将其关于二次登记和国际登记的立法修正案通知它。②被告辩称这一主张不能被认为比船旗国的授权证书的限制性要小。这是因为欧盟委员会不能保证它总是能够向东道国提供最新的准确信息。③

欧盟法院指出，要求未在初始登记中登记的共同体船舶出示船旗国的证书，以确认其有资格提供沿海运输服务，这一要求显然具有歧视性。在此前提下，这种要求通常会构成对提供海上运输服务自由的限制。欧盟理事会第 3577/92 号条例第 1 条并没有规定如何证明船舶符合在船旗国进行沿海运输的所有条件。因此法院认为，如果不是出于东道国的公共利益有正当的压倒一切的理由，一国不能限制提供服务的自由。④然而，所采取的国家措施必须与所寻求的目标相称，并且不得超出实现该目标所需的范围。欧盟委员会提出的解决方案无法实现所寻求的目标，拟议的解决方案比有争议的证书制度更复杂，对提供沿海服务的自由限制更大。因此，欧

---

① 参见欧盟理事会第 3577/92 号条例第 10 条的规定。

② See the judgement in: Asociacion Profesional de Emresas Navieras de Lineas Regulares (Analir) and others v. Admninstration General Del Esado(Case C-205/99)(2001), ECR 1271.

③ See European Commission COM(2014) 232 final, Brussels, 22 April 2014.

④ Cases C-15/98 and C-105/99 Sardegna Lines v. Commission(2000) ECR I-8855.

洲法院决定，欧盟委员会不能证明希腊共和国要求出示证书是没有履行其在条例下的义务。对于成员国之间提供沿海运输服务的自由而言，要求未在初次登记中记录的共同体船舶出示船旗国出具的证明其有资格从事沿海运输的证书，不能被视为多余。①

欧盟委员会在其第三项诉请中声称，希腊共和国赋予 Peloponnese 岛以岛屿地位是错误的。因此，欧盟委员会指控希腊政府对该地区的港口非法适用欧盟理事会第 3577/92 号条例第 6(3) 条。委员会还指责希腊人为地将第 6(3) 条的减损范围扩大到 Peloponnese 半岛的港口之间以及位于大陆的港口和 Peloponnese 半岛的港口之间的沿海运输服务。Peloponnese 半岛不能被视为一个岛屿，因为它虽然与希腊大陆分开，但只是被一条人工运河分开。此外，Peloponnese 半岛和希腊大陆由 Corinth 运河上方的一条铁路线和一条国道连接。相比之下，希腊政府认为 Peloponnese 半岛构成了一个实际的岛屿，因为它完全被水包围，尽管是人为修建的。它提到了意大利和 Sardegna 航运公司诉欧盟委员会案，并表示根据该案确定构成岛屿的决定性标准取决于对海上贸易的统计分析。然而，与被告的论点相反，法院并没有对该案中的"岛屿"一词发表看法。此外，希腊政府指出位于非洲大陆的 Ceuta 和 Melilla 港口被欧盟理事会第 3577/92 号条例第 2(1)(c) 条视为岛屿港口。因此，将这些港口视为岛屿港口，而将位于 Peloponnese 半岛、完全被水包围的港口称为大陆港口是自相矛盾的。此外，根据欧盟理事会第 3577/92 号条例第 6(3) 条给予它的减损是基于社会经济的凝聚力，将该减损的适用范围扩大到 Peloponnese 半岛这一发展指数较低的地区，并不与这一目标相悖。②

法院认为，欧盟理事会第 3577/92 号条例中没有明确界定"岛屿"一词。然而，法院采用了"岛屿"一词在海洋环境中的常见含义。它将岛屿描述为从海上永久升起的一大片土地。关于 Ceuta 和 Melilla 的港口以及

---

① 参见欧盟理事会通讯第 1151.65/2/98 第 2.4.1 段落。
② 参见欧盟理事会第 3577/92 号条例第 9 条的规定。

Peloponnese 的港口，法院的结论是，Ceuta 和 Melilla 仅在欧盟理事会第 3577/92 号条例第 2 条的范围内构成岛屿港口。因此，它们在性质上仍然是大陆港口。由于 Peloponnese 半岛没有被第 3577/92 号条例构成岛屿，希腊政府未能证实其主张。欧盟委员会抗议希腊作为东道国对 650 吨以上的共同体邮轮的人员配备适用其国家立法。委员会声称这不符合欧盟理事会第 3577/92 号条例第 3(1)条。该条款规定对于从事大陆沿海运输的船舶和邮轮与人员配备有关的所有事项均应由船旗国负责。欧盟委员会认为第 3(1)条适用于共同体邮轮，而无论其是从事大陆或岛屿的沿海运输。相反，希腊政府认为根据欧盟理事会第 3577/92 号条例第 3(1)条，船旗国的人员配备规则只适用于停靠大陆港口的邮轮。①

在裁决中，欧洲法院承认在欧盟理事会第 3577/92 号条例第 3(1)条中没有对邮轮进行明确分类。然而，法院推断如果将从事岛屿沿海运输的邮轮纳入第 3(2)条，那么第 3(1)条对于邮轮的提及则毫无意义。法院声称，"从事大陆沿海运输的邮轮"已经被"从事大陆沿海运输的船舶"这一通用短语所涵盖。因此，没有必要在条例第 3(1)条中具体提及"邮轮"，而在第 3(2)条中却不提及。因此，第 3(1)条中具体提及"邮轮"为其提供了有效的独立解释，该解释将责任赋予船旗国。它规定了与在岛屿港口进行沿海航行的 650 总吨以上游轮的人员配备有关的所有事项的规则。因此，法院宣布希腊没有履行欧盟理事会第 3577/92 号条例第 1、3 和 6 条规定的义务。②

4. Agip Petroli SPA 案

本案关涉欧盟理事会第 3577/92 号条例对船员的限制。更具体地说，欧盟法院面临的问题是正确解释并澄清欧盟理事会第 357792 号条例第 3(3)条的规定。对于超过 650 总吨的货船，在进出另一个国家的航程开始之前和结束之后进行岛屿沿海运输的，所有与人员配备有关的事项应由船

---

① 参见欧盟理事会第 3577/92 号条例第 10 条规定。

② 参见欧盟理事会第 3577/92 号条例第 1 条规定。

旗国负责。Agip Petroli 公司租用了在希腊注册的 Theodoros Ⅳ号油轮，将一批原油从 Magnisi 运到 Gela，起运港和目的地都在西西里岛。Agip Petroli 公司以欧盟理事会第 3577/92 号条例第 3(3) 条为依据，证明减损适用东道国意大利的立法是合理的。原告的目的是要适用船旗国希腊共和国的法律。在申请许可进行该岛的沿海航行时，原告认为该船随后将直接航行到外国，尽管船上没有任何货物，即所谓的"压载"航行。意大利当局拒绝了执行这次航行的申请，因为该船的船员包括来自菲律宾的非欧盟国民。允许外国船员进行岛屿航行被认为是违反了《意大利航运法》第 318 条。正是由于意大利当局的这一拒绝，Agip Petroli 开始了法律诉讼。法院认为，根据欧盟理事会第 3577/92 号条例第 3(3) 条的规定，在沿海航行之后或之前的航行是否只指功能和商业上独立的航行，即船上有货物的航行，目的地是外国港口或来自外国港口。或者说"压载"航行是否构成欧盟理事会第 3577/92 号条例第 3(3) 条所考虑的有效航行。①

意大利当局辩称，欧盟理事会第 3577/9 号条例第 3(3) 条只适用于前一个或后一个航程是载重船的航行。因此，如果船舶已经完成或将在岛内航行后完成"压载"航行或装载货物的航行，而这些货物在质量和数量上不能使航行具有自主功能和商业价值，则不能援引第 3(3) 条。此外，由于后续航行是"压载"航行，欧盟理事会第 3577/9 号条例第 3(2) 条应该适用。欧盟理事会第 3577/92 号条例第 3(2) 条规定，对于从事岛屿沿海运输的船舶，所有与人员配备有关的事项应由该船舶从事海上运输服务的东道国负责。欧洲法院裁定，第 3(3) 条涵盖了船只在"压载"航行到另一个国家的情况。这一决定与欧盟委员会在 2003 年的解释公告中的立场形成鲜明对比。委员会指出，如果在岛屿沿海航行之后或之前的国际航行是"压载"航行，则适用东道国的规则。尽管如此，法院进一步推断，船舶在"压载"状态下航行是常见的航运惯例。②然而，法院接受了蓄意规避第

---

① Case C-456/04（2006）Agip Petroli SPA v. Capitaneria di Porto di Siracusa et seq ECR I-3395（Second Chamber）.

② Case 125/76 Cremer（1977）ECR 1593，paragraph 21.

3(3)条规定的可能性。因此，法院承认，如果前面或后续"压载"航行到另一个国家显然是为了阻挠东道国关于船员的规则，那么船旗国将被禁止援引欧盟理事会第 3577/92 号条例第 3(3)条。欧盟法律的范围在任何情况下都不能扩大到包括任何一方的滥用行为。这包括旨在规避欧盟法律规则的活动，以及不在正常商业交易中进行的活动。因此，证明上述航行是合法或非法的举证责任由东道国承担。本案证实，欧盟实施自由主义沿海运输权立法旨在建立在欧盟国家范围内提供海上运输服务的自由。然而，欧盟的自由主义沿海运输权立法和政策，不是绝对的自由主义，而保护主义的色彩仍然浓厚。此外，欧盟沿海运输法和政策的这些微妙的保护主义色彩得到了法律的默许。可以说，在适用东道国规则的情况下，欧盟的船舶所有人可以预期会面临不同程度的竞争。①

5. 西班牙王国案

这是由欧盟委员会对西班牙王国提起的诉讼。欧盟委员会在起诉书中宣称，西班牙坚持其国家立法未能履行《欧共体条约》和第欧盟理事会第 577/92 号条例第 1、4、7、9 条规定的义务。为此，欧盟委员会诉请如下：(1)允许将 Vigo 河口的海上运输服务特许权授予单一运营商，期限为 20 年，并将在 Vigo 河口的运输经验作为特许权的标准，从而违反了条例第 1 条。(2)允许对与岛屿之间的季节性运输服务和大陆港口之间的定期运输服务施加公共服务义务，从而违反了条例第 4 条。(3)允许采用比欧盟理事会第 3577/92 号条例生效之日更为严格的制度，因此违反了该条例第 7 条。(4)在没有与欧盟委员会协商的情况下批准，因此违反了欧盟理事会第 3577/92 号条例第 9 条。第 4/1999 号法律是 Galicia 自治区在 1999 年通过的，即欧盟理事会第 3577/92 号条例生效 6 年之后。第 4/1999 号法律宣布 Vigo 河口的海上客运是属于 Galicia 地区政府的公共服务。②

在处理欧盟委员会提出的四项诉请之前，法院审理了西班牙政府提出

---

① Case C-515/03 Eichsfelder Schlachtbetrieb(2005) ECR I-7355，paragraph 40，76.

② Case 323/03 Commission of the European Communities v. Kingdom of Spain(2006). Judgement of the Court(Second Chambers)，9 March 2006.

的一个初步事项。被告对欧盟理事会第 3577/92 号条例适用于 Vigo 河口的运输服务提出异议，该河口受第 4/1999 号法律管辖。西班牙政府辩称，沿海运输必须被理解为"港口之间"的海上客货运输。在此基础上，被告将 Vigo 河口的海上运输描述为既不是海上运输，也不是欧盟理事会第 3577/92 条例中赋予这些术语的意义上的港口之间的运输。被告主张，"海上运输"应被理解为指外部海域，而不是内水。据此 Vigo 河口的运输服务只构成内水的运输。因此，与欧盟理事会第 3577/92 号条例相反，Vigo 河口的运输不能被视为建立内部市场的必要组成部分。此外，Vigo 河口的航运不构成港口之间的航运。根据适用的国家法规，河口是 Vigo 港口服务区的一部分，只有一个停泊能力有限的码头。西班牙政府提到理事会第 98/18/EC 号指令，声称即使是共同体的规则也不把 Vigo 河口的水域视为海域。[①]

法院裁定，在解释共同体法律条款时，不应限于考虑该条款的措辞，还应考虑该条款的适用背景及其所属规则的目标。因此，"港口间海上运输"一词应根据欧盟理事会第 3577/92 号条例第 2(1)(a)和(c)条的目标来解释，其目的是争取提供海上运输服务的自由。因此，将欧盟理事会第 3577/92 号条例意义上的"海洋"一词与 1982 年《联合国海洋法公约》意义上的"领海"一词等同起来，可能会破坏这一目标。此外，没有迹象表明欧盟理事会第 3577/92 号条例旨在将其范围限制在 1982 年《联合国海洋法公约》意义内的领海，因此，将这些术语等同起来没有任何意义。[②]

关于 Vigo 河口的航运对建立内部市场的目标影响甚微的论点，有学者认为欧盟理事会第 3577/92 号条例中没有任何规定表明，其范围取决于特定地区的航运对设立内部市场的经济和社会影响。因此，根据欧共体指令 98/18，声称 Vigo 河口的海上运输服务不构成欧盟理事会第 3577/92 号条例意义上的"港口间"运输服务是无效的。此外，该条例的范围并不受

[①] Aniekan Akpan, *Maritime Cabotage Law*, London: Routledge, 2019, p.206.

[②] Case C-175/97 Commission v. France(1998) ECR I-963.

制于任何成员国的法律。欧盟理事会第 3577/92 号条例中的"港口"一词包括便利海运货物装卸的基础设施，尽管规模较小。根据既定判例法，因此必须对"港口"一词作出自主和统一的解释，以反映使用该词的立法的背景和目的。①Cíes Isles，Vigo，Cangas 和 Moañ 现有的基础设施必须视为欧盟理事会第 3577/92 号条例意义上的港口。因此，法院决定第 4/1999 号法律管辖的 Vigo 河口运输服务属于理事会第 3577/92 号条例的范围。②

欧盟委员会认为，第 4/1999 号法律在两个方面违反了欧盟理事会第 3577/92 号条例第 1 条。该法律将 Vigo 河口的海上客运服务保留给单一运营商并授予行政特许权。欧盟委员会诉称，允许这种保留在特许期内阻碍了市场准入。同时，第 4/1999 号法律规定在维戈河口运营运输服务的经验是授予特许权的标准，这有利于现有运营商并歧视其他成员国的新运营商。西班牙政府在辩护中称，法院判例法意义上的公共利益压倒一切的理由证明了特许权安排的正当性。西班牙政府主张，Cíes 群岛的海上运输服务是与这些岛屿的唯一可能联系。因此，出于环境保护原因，该区域内的海洋活动必须受到限制。此外，这些岛屿上的码头无法支持大量的海上交通。因此，西班牙政府辩称，使用配额制度是控制允许每天访问 Cíes 群岛的交通量的唯一合理手段。同时，关于 Vigo、Cangas 和 Moaña 镇之间的海上连接，西班牙政府认为这是最直接和最经济的运输方式。因此，它的停止将对 Vigo 和 Morrazo 半岛的交通组织产生负面影响。③

法院认为，将 Vigo 河口的海上运输服务保留给单一运营商至少 20 年的国家措施可能构成对提供服务自由的限制。它驳斥了西班牙政府的论点，即这项措施是基于公共利益的压倒一切的理由。关于监测 Cíes 群岛的交通量以符合环境要求，法院认为，与最低 20 年的特许权相比，被告可选择的限制性较小。例如，它可以使用预先预订和出售该目的地可用位置的系统。此外，法院认定，西班牙政府无法证明给予一家运营商 20 年的特许

---

① Case C-205/99 Analir and Others(2001) ECR I-1271，paragraph 19.

② Ministerial Decree of 23 December 1966，BOE of 23 January 1967.

③ Case C-205/99 Analir and Others(2001).

权是保证每年在 Vigo 河口提供 100 多万名乘客的服务仍然有利可图的唯一途径。[1]法院认为，在授予特许权时，标准在多大程度上起决定作用并不相关。这是因为对一个成员国未能履行其义务的认定与由此产生的损害的认定无关。[2]此外，第 9/2003 号法律撤销该标准被认为无关紧要。任何一方都没有因该标准而遭受损失，这一点也不重要。法院认为，关于成员国是否未能履行义务的问题必须参照合理意见到期时成员国的普遍情况来确定。因此，法院没有考虑到 随后的任何变动。故而，第一项诉请得到维持。

在第二项诉请中，欧盟委员会声称西班牙违反了欧盟理事会第 3577/92 号条例的第 4 条。第 4 条明确规定，成员国应与只从事往返于岛屿和岛屿之间的定期服务的运营商签订公共服务合同（PSC）或对其施加公共服务义务（PSO）。然而，欧盟委员会指出 Vigo 河口的运输服务并不是通往岛屿或岛屿之间的定期运输服务。Vigo-Cangas 和 Vigo-Moaña 路线上的定期服务不是岛屿服务，前往 Cies 岛的服务是季节性的旅游服务。这与欧盟理事会第 3577/92 号条例第 4 条所设想的"定期"要求相悖。[3]对此，西班牙政府辩称，第 4 条的前提是 PSC 或 PSO 是连接有关地区的岛屿之间或岛屿与大陆之间的唯一手段。现有的陆地连接是困难的。因此，将欧盟理事会第 3577/92 条例第 4 条的原则适用于 Vigo 河口的航运连接是合理的。欧盟委员会承认在特殊情况下有可能扩大第 4 条的适用范围。这将适用于通往岛屿或岛屿之间的海上运输服务的替代方案带来的挑战，以至于它们实际上不再构成海上连接的真正替代方案。然而，欧盟委员会断然拒绝在本案中适用这种特殊情况。[4]

法院认为 Vigo、Cangas 和 Moaña 镇之间的定期海上运输服务不能被视为通往岛屿或岛屿之间的海上运输服务。这是因为除了海上连接外，还

---

[1]　Case C-55/02 Commission v. Portugal(2004) ECR I-9387.

[2]　Case C-76/90 Sager(1991) ECR I-4221.

[3]　Case C-19/92 Kraus(1993) ECR I-1663.

[4]　Case C-55/94 Gebhard(1995) ECR I-4165.

有一个直接连接各城镇的功能性公路网，可以随时进入各城镇。此外，西班牙政府对往返于 Cies 岛的海上运输服务不是定期服务这一点没有异议。①欧盟委员会主张被告通过的第 4/1999 号法律，违反了欧盟理事会第 3577/92 号条例第 7 条。该条例第 7 条款遵从了欧共体条约第 62 条。欧共体条约的这项规定禁止成员国采取比欧盟理事会第 3577/92 号条例生效之日适用的限制性措施更多的措施。根据 Galicia 自治区 1984 年的决定所作的安排比通过第 4/1999 号法律所作的限制性更小。应当指出，第 62 条在1999 年被《阿姆斯特丹条约》废除，这反映在欧盟理事会第 3577/92 号条例第 7 条中。欧盟理事会第 3577/92 号条例第 6 条不包括 Vigo 河口的海上运输服务。这是因为在合理意见的有效期内，第 4/1999 号法律的通过不可能违反欧盟理事会第 3577/92 号条例的第 6 条和第 7 条。②因此，欧盟委员会的第三项诉请被驳回。欧盟委员会在其第四项诉请中提出，西班牙政府在通过第 4/1999 号法律之前没有征求欧盟委员会的意见，因此违反了欧盟理事会第 3577/92 号条例第 9 条。西班牙政府承认，它在通过第 4/1999 号法律之前没有根据欧盟理事会第 3577/92 号条例第 9 条的规定通知委员会。因此，第四项诉请得到了支持。综上所述，法院认为西班牙王国违反了欧盟理事会第 3577/92 号条例第 1 条、第 4 条和 第 9 条的规定，没有履行欧盟共同体规则的义务。③

三、自由主义沿海运输权立法之比较考察

1. 南非的相关立法

南非共和国采取了强有力的航运市场驱动政策。南非实行非常自由的海事政策，允许从事国际贸易的外国船舶参与其沿海运输服务。然而在南非，关于是否需要尝试实行保护主义的沿海航行权立法的讨论越来越多。1996 年，一份关于国家运输政策的政府白皮书考虑了南非的沿海运输权立

---

① Case C-272/94 Guiot(1996) ECR I-1905.

② Case C-175/97 Commission v. France(1998) ECR I-963.

③ Case C-209/02 Commission v. Austria(2004) ECR I-1211.

法。白皮书强调，政府打算根据不断变化的国际海上货物运输惯例，对各种海上货物运输的选择进行评估。2003 年，《南非海事黑人经济赋权宪章》被签署成为法律。该宪章旨在说服国内贸易商在运输货物时优先选择南非船舶，还主张实行一项沿海运输政策，即通过南非港口的货物由南非船舶运输。尽管南非的贸易量巨大，但是并没有反映在其船舶保有量和船舶运营能力上。因此南非政府认为，实行保护主义沿海运输权政策将振兴悬挂本国船旗的船舶承运人并刺激当地的海运业。①在考虑采取何种沿海运输权政策时，南非的巨大贸易量将是一个重要因素。然而，拥有庞大的贸易量本身并不足以作为制定和颁布沿海运输权法律和政策的充分依据。2008 年《南非海运政策草案》要求在南非采取保护主义的沿海运输权政策，该政策的第 3.3.4 条规定，南非政府应根据联合国贸易和发展委员会（UNCTAD）制定的指导方针出台沿海运输政策。此外，南非的经济增长和发展与非洲地区的同步增长和发展有着密不可分的关系。因此，南非必须重新思考其国内的海运政策，因为区域沿海运输已经成为促进区域内贸易和发展的一个重要因素。南非政府意图考察区域沿海运输潜力，并将其与非洲发展共同体（SADC）的沿海运输政策相结合。同时，考量沿海运输在该地区近海产业发展中可以发挥的作用。②

　　然而，2008 年《南非海运政策草案》必须与其他运输部门的类似政策发展相适应，否则这些改革将形同虚设。事实上，南非面临的难题是，其海上运输政策必须符合 1994 年《非洲海上运输宪章》和 1996 年《南部非洲发展共同体运输、通信和气象议定书》。《非洲海上运输宪章》主张在非洲区域内实行类似于欧洲联盟的海上运输政策。此外，《南部非洲发展共同体议定书》要求成员国逐步取消对在成员国登记的船舶的航行限制。③

---

①　参见 2003 年《南非海事黑人经济赋权宪章》第 2.3.1 部分规定。

②　参见 2003 年《南非海事黑人经济赋权宪章》第 2.3.2 部分规定。

③　Department of Transport，"Draft South African Maritime Transport Policy"，DOT，2008，p.25.

南非任何海运业政策的成功都取决于设计一个稳健但灵活的框架，以兼顾这两个法律框架的目标。因此，南非采取保护主义海运政策的倾向很可能取决于她是否有能力说服其南非发展共同体伙伴效仿南非，采取类似的保护主义沿海运输政策。然而，这意味着南非及其伙伴在《非洲海运公约》生效时将不会遵守该公约的目标和要求。①然而，南非并没有明确的理由放弃其自由的沿海运输权政策。此外，采取保护主义的沿海运输权政策将意味着背离非洲发展共同体的原则。

2. 新西兰的相关立法

新西兰是深入实施经济自由化政策的国家。1994 年之前，新西兰的沿海运输受 1952 年《航运和海员法》的调整。该法将新西兰的沿海运输权保留给国内船舶，除非国内没有适当吨位的船舶。如果由于缺乏合适吨位的国内船舶而允许外国船舶从事新西兰沿海运输服务，则外国船舶须遵守严格的条件，例如仅限于运输特定货物。同时，根据 2006 年《海事劳工公约》，新西兰保留了外籍船员的福利和工资要求。1984 年至 1994 年期间，在新西兰经济改革期间，保护主义沿海运输权被逐渐放宽。这项改革见证了 1993 年《运输法改革法案》的出台，该法案提议允许外国船舶不受任何限制地参与新西兰的沿海贸易和服务。该法案的相关部分明确规定，在新西兰任何港口装载的货物或登船的乘客，如果持有所有适当的海事文件，可由任何船舶运载，包括船舶和海员，最终在新西兰任何港口卸载或登岸。②

然而，1993 年《运输法改革法案》中提出的自由的开放海岸政策未能在立法院获得足够的支持。开放海岸政策的提议遭到了强烈的反对，有人认为这样的政策会对本土就业、国防和国民经济发展产生不利影响。这导致该法案被大幅修改。经修订的法案建议允许在国际航行中经过新西兰海

---

① South African Maritime Safety Authority，"Maritime Sector Skills Development Study"，Department of Transport，Pretoria，21 September 2011.

② T. Hazledine(1993)，"New Zealand Trade Patterns and Policy"，*Australian Economic Review*，26(4)，pp.23—27.

岸的外国船舶参与新西兰的沿海运输服务。目前，新西兰的沿海运输权政策由 1994 年《航运法》调整。1994 年《航运法》包含了对完全开放海岸政策负面影响的担忧，但在很大程度上仍然是一种自由的沿海运输政策。[①]该法第 198 条（C、D 款）表明，只要外国船舶从外国港口卸货或为外国港口装载货物，就可以不受限制地进入新西兰沿海水域。然而，这与新西兰移民规则的规定相反。[②]新西兰《2010 年移民条例》附表 3 规定，"由于符合1994 年《航运法》第 198 节的条件，从事沿海贸易的外国船舶上的船员每次国际航行的工作许可期仅限于 28 天"。新西兰《2010 年移民条例》附表3 中关于"外国船舶上的船员"的措辞只适用于外国船员，而不适用于外国船舶。因此，并不清楚一艘拥有本土船员的外国船舶是否会违反法律规定。此外，1994 年《航运法》第 198（2）条允许不能满足第 198（1）条要求的外国船舶在没有合适的悬挂国内船旗的船舶的情况下，从事海上运输服务。这一豁免预计会受到新西兰劳工和海事联盟的强烈谴责。他们反对宽松的开放海岸政策的前提是，外国船舶所有人可以在不缴税的情况下从事新西兰的沿海贸易。此外，他们还担心外国船舶对生物安全造成的额外风险。[③]

新西兰的经济改革最终导致世界上最严格管控的经济体之一被最自由的市场经济体之一所取代。这些改革的标志之一是消除了商品和服务的国际竞争障碍。新西兰政府认为，放松管制的政策给经济带来的海运优势包括降低国内运输成本和降低货物价格。有观点认为，宽松的沿海运输权政策将为贸易商带来一系列的航运利益，包括因国际竞争而提高服务质量。当然，新西兰自由的沿海运输权制度也受到质疑和反对，这些反对理由在

---

① M. Brooks，"Maritime Cabotage: International Market Issues in the Liberalisation of Domestic Shipping", in A. Chircop et al. (eds), *The Regulation of International Shipping: International and Comparative Perspectives*, Martinus Nijhoff 2012, pp.293—324.

② S. Goldfinch(2004), "Economic Reform in New Zealand: Radical Liberalisation in a Small Economy", *Otemon Journal of Australian Studies*, 30(1), 75—98.

③ R. May et al.(2001), "Unions and Union Membership in New Zealand: Annual Review for 2000", *New Zealand Journal of Industrial Relations*, 26(3), 317—329.

于，新西兰担心外国船舶会利用宽松的税收制度而从中获利。这使得船舶所有人雇佣外国船员比雇佣本土船员更有利可图。然而，这些问题中的许多问题特别是船员福利和工资问题已经得到解决。①

第三节　灵活主义沿海运输权：立法与判例

一般而言，对于一个主权国家来说，选择不同的沿海运输权模式和立法基本上是选择保护主义模式或自由主义模式。然而，在两者之间确实存在被称为"灵活主义沿海运输权"的立法或政策。灵活主义沿海运输权的基本特征是一个主权国家可以根据本国具体情况需要而交替选择保护主义和自由主义的沿海运输权。

一、俄罗斯联邦的灵活主义沿海运输权

俄罗斯横跨整个亚洲北部和东欧大部分地区，与这两个大陆上的一些国家共享陆地和海洋边界。因此，俄罗斯在地理上通常被认定为处于欧亚大陆。②俄罗斯的地域特征决定了该国无法单纯适用于欧盟理事会第3577/92号条例，也无法单纯适用于一些亚洲国家沿海运输权的协议。俄罗斯的沿海运输政策由俄罗斯联邦1999年《商船航运法》规范。该法第4条规定了俄罗斯执行的沿海运输权法律和政策。主要包括俄罗斯联邦海港之间的运输和拖航应由悬挂俄罗斯联邦国旗的船舶进行。但是，根据俄罗斯联邦缔结和参加的国际条约，或在某些情况下，按照俄罗斯联邦政府规定的程序，可由悬挂外国国旗的船舶从事沿海运输和拖航。③

1999年《商船航运法》并不是俄罗斯第一部旨在规范其沿海运输权秩

---

① A. Bollard，"New Zealand"，in J. Williamson(ed.)，*The Political Economy of Policy Reform*，Institute for International Economics 1994，pp.73—110.

② M. Brooks，"Maritime Cabotage：International Market Issues in the Liberalisation of Domestic Shipping"，in A. Chircop et al.(eds)，*The Regulation of International Shipping：International and Comparative Perspectives*，Martinus Nijhoff 2012，pp.293—324.

③ 参见1999年《俄罗斯联邦航运法》第4条规定。

序的法律。在颁布该法案之前，早在 1830 年俄罗斯就通过了一项法律，将沿海贸易运输权留给悬挂俄罗斯国旗并雇佣俄罗斯船员的船舶。然而，该法律从未被实施。此外，1897 年俄罗斯还通过了另一部沿海运输法。俄罗斯选择灵活的沿海运输权模式，也许是受到其地理特征的影响。然而，俄罗斯也热衷于发展其沿海运输权立法并试图形成稳定的沿海运输权政策。①在俄罗斯，沿海运输权通常只适用于悬挂俄罗斯国旗的船舶，除非需要专门运输的船舶，但没有合适的俄罗斯旗船舶，或者在紧急需要船舶实施拖航的情况下。

因此，外国籍船舶可以提供俄罗斯沿海运输服务。此外，俄罗斯交通部还实行沿海运输许可制度，通过向外国船舶发放沿海贸易许可证允许外国船舶从事俄罗斯沿海运输和服务。然而，专门为国家项目建造或采购的船舶，如近海凝析气和油气田的勘探，可以在这些长期合同的有效期内获得沿海运输许可证。②从事俄罗斯沿海运输的大部分外国船舶是在萨哈林油田和其他石油和天然气项目中工作的近海船舶。这是因为俄罗斯缺少或没有合适的本国船舶。③

二、澳大利亚实施的沿海运输权：政策与判例

澳大利亚的沿海运输法律和政策此后经历了过山车式的改革。历届澳大利亚政府都喜欢采取以一种沿海运输权模式去取代另一种沿海运输权模式。经过一波又一波的改革，澳大利亚的沿海运输业已经从一个总体上不受监管的领域逐渐过渡到一个更加规范的领域。在这些改革之前，澳大利亚的沿海运输权政策的重点是确保在澳大利亚领海内的船舶上工作的所有船员都能得到公平待遇，以及确保在澳大利亚沿海水域提供海事服务的船舶具有一定的自由。2012 年《澳大利亚沿海贸易法》是后续规范澳大利亚

---

① N. Prisekina, "Cabotage: Frequent Legal Issues for Contractors on Sakhalin Oil and Gas Projects", Russin & Vecchi, London, 18 November 2003.

② 参见《俄罗斯联邦政府第 204 号决议》第 8 条。

③ G. Curtis, Russia: A Country Study, Library of Congress 1998.

沿海运输的法律。①该法的目标之一是在沿海贸易中最大限度地使用在澳大利亚登记的船舶。该法案标志着澳大利亚沿海运输法正朝着新的、更严格的方向发展，该法是在2009年《公平工作法》的基础上制定的，已经对在澳大利亚沿海运输业中雇佣外国船员的外国注册船舶适用澳大利亚的劳动标准。根据2009年《公平工作法》，在沿海贸易中雇佣外国船员的成本仅为雇用澳大利亚海员的26%。②随着2012年《澳大利亚沿海贸易法》的出台，被允许进入澳大利亚沿海贸易的情况将不再发生。这导致新法中的沿海运输法进一步得到改革。2014年，澳大利亚国家审计委员会建议，澳大利亚的沿海运输法和政策应完全废除。该审查报告认为，除非能够证明以下情况，否则应废除沿海运输的限制。这些情况包括限制措施给澳大利亚社会经济带来的好处超过了成本，以及该政策的目标只能通过限制竞争来实现等。③

　　与其他国家一样，澳大利亚实施沿海贸易权法律自然也会影响到澳大利亚本土贸易商的利益。比如，根据有关机构的研究表明，悬挂外国国旗的船舶在澳大利亚沿海贸易中的参与度急剧下降，意味着澳大利亚企业的竞争减少。同时，由于缺乏竞争导致澳大利亚贸易商支付的运费增加，航运成本大幅增加。很多贸易商因业务或外部因素的不可预见的变化无法灵活选择沿海航运需求。④为此，澳大利亚采取了分别颁发沿海运输权一般许可、临时许可以及紧急许可的模式，形成了具有本国特色的灵活主义沿海运输权模式。在一般许可模式下，所有申请一般许可的船舶都必须在澳大利亚一般航运注册处（AGSR）注册并保持注册状态。一般许

---

① S. Thompson R. Springall and H. Brewar，A Guide to the Coastal Trading Reforms in Australia，Holman Fenwick Willan 2012.

② Rio Tinto，"Submission to Senate Standing Committees on Economics Inquiry into the Shipping Reform Bills(Supplementary)"，Government Office，2008，p.5.

③ I. Harper et al.，Competition Policy Review：Final Report(The Harper Review)，Commonwealth of Australia 2015.

④ C. Keane，M. Thompson and J. Cockerell，"Harper Review Recommends Changes to Australia's Cabotage Regime and Liner Shipping Exemption"，Clyde & Co Newsletter，Melbourne，2 April 2015.

可证持有人可以不受限制地进入澳大利亚沿海海域进行沿海贸易运输，期限最长为五年。①一般许可证制度下的船舶经营者必须确保其船舶上的每个海员在澳大利亚沿海水域作业时不被禁止工作。这意味着这些海员必须是澳大利亚公民、澳大利亚永久签证的持有者，或在澳大利亚拥有工作权利。在临时许可证模式之下，临时许可证允许船舶从事澳大利亚的沿海运输贸易，并且期限最长为 12 个月。②2012 年《澳大利亚沿海贸易法》第 40(a)条规定任何用于进行临时许可证授权航行的船舶必须在澳大利亚国际船舶注册处（AISR）注册，或已经根据外国法律注册。一旦申请了临时许可证，就必须以公告的方式向每个一般许可证的持有人发出通知。③

就紧急许可模式而言，根据任何国家的法律注册的船舶都可以申请紧急许可证，以便在紧急情况下如在灾害期间，实施货物或乘客的沿海运输活动。通常而言，紧急许可证的期限最长为 30 天。新法下紧急许可证持有人必须遵守适用于其他许可证持有人的同样的强制性报告要求。这些要求包括货物类型、船上乘客人数以及船舶的装货港和卸货港口等信息。④然而，澳大利亚政府在沿海运输权政策的实施上，不断尝试改革。2017 年 9 月，一项新的立法《沿海贸易法修正案》被提交给澳大利亚议会，以取代2012 年《澳大利亚沿海贸易法》。拟议的法案旨在调整现有的沿海运输权法律框架，使其更加有效。新法的目的是通过简化临时许可证申请程序来减少沿海航运业的障碍，以鼓励利用航运来促进澳大利亚的沿海货物运输水平的提升。⑤

由于适用澳大利亚沿海运输权立法和政策而引发若干起法律争端和纠纷。在 Re the Maritime Union of Australia & Ors; Ex parte CSL Pacific

---

① 参见 2012 年《澳大利亚沿海贸易法案》第 3(2a) 和 16(1) 的规定。

② 参见 2012 年《澳大利亚沿海贸易法案》第 28(1) 和 28(2) 的规定。

③ 参见 2012 年《澳大利亚沿海贸易法案》第 30(b) 和 33 的规定。

④ C. Berg and A. Lane, "Coastal Shipping Reform: Industry Reform or Regulatory Nightmare?" Institute of Public Affairs, 2013.

⑤ M. Ganter(1997), "Australian Coastal Shipping: The Vital Link", *Australian Maritime Affairs*, No.3.

Shipping Inc.案中,①显示了许可制度下沿海运输权的变迁,反映了当时澳大利亚海上运输法的重点是在沿海贸易中工作的外国船员报酬与澳大利亚船员报酬同等。托伦斯河号(River Torrens)是一艘在澳大利亚注册的船,根据1912年《澳大利亚沿海贸易法》第288条的规定,该船在沿海贸易中使用澳大利亚船员。许可证规定经营人澳大利亚国家航运公司有义务向船员支付澳大利亚的现行工资。该船后来卖给了加拿大CSL集团,并更名为CSL Pacific,并在巴哈马注册。后来该船回到澳大利亚海岸从事沿海运输,且一个乌克兰船员取代了澳大利亚船员,根据1912年《澳大利亚沿海贸易法》第286条被允许沿海贸易。重要的是,乌克兰船员的工资标准符合国际运输联盟(ITF)的标准,但低于澳大利亚的工资标准。沿海运输许可使运营商可以避免支付澳大利亚工资标准的要求。然而,澳大利亚海事联盟向澳大利亚劳资关系委员会(AIRC)申请对CSL太平洋公司实施澳大利亚劳工标准,CSL向高等法院提出上诉。法院面临的问题是,AIRC改变关于劳动标准的裁决的管辖权是否也适用于一家经营着一艘外国船舶、有外国船员并且被允许在澳大利亚水域贸易往来的外国公司。②一般的理解是,AIRC的管辖权只限于澳大利亚港口之间的沿海航行。法院裁定,尽管是一艘外国船舶,AIRC在宪法上有权管辖对乌克兰船员实行澳大利亚的工资标准。法院接受CLS所主张的"内部经济"规则是国际法的一个有效原则,也是澳大利亚的有效法律。然而,法院认为,该规则并不能取代1996年《工作场所关系法》第5(3)(b)条赋予澳大利亚劳资关系委员会的明确管辖权。虽然裁定AIRC对CSL实施澳大利亚工资标准有管辖权,但澳大利亚劳资关系委员会选择不这样做。其理由是,这种行动可能会对生产力和工作积极性产生负面影响。③

CSL Australia Pty Ltd v. Minister for Infrastructure & Transport and

---

① Re The Maritime Union of Australia & Ors; Ex parte CSL Pacific Shipping Inc(2003) HCA 43; 214 CLR 397, 7 August 2003.

② 参见 2012 年《澳大利亚沿海贸易法案》第 33 和 34(3)的规定。

③ 参见 2012 年《澳大利亚沿海贸易法案》第 64(3a) 和 72(a)的规定。

Braemar Seascope Pty Ltd 案中，①本案中的上诉人是一个一般许可证经营者，有资格从事一般沿海贸易。第二被告 Braemar Seascope 是一家船舶经纪公司，于 2012 年 8 月向第一被告（部长）申请临时许可，以从事 17 个特定航次。在填写申请表时，Braemar 知道它在申请中指定的所有 17 个航次都是虚构的。此外，Braemar 在 2013 年 3 月又提出申请，要求在其临时许可证上再增加 7 个航次。在这份申请中，为每个航次提供的细节，包括货物类型、数量、装载和卸货港口、日期和船舶细节都是虚构的。Braemar 公司还知情，它不拥有或租用任何船舶，不是任何船舶的代理，也不是任何虚构货物的托运人。相反，它预计在 12 个月的临时许可到期之前，会有机会让它使用未在总登记册上的船舶来运输货物。它还希望能找到希望提供的比普通许可证上的船只更便宜的价格运输货物的托运人。当这些机会出现时，Braemar 打算并确实向第一被告人申请更改其临时许可中授权的一个或几个虚构的航程。更改后的许可证将批准 Braemar 公司想要安排的实际航行。因此，之前虚构的从奥尔巴尼到墨尔本装载 20 000 吨谷物的授权航次被修改为从肯布拉港到威亚拉装载 45 000 吨煤炭的航次，装载日期为 2013 年 8 月 2 日。2013 年 7 月变更的临时许可证授权了 21 个航次。其中四个航次，包括第 23 航次，尚未执行。②

上诉人 CSL 要求法院宣布，部长代表向 Braemar 发放临时许可证并在 2013 年 4 月和 2013 年 7 月两次更改许可的决定是无效的，因为 Braemar 没有资格申请临时许可证或更改许可。此外，他们要求法院裁定，2013 年 7 月 9 日批准的变更是无效的，因为部长的代表没有遵循法律规定的适当程序。上诉人还要求法院宣布 Braemar 公司使用其临时许可证的方式规避了一般许可证条款的目的或 2012 年《澳大利亚沿海贸易法》第 63 条所设想的目标。③

---

① CSL Australia Pty Limited v. Minister for Infrastructure & Transport and Braemar Seascope Pty Ltd(2014) FCA 1160，3 November 2014.

② Re The Maritime Union of Australia & Ors；Ex parte CSL Pacific Shipping Inc(2003) HCA 43.

③ D. Maybury and M. Tang，"Australian Shipping Industry Reform：Coastal Trading Bill"(2012)，Legalseas，February.

法院面临的问题是，根据 2012 年《澳大利亚沿海贸易法》的规定，基于虚构航程的临时许可证申请是否有效。此外，这种授权的临时许可在随后为真实或进一步的虚构航程而进行修改时，修改是否有效。如果获得和更改临时许可的申请是无效的，那么部长是否有权批准这些申请和随后的更改。Braemar 公司承认，在申请之初它没有成为任何航程的一般许可证持有人。同时，他们也承认在申请之初，没有一个航次是真实的。然而，他们声称，这是他们根据行业知识的最佳猜测。重要的是 Braemar 公司承认，其申请并获得临时许可证的最初 17 个航次中，没有一个航次被执行。根据 2012 年《澳大利亚沿海贸易法》第 28(1) 条，Braemar 公司获得并使用其临时许可证，计划在不需要一般许可证持有人运输沿海货物的机会出现时获得专门变更。这种专门使用临时许可证的行为违反了该法第 3(2b) 条的规定。[1]此外，第二被告的行为规避了一般许可证规定的目标和 2012 年《澳大利亚沿海贸易法》第 63(1) 条所设想的目标。2012 年《澳大利亚沿海贸易法》并没有预设一般许可证持有者的权利会受到基于虚构航程的临时许可证申请和随后根据可能出现的商业机会对该许可证进行变更的影响。

根据 2012 年《澳大利亚沿海贸易法》第 35 条，第一被告 2012 年批准第二被告临时许可证申请的决定是无效的。此外，根据该法第 28(1) 条，第一被告缺乏向第二被告发放临时许可证的管辖权，因为第二被告没有资格申请有关的许可证。第一被告 2013 年 4 月决定批准第二被告根据该法第 55 条提出的变更许可证的申请是无效的。因为许可本身是不可变更的，第一被告没有管辖权。这是由于根据该法第 35 条，2012 年的原始申请基于虚构的事实而无效的。第一被告决定批准第二被告 2013 年 7 月根据该法第 47 条提出的将第 23 航次的许可证从虚构航次改为实际航次的申请是无效的，同样，因为许可本身是不可变更的，第一被告没有管辖权。这是由于根据该法第 35 条，2012 年的原始申请基于虚构的事实而无效。[2]此外，由

---

[1]　参见 2012 年《澳大利亚沿海贸易法》第 2 部分第 4 节规定。

[2]　Australian Dry Bulk Shipping Users(ADBSU)，"Submission to Senate Standing Committees on Economics Inquiry into the Shipping Reform Bills"，Canberra，19 April 2012，pp.1—5.

于变更并非基于许可证授权的事项，因此根据该法第 47 条不能批准变更。法院裁定第二被告专门变更临时许可证的做法很聪明，但旨在破坏一般许可证条款的目标和 2012 年《澳大利亚沿海贸易法》第 63(1)条所设想的该法的目标。[①]

　　澳大利亚实施新的 2012 年《澳大利亚沿海贸易法》及其简化的三级许可制度与加拿大的沿海运输权框架有一些共同的特点。新的立法为澳大利亚的沿海贸易提供了一个监管框架，提高了澳大利亚的整体海运能力，为澳大利亚海洋经济做出贡献。此外，它还使在澳大利亚注册的船舶能够获得拟议的澳大利亚税收优惠，特别是在新的澳大利亚国际船舶注册制度（AISR）下，从而最大限度地利用了这些船舶。新法律规定的免税措施是否足以说服海运企业在澳大利亚海运业投资，是值得商榷的。如果税收优惠政策不伴有明显的成本节约，就不可能吸引船舶前往澳大利亚国际航运注册。此外，新的沿海运输法的成功与否主要取决于澳大利亚国际航运登记册对本土和国际航运界的吸引力。但新法不允许在澳大利亚国际航运登记册上的船舶获得一般沿海贸易许可证，这阻碍了新法的成功。[②]因此，澳大利亚的沿海航运经历了两个独立但相互影响的变化，在保护澳大利亚注册船舶的同时，大大增加了对外国船舶的监管负担。2009 年《公平工作法》对从事澳大利亚沿海贸易运输的外国船舶及其船员实施了澳大利亚的劳动标准。此前，1996 年《工作场所关系法》规定，被允许经营的外国船舶可以不执行澳大利亚的劳工标准。澳大利亚海事联盟将较低的外国劳工标准称为不公平竞争。从旧的许可和允许制度转为三级执照制度，重新界定了从事澳大利亚沿海贸易的程序，这有利于在澳大利亚注册的船舶。

———————————

　　① See：A. Shepherd et al.，Towards Responsible Government：The Report of the National Commission of Audit，Phase II(Commonwealth of Australia 2014). See also：L. Kennedy and J. Leslie，"Options Paper：Approaches to Regulating Coastal Shipping in Australia"，Commonwealth of Australia，2014.

　　② 参见 2012 年《澳大利亚沿海贸易法案》第 33 条和 34 条第(3)款的规定。

三、智利的灵活主义沿海运输权

历史上，智利所实施的灵活沿海运输政策被称做沿海运输权的典范。传统上，智利采取的是保护主义沿海运输权立法。智利的沿海运输法律框架是由几项立法组成的。然而，该法律框架的设计既稳健又灵活，以适应智利国内海上运输服务的起伏变化。在智利，沿海运输权通常仅由智利船舶享有。①1836年《智利航海法》第1条对智利船舶的界定为"在智利共和国或其他国家的造船厂建造，并由智利的自然人或法人通过合法合同拥有的船舶"。1974年智利第466号法律第3条进一步保证了智利水域的沿海贸易和服务由智利船舶享有，以促进国内造船业和本地船舶拥有能力。②目前，智利的海上运输法是1978年的智利2222号法令。

根据智利2222号法令第11条规定，只能由智利公民或在智利注册的法人在智利注册船舶。如果一个外国公司在智利有住所，并且其主要营业地在智利，那么他就有资格注册船舶。但是，外国公司的负责人和大多数董事必须是智利国民。此外，一半以上的资本必须属于智利的自然人或法人。并且悬挂智利国旗的船只必须确保船长、官员和船员是智利公民。③智利第3059/79号法令第3条延续了为智利船只保留智利领海内的沿海运输服务的传统。但是根据这一规定，如果托运人为900吨以上的货物运输发布国际招标广告，外国船只可以通过参加公开招标在智利水域进行贸易。此外，在没有合适的悬挂智利国旗的船舶情况下，国家海事局可以给予外国船舶豁免权，让其在沿海运输中承担低于900吨的货物。④另外，在互惠的基础上，外国船舶可以在两个或更多的国内港口之间运载空集装箱。从事智利沿海运输服务的外国船舶必须雇佣智利船员，而且对这些外国船征收的税率要高于智利船舶。智利政府已经公布了修改智利第3059/79号法

---

① 参见1939年《智利沿海运输法》第1条规定。
② 参见1836年《智利航海法》第1条规定。
③ 参见1978年智利第2222号法令第14条规定。
④ 参见1979年智利第3059号法令第3部分规定。

令第 3 条规定，在符合以下条件的情况下，将海上运输权扩大到外国船舶：（1）船舶必须是定期服务的外国商船。（2）船舶必须运输集装箱货物。（3）船舶必须在两个或更多的智利港口之间航行，并将这些港口登记为船舶的定期停靠港。[①]

　　为了降低国内海上货物运输的成本，智利政府鼓励人们优先选择海上运输方式。智利认为，这将优化智利沿海运输和服务领域的公平和效率。然而，智利本土航运公司反对拟议的改革，因为这将使智利的沿海运输服务向邻国开放，而智利邻国却没有实施对外国优惠的沿海运输政策，这将阻碍智利的经济发展。此外，长期以来，智利船舶所有人一直认为，沿海运输自由化的提议对海员的工作和智利航运业的生存构成了威胁。他们还认为，邻国实施的是保护主义沿海运输权政策，这对智利计划中的开放沿海运输政策没有任何好处。此外，有学者认为，智利关于沿海运输权的立法已经足够灵活，因为外国船舶在某些情况下被允许参与智利的沿海运输权贸易。[②]

四、印度的灵活主义沿海运输权

　　自从独立于英国以来，印度一直试图将所有的海上运输服务保留给悬挂本国国旗的船舶。此外，印度政府在 1945 年成立了一个"航运重建政策小组委员会"。该委员会建议印度的沿海运输服务应完全保留给印度船舶。因此，1958 年《印度商船航运法》第 407（1）条对印度的沿海运输权予以立法强化。除印度船舶或由印度公民或符合第 21 条（b）款要求的公司租用的船舶外，任何船舶都不得从事印度的沿海贸易，除非有总干事根据本条颁发的许可证。1958 年《印度商船航运法》第 21 条涉及印度船舶的注册和定义，其（b）款特别规定公司的主要营业地必须在印度，同时要求印度公

---

① 　参见 1974 年智利第 466 号法令第 3 条规定。

② 　R. Rozas, "Shipping and Transport: Chile: Potential Regulatory Changes in the Cabotage Trade", *International Law Office*, London, 22 June 2011.

民必须至少持有公司 75％的股份。①

与此同时，1958 年《印度商船航运法》第 407(2)条显示了印度沿海运输法律和政策框架的灵活性。该法案规定可以通过发放许可证允许外国船舶参与印度沿海运输服务。此外，印度有关外汇管制的法律允许印度公民租用外国船舶在印度沿海水域进行贸易运输。同时，该法规还允许印度航运公司 100％由外国资本投资。②因此，这些公司所拥有的船舶不受任何通常对外国船舶进行的限制。这显示印度所实施的沿海运输权属于灵活主义的沿海运输权。

当然，要获得在印度从事沿海运输服务的许可证，必须满足严格的条件，其中包括外国企业要证明没有合适的悬挂印度国旗的船舶可用。然而，外汇管制的宽松政策与 1958 年《印度商船航运法》第 21 条(b)款的明确规定形成对比。这两种相反的立场的调和是一个令人棘手的挑战。此外，在两者同时适用的情况下，也不清楚何者优先适用。一般地，印度政府决定放宽班轮的沿海运输规制，主要是为了鼓励集装箱在印度港口的聚集。如果是这样，外国船舶将被允许从事印度沿海海域的集装箱货物的运输业务，前提是这些集装箱必须直接运往外国目的港，而不需要再进行转运。③同样地，进口集装箱也可以由外国船舶从国外主要港口运输到印度目的港。这也受制于一个前提条件，即集装箱从外国港口直接到达印度的港口，而不需要事先进行任何转运。此设想符合印度政府在 1991 年制定的经济自由化改革计划。当启动自由市场驱动路径时，如果没有悬挂印度国旗的船舶时，可以租用外国船舶。

此外，如果印度船舶和外国船舶之间的租价差异小于 10％，印度船舶必须匹配较低的租金。任何悬挂印度国旗的船舶，无论其所有权如何，都

---

① 参见 1850 年《印度沿海贸易法案》第 5 号法令。

② I-maritime, "Indian Shipping Industry Report 2000", Research & information Division, 2000.

③ N. Vasuki Rao(2005), "India Relaxes Cabotage Law to Ease Nehru Congestion", *Journal of Commerce*, 10 January.

将获得与印度船舶同等的待遇。^①为此，有学者认为印度现行的沿海运输法将进一步放宽，甚至被彻底改革。其主要动机在于这种改革将刺激印度的海上运输贸易和服务的商业增长。^②当然，印度这种放开沿海运输权的政策，引发本国船舶所有人的反对，本国船舶所有人认为进一步放宽沿海运输权并不能鼓励沿海贸易的发展。相反，印度本国船舶所有人认为应采取比现在更严格的沿海运输法。总体而言，印度所实施的沿海运输权基本上属于灵活主义模式。

①　P. Ghosh and S. Narayan，"Maritime Capacity of India：Strengths and Challenges"，Observer Research Foundation，2012.

②　India's Directorate General of Shipping，Shipping Manual：Liberalization in Shipping，DGS 2012.

第5章　沿海运输权视阈下沿海捎带问题探析

第一节　问题与挑战

《中国(上海)自由贸易试验区总体方案》试点施行沿海捎带业务政策，旨在促进航运管理模式创新、实现贸易投资便利化以及提升我国航运服务水平。沿海捎带业务政策实质是作为传统航运政策沿海运输权的适度开放。世界主要航运国家依据本国航运经济实际情况实施了不同模式的沿海运输权，这为探索自贸区实施沿海捎带业务政策提供了某种视角的借鉴。由于沿海运输权是与国家安全、政治互信、船舶登记、海运服务自由化以及海员就业等息息相关，导致沿海捎带业务政策的正面和负面影响兼具。在比较研究和实证分析的模式下认知实施沿海捎带业务政策，基于我国航运服务水平、国内和国际集装箱运输市场和运力实际情况的考察，笔者认为实施管制—开放沿海运输权模式下的沿海捎带业务政策，对中国而言不失为一种理性的选择。

《中国(上海)自由贸易试验区总体方案》(以下简称"总体方案")勾勒了旨在"加快政府职能转变、探讨管理模式创新以及促进贸易和投资便利化"的新图景。根据总体方案，交通运输部与上海市人民政府联合制定实施意见以强化创新航运政策的积极效益。作为一项重要的航运政策创新，总体方案实施意见第6条规定实施沿海捎带试点政策，积极推动中转集拼业务发展，允许中资航运公司利用自有或者控股拥有的非五星旗国际航行船舶先行先试外贸出口集装箱在国内开放港口与上海港之间（以上海港为中转港）的捎带业务。①为了增加实施意见的可操作性和规范性，交通运输部发布《关于在上海实行中资非五星旗国际航运船舶沿海捎带的公告》（2013 年第 55 号），明确了认定"中资航运公司"的标准、实施试点捎带业务备案制、转租限制以及处罚等内容。②然而，由于沿海捎带业务在我国并没有积累丰富的实践，目前没有形成成熟的沿海捎带业务政策的实施效果评估机制，因此，实施沿海捎带业务政策必然会衍生诸多问题。这些问题可能包括沿海捎带业务政策对国内国际航运市场的积极或者消极影响、沿海捎带业务政策的执行、沿海捎带业务政策与海运服务自由化、国家安全等的关联性问题等。

一般地，沿海捎带业务被认为属于沿海运输权范畴。而沿海运输权是否开放、开放程度和方式，是一个颇为复杂的问题。故此，探讨沿海捎带业务政策问题的切入点是从沿海运输权入手，以资考察该政策的实施效果。基于沿海运输权的立法与实践在国际上没有形成统一的模式，因此，沿海捎带业务政策在执行中必然会受制于沿海运输权的理论与实践，同时其亦面临沿海运输权所固有的风险和挑战。特别是实施沿海捎带业务政策的监督机制，如何理性地评估该政策风险和挑战，尝试国际航运政策的创新以实现国际贸易的便利化，显然是自贸试验区法治建设的重要范畴，亦是本章初略探究的问题。

第二节　沿海捎带业务政策的实质及其历史渊源考察

一、沿海捎带业务政策的实质

很显然，交通运输部 2013 年第 55 号公告实质是一种传统的航运政策，

---

①　参见交通运输部和上海市人民政府《关于落实中国（上海）自由贸易试验区总体方案，加快推进上海国际航运中心建设的实施方案》（交水发［2013］584 号）。

②　参见交通运输部《关于在上海实行中资非五星旗国际航运船舶沿海捎带的公告》相关规定。

从其文义和政策动向来审视，沿海捎带业务显然具有传统的航运政策——沿海运输权（cabotage）的特征，属于沿海运输权范畴。[①]然而，沿海运输权在不同国家的立法（cabotage laws or acts）表述亦有差异，而且其在不同历史阶段内涵有所不同。影响比较大的沿海运输权的立法当属美国 1920 年《琼斯法案》（*Jones Act*）对沿海运输权的界定。该法案明确规定在美国境内航行的船舶必须由美国制造，并在美国登记注册；船舶的所有权至少有75％是美国公民拥有；船员必须是美国公民。[②]1920 年《琼斯法案》实施近百年来可以说为美国的国民经济发展做出了巨大贡献，保障了国家经济安全和国防安全。[③]美国的 1920 年《琼斯法案》体系比较复杂，其为了实现立法政策，通过造船、船旗悬挂、船舶登记、船员雇佣以及税收等方面来限制外国船队运力介入美国的国内航运市场。然而，作为一项古老的传统航运管理政策，据考证，沿海运输权起源于西班牙，经过数个世纪的变迁，其不仅适用于沿海运输，而且也适用于航空运输、铁路运输以及公路运输领域。（Rong-Her Chiu，2013）

根据我国《海商法》第 4 条、《中华人民共和国国际海运条例》第 28 条第 2 款的规定，我国法下的沿海运输权所规制的范围似乎比较窄，即强调"海上运输和拖航"或者"船舶运输业务"。[④]相比而言，美国法下的沿海运输权愈加严格和周密，其创设了从多个方面和角度来限制外国船舶介

---

① 交通运输部 2013 年第 55 号公告对沿海捎带业务政策的描述为："为推动上海国际航运中心和中国（上海）自由贸易试验区建设，根据我国相关法律法规和规定，我部决定，允许中资航运公司利用全资或控股拥有的非五星旗国际航行船舶，经营以上海港为国际中转港的外贸进出口集装箱在国内对外开放港口与上海港之间的捎带业务。"

② See Gibson & Donovan, supra note 41, at 119; Lawrence, supra note 26, at 41. Section 1 of the Merchant Marine Act, 1920, containing those goals, is codified at 46 U.S.C. app. § 861 (repealed 2006).

③ See Constantine G. Papavizas, Bryant E. Gardnet, Is the Jones Act Redundant? University of San Francisco Maritime Journal 2008—2009, 21u.s.f Mar.

④ 我国《海商法》第 4 条规定："中华人民共和国港口之间的海上运输和拖航，由悬挂中华人民共和国国旗的船舶经营。但是，法律、行政法规另有规定的除外。非经国务院交通主管部门批准，外国籍船舶不得经营中华人民共和国港口之间的海上运输和拖航。"我国《国际海运条例》第 28 条第 2 款规定："外国国际船舶运输经营者不得经营中国港口之间的船舶运输业务，也不得利用租用的中国籍船舶或者舱位，或者以互换舱位等方式变相经营中国港口之间的船舶运输业务。"

入美国国内运输的体制，与我国法下的沿海运输权具有一定的差异。即便如此，依据交通运输部第 55 号公告，将沿海捎带业务视为沿海运输权框架下的范畴，是不存在法律障碍的。沿海捎带政策是以国内开放港口与上海港之间为适用范围的沿海运输权，某种意义上，是一种在多方面受到限制的沿海运输权。目前沿海捎带业务只是局限于集装箱运输，而其他类型的沿海运输没有包括在内。因此，沿海捎带业务政策的本质仍然是沿海运输权问题，是传统沿海运输权的适度开放。

二、沿海捎带业务的历史变迁考察

1. "捎带空箱"的实践：沿海捎带业务政策的雏形

早在 10 余年前，我国曾经一度流行"捎带空箱"业务。实质上这是沿海捎带业务的雏形。根据当时交通部发布的《关于同意国际班轮公司在我国沿海主要港口之间调运空集装箱的函》，允许国际班轮公司在我国沿海港口调拨空集装箱。此种业务即所谓的"捎带空箱"业务。由于学理上将集装箱解释为船舶的有机组成部分，故此，人们将"捎带空箱"业务设想为国际班轮公司在我国国内港口之间实质性地存在着运输服务业务。如此，"捎带空箱"业务为"捎带重箱"业务的开展奠定了基础和前提。①当时我国从事运输管理人士呼吁我国大力开展"捎带重箱"业务，主要目的在于遏制我国外贸货物流失境外港口日益严重的局面，充分利用支线班轮的闲置运力、优化航线布局，以实现降低干线班轮的营运成本和提升我国中转港口的竞争力之目的。虽然由于种种政策性因素、贸易体制以及软环境的限制的考虑，"空箱捎带"业务没有转变为"捎带重箱"实践，没有形成相关的经验，但是"捎带重箱"的动议深刻地影响着我国国内港口之间集装箱运输的管理体制，为后来探索沿海捎带业务政策提供了可资借鉴的构想。

2. 沿海内贸船舶捎带模式的实践：突破船舶规范法律障碍的尝试

2005 年为了破解航运于长江水域的江轮禁止驶入海域的难题，解决上

---

① 所谓"捎带重箱"业务就是捎带承载了货物的集装箱业务。

海洋山深水港和长江内支线中转集装箱运输的方案一直在酝酿。该方案核心问题是船舶规范所导致的船舶航行障碍问题，但是，其思路为沿海捎带业务的开展提供了重要启迪。根据国家有关规定江轮禁止驶入海域，然而江轮是长江内支线集装箱的主要运输船型，几乎全部的长江内支线集装箱的运输船舶都是江轮。江轮承载的长江内支线中转箱必须经换装海轮后运往洋山深水港。基于我国内贸运输市场运力格局和内贸集装箱运输发展趋势的分析，有人士认为随着政策进一步放开和充分利用运输能力的趋势，①在条件成熟的情况下内外贸集装箱混装将成为可能。为此，建议首先选择有实力的船公司进行试点。试点船公司中同时包含内支线船公司和内贸船公司，这样有利于长江内支线和内贸航线的衔接。其次，长江沿岸中指定拥有现代集装箱作业能力、规模相对较大的港口进行试点，以减少港口间恶性竞争为中转点带来不利影响。最后，允许洋山深水港同时进行内贸集装箱中转作业，使洋山深水港成为上海港最重要的水水中转港区。②上述业务就是内贸海船捎带方案。内贸海船捎带业务政策很好地解决了因为船舶规范的法律障碍所引发的运输中转问题，不仅有效配置了长江内支线的运力资源，而且一定程度上增强了上海洋山港吸收和中转长江流域所辐射的货源的能力。内贸海船捎带方案虽然迥异于沿海捎带业务，但是其基本理念被传统的沿海运输权所包容，因此，内贸海船捎带方案为实施沿海捎带业务政策提供了经验和制度资源。

3. 沿海捎带业务政策的推出及其原因简析

近年来，上海国际航运中心的建设取得重大突破。然而，上海国际航运中心的建设也存在值得反思的地方。在强化国际航运中心硬环境建设的同时，某些软环境诸如航运服务能力、航运法律环境以及管理体制的创新方面值得进一步检讨和反思。根据总体方案和交通运输部的公告，国际班轮公司沿海捎带业务正式试点运行，其主要考量在于我国主要港口来自日

---

① 近年来，从事我国长江内支线的运力显著增强，诸多著名的大船公司都有大规模船队从事长江内支线的运输服务。

② 林松、陈世英：《沿海内贸船舶捎带模式》，《中国港口》2005 年第 7 期。

益严峻的周边国家大港口的压力剧增，实施该政策以提升我国港口的国际竞争力。当然，实施沿海捎带业务政策是一个复杂问题，绝不是非此即彼这么简单。根据学者的研究，对中资外籍船放开外贸集装箱沿海捎带业务的呼声，既有来自外部的竞争压力，又有某些港口本位利益的表现。外部的竞争压力主要来自我国周边大港口的竞争压力。①促成实施沿海捎带业务政策的内因是我国部分港口进一步扩大竞争优势的需要。如果放开内贸集装箱的沿海捎带业务，不仅吸引周边更多中小型港口的集装箱的中转，而且进一步加强港口的枢纽港地位。另外，实施沿海捎带业务政策，可以为大型中资航运公司带来利益。航运公司的运营范围进一步覆盖到了国内航线，闲置运力可以得到合理的调配。②中资航运公司控股的非五星旗船舶进行"外轮捎带"业务的成本较小。因此，沿海捎带业务能提升国际大型航运公司的竞争力。

在认知沿海捎带业务政策的本质、政策导向和目的的基础上，由于我国实施沿海捎带业务政策的经验和实践不足，给该政策一个精准的界定，或者完全认清楚实施该政策的正面影响和负面影响，都将不是一蹴而就的，更不能一劳永逸。本书以为，沿海捎带业务政策不是孤立的，而是与其他问题互为制约的。同时，系统考察作为传统航运政策的沿海运输权问题，也是有助于认识沿海捎带业务政策的实施效果。

第三节　主要国家沿海运输权之立法与实践考察

一、美国 1920 年《琼斯法案》及其存废之争

美国 1920 年《琼斯法案》被认为是对沿海运输权影响极大的法案。历

---

① 根据釜山港湾公社 2012 年的数据，釜山港当年计划完成集装箱吞吐量约为 1 750 万 TEU，其中集装箱中转量为 850 万 TEU 左右，源自我国的中转箱所占比例就达到了 30％以上。外贸集装箱的流失不仅使我国沿海港口损失了相应的集装箱中转收益，也使釜山港在东北亚枢纽港的竞争当中抢占了先机。

② 王利：《放开"沿海捎带"业务对天津港的影响探讨》，《滨海时报》2013 年 11 月 25 日。

史上，1920 年《琼斯法案》对美国国内水路运输和国民经济贡献巨大。由于与国内水路运输直接相关的经济活动对美国直接经济贡献很大，因此该法案在促进美国的就业、国家安全、贸易竞争力、船舶工业、军事保障和补救以及交通顺畅方面发挥了积极的法律效应。1920 年《琼斯法案》的立法价值一直比较侧重国家安全的保障。美国航运业是一个包含安全和经济的产业，《琼斯法案》则是让它保持健康和强大的法宝。美国 1920 年《琼斯法案》下的沿海运输权比较严格，而且给美国有关利益方带来了负面影响。因此。美国 1920 年《琼斯法案》自其诞生之日起就争议不断。该法案对美国的造船业产生的负面作用日益明显。肇始于 2008 年的航运市场持续低迷使得深受美国造船价格和船员成本直线攀升困扰的船东和货主开始迁怒于 1920 年《琼斯法案》。[1]此外，1920 年《琼斯法案》还造成远洋货箱在美国港口间的转运受限且成本较高，国内支线行业不见繁荣等诸多不利影响。[2]然而，1920 年《琼斯法案》废除之争没有定论，而且有足够的证据和迹象表明，美国不会轻易放弃实施近一个世纪之久的法案，支持该法案的力量似乎更加强大一些。[3]1920 年《琼斯法案》一直以追求维护美国的航运安全和国家安全为核心价值，其主流不因美国和他国的航运格局变迁而变化。

二、欧盟的沿海运输权立法与实践

与美国 1920 年《琼斯法案》不同，欧盟有关法令和指令关于沿海运输权的规制具有开放与包容的色彩。2007 年 10 月 10 日，欧盟执行委员会发布了题为"一个综合的欧盟海运政策"的行动计划，宣布了未来海事领域将开展的工作和执行的计划。根据欧盟《关于成员国之间和成员国与第三国之间适用自由提供服务原则的 4055 号理事会决议》（4055/86 号法规），欧盟在货物流动和服务上力求实现不受限制的内部市场。根据 4055/86 号法规，只要是欧盟成员国公民，任何提供海运服务的人和接受他们服务的

---

[1] 美国船厂和亚洲船厂之间的造价差距以及船员薪资差距正在拉大，随着航商运营的成本上升，以保护主义为目的的《琼斯法案》给国内船东和货主所带来的成本压力已经愈发明显。

[2] 胥苗苗：《琼斯法案存废之争》，《中国船检》2014 年第 2 期。

[3] See Rob Quartel, The Jones Act? Gimme a Break, J. Com.(New York, N.Y.), Oct.8, 1991.

人都有自由的准入权。各国国内沿海运输权的问题则由欧盟理事会第3577/92 号法规来约束。欧盟理事会第 3577/92 号条例主要针对欧共体成员国的国内沿海运输权问题，其要求只有在船公司为"共同体船舶所有人"（community shipowner），①并且其经营的船舶在欧盟内某一成员国登记的情况下，该公司拥有在欧共体内部从事沿海运输的权利。同时，这些船舶还必须完全符合其登记国对经营沿海运输船舶的各项要求。②欧盟理事会第 3577/92 号条例建立的基础是"提供服务自由"原则。但是基于沿海运输的特殊性考虑，有如下限制：第一，一成员国可以要求其他从事该国沿海运输的成员国承担所谓的"公共服务"义务，即其他成员国必须保证在所谓的"经济效益差的航线"（thin route）上等同地提供服务。第二，从事一成员国岛屿之间的运输的其他成员国的船舶必须根据该国的法律规定来配备船员。③第三，欧盟理事会第 3577/92 号条例建立一个所谓的"应急机制"（crisis mechanism）以应付因沿海运输权放开而引起严重混乱。该机制规定了欧盟委员会有权对此采取行动。如果欧盟委员会未采取措施，则该国有权单方面采取措施，但是该措施的实施时间不得超过三个月。④

由此观之，欧盟成员国的沿海运输权向在任何成员国登记或悬挂任何一个成员国国旗的船舶开放。但考虑到沿海运输对欧盟地中海国家特别是希腊、西班牙、葡萄牙、法国的特殊利益，对以上国家的某些领域则暂停适用该规则。⑤就欧盟成员国之间而言，实施的沿海运输权具有很

①　"共同体船舶所有人"（community shipowner）是指在一欧盟成员国注册，其主要的营业场所也在一成员国内，并且在该国的经营确定是有效的和控制之下的船公司。

②　Malgorzata Nesterowicz, Freedom to Provide Maritime Transport Services in European Community Law. *Journal of Maritime Law and Commerce*. October, 2003. 34 J. Mar. L. & Com.629.

③　从 1999 年 1 月 1 日起，这项规定将有所放松，即如果岛屿之间的航线有前续或后继航线往来于另一成员国，也就是岛屿间航线仅是一个完整的航线的一部分时，船员的配备可以依据船舶登记国的规定。

④　吴宇：《欧盟海运立法的基石：自由提供服务》，《中国远洋航务公告》1998 年 12 月 1 日。

⑤　欧洲国家实行沿海运输权的情况为：丹麦、英国、荷兰、爱尔兰、比利时、冰岛和挪威对船舶船旗没有任何限制；芬兰、德国、希腊、意大利、葡萄牙和瑞典仅限于对挂欧盟成员国国旗的船舶开放，对于仅是在欧盟成员国登记的船舶不享有该权利；在意大利和西班牙，不论是挂欧盟成员国国旗还是挂方便旗的成员国船舶，只要是捎带有国际货物的船舶都可获得沿海航行权；在法国，无论是挂什么旗的船舶（包括欧盟成员国的船舶）都没有得到沿海运输的国际航行权。参见魏明：《欧洲国家航运政策的新发展》，《水运科学研究》2007 年第 4 期。

大的自由。①从该角度看，欧盟成员国之间的沿海运输权是有条件的开放式沿海运输权。

三、菲律宾等东南亚国家实施沿海运输权的立法与实践

历史上菲律宾是美国的殖民地。因此，菲律宾所实施的沿海运输权政策基本上是以美国的相关法案为蓝本的。根据菲律宾《关税和海关法》的规定，只有在菲律宾登记注册的船舶才有权从事该国沿海的运输贸易。同时根据《菲律宾宪法》和《公用事业法》相关规定，公用事业的所有权或者经营权归属于菲律宾人，而沿海运输被认定为属于公用事业范畴。然而，近年来由于该国沿海运输业服务质量低下，导致实践中并没有严格执行沿海运输法律，甚至产生了某些变通的做法。②上述做法引起了从事国内运输的船公司的强烈反对。可见，在菲律宾沿海运输的法律和实践并不是很稳定，经常出现背离沿海运输权政策的情境。就东南亚国家而言，印度尼西亚的沿海运输业属于比较开放的。1990 年开始有条件开放该国的沿海运输，允许外国船公司从事该国的沿海运输业务。有数据显示，自从开放沿海运输以降，该国国内航运公司在国内运输市场上的占有率从 71％下降至 51％，而在 1989 年至 1994 年期间，外国籍船舶在印度尼西亚境内的运力显著增长。③实践表明，一国一旦开放沿海运输，必然对该国从事国内沿海运输的船公司形成竞争，进而影响该国沿海运输市场的运力格局。马来西亚于 1980 年 1 月 1 日开始实施沿海运输权政策。根据该国《1952 年航运法》(the Merchant Shipping Act 1952，MSO 1952)的规定，马来西亚国内海上运输由悬挂马来西亚国旗的船舶专属经营。后来经过修订的法案更加强化了马来西亚政府对从事该国国内沿海运

---

① Case C-160/99，Commission v. France，(2000) E.C.R. 1-06137.

② 为了节省有关费用，在菲律宾出现了定期挂靠马尼拉港和菲律宾其他外贸输出港口的国际贸易运输船舶可以使用任何外国船公司的空集装箱。另外，从事国际航线的船舶可以从事转船业务。参见蔡先凤：《菲律宾沿海运输现状》，《中国远洋航务公告》1997 年 6 月 1 日。

③ 蔡先凤：《菲律宾沿海运输现状》，《中国远洋航务公告》1997 年 6 月 1 日。

输的控制。①

第四节　沿海捎带业务政策的法律解读：管制—开放模式的构架

一、沿海捎带业务政策是沿海运输权的适度开放

据美国海运管理局运输部对 54 个国家进行调查，其中 47 个国家具有限制外国介入国内水路运输的相关法律，具有严格航行权条款的国家有 40 个。各国对进入国内运输的限制内容有所差别，其中 6 个国家要求从事国内运输的船舶必须由国内建造，38 个国家要求必须使用本国籍船舶运输，42 个国家要求使用本国籍船员。②可见，无论是历史上还是当今时代，作为一项相对传统的航运政策，沿海运输权为各国高度重视，并通过立法予以明确。通常而言，沿海运输权政策的立法严与宽、管制抑或放开都不是一成不变的。一般而言，以美国 1920 年《琼斯法案》为代表的美国沿海运输权比较严格，而且鲜有修订；而欧盟基于政治上的互信、地缘上特征、沿海运输状况等因素使然，沿海运输权相对而言形成了区域性的开放式的沿海运输权。欧盟各成员国在构建"统一欧洲"宏大目标驱使下，在有共同的政治文件为纲领的指引下，在欧盟各成员国之间实施较为开放的沿海运输权。③即便是美国 1920 年《琼斯法案》，也曾因第一次世界大战的缘故暂停实施。第一次世界大战期间，由于战争的因素导致美国沿海运输的市场格局发生重大变化，美国国会于 1914 年 8 月 8 日不得不改变《琼斯法案》在战争期间的实施。④除此以外，自从 1935 年以降，美国 1920 年《琼

---

① See Tee Johnson. "Reviewing Cabotage Policy for Shipping". http：//sdc.net.my/sdc/index2.php?option＝com _ content&do _ pdf＝1&id＝129，最后访问日期 2014-06-22。

② 孙俊岩：《琼斯法案对美国经济的影响》，《中国水运》2004 年第 6 期。

③ See John W. McConnell，Jr.，A Corporate "Citizen of the United States" for Maritime Law Purposes，25 J. Mar. L. & Com.159，203(1994).

④ See Clinton H. Whitehurst，Jr.，American Domestic Shipping in American Ships—Jones Act Costs，Benefits，and Options 13(1985).

斯法案》一度在符合某些条件的前提下或者更加严格，或者适当开放。①可见，各国的沿海运输权在执行过程中，某种角度上是变动不居的。一国通常基于自身的具体情况而实施更加严格或相对开放的沿海运输权政策。

《中国（上海）自由贸易试验实施方案》下的沿海捎带业务政策得到我国法律的支持。通过对我国《海商法》第4条的文义解释和目的解释，我们不难推断出外国籍船舶经过法律、行政法规的特别授权，是可以从事我国港口之间的运输和拖航。虽然"外国籍船舶"的认定可能会影响到沿海运输权问题，但是，我国《海商法》下的沿海运输权应该属于一种比较开放的形态。但是《中华人民共和国国际海运条例》第28条第2款的措辞显示了我国实施比较严格的沿海运输权政策。由此推理，沿海捎带业务政策遇到了法律障碍。然而，由于现代航运市场形态多元化趋势日益显著，各种商业合作频出，如何界定"外国国际船舶运输经营者"，以及"外国国际船舶运输经营者"是否属于"中资航运公司利用全资或控股拥有的非五星旗国际航行船舶"的经营者范畴，都需要进一步的解释和认定。尽管有《国际海运条例》的规定，沿海捎带业务政策基本上属于一种先对开放的沿海运输权。因此，自贸试验区实行的沿海捎带业务政策乃涉及其他问题，诸如船舶身份的认定和界定等问题。通过对船舶身份等问题的界定，实现适用沿海运输权的适度开放。

二、沿海捎带业务政策是具有系统性属性的法律问题

1. 沿海捎带业务政策与船舶登记

根据交通部2013年第55号公告，"中资航运公司"是指注册在境内，依据《中华人民共和国国际海运条例》取得国际班轮运输经营资格登记证、从事国际海上运输业务的企业法人。可见该公告采用注册地主义来认

---

① 1935年美国《〈琼斯法案〉修订案》规定，如果享有美国沿海运输权的美国船舶在外国出现了"整体或部分出售"（sold foreign in whole or in part）或者"重新建造"（rebuilt）的情境，那么该船舶将丧失美国的沿海运输优先权。See C. Todd Jones, The Practical Effects on Labor of Repealing American Cabotage Laws, 22 Transp. L.J. 403, 410—411, Spring 1995.

定"中资航运公司"的标准，其法律依据是《中华人民共和国国际海运条例》。该公告同时规定了中资航运公司拟开展试点捎带业务船舶的相关要求，诸如国籍证书(Certificate of Registry)、入级证(Certificate of Classification)，以及船舶所有权关系证明材料等。如船舶为中资航运公司通过境外独资投资企业间接拥有的，还需提供中资航运公司投资该境外独资企业的证明文件、该境外独资投资企业全资或控股拥有船舶的证明，以及中资航运公司租赁船舶的证明文件。①这是从船舶的角度来认定沿海捎带业务政策的实施对象。根据我国《船舶登记条例》的相关规定，如果船舶获得中国国籍，必须满足一定的条件。②为扩大国有船队规模并加强船舶安全监管，中国在上海等港口推出了特案免税政策，对符合条件的船舶免征关税和进口环节增值税，以鼓励中资外籍船舶移籍回国，悬挂五星红旗航行。2012 年，洋山保税港区成为我国首个"保税船舶登记"试点区域，允许为注册在洋山保税港区航运企业所拥有的从事国际航运业务的保税船舶(办理了出口退税或进境备案手续)办理船舶登记业务。③实施意见提出在上海自贸试验区实施创新国际船舶登记制度，在洋山港保税船舶登记的基础上，研究并推动实施高效便捷的国际船舶登记制度，简化国家船舶运输经营许可程序，适当放宽登记主体、船龄范围等限制条件，完善船员配备、登记种类、登记收费、船舶航行区域等内容，优化船舶运营、检查与登记业务的相关流程。④

　　如此，实施沿海捎带业务政策下的"中资航运公司"的认定与实施意见下船舶登记制度的创新必须吻合，否则"中资航运公司"的认定会带来法律上的困惑。由于对"中资船舶"的定义存在法律上的争议，所以极可能导致在实践中产生操作上的困境。从这个角度看，实施沿海捎带业务政

---

① 参见交通运输部 2013 年第 55 号公告第三项。
② 参见《中华人民共和国船舶登记条例》第 2 条。
③ 王杰、李艳君、白玮玮：《中国(上海)自贸试验区下航运政策解析》，《世界海运》2014 年第 2 期。
④ 参见交通运输部交水发［2013］584 号实施意见。

策适宜局限于自贸区内，而不是任意地扩大范围。由于实施沿海捎带业务政策与船舶登记制度息息相关，因此建议在"中资非五星旗船舶"的界定上必须明确且增强其可操作性。随着航运业的发展，航运公司之间相互渗透、相互合作的现象越来越普遍，船舶大型化又加剧了航运公司联盟化的趋势。航运公司之间通过联盟、联营、融舱以及相互持股、合并兼并、合并经营、合并收入等方式抱团取暖已不是新鲜现象。仅针对中资非五星旗船开放此项业务，很有可能会出现第三方根据世贸规则要求享有同等待遇。[1]因此，实施沿海捎带业务政策具有系统性，必须与船舶登记制度协调一致。船舶登记制度的创新必须与实施沿海捎带业务政策协调起来，否则必将形成操作上的困惑。实施方案鼓励积极创新船舶登记制度，在一定程度是需要与沿海捎带业务政策协调一致。

2. 沿海捎带业务政策与国家安全、政治互信

作为一项古老和传统的航运政策，沿海运输权历来与国家的安全和政治理念纠缠在一起。欧盟沿海运输权的开放是与欧盟政治和经济一体化发展同步的，其内部开放沿海运输权是在经历了 40 多年发展的基础上提出的。欧盟实施的沿海运输权政毫无疑问彰显了国家安全理念与政治互信的高度融合与重视。就国际海运业而言，欧盟早在 1986 年欧盟理事会 4055 号规则中便做出具有前瞻性的规划，当然，零欧盟棘手的问题是成员国间的沿海航运权问题。[2]欧盟的沿海运输权立法与实践，是在充分保障国家安全和共同政治理念的框架下形成的区域性航运政策。

然而，审视亚洲主要航运国家在沿海运输权开放与合作问题，则令人倍感失落与灰心。与欧盟国家基于国家安全与政治互信而适度开放沿海运输权一样，亚洲国家诸如中国、日本和韩国亦是基于同样的原因而实施互相不开放的沿海运输政策。目前，中日韩三国沿海运输权的开放程度不同。根据中国现行法律、法规规定和入世承诺，中国已经在一定程度上开

---

① 王利：《放开"沿海捎带"业务对天津港的影响探讨》，《滨海时报》2013 年 11 月 25 日。
② 林晖：《欧共体航运经济法律制度评介》，《水运管理》2008 年第 3 期。

放了港口之间的沿海运输权。根据我国《海商法》第 4 条，在特定情况下得到中国国务院交通部允许，外籍船舶可以从事中国沿海运输。根据中国入世谈判签署的《中华人民共和国服务贸易具体承诺减让表》第 2 条最惠国豁免清单内容，外国投资者可以通过采取合资或合营的方式在中国建立商业存在，成立合资公司、合营公司的船舶可以在中国登记注册并取得中国国籍。综上所述，外国公司可以通过参股在中国成立合资航运公司参与中国的沿海运输。沿海运输开放问题必然与其他因素联系在一起。因此，中日韩国之间的政治互信和政治基础和国家安全问题是制约沿海运输权能否开发的重要因素。由于我国与日本岛屿与海洋划界争端、日本侵华历史问题以及意识形态等问题，而韩国与日本之间同样存在严重的历史问题，导致中日韩三国之间失去开放沿海运输权的政治基础和政治互信。这样，根据总体方案，中资非五星旗国际航行船舶从事国内港口与上海港之间的沿海集装箱运输必然会将"外国因素"带入国内沿海运输服务中，这些影响国际安全的因素包括集装箱反恐、集装箱危害国家安全、集装箱偷渡、本国海员就业以及海关通关秩序等。因此，沿海捎带业务政策的实施务必顾及其他系列问题。

3. 沿海捎带业务政策与海运服务贸易(GATS)

海运服务贸易自由化的程度历来较高。但是就一国的沿海运输服务而言，各国基于本国安全考虑，都没有实现沿海运输领域的自由化。几乎所有的海运国家都实施沿海运输权政策。[①]这实质是与 GATS 的宗旨背道而驰的。海运业的调整市场准入在 GATS 中属于特定义务，即并不是适用所有部门，而是针对每一缔约方在承诺义务的计划表中所列的部门。商业性存在方面的限制，包括在运输及运输辅助行业对外国企业设立机构的限制，对船舶及其他海运实体中外资比例和存在形式的限制以及沿海运输权的限制等。随着集装箱运输业的发展，特别是门到门、仓到仓运输服务需

---

① Hannu Honka, European Union Shipping Policies, in United States Shipping Policies and the World Market 127(William A. Lovett ed., 1996).

求的增加，海洋运输问题还涉及境内的陆上或水上运输、专用集装箱码头或港口，以及相应的基础设施、装卸设备等的建设使用问题。所以，现代的海运服务贸易的开放又显得重要起来。沿海运输权关系到国家的主权和安全，著名的海洋战略理论家马汉曾经提到："一个国家为了确保本国人民能够获得不均衡的海上贸易利益，或是采用平时立法实施垄断，或是制定一些禁令来限制外国的贸易，或是直接采取暴力行动来尽力排除外国人的贸易。"[①] 对我国沿海运输权采取一定的保护政策是十分必要的。事实上，世界大多数国家基于同样的原因，也是对本国沿海运输权采取严格保护政策的。[②] 沿海捎带业务政策终究是沿海运输权一定程度的开放，理论上其可能被纳入到 GATS 框架之下，或者一定程度被纳入到海运服务自由化体系之中。

就中国的利益而言，在实施沿海捎带业务政策获得一定利益的同时，应该积极探索和评估实施该政策带来的负面影响以及负面影响的程度、方式、后果以及应对对策。诸如如何在立法上完善"中资航运公司"的认定，或者界定"外国国际船舶运输经营者"等。同时，也应该在 GATS 框架下探讨对等原则，以防止被某些利益主体利用我国的沿海捎带业务政策获取"搭便车"的利益。根据学者的研究，海运业开放程度越深，我国海运服务贸易出口额越大。开放程度对海运服务贸易的影响要基于发展成熟的海运市场和政府的政策支持。按照 GATS 框架下关于"自由化"的原则要求，各国的航运保护政策应该逐渐减少。但是沿海运输权属于例外。沿海运输权只是在区域性集团的成员国之间相互开放，诸如欧盟成员国之间。为了提高我国海运服务贸易的竞争力，减少海运服务贸易逆差，应当抓住 GATS 框架下"逐步自由化原则"，利用某些"豁免和例外"条款和未纳入规则范围的制度空白点，在世界航运自由化的趋势推动下，深化我国的海运开放程度，将促进我国海运服务贸易的发展。[③]本书以为，根据我

---

① ［美］A.T.马汉：《海权对历史的影响》，安常客、成忠勤译，解放军出版社 1998 年版，第 1 页。

② 许民强：《符合 GATS 的我国航运市场准入的立法建议》，《世界海运》1999 年第 6 期。

③ 李晨、郭浩然：《我国海运服务贸易竞争力影响因素的实证研究》，《国际商务研究》2013 年第 3 期。

国的航运服务能力，在自贸试验区内探索沿海捎带业务政策，必将对海运服务自由化进程产生一定程度的影响，为海运服务自由化的例外提供实践素材。

三、实施沿海捎带业务政策的"双刃剑"属性

沿海捎带业务政策的实施恰似一把"双刃剑"。通常沿海捎带业务政策的实施给我国航运业的冲击或者影响是复杂的，既有正面影响又有负面影响。现行沿海捎带试点政策允许中资非五星旗船舶在国内开放港口与上海港之间开展进出口集装箱捎带业务，进一步开放了中国沿海运输市场。从技术上讲，支线运输的干线衔接，进而形成干支网络，是集装箱运输的客观要求，沿海捎带政策满足了这一要求；但从政策角度来说，沿海捎带政策打开了中国沿海运输市场的封闭闸门，未来是否会继续扩大，集装箱班轮运输的国内市场和国际市场是否会合成一个，这一问题必将成为多方博弈的焦点。多数国家并未放开"沿海捎带"业务。允许非五星旗船开展沿海港口集装箱捎带业务是指允许外籍船舶在我国沿海港口之间从事外贸集装箱的国内段运输，性质属于国内沿海运输。

针对是否放开"沿海捎带"业务的争论，交通运输部于 2010 年还公开表示"禁止外轮捎带的政策没有改变"。除了出于主权和国家安全的考虑以外，禁止"沿海捎带"还有对本国从事沿海运输的航运企业保护的考虑。"沿海捎带"业务放开将造成国内港口集装箱运输量转移。我国某些港口国际集装箱中转业务能力不强，不但不能从中受益，甚至本港的集装箱还可能被转运到其他港口中转，从而对本港的干线航班发展产生不利影响。同时，"外轮捎带"将严重影响内支线运营市场，直接冲击我国的内贸航运企业。[①]当然，沿海捎带业务政策一定程度上必然刺激国内沿海运输力量之间的竞争力，导致国内沿海运输服务水平的提升。当然，上述分析只是居于理论上的预测和评估，由于沿海捎带业务政策属于试点阶段，没

---

① 王利：《放开"沿海捎带"业务对天津港的影响探讨》，《滨海时报》2013 年 11 月 25 日。

有足够的实证数据来支撑根据推理得出的结论，因此，某些结论和分析只是具有参考的价值。

四、构建管制—开放沿海运输权模式

显然，前文对沿海捎带业务政策的法律解读，显示了沿海运输权问题的系统性与复杂性。因此，美国1920年《琼斯法案》下的沿海运输权模式与欧盟成员国之间的沿海运输权，无不显示构建一个灵活、务实、动态的沿海运输权体制实属必要。本书称之为"管制—开放沿海运输权模式"，即在坚持沿海运输权的管制的前提和基础下，根据我国的航运格局等具体情况，可以在满足一定条件下实施开放的沿海运输权政策。

1. 管制—开放沿海运输权模式的经济基础

我国国际海运服务业的开发程度日益扩大。就作为比较敏感领域的沿海运输权而言，我国的立法与实践也是相对开放的。[1]从竞争的角度而言，在一定范围内引进外资，对于改善运输服务质量，保证贸易运输需求和确保合理的运输价格，促进国内运输业的发展具有积极的作用。但外资航运企业的进入也对我国航运市场带来冲击。[2]有关数据显示，截至2008年，我国海运服务贸易出口额从20.12亿美元增长到254.51亿美元，增长了12倍。我国海运服务贸易获得了飞速发展，但是飞速增长的贸易总额背后却存在着巨大逆差，而且逆差额也呈现了逐年扩大的趋势。我国海运服务贸易竞争力受到国内市场的需求和海运开放程度的影响。由于我国的海运业是服务贸易中开放最广、开放程度最深的一个行业，外资企业占有很大一部分市场份额，外籍船舶对货物的承运量也相应地大于我国的自有船舶。[3]基于此，本书以为，在实施沿海捎带业务政策要充分评估该政策的实施效

---

① 1984年，我国批准第一家外国航运公司班轮挂靠我国港口。1986年，我国批准了第一家外国航运公司在华设立代表处，同年批准成立第一家中外合资国际航运企业和第一家中外合资国内航运企业。1994年，我国批准了第一家外国航运公司在华设立独资船务公司。

② 许民强：《符合GATS的我国航运市场准入的立法建议》，《世界海运》1999年第6期。

③ 李晨、郭浩然：《我国海运服务贸易竞争力影响因素的实证研究》，《国际商务研究》2013年第3期。

果，沿海捎带政策在"回归五星旗"上的效应如何，都是值得认真研究。

2. 管制—开放沿海运输权模式的法律基础

在我国，规制沿海捎带业务的法律体系相对而言是健全的。我国的《海商法》《水路运输管理条例》以及《中华人民共和国国际海运条例》都有沿海输运权的规定。上述法律显示了中国的沿海运输政策比美国的1920年《琼斯法案》更为宽松。沿海运输的立法核心问题是追求何种立法目的。很显然，世界范围内沿海运输权立法徘徊在国家经济利益与国家安全之间，而立法者更看重的是哪一个价值，可能与该国在特定历史阶段的航运经济格局和该国的国家安全形势相关。就美国的1920年《琼斯法案》而言，其主流是维护美国的海运安全，而将航运经济效益置于次要位阶；而就欧盟成员国而言，由于成员国之间的国家安全得到了欧盟一体化的保障，各成员看重的是本国在开放沿海运输权中获得的经济利益。我国的航运经济实力与竞争力既不同于美国，又不存在与周边海运国家构建沿海运输自由区域的政治互信机制，加之历史上我国在海洋权益上备受侵略和侵害，我国自然高度重视航运实力的提升。但是沿海捎带业务政策开放的模式与程度必须依赖我国航运法律的完善。本书以为，应该将沿海捎带业务政策进行国家立法的顶层设计。同时，在现阶段充分意识到沿海捎带业务绝非是一个孤立的政策，其法律基础不仅涉及私法诸如海商法典的完善，而且更关涉公法诸如《中华人民共和国国际海运条例》、《船舶登记条例》以及《水路运输管理条例》等法律，是一个互相制约的体系。

3. 管制—开放沿海运输权模式下沿海捎带业务政策的构架

沿海捎带业务政策是否成熟的问题，是一个价值判断和抉择的问题。管制—开放沿海运输权模式下沿海捎带业务政策的构成要素，应该与航运经济效益、国家安全、海洋环境、海员就业、海运服务业自由化、船舶登记制度、海关制度以及航运业补贴等系列问题相关联。这显然是一个复杂的问题。但就我国而言，我国航运业软实力不足、软环境亟待提升、海员群体庞大、沿海运输关系到内河水域的航运、与周边国家存在海洋争议等诸多复杂的因素，决定了我国选择偏重管制的沿海运输权是合理的，符合我国的基本航运业国情。沿海捎带业务政策的试点实施，需要细化一些重要的问题，诸如船舶登记、中资航运公司的认定等。在强化管制色彩的沿海运输权的同时，也要以沿海捎带业务等多种形式来丰富沿海运输权的模式和内涵，构建灵活、适度开放以及多元的沿海运输权模式。

中国（上海）自由贸易试验区的总体方案下的航运政策创新包括了一揽子相关问题。其旨在促进航运管理制度创新、优化和提升我国航运服务竞争力水平。总体方案下的实施沿海捎带业务试点政策无疑是探索航运政策变革的重要举措之一。沿海捎带业务政策的法律解读为合理和科学地实施该政策提供了法律依据、法律价值判断的导向以及政策的正面与负面的影响的法律根源。实践是法律理性。基于我国尚未积累相关的实际经验，某些观点和结论有待于进一步的检视。

作为一项传统的航运政策，沿海运输权不是一成不变的，其法律内涵与外延因不同国情和历史阶段而存有变迁。美国 1920 年《琼斯法案》的变迁历史表明了这一点。近期，美国积极修订"能源法案"以鼓励沿海运输和鼓励船东扩张船队规模，并且允许美国国内船公司利用美国建设资本基金（CCF），新建集装箱滚装船用于美国沿海和五大湖区的运输。而欧盟是主张废除 1920 年《琼斯法案》的重要力量，原因是欧洲国家的海运实力较强，希望更多的国家和地区放开沿海控制权而从中获益。因此，以欧盟为代表的多个国家开始积极向世人展示他们在海运贸易保护问题上正在变得更明智更开放的态度。[1] 可见，无论是美国 1920 年《琼斯法案》，还是欧盟理事会第 3577/92 号条例，对我国而言，皆不能简单和机械地复制和模仿。

在尝试实施沿海捎带业务政策的过程中，应该积极调整我国的海运业结构，提高海运行业竞争力。我国拥有丰富的国内和国际航运资源，应该统筹配置各种类型的航运资源和力量。探索远洋运输量的提高带动海运服务贸易出口额增加的法律机制，积极优化我国的运力结构与我国货物贸易

---

① 胥苗苗：《琼斯法案存废之争》，《中国船检》2014 年第 2 期。

的运输需求相适应的体制和制度。同时，基于环境保护和陆运成本增加的
因素考量，认真探索沿海运输服务新模式和新手段。①这也是检验沿海捎带
业务政策是否成功的重要途径，反之，不断涌现的沿海运输模式也有利于
完善沿海运输权立法，提升立法水平。作为沿海运输"晴雨表"的沿海运
输指数体系，在沿海运输市场秩序规则方面具有重要的导向和参考功能。②
在沿海捎带业务政策的驱动下，尝试构建专门的沿海集装箱运输运价指数
体系也有助于评估该政策的实施效果。

---

　　①　近年来澳大利益为了规避公路交通事故频发的风险，也鼓励州际货物运输从拥挤的公路
转向沿海运输，而日本积极探索该国沿海运输的发展模式，特别是日本大力发展沿海滚装船运力。
参见 Michael Grey：Technology Makes Possible the Coastal Cargo "BUS". Lloyd's List Maritime
Asia，Apr. 1994。

　　②　早在 2001 年 11 月，我国便实施和公布了中国沿海（散货）运价指数，构建了我国沿海运
输市场的价格标尺，引导我国沿海运输步入了竞争有序、规范健康的轨道。中国沿海（散货）运价
指数是我国航运界继中国出口集装箱运价指数之后推出的第二大指数。参见敏华：《沿海运输市场
亮出"晴雨表"》，《中国远洋航务公告》2002 年第 1 期。

第6章 代结论：海商法典的体系化和民族性

海商法典演进中呈现出勃兴、扩张与简约的趋向。海商法法典体系存在一定的差异性，但其体系演进中一直维系着海上货物运输合同的强制性体制。作为提单或者运输单证所证明的合同，海上货物运输合同迥异于航次租船合同。海商法典内部体系下我国《海商法》关于航次租船合同立法例存在瑕疵，这是由我国《海商法》下海上货物运输合同的本质和范围决定的。作为海商法典体系化中衍生品的民族性，为理解内河航运纳入我国《海商法》下海上货物运输立法的可能性和可行性提供了合理路径。因此，通过规范配置等立法技术和立法理念的革新，厘清和重构我国《海商法》下海上货物运输立法是可行的。

我国积极推动"一带一路"倡议的核心内涵是坚持共商、共建、共享原则，加强经济政策协调和发展战略对接，促进协调联动发展，共同构建人类命运共同体。①其中，为国际贸易运输的便利化提供重要法治保障构成"一带一路"倡议的重要范畴。我国《海商法》移植国际立法和行业惯例的立法模式，表面上使我国《海商法》具有先进性和国际统一性，但由于法律制度在移植过程中发生的肢解、丢失与变形，导致所移植法律制度与本土法律制度和文化之间产生矛盾和冲突。②实施近30年的我国《海商法》暴露出其内容与体系范畴上的缺陷。为此，2017年我国正

① 中共中央党史和文献研究院编：《习近平新时代中国特色社会主义思想学习论丛（第四辑）》，中央文献出版社2020年版，第71页。

② 张湘兰主编：《海商法问题专论》，武汉大学出版社2007年版，第2页。

式启动《海商法》修改工作并于 2018 年 9 月被列为全国人大常委会五年立法规划，我国《海商法》修改被列为二类项目。①作为我国《海商法》重要的组成部分，该法第四章构成海商法典修改的核心和重点。其中，该章第7 节"航次租船合同的特别规定"是否应该维系原来的立法模式不变，抑或展开修正，构成我国《海商法》修改的关切。内河航运问题是否纳入我国《海商法》体系，亦构成我国《海商法》修改中备受关注的问题。如果将上述两个问题统筹考量，将转化为我国《海商法》第四章的调整范围。

　　然而，上述两个基本问题并非互为独立，而是属于海商法典的体系问题。本书试图将内河航运是否纳入海商法典调整范围和航次租船合同立法例问题，置于海商法典体系性这一语境之下展开探讨，以回应我国《海商法》的调整范围问题。大陆法系立法文化非常崇尚法律的体系化。不仅如此，在海商法典体系化进程中，不断衍生其民族性的属性。海商法典的民族性是体系化中基于立法者特定的国情、社会经济、航运传统等本土因素考虑而形成的体系化立法趋向。海商法典的民族性实质上属于体系化的一个表征，但是具有很强的独立性，其主要用来描述海商法典体系化中调整范围是否扩张及其如何扩张的问题。例如，一国的内河航运是否应该纳入海商法典调整范围的问题。就海商法典而言，其体系化问题、民族性问题与我国《海商法》第四章的调整范围互为关联。故此，本书以海商法典体系演进规律为脉络，聚焦海上货物运输合同立法的实证分析，以此进一步探究海商法典的体系化和民族性。

一、海商法典体系演进与海上货物运输合同的强制性

（一）海商法典体系及其演进

西方启蒙运动推崇法典的体系性，体系性是法典编纂中的最高价值之

---

① 郭萍：《海商法"海上旅客运输合同"章修改：现实困惑与价值选择》，《地方立法研究》2020 年第 3 期。

一。19世纪初期，英国人边沁创设"法典化"一词，用以表达兼具整全性和体系性的理想法典。①随着法典编纂实践的变迁，人们对于法典体系化的理解日渐达成基本共识。通常法典的编纂或形成强调两个根本特征——综合性和体系性，前者要求法典调整其权限内的全部事项，后者强调法条之间的融贯性和关联性。②海商法一度被学者认为是"非常特别的特别法"。③虽然海商法自成一个完整的法律体系，但是普通法和民法法域都有海商法体系的存在。普通法和民法均对海商法体系的形成产生重要影响，因此，海商法构成普通法和民法历史和当代的融合，由此导致海商法体系与民法体系或者普通法体系在很大程度上具有相通性。海商法体系的基本内涵，主要聚焦海商法体系在法典调整范围的大小和规范配置等领域。海商法体系的演进，也彰显了法典编纂中追求体系化所体现的价值与规律。

通常而言，海商法体系的变迁与发展，可以通过考察各个历史时期各国海商法典的编纂和形成来获得认知。总体而言，海商法典化演进中呈现了勃兴、扩张与简约的趋向。公元7—8世纪，流行于地中海的《罗得海法》一度开启了拜占庭时期海商法典的勃兴。④而后，该法典以相当丰富的海商法体系深刻影响后世海商法典的逐渐成型和发展。1536年出版于英国的《奥利隆裁判集》和1681年法国颁布的《海事条例》，汇编了欧洲主要港口的法律。《海事条例》与其他海商法的区别在于它是由国家赞助编纂的整个国家的法律与习惯，宣示海商法在法国作为整体的重要性。海商法典体系化的勃兴，其主要的特征在于法典体例的包容和开放。法典的规范设计并非完全由私法规范构成，而是私法规范与公法规范的相互掺杂。⑤这

---

① Dru Stevenson，"Costs of Codification"，*University of Illinois Law Review*，2014(4)，pp.1129—1174.

② McAuley Michael，"Proposal for a Theory and a Method of Recodification"，*Loyola Law Review*，2003，49(2)，pp.261—286.

③ 郭瑜：《海商法的精神——中国的实践和理论》，北京大学出版社2005年版，第64页。

④ R.D.Benedict，"The Historical Position of the Rhodian Law"，*Yale Law Journal*，1909，18(4)，pp.223—242.

⑤ B. Obinna，Okere，"The Technique of International Maritime Legislation"，*The International and Comparative Law Quarterly*，1981，30(3)，pp.513—536.

一点也深刻反映在公元 14 世纪流行于地中海西部区域的一些商人法的编纂体例上。

航运贸易发展的日新月异以及民法法系法典编纂活动的涌动，对海商法典扩张产生了重大影响。这一时期，海商法典体系的扩张最为典型的当属于法国商法典纳入海商法部分，开创了商法典融入海商法法典体例的先河。法国商法典包容海商法的实践，是法国丰厚海商法文化传统法典化诉求的反映，也迎合了法国人当初尽心尽力编纂一部有世界影响力商法典的心态。[①]受到法国商法典的鼓舞，一些大陆法系国家纷纷启动本国商法典的编纂，同时将涉及航运实务和海商法的内容囊括到本国法典之中。除了法国商法典以外，比较典型的当属德国商法典下海商法体系，构成海商法体系扩张体例的圭臬。[②]新的德国商法典触及货运代理和仓储的立法。[③]德国商法下的海商法体例比较宏大，立法内容具有很浓厚的本土色彩。晚近，海商法典的扩张并没有消歇，有两部重要海商法典的编纂也值得关注——荷兰海商法典和俄罗斯海商法典。俄罗斯海商法典不仅对传统海商法典的体系进行制度设计，而且在其他海商法典所遗忘的领域也给予了关注。[④]

海商法典的扩张并非毫无节制。晚近以来，海商法典涌现出一股"瘦身"与追求简约的趋向。海商法典体系的变迁昭示着航运领域立法理念与立法技术的变革。就海商法典体系范畴或者立法调整的社会关系领域而言，无疑，海上货物运输合同构成海商法典的核心和重点内容。作为代表承运人力量的英国与代表托运人力量的美国博弈的结果，诞生于 1893 年的

---

① Malcolm Alistair Clarke, *Aspects of the Hague Rules: A Comparative Study in English and French Law*, The Hague: Martinus Nijhoff, 1976. p.4.

② G. H. B. Kenrick, "The New Commercial Code of Germany", *Journal of the Society of Comparative Legislation*, 1900, 2(2), pp.342—347.

③ 《各国（地区）海商法汇编》，韩立新、王秀芬编译，大连海事大学出版社 2003 年版，第982 页。

④ 主要是俄罗斯海商法典在船舶、港口国监管、海事引航员、沉没财产、海事代理合同、船舶油污损害赔偿、海事声明以及时效上给予立法，形成海商法典下公法规范和私法规范掺杂的格局。参见俄罗斯联邦《商船航运法典》相关规定；也可参见曹兴国、初北平：《作为特别法的〈海商法〉的修改》，《政法论丛》2018 年第 1 期。

美国国内法——哈特法，奠定了海上货物运输合同立法的基础，为当代海商法典的成型提供了立法蓝本。①在当代海商法典的演进过程，其简约的趋向不断凸显。所谓海商法典的简约趋向，是指导致某些海商法典所规制的传统范畴被废除，或者海商法典从商法典体系中独立出来。海商法典的简约趋向，在德国商法体系之下的海商法典和日本商法体系之下的海商法典的现代化中得到了充分体现。②新近德国商法典实现了立法结构和立法内容的重大变化，法典条文被缩减到143条，显得更加精练和实用。③2018年日本对商法典运输总则大修改，修改后的日本商法典运输总则追求法典体系化、水上运输的双轨制以及海商法"上岸"等。④事实上，我国也有学者对于商法典的扩张式移植持有谨慎的态度，即便是对于比较先进国际立法如2008年《鹿特丹规则》的吸收亦然。海商法典对于国际运输立法的吸收，应该秉承顾及当事人利益平衡、国家贸易利益、贸易伙伴立场以及法律技术等因素的制约。⑤

（二）海商法典体系演进中的特质：海上货物运输合同的强制性

纵观各国海商法典体系的演进，其主要受制于环保主义理念驱使而形成的"绿色海商法典"趋向、崇尚高效综合运输而形成的海商法典重视多式联运立法以及作为海商法典核心的海上货物运输合同的本质而形成的简约趋势。对此，有学者认为当代海商法日益呈现服务海洋环境保护的趋势，海洋环境保护逐渐成为海商法的价值取向之一。⑥多式联运在未来运输模式中具有重要的战略地位，故此，完善多式联运法治并融入海商法典的

---

① John Macdonell，"The Codification of the Commercial Law of the Empire"，*Journal of the Society of Comparative Legislation*，1916，16(2)，pp.265—282.

② 一些国家并不存在独立的海商法典，海商法典以"章"或者"编"的形式存在于该国的商法典之中，比如德国和日本。基于行文方便的考量，本书所指的海商法典采用比较广义和宽泛的角度。

③ 王彦：《德国海商法的改革及评价》，《中国海商法研究》2015年第2期。

④ 陈昊泽、何丽新：《日本海商法修改中的本土性、国际化及其协调》，《大连海事大学学报（社会科学版）》2021年第6期。

⑤ 张辉：《2020年的国际海上货物运输立法——从海牙时代到鹿特丹时代?》，《武大国际法评论》2012年第15卷第1期。

⑥ 胡正良：《海事法》（第3版），北京大学出版社2016年版，第21—24页。

体系之中非常必要。①

海上货物运输合同的强制性构成海商法典体系演进的特质和核心。海上货物运输合同的强制性意指调整海上货物运输的某些法律规则不能由合同当事人减损，否则与这些规则相冲突的合同约定将归于无效。②海上货物运输合同的强制性规则主要规定承运人的责任并构成公共政策，其宗旨在于为承运人的责任确立最低程度的标准，从而保护托运人的利益。在海上货物运输领域确立和实施强制性体制的实质，就是以国家的立法和司法干预排除合同当事人的合同自由。从商业的角度看，这种干预客观上限制了承运人和托运人通过讨价还价实现预期商业利润的自由。③在海上货物运输领域，国际统一立法努力从未间断过。强制性法律规范是海上货物运输法的重要特点和核心内容，并且贯穿于国内国际立法始终，是一个十分重要的法律现象。④

在海商法典体系变迁中，海上货物运输合同的强制性体制构成海商法典体系的主线索，引领着海商法典体系的扩张或者减缩。⑤不仅如此，海上货物运输合同的强制性体制在主导海商法典体系演进中衍生出海商法典体系的丰富性。诸如，代表着海上货物运输最新立法的 2008 年《鹿特丹规则》为了应对国际贸易运输实践的复杂性而采取对海上货物运输合同强制性体制的软化处理——根据美国提案增设海上运输批量合同。批量合同虽然可以背离强制性体制的大部分内容，但仍有若干"超级强制条款"不允许当事人背离，自由依然是有限制的。⑥

---

① 周灵、刘水林：《"一带一路"背景下我国国际多式联运责任制度的完善》，《上海财经大学学报》2019 年第 5 期。

② Hannu Honka, "Validity of Contractual Terms", Alexander von Ziegler, Johan Schelin and Stefano Zunarelli(eds), *The Rotterdam Rules 2008*: *Commentary to the United Nations Convention on Contracts for the International Carriage of Goods Wholly or Partly by Sea*, Alphen aan den Rijn: Kluwer Law International, 2010, pp.331—348.

③ 左海聪：《国际经济法的理论与实践》，武汉大学出版社 2003 年版，第 219 页。

④ 杨洪：《论海上货物运输强制性法律规范的性质与功能》，《中外法学》2007 年第 4 期。

⑤ M. J. Shah, "The Revision of the Hague Rules on Bills of Lading within the UN System-Issues", Samir Mankabady(eds), *The Hamburg Rules on the Carriage of Goods by Sea*, Leyden/Boston: A. W. Sijthoff International Publishing Company, 2018, pp.211—220.

⑥ 胡绪雨：《国际海上货物运输承运人责任基础的强制性发展》，《现代法学》2016 年第 1 期。

单纯考察我国《海商法》第四章下海上货物运输合同的本质与范围，进而探究该法第四章调整范围问题，可能会陷入一种针锋相对的学术争论旋涡之中。如果将我国《海商法》第四章调整范围问题置于海商法典体系视域之下予以考量，分别从海商法典内部体系和外部体系两个路径展开考察，不失为对我国《海商法》第四章调整范围一个理性的回应。

从学理上审视，海商法典的体系化问题原本与海上货物运输合同立法属于不同范畴。然而，从海商法属于民法特别法的视角看，海商法典的体系化与海上货物运输合同的强制性具有某种意义上的"关联性"。从海商法典的历史演变中我们看到，由于受到不同历史时期立法理念和立法政策的影响，其调整范围是变动不居的，进而海上货物运输合同的范围和含义也不是一成不变的。然而，海上货物运输合同立法一直秉承"强制性体制"这一立法理念。仅就国际立法而言，从1924年《海牙规则》、1968年《海牙—维斯比规则》、1978年《汉堡规则》到2008年《鹿特丹规则》，运输合同的强制性体制宛如一条主线索引领着立法。上述体制几乎为各国海商法典所移植和参照。考察上述立法例所涵盖的调整范围，则存在着差异性，这种差异性主要体现在海上货物运输合同含义与范围的界定上，进而引发不同航次租船合同的立法例问题。海商法典体系化与海上货物运输合同立法的"关联性"，主要反映在维系海上货物运输合同强制性体制的"不变"，而允许海商法典调整其他事项范围的"变"，这便是海商法典内部体系的问题，包括运输合同的本质与范围、航次租船合同立法例及其合理性以及规范配置等系列问题。

二、海商法典内部体系：海上货物运输合同立法例审视

(一) 海商法典内部体系下海上货物运输合同的本质与范围

正如民法典编纂中面对体系化问题一样，作为自足性十足的海商法典，其体系化的形成同样也面临着海商法典内部体系的合理性问题。按照理解私法法典体系的逻辑路径，海商法典的内部体系主要考察法典规范

（法条）设计，并从私法性规范与公法性规范、任意性规范与强制性规范等展开。此种认知也迎合了西方学者认为海商法的组成部分应该包括船舶、海运中的基本合同以及海商法基本主题的观点。[①]当然，这种学理上的关于海商法组成的认识，并不必然成为海商法典体系构成的唯一基础和标准。

海商法典的内部体系主要侧重于法典规范设计的考察，基本上审视海上货物运输合同规范是私法性规范还是公法性规范，是任意性规范抑或强制性规范。毫无疑问，作为调整国际贸易运输领域的法律体系，海上货物运输合同基本上应该由私法性规范所组成。而对于任意性规范与强制性规范的选择，海上货物运输合同的强制性体制决定了其主要采用后者的必然性。海商法典简约化的演进趋向，导致海商法典内部体系下的规范设计和条文配置发生重大变化，但是海上货物运输合同的强制性体制并没有变化。因此，从该意义上看，海商法典内部体系下的海上货物运输合同的本质，在于其基本上是由强制性规范所构建，这也是前文所提及的海商法典体系演进中的特质所使然。决定海上货物运输合同的强制性体制的根源，在于海商法典内部体系下的海上货物运输合同几乎具有一个共性：是提单或者运输单证所证明的合同，而断然排除了其他类型的海上货物运输合同，当然也包括航次租船合同。[②]虽然，提单或者运输单证的国内立法与国际立法在不断发展，然而，无论其如何发展和演进，为提单或者运输单证所证明的海上货物运输合同的本质——强制性体制一如既往得到维系。很显然，相关重要国际立法下的海上货物运输合同的本质与范围得到非常明确的界分（见表 6.1）。

不仅如此，海上货物运输合同的本质与范围也为相关国内立法和相关理论所确认。2013 年德国根据《海牙—维斯比规则》和《鹿特丹规则》修订了商法典。其中，该法典第二章"运输合同"纳入定期租船合同，而没

---

① M. G. Bridge. *Personal Property Law*（2ed），London：Blackstone，1996，pp.29—30.

② Sir Guenter Treitel, *Carver on Bills of Lading*, Second Edition, London：Sweet & Maxwell, 2005, p.214.

表 6.1 重要国际公约关于合同本质和范围的立法

	1924 年《海牙规则》	1978 年《汉堡规则》	2008 年《鹿特丹规则》
合同的本质	第 1 条(b)规定："运输合同"仅适用于由提单或者只要是与海上货物运输有关的任何类似的物权凭证所包含的运输合同，而对在租船合同下或依据租船合同所签发的上述任何提单或任何类似的物权凭证，则自此种提单或类似的凭证从调整承运人与凭证持有人之间的关系之时起，亦包括在内。第 3 条第 8 项："运输合同中的任何条款、约定或协议，凡是免除承运人或船舶对由于疏忽、过失或未履行本条规定的责任与义务而引起货物的或与货物有关的灭失或损害的责任，或以本公约规定以外的方式减轻这种责任的，都应作废并无效。"	第 1 条第 6 项规定："海上运输合同是指承运人收取运费据以将货物从一个港口运往另一个港口的合同；但是，对于既涉及海上运输又涉及某些其他运输方式的合同而言，只有在其涉及海上运输时，才应视为本公约所指的海上运输合同。"	第 1 条第 1 款规定："运输合同"是指承运人收取运费，承诺将货物从一地运至另一地的合同。此种合同应当就海上运输作出约定，且可以对海上运输以外的其他运输方式作出约定。第 79 条第 1 款和第 2 款分别赋予公约的强制性体制。
合同的范围	第 5 条规定："本公约中的规定不适用于租船合同，但如提单是在船舶处于租船合同的情况下签发，应符合本公约的规定。"	第 2 条第 3 项规定："本公约各项规定不适用于租船合同。但是，如果提单是根据租船合同签发，并对承运人和非属承租人的提单持有人之间的关系加以制约，则本公约各项规定应适用于此种提单。"	第 6 条第 1 款规定："本公约不适用于班轮运输中的下列合同：(a)租船合同和(b)使用船舶或者其中任何舱位的其他合同。"第 2 款规定："本公约不适用于非班轮运输中的运输合同，但是下列情形除外：(a)当事人之间不存在使用船舶或其中任何舱位的租船合同或者其他合同；并且(b)签发了运输单证或者电子运输记录。"

有将光船租赁合同与航次租船合同纳入法典之中。日本商法典体系之下的民商租赁无法涵盖国际光船租赁合同，也缺位于光船租赁合同和航次租船合同。①英美法学者认为，航次租船合同意指船舶所有人同意将船舶全部舱位于某一时限内供人使用。但是，如果将船舶提供给班轮运输，则为提单合同。②在航次租船合同之下，承租人在一定权限范围内安排船舶所有人提供的船舶，但是船舶所有人仍然控制与管理船舶。船舶所有人以承运人身份依照约定条件运送货物。③故此，船舶租用合同应该涵盖定期租船合同、航次租船合同以及光船租赁合同。④

（二）航次租船合同的立法例考察

世界主要航运大国特别是具有大陆民法法系传统的国家，对于航次租船合同的法律规制在立法体例上各有千秋，体例比较多样化（见表 6.2）。有的立法例没有明确对航次租船合同予以规制，而是明确规定"租船合同"，将其置于"运输"名目之下，如日本《商法》第四编"海商"即采用这种方式。该法典将租船划分为整船租船合同、部分租船合同以及件杂货运输等。⑤而于 1957 年公布的日本《国际海上货物运输法》并没有涉及航次租船合同，这是因为日本立法者将该法定位于调整提单项下的海上货物运输。韩国《商法典》将运输合同划分为两种，即租船合同和以件杂货运输为目的的合同。⑥瑞典《海商法》对航次租船合同进行了详细的规定，并且置于第 14 章"租船"名目之下。

其他各国海商法典下航次租船合同的规定也是各有千秋。希腊《海事私法典》在其第 6 章"运输"中没有专门提到航次租船合同，而是在第

①　王肖卿：《船舶航次租用的本质是"租"不是"运"》，《中国海商法研究》2019 年第 4 期。

②　John F. Wilson, *Carriage of Goods by Sea*, 7th ed, New York：Pearson Education Limited，2010，p.3.

③　Raoul Colinvaux & Carver, *Carver's Carriage by Sea*，12th edition，New York：Stevens & Sons，1973，p.272.

④　Bernard Eder et al., *Scrutton on Charterparties and Bills of Lading*（22nd ed），London：Sweet & Maxwell，2011，p.1.

⑤　参见《日本商法典》第 3 章第 1 节。

⑥　参见《韩国商法典》第 780 条。

表 6.2　航次租船合同立法例①

国　别	对航次租船合同的立法规制
美　国	1. 1936 年《海上货物运输法》没有明确涉及航次租船合同；2. 1999 年《海上货物运输法》（草案）第 2 条排除了租船合同的适用。
澳大利亚	1998 年《海上货物运输法》没有明确涉及航次租船合同。
南　非	1986 年《海上货物运输法》没有明确涉及航次租船合同。
加拿大	2001 年《海事责任法》没有明确涉及航次租船合同。
日　本	1957 年《国际海上货物运输法》没有明确涉及航次租船合同。
瑞　典	1994 年瑞典《海商法》第 14 章第 322 条以"合同自由"为题规定："合同中如果另有规定，或双方之间形成的习惯或贸易惯例以及其他必须考虑的约束当事各方的习惯有不同的内容，则本章规定不适用。"第 327 条规定："出租人应保证船舶适航，包括妥善配备船员与设备，使其货舱、冷冻舱以及其他载货舱处于良好状态，适于货物的接受、运送及储存。"
韩　国	1990 年韩国《商法典》涉及"租船合同"，但没有明确涉及"航次租船合同"。
荷　兰	荷兰《海商法》第 5 章是"船舶出租和承租"，该法第 453 条规定："三、航次租船是指一方（出租人）确保将约定的船舶全部或部分提供给另一方（租船人），有租船人用于在海上进行约定的一个或多个航次的客货运输，并为此种运输支付一定租金的合同。"这一点与我国海商法对航次租船合同的界定有差异，主要是"运费"和"租金"的差异。同时，该法专门以一节规范了"航次租船合同"（从第 518h 条到 520f 条）。
挪　威	1994 年挪威《海商法》涉及航次租船合同。但该法第 14 章"租船"第 322 条"合同自由"规定，本章条款不适用，如合同、当事人的习惯做法、行业惯例或其他约束双方的做法有另外规定。
德　国	德国《海商法》没有直接规定航次租船合同，但在其第 577 条涉及"租船合同"。
俄罗斯	1999 年俄罗斯联邦《商船航运法》比较有特色。该法第 116 条规定了"本章规定的适用范围"，"除非双方另有约定，本章规定均应该适用。在本章有明确规定的情况下，与之相冲突的约定无效"。 该法在第 10 章、第 11 章分别规定了"定期租船合同"和"光船租赁合同"，没有专门规定"航次租船合同"，而是并入提单下的运输。
意大利	意大利《航海法典》第 2 章是"包运合同"，其中第 386 条规定，出租人应当在开航前使船舶处于能完成本航次的适航状态，装备船舶并提供必要的文件。该法典将运输分为"租船"与"运输"，即（一）船舶的租赁；（二）包运租船；（三）件杂货运输；（四）整船运输或部分货物运输。

---

① 关于各国立法例的情形和相关资料，参见《世界著名法典选编》《海商法资料选编》以及《各国（地区）海商法汇编》等。

107 条通过对运输合同标的进行分类，有机地将整船租船和部分租船统一到海上货物运输之中。①荷兰《海商法》单独规制"航次租船"，但是在"船舶出租和承租"名目下规定，且与"定期租船"并列规定。挪威《海商法》与瑞典《海商法》对于航次租船合同的规定相类似，也比较细致，而且通过第 322 条"合同自由"的规定，使得第 2 节"航次租船"的条款规定是任意性规定。②

(三) 我国《海商法》下航次租船合同立法的合理性问题

我国《海商法》第四章以"海上货物运输合同"为题对海上货物运输予以调整，并且该法第 44 条规定奠定了我国海上货物运输合同的"全面"强制性体制。③除此以外，我国《海商法》第四章的其他条款分别以强制性规范和任意性规范的条款设计来规制海上货物运输合同(见表 6.3)。虽然，我国《海商法》第四章冠以"海上货物运输合同"之名，但在其名下又以"航次租船合同的特别规定"作为一节来调整航次租船合同。④

表 6.3　我国《海商法》第四章立法规范

强制性规范		任意性规范	
"应当"	43	"可以"	18
"不得"	4	"除外"	6
总计	47	总计	24

①　希腊《海事私法典》第 107 条规定："运输合同的标的为：1.为进行海上运输而使用整船(整船租船)或部分船舶(部分租船)；2.海上货物运输(货物运输合同)；3.海上旅客运输(旅客运输合同)，除非法律另有规定外，或合同明确规定，或性质明显不同，有关整船租船或部分租船的规定适用于货物运输合同。"参见韩立新、王秀芬编译：《各国(地区)海商法汇编(中英文对照)》，大连海事大学出版社 2003 年版，第 953 页。

②　马得懿：《海上货物运输法强制性体制论》，中国社会科学出版社 2010 年版，第 262—264 页。

③　我国《海商法》第 44 条规定："海上货物运输合同和作为合同凭证的提单或者其他运输单证中的条款，违反本章规定的，无效。此类条款的无效，不影响该合同和提单或者其他运输单证中其他条款的效力。将货物的保险利益转让给承运人的条款或者类似条款，无效。"

④　严谨地说，我国《海商法》对航次租船合同的法律规则所适用的法律规范应该是一种所谓"倡导性规范"，即提倡和诱导当事人采用特定行为模式的法律规范。参见王轶：《论倡导性规范——以〈合同法〉为背景的分析》，《清华法学》2007 年第 1 期。

从法律规范的标志性措辞来看，表 3 中的统计数字表明，我国《海商法》下海上货物运输合同的强制性规范字句为 47 处，而任意性规范则为 24 处。就这一角度而言，我国海上货物运输合同立法被视为一种全面的强制性体制。根据文义解释，凡是海上货物运输合同和作为合同凭证的提单或者其他运输单证中的条款，违反本章规定的，一律是无效的。然而，考虑到航次租船合同的此种立法安排，从海商法典内部体系的逻辑要求来看，我国《海商法》第 44 条的合理性值得进一步探讨。

第一，与我国《海商法》第 94 条在效力上的混乱和冲突。我国《海商法》第 94 条共分两款，第 1 款表明本法第 47 条和第 49 条的规定适用于航次租船合同的出租人。根据一般的解释，由于本章第 47 条和第 49 条是一种强制性规定，不容当事人依照意思自治变更，因而得出的结论是：航次租船合同的出租人应该负有谨慎处理使船舶适航和不得进行不合理绕航的义务，即与海上货物运输法下对承运人的强制性义务是一致的。①而从我国《海商法》第 94 条第 2 款的措辞可以看出，如果航次租船合同的出租人和承租人依据契约自由原则约定各自的权利和义务，则这种约定即便和第四章的关于合同当事人的权利义务的约定不同，也是有效的。换言之，我国《海商法》下航次租船合同的特别规定除了第 94 条第 1 款的规制之外，是任意性规范范畴。根据第 44 条所使用"本章"的措辞，自然是囊括了包括第四章中的第 7 节"航次租船合同的特别规定"，如此，两种规定产生前后矛盾和逻辑上的混乱。

不仅如此，我国《海商法》下航次租船合同立法合理性与海商法典内部体系的基本要求相悖。追求海商法典体系下各类规范配置富有逻辑和法理支持，是海商法典内部体系的基本要求。然而，由于我国《海商法》第 94 条第 2 款规定不仅造成该款与《海商法》第 95 条的不协调，而且通过我国《海商法》第 94 条第 2 款的规定打开两个合同的"壁垒"，开启承租

---

① 正是这种意义上，有一种通说认为在我国《海商法》下的"航次租船合同"是海上货物运输合同。

人选择提单法律关系的"通道"。在"华建公司与南京远洋公司等海上货物运输合同纠纷上诉案"中，法院认为："《海商法》第 95 条仅规制提单持有人与承租人不属同一主体的情形，不能对该条款进行反面推论，即认定在提单持有人同时属于承租人情形下仅能适用航次租船合同的约定，从而否定该主体依据提单寻求救济的权利。"①这进一步印证了海商法典内部体系合理性下我国《海商法》关于航次租船合同立法合理性存在的问题。

第二，从海商法典体系视野下法律规范的合理配置上看，我国《海商法》下海上货物运输合同强制性体制的规定也有值得商榷的地方。由于我国立法深受大陆法下强制性规范理论体系的影响，导致我国合同法体系下基本形成了一种共识，即合同法体系不能简单地将法律规范划分为强制性规范和任意性规范，而是应该在这两者之间予以细化。②虽然上述关于法律规范的合理配置存有争议，但我国合同法下法律规范的配置已逐渐呈现出多样化的特征。就法律规范的效力而言，总的趋势是意思自治原则越来越多样化和注重实际的效能，公序良俗原则越来越定位合理，鼓励交易原则越来越多样化。③因此，我国《海商法》下海上货物运输合同强制性规范的配置和合理表达，存有改进的必要性。这并不是一个单纯的法律规范的配置问题，而是一个与法典体系合理性相关联的问题。

由此观之，航次租船合同立法例问题绝非一个单纯的立法例问题，而是一个关涉海商法典体系膨胀或减缩的问题。该问题在立法技术尤其是立法规范配置上的直接反映，便是一个通过规范配置彰显海商法典内部体系的问题。

三、海商法典外部体系：海商法典的民族性与内河航运是否纳入《海商法》调整范围

在本书的语境之下，海商法典的外部体系，主要关涉海商法典是否扩

---

① 参见"(2011)津海商初字第 117(一审)""(2013)津高民终字第 84 号(二审)"。
② 这七种分别为资格型强制性规范、权限型强制性规范、要件型强制性规范、伦理型强制性规范、政策型强制性规范、管理型强制性规范和技术型强制性规范。参见钟瑞栋：《民法中的强制性规范》，法律出版社 2009 年版，第 178 页。
③ 崔建远：《我国合同效力制度的演变》，《河南省政法管理干部学院学报》2007 年第 2 期。

张以及如何扩张的问题，或者海商法典所应该调整的社会法律关系等问题。就立法学的发展规律而言，法典外部体系的发展通常受制于社会经济发展的各种因素。当然，有学者认为，法律的外部体系效益的基础之一是调整事项的综合性，即将立法者预见的全部社会事实涵摄于法体系。不同风格的法典完成这一任务路径并不完全相同。①虽然海商法典具有一定程度的自体性，导致其外部体系的更迭可能具有自身的特点，但是，海商法典外部体系的更新也是有规律可循的。为了聚集本书的研究目的，我们将海商法典民族性与内河航运问题展开联动探讨，并且重视海事司法实证的分析与阐释。这是海商法典外部体系所使然。

（一）海商法典是否具有民族性？

为国际贸易保驾护航的海商法典是否具有法典编纂中的民族性？海商法典具有浓郁的基于应对海上风险而形成的自足性。即便如此，海商法典终究是属于民商事范畴的法典。在海商法体系归属问题的争论中，我国很多学者倾向于海商法体系属于民商法体系，这是由海商法的调整对象多属于民商事法律关系所使然。②因此，在一定程度上，民法典编纂中的民族性同样也可以用来描述海商法典的民族性。民法典的民族性正是基于民族社会的精神气质，是内在品质的集中体现，反映了一个民族的政治立场、经济水平与文化传统。③无独有偶，海商法典体系化进程中也不断衍生出一定的民族性。以1681年法国《海事条例》为例，该法典体系不断演进，最终被《法国商法典》所吸收。同样，一些欧陆国家的海商法典体系演进中也印上了民族性的烙印。因此可以断言，海商法典体系演进中的民族性是不容漠视的。

为此，本书将内河航运是否可以纳入我国《海商法》调整范围的问题置于海商法典体系化中民族性的角度予以审视。海商法典体系的简约化曾

①　谢鸿飞：《民法典的外部体系效益及其扩张》，《环球法律评论》2018年第2期。
②　何丽新、梁嘉诚：《海商法实施25年司法运用研究报告》，《中国海商法研究》2018年第2期。
③　许中缘：《政治性、民族性、体系性与中国民法典》，《法学家》2018年第6期。

引发法典调整内容或范畴的变革。根据历史上意大利《航海法典》第 6 章"内水运输合同"的规定："本部分规定适用于使用船舶从事内水运输的合同，另有规定除外。"可见，其内河航运法治有条件地纳入意大利《航海法典》体系之内。同样，俄罗斯联邦《商船航运法》在"一般规定"中，亦将法典规定的适用范围有条件纳入俄罗斯的内水。这是海商法典体系化中重视民族性因素的结果。意大利和俄罗斯在海商法典体系化中充分考虑到两国的内河航运法治现实和诉求，由此可见，两国海商法典作出如此安排是海商法典民族性外露所使然。一国海商法典体系的演进模式并非千篇一律。考察欧陆有关国家如德国海商法典体系、意大利海商法典体系、俄罗斯海商法典体系以及荷兰海商法典体系的现代化模式，具有很大的差异性，这主要是由于各国海商法典体系演进中的民族性差异所导致的。海商法典体系的民族性并非新鲜事物，而是伴随着海商法典体系的发生和发展。尤其是古希腊时期盛行于地中海区域的海商法典，便孕育着强劲的民族性。[1]

内河航运是否纳入海商法典体系可能与海商法典体系演进中的民族性与政策性息息相关。俄罗斯海商法典或意大利海商法典纳入内河航运法治，是民族性在海商法典演进中发挥其立法上功能的勃发。海商法典体系的民族性可能导致法典体系的变异，这也是各国海商法典体系的立法例存在很大差异的根本动因。历史上，俄罗斯海商法典体系遵循民族性的立法例发端于 20 世纪 20 年代。1929 年苏联海商法典在立法体例、调整范围以及立法技术上都具有强烈的国情甚至政治意识色彩。[2]同样，德国、荷兰以及日本立法者尚未将内河航运纳入本国海商法典体系之中，是由于这些国家海商法典体系形成中融入相当浓厚的政策性因素。从海商法典的历史渊源看，海商法是一个关注涉及各种形式的海上和水上运输的私法体系。海

---

① Panajotis, Perdicas, "On History and Outlines of Greek Maritime Law", *Transactions of the Grotius Society*, 1939, 25(1), pp.1—50.

② S. Dobrin, "The Soviet Maritime Code, 1929", *Journal of Comparative Legislation and International Law*, 1934, 16(4), pp.252—268.

商法虽然渊源于民法法系传统，但是普通法和民法法系对海商法典体系的形成具有重大贡献。海商法典体系具有私法与公法共存的形态。上述各国在架构海商法典体系之外，同时也构建体系完备的关涉内河航运管理的公法性的法律体系，使得其失去凸显或者强化海商法典体系政策性的可能性和前提。德国非常重视水资源的综合利用，不断强化公路、铁路和水路的联合运输的整合，并且采取行政和经济手段鼓励公路货物向水运分流，推动内河水运可持续发展。①这导致德国海商法典体系失去在其法典体系中加入大量公法性规范的基础和可能性。由此可见，内河航运是否纳入海商法典体系的问题，其实质属于海商法典体系形成中的民族性和政策性的立法表达问题。

（二）内河航运纳入《海商法》调整范围的可能性：武汉海事法院的司法实证

素有"黄金水道"之称的长江，是横贯中国东西第一河，具有航运、生态维系、防洪以及灌溉等多种功能。长江在我国经济发展战略实施中居于重要地位，被誉为中国经济和生产力布局的最重要的主轴线之一。②内河航运法治是否应该纳入海商法典体系之下？为了回应该问题，本书以近年武汉海事法院的司法实践展开实证分析，明确中国内河航运法治的瓶颈以及解决问题的出路。本书整理和分析了武汉海事法院 2018 年至 2019 年期间审理的主要案例。根据武汉海事法院近两年的司法实践，长江航运秩序不容乐观，案例争议类型反映的长江水域航运的主要问题是：其一，船员劳动报酬(包括人身伤害)纠纷比较突出；其二，由于不遵守有关长江航行管理规则而诱发的船舶侵权案件比较凸显；其三，船舶买卖和担保纠纷比较突出(参见图 6.1)。③从武汉海事法院审理案件所适用的法律看，存在法

① 王玉芬：《关于推进内河水运科学发展的探讨》，《交通运输部管理干部学院学报》2015 年第 3 期。

② 沈培钧、张菁：《长江航运在综合运输体系中的地位和作用》，《综合运输》2005 年第 1 期。

③ 图 6.1 为武汉海事法院近两年来审理案件的类型统计，其数据来源于中国裁判文书官网。

官引用或者类比适用我国《海商法》的案例具有增长趋势，这彰显内河航运的法律法规存在很大薄弱或者空白，也预示着海商法典的民族性催生内河航运纳入海商法典体系的可能性。为了完善和健全长江航运法律体系，有必要修改我国《海商法》第四章的调整范围，从而实现将内河航运法治纳入海商法典体系。

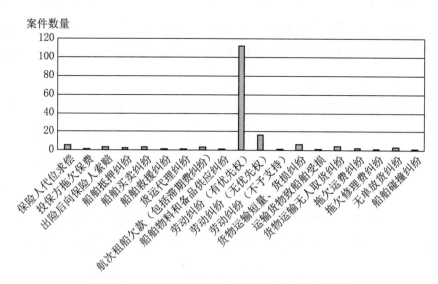

图 6.1　适用或者争议适用《海商法》案件案由统计

虽然内河航运纳入我国《海商法》体系具有内生动力，但这是一个融立法技术、规范配置以及立法理念等法典体系问题于一身的复杂问题。根据交通运输部《海商法》修改课题组提供的《海商法》修改稿第五章"国内水路货物运输合同"的草案，该修改稿下国内水路货物运输合同似乎是复制或者全盘借鉴国际海上货物运输合同下的内容，单独成立一章。此种立法技术显然比较浅陋，不值得推崇。2019 年 12 月 21 日《海商法》修改小组继续优化和完善修改稿，将征求意见稿"国内水路货物运输合同"调整为"海上货物运输合同"下的一节"国内水路货物运输合同"，采用"最小双轨制"和引入"援引条款"的立法技术。①这一立法模式的优劣难

①　参见交通运输部《海商法》修改小组公布的 2019 年 12 月 21 日《海商法征求意见稿》，内部材料。

辨，缺乏实践检验。事实上，就目前中国海商法典体系而言，并没有完全排除"内河航运"的适用，通过法律解释学可以在一定程度上解决内河航运问题。就内河船舶是否可以适用于海商法典体系下的特别制度而言，原本肇始于海船或者调控海洋风险的海商制度，诸如海事优先权等，也可以通过立法推广到内河船舶。①因此，从海商法典体系编纂上看，"内河航运纳入海商法典体系"是一个不严谨的表达。其不应该是大批量地将内河航运领域的事项（调整范围）不加选择地纳入海商法典体系中，而应该注重立法技术和立法理念的创新。

将该问题引入海商法典体系性语境下考虑，内河航运纳入海商法典体系问题将演变成为中国海商法典体系在追求民族性中的立法技术问题。目前，属于海商法典内部体系的范畴应该是公法规范与私法规范的配置、任意性规范与强制性规范等问题。就内河航运法治而言，应该以任意性规范设计，抑或以私法规范设计。显然，采用"国内水路货物运输合同"模式大面积复制国际海上货物运输合同的内容，将导致海商法典体系的无限扩张，这显然是不足取的，也背离海商法典体系简约化的发展趋势。由此观之，内河航运纳入海商法典体系的可行性和合理性，在于厘清内河航运纳入海商法典体系的具体范畴或者内容，而其立法技术尤其是规范配置的合理性和立法理念的更新则构成问题的关键所在。

四、海商法典体系下我国《海商法》第四章调整范围的厘清与重构

前文分别从海商法典内部体系和民族性两个路径展开考察，为我们进一步探究海商法典体系视域下我国《海商法》第四章的调整范围奠定了基础和前提。考量并探析我国《海商法》第四章调整范围问题，其逻辑原点

---

① 1988年《斯特拉斯堡公约》赋予内河船舶享受海事责任限制的权利。此外，根据本国航运实践和航运政策，《法国运输法典》《德国内河航运法》《荷兰民法典》等法典均规定海事赔偿责任限制、船舶优先权等制度适用于内河船舶。

在于完善我国《海商法》第四章调整范围是根植于现行《海商法》第四章
的规定和条文规范。①因此，海商法典体系视域下我国《海商法》第四章的
调整范围，应以我国《海商法》第四章第 7 节"航次租船合同的特别规定"
和第 8 节"多式联运合同的特别规定"为逻辑原点。

(一) 规范的配置

就海商法典内部体系而言，主要聚焦了海商法典体系的规范配置问
题，尤其是从任意性规范与强制性规范的配置、私法规范和公法规范的配
置角度审视内河航运纳入海商法典体系的可行性。当然，这同时也是海商
法典体系的立法技术问题。目前，包括我国《海商法》在内，世界上很多
国家海商法典体系都是私法规范与公法规范交叉、任意性规范与强制性规
范并存甚至包括大量示范性规范的模式。诸如船员与船长劳动立法、沿海
运输权政策、海事声明以及海事诉讼程序法的内容，不同程度存在于不同
国家的海商法典中。

就海商法典体系下的任意性规范与强制性规范的合理配置而言，正如
前文所言，我国《海商法》第 7 节关涉航次租船合同的特别规定存在某种
意义上的缺憾。我国《海商法》第四章下的海上货物运输合同是作为提单
或者运输单证所证明的合同，故此，其本质与范围在于海上货物运输合同
的强制性体制和排除航次租船合同的适用。从现行我国《海商法》第四章
所调整的海上货物运输法的法律规范看，基本上是海上运输当事人之间的
利益关系、海上运输当事人与运输合同之外的第三人之间的利益关系以及
运输合同当事人的利益与社会公共利益之间的利益关系，这是由海上货物
运输法对托运人或者提单持有人等利益的维护所形成的历史性调整机制的
结果。但是，现行我国《海商法》的规范配置和表达存有一些缺憾：（1）
属于运输合同当事人之间的权利和义务的规范在现行规范的配置之下一概
配置为强制性规范。（2）本来非属于调整"权利—义务"型的法律规范也

① 我国现行《海商法》第四章共包括八节，主要调整一般规定、承运人的责任、托运人的
责任、运输单证、货物交付、合同的解除以及两个"特别规定"。其中，第 7 节为"航次租船合同
的特别规定"，第 8 节为"多式联运合同的特别规定"。

被视为强制性规范的范畴。我国《海商法》第44条实际上发挥着同时调整两种利益关系类型的功能，即通过"管制"当事人的行为来优先"保护"社会公共利益，通过"管制"一方当事人的行为来优先"保护"处于弱者地位的另一方当事人利益或者善意的第三方利益。因此，本书建议优化我国《海商法》第44条的规定，将其修改为"本章中关于承运人和托运人或提单持有人的义务和责任"。同时，在原条文的基础上增加例外的表达条文，即不适用于某些不属于承运人和托运人的义务和责任的规范。为了立法体例上的合理性，有必要将航次租船合同的任意性规范单列为独立于"海上货物运输合同"一章，即关涉航次租船合同法律规范纳入现行《海商法》第六章"船舶租用合同"中。或者，在完善《海商法》第44条的配置与表达基础上，删除所有关于航次租船合同的任意性规范。

就内河航运纳入我国《海商法》体系而言，从法律规范配置的角度看，本书建议淡化"援引条款"的规范设计，强化"转介条款"的采用。[①]从目前部分海商法典体系可认可和容忍大量任意性规范存在于海商法典体系中的现实看，"内河航运纳入海商法典"具有可能性。就海商法典内部体系下公法规范与私法规范配置而言，通过配置一些公私法"转介条款"可以达到完善内河航运法治秩序的立法目的。海运同时促进了公法和私法等重要法律领域的发展。在国家干预私法和公法生活的当今世界，提单、租船合同、救助协议和拖航合同等，都在各种程度上以服从公共秩序的默示条件为前提，同时还要遵守与船舶和船员安全以及环境保护相关的各种强制性规定。[②]在未来完善我国《海商法》时，可以适当配置公私法"转介条款"。这不仅是完善内河航运法治的需要，而且也具有相关立法支撑。2015年3月1日实施的《航道法》，其立法理念由原有的管理到共治的跃升，实现了航道治理权的优化。[③]由此可见，通过私法体系下的"转介条

---

① 苏永钦：《以公法规范控制私法契约——两岸转介条款的比较与操作建议》，《人大法律评论：民法规范论》，2010年第1期。

② 威廉·泰特雷：《国际海商法》，张永坚等译，法律出版社2005年版，第22、46页。

③ 何平：《从管理到共治：航道法的理念跃升与制度完善》，《武汉理工大学学报（社会科学版）》2018年第1期。

款"，可以强化内河航运法治的社会治理功效。

（二）多式联运合同的扩张性解释

就内河航运是否纳入我国《海商法》而言，通过对多式联运合同的扩张性解释，为我们理解我国《海商法》第四章调整范围提供了另一种路径。这一路径的展开以我国《海商法》第四章第 8 节为逻辑原点。目前，界定多式联运的学理标准尚未统一。传统上，国际贸易运输实务多以不同运输工具的采用即运输方式为标准来识别多式联运合同。我国货物运输立法一度形成"重海轻水"局面：涉海立法相对完善健全，而内河航运的专门立法则相对落后甚至为空白。以中国国情作为立法的根本出发点和立足点，并不意味着要关起门来立法，而是要在借鉴各国优秀立法成果的基础上找到适合自己国情实际的立法发展路径。[1]为此，交通运输部《海商法》修改送审稿第 129 条在原条文基础上嵌入了"国内水路运输方式"。[2]由于缺位于司法实践的验证，其修改效果还不得而知。在完善我国《海商法》第四章调整范围视域下考察该问题，重塑多式联运合同的法律涵义，为内河航运纳入我国《海商法》体系提供了可能性。当然，这需要在立法理念和立法技术上尝试突破和更新，同时这也是海商法典体系化中凸显政策性的需要。为了服务和保障长江经济带发展，2017 年武汉海事法院发布《2017 年长江海事审判白皮书》。其中，"金东纸业与重庆轮船公司、重轮乐山公司、九五船运公司多式联运合同纠纷案"被列为典型案例。该案对如何为集装箱江海中转联运和江海直达运输确立法治保障提供了重要的司法价值和立法参考，同时也在一定程度上厘清了内河货物运输规则的适用规则。[3]

---

① 封丽霞：《新时代中国立法发展的理念与实践》，《山东大学学报（哲学社会科学版）》2018年第 5 期。

② 交通运输部《海商法》修改送审稿第 129 条第 1 款规定："本法所称货物多式联运合同，是指多式联运经营人以两种以上的不同运输方式，其中一种是国际海上运输或者国内水路运输方式，负责将货物从接收地运至目的地交付收货人，并收取全程运费的合同。"

③ 武汉海事法院：《2017 年长江海事审批白皮书》，http://whhsfy.hbfy.gov.cn/DocManage/ViewDoc?docId=0681720f-32d6-4787-adb4-d13dc0c268d7，2020-05-06。

目的解释理论认为，制定法条文的字面含义仅仅是立法者目的的表面判断标准，而字面含义经常没有办法准确地反映立法者的目的。任何一种制定良好的法律文本都会存在"漏洞"。①由此，对多式联运合同的扩张性解释构成理解内河航运纳入我国《海商法》的理性路径。当前，以运输工具或运输方式所适用的法律制度为标准来界定多式联运日渐流行。如果采用此种模式来界定多式联运，那么，海上货物运输与内河货物运输则可以构成多式联运合同所调整的范畴。事实上，运输方式的本质在于该运输方式所适用的法律，而非运输工具的类型。因为多式联运下决定当事人法律地位的是该法律所适用的责任基础和责任限制等问题，而不是其采用运输工具的类型。②1973 年《多式联运单证统一规则》明确了内河运输不同于海上货物运输，开创了江海联运合同属于多式联运合同的国际立法新认知，这是对多式联运合同的扩张性解释，同时也为理解我国《海商法》第四章第 8 节提供了新视野。

显然，内河货物运输合同所适用的法律不同于国际海上货物运输合同所适用的法律。由此观之，在维系我国《海商法》第四章的基本逻辑和框架下，可以通过对多式联运合同的扩张性解释，将内河航运纳入我国《海商法》体系之下。由于内河航运所涉及的问题并非仅仅涵盖内河货物运输合同问题，还包括内河船舶是否适用于海事赔偿责任限制、海难救助以及共同海损分担等特殊制度，因此，海商法典的体系化要求在适用海商法典时善于通过法律解释应对空白，尤其是扩张性解释在国际海难救助、船舶碰撞以及海事赔偿责任限制等领域需要对"船舶"给予扩张性解释，从而实现立法的目的。

海商活动具有基于应对海洋贸易运输风险而形成的固有特殊性，其相关的制度建构与其他部门法有着密切的关联。因此，必须将海商立法

---

① 王云清：《制定法中的目的解释——以英美国家为中心》，《法制与社会发展》2020 年第 1 期。

② 黄晶：《我国〈海商法〉对国内水路货物运输的适用》，《上海海事大学学报》2018 年第 1 期。

置于整个法律体系之内通盘考虑，并且要在各个层级、各个环节之间做好协调。①我国《海商法》第四章调整范围的界定，并不是非此即彼的简单问题，否则极有可能导致立法者纵容我国《海商法》的体系无限扩容，滋生立法的"头痛医头、脚痛医脚"的低水平法治局面。海商法典体系演进的趋向和规律性，彰显了海上货物运输合同具有强制性的特质，其贯穿于海商法典体系下海上货物运输合同立法的始终。这是作为提单或者运输单证所证明的海上货物运输合同迥异于航次租船合同的特质所使然。

海商法典体系下的内部体系决定了我国《海商法》第四章可以果断地将该章第 7 节"航次租船合同的特别规定"移位，这是基于航次租船合同立法例瑕疵的考量。而海商法典的民族性，强烈预示着我国《海商法》纳入内河航运的合理性和可能性，这是基于对多式联运合同扩张性解释存在合理性的学术展望和学术预判的结果。当然，我国《海商法》第四章调整范围的立法质量的优劣，仍然取决于对海商法典体系演进规律的掌握、立法理念的更新以及规范配置的合理运用。

---

① 傅廷中：《海商立法中若干层级与环节的协调》，《地方立法研究》2018 年第 5 期。

参考文献

一、中文论文

[1] 傅廷中：《海商立法中若干层级与环节的协调》，《地方立法研究》2018 年第 5 期。

[2] 马得懿、王幸子：《我国航运补贴的制度构架》，《国际经贸探索》2011 年第 11 期。

[3] 马得懿：《普通承运人、公共承运人与"从事公共运输的承运人"：渊源、流变与立法探究》，《社会科学》2016 年第 8 期。

[4] 马得懿：《中国（上海）自贸试验区实施沿海捎带业务政策之法律解读》，《上海经济研究》2014 年第 10 期。

[5] 马得懿：《海商法典的体系化与民族性：海上货物运输合同立法的实证研究》，《厦门大学学报（哲社版）》2023 年第 1 期。

[6] 封丽霞：《新时代中国立法发展的理念与实践》，《山东大学学报（哲学社会科学版）》2018 年第 5 期。

[7] 何平：《从管理到共治：航道法的理念跃升与制度完善》，《武汉理工大学学报（社会科学版）》2018 年第 1 期。

[8] 王云清：《制定法中的目的解释——以英美国家为中心》，《法制与社会发展》2020 年第 1 期。

[9] 黄晶：《我国海商法对国内水路货物运输的适用》，《上海海事大学学报》2018 年第 1 期。

［10］朱岩：《强制缔约制度研究》，《清华法学》2011 年第 1 期。

［11］彭阳：《国际班轮运输公司强制缔约义务否定论》，《中国海商法研究》2015 年第 2 期。

［12］翟艳：《强制缔约制度与经济法的契合性解读》，《政治与法律》2013 年第 7 期。

［13］万俊人：《公共性的政治伦理理解》，《读书》2009 年第 12 期。

［14］于立、吴绪亮：《运输产业中的反垄断与规制问题》，《中国工业经济》2008 年第 2 期。

［15］陈继红、真虹等：《基于交易费用的航运组织制度演进机理》，《交通运输工程学报》2009 年第 9 期。

［16］谢燮、王勇昌：《航运联盟的行业监管之道》，《中国港口》2014 年第 11 期。

［17］陈继红：《论集装箱班轮运输企业联盟的管理协同机制》，《大连海事大学学报（社会科学版）》2012 年第 1 期。

［18］朱意秋、张琦：《我国集装箱班轮运输市场垄断程度研究》，《上海船舶运输科学研究所学报》2006 年第 2 期。

［19］邹盈颖、丁莲芝、张敏：《国际班轮运输业反垄断豁免政策和立法之态势与启示》，《上海海事大学学报》2012 年第 2 期。

［20］颜晨广、岳金卫：《国际航运市场反垄断豁免合理性研究》，《交通企业管理》2014 年第 1 期。

［21］曾祥生：《服务合同立法的比较研究》，《求索》2011 年第 12 期。

［22］王利明：《典型合同立法的发展趋势》，《法制与社会发展》2014 年第 2 期。

［23］周灵、刘水林：《"一带一路"背景下我国国际多式联运责任制度的完善》，《上海财经大学学报》2019 年第 5 期。

［24］杨洪：《论海上货物运输强制性法律规范的性质与功能》，《中外法学》2007 年第 4 期。

[25] 胡绪雨:《国际海上货物运输承运人责任基础的强制性发展》,《现代法学》2016 年第 1 期。

[26] 王肖卿:《船舶航次租用的本质是"租"不是"运"》,《中国海商法研究》2019 年第 4 期。

[27] 王轶:《论倡导性规范——以〈合同法〉为背景的分析》,《清华法学》2007 年第 1 期。

[28] 崔建远:《我国合同效力制度的演变》,《河南省政法管理干部学院学报》2007 年第 2 期。

[29] 谢鸿飞:《民法典的外部体系效益及其扩张》,《环球法律评论》2018 年第 2 期。

[30] 何丽新、梁嘉诚:《海商法实施 25 年司法运用研究报告》,《中国海商法研究》2018 年第 2 期。

[31] 许中缘:《政治性、民族性、体系性与中国民法典》,《法学家》2018 年第 6 期。

[32] 王玉芬:《关于推进内河水运科学发展的探讨》,《交通运输部管理干部学院学报》2015 年第 3 期。

[33] 沈培钧、张菁:《长江航运在综合运输体系中的地位和作用》,《综合运输》2005 年第 1 期。

[34] 苏永钦:《以公法规范控制私法契约——两岸转介条款的比较与操作建议》,《人大法律评论:民法规范论》2010 年卷。

[35] 陈亚:《国际班轮公司作为公共承运人的强制缔约义务》,《人民司法》2011 年第 14 期。

[36] 最高人民法院民事审判第四庭:《最高人民法院海事海商审判综述》,《武大国际法评论》2010—2011 年第 2 期。

[37] 蔡宏波:《WTO 框架下战略性补贴政策的制约因素与应对策略》,《世界经济研究》2007 年第 5 期。

[38] 林松、陈世英:《沿海内贸船舶捎带模式》,《中国港口》2005 年

第 7 期。

[39] 胥苗苗：《琼斯法案存废之争》，《中国船检》2014 年第 2 期。

[40] 魏明：《欧洲国家航运政策的新发展》，《水运科学研究》2007 年第 4 期。

[41] 孙俊岩：《琼斯法案对美国经济的影响》，《中国水运》2004 年第 6 期。

[42] 王杰、李艳君、白玮玮：《中国（上海）自贸试验区下航运政策解析》，《世界海运》2014 年第 2 期。

[43] 林晖：《欧共体航运经济法律制度评介》，《水运管理》2008 年第 3 期。

[44] 许民强：《符合 GATS 的我国航运市场准入的立法建议》，《世界海运》1999 年第 6 期。

[45] 李晨、郭浩然：《我国海运服务贸易竞争力影响因素的实证研究》，《国际商务研究》2013 年第 3 期。

[46] 曹兴国、初北平：《作为特别法的〈海商法〉的修改制度体系、修法时机及规范设计》，《政法论丛》2018 年第 1 期。

[47] 王彦：《德国海商法的改革及评价》，《中国海商法研究》2015 年第 2 期。

[48] 陈昊泽、何丽新：《日本海商法修改中的本土性、国际化及其协调》，《大连海事大学学报（社会科学版）》2021 年第 6 期。

[49] 张辉：《2020 年的国际海上货物运输立法——从海牙时代到鹿特丹时代?》，《武大国际法评论》2012 年第 1 期。

[50] 于谨凯、侯瑞青：《海洋运输业竞争力提升中的政府补贴机制研究》，《内蒙古财经学院学报》2009 年第 6 期。

[51] 尹立、张阿红：《WTO 框架下中国工业补贴方式改进之探讨》，《法学家》2008 年第 6 期。

[52] 郭艳、张蔚蔚：《中国航运企业发展现状及对策研究》，《中国水

运》2007年第1期。

[53] 郭萍：《海商法"海上旅客运输合同"章修改：现实困惑与价值选择》，《地方立法研究》2020年第3期。

[54] 林惠玲：《美国反补贴实体法律实施问题研究》，上海人民出版社2019年版。

二、中文著作

[1] 傅廷中：《海商法论》，法律出版社2012年版。

[2] 吴焕宁：《海商法学》，法律出版社1996年版。

[3] 卜海：《国际经济中的补贴与反补贴》，中国经济出版社2009年版。

[4] 薛波主编：《元照英美法词典》，法律出版社2003年版。

[5] 杨良宜：《提单及其付运单证》，中国政法大学出版社2001年版。

[6] 马得懿：《海上货物运输法强制性体制论》，中国社会科学出版社2010年版。

[7] 吴玉岭：《遏制市场之恶——美国反垄断政策解读》，南京大学出版社2007年版。

[8] 李国安：《WTO服务贸易多边规则》，北京大学出版社2007年版。

[9] 孙光圻：《国际海运政策》，大连海事大学出版社1998年版。

[10] 中共中央党史和文献研究院编：《习近平新时代中国特色社会主义思想学习论丛》（第四辑），中央文献出版社2020年版。

[11] 张湘兰主编：《海商法问题专论》，武汉大学出版社2007年版。

[12] 胡正良：《海事法》（第3版），北京大学出版社2016年版。

[13] 左海聪：《国际经济法的理论与实践》，武汉大学出版社2003年版。

[14] 钟瑞栋：《民法中的强制性规范》，法律出版社2009年版。

[15] 郭瑜：《海商法的精神——中国的实践和理论》，北京大学出版社

2005 年版。

[16] 韩立新、王秀芬编译：《各国（地区）海商法汇编》，大连海事大学出版社 2003 年版。

三、中译版著作

[1] ［美］威廉姆森：《反托拉斯经济学——兼并、协约和策略行为》，张群群、黄涛译，经济科学出版社 1999 年版。

[2] ［苏］小奥利弗·温德尔·霍姆斯：《普通法》，冉昊、姚中秋译，中国政法大学出版社 2006 年版。

[3] ［德］迪特尔梅·迪库斯：《德国债法总论》，杜景林、卢谌译，法律出版社 2004 年版。

[4] ［美］罗伯特·A.希尔曼：《合同法的丰富性：当代合同法理论的分析与批判》，郑云端译，北京大学出版社 2005 年版。

[5] ［加］彼得·柏森：《合同法理论》，易继明译，北京大学出版社 2004 年版。

[6] ［美］乌戈马太：《比较法律经济学》，沈宗灵译，北京大学出版社 2005 年版。

[7] ［英］约翰·哈德森：《英国普通法的形成——从诺曼征服到大宪章时期英格兰的法律与社会》，刘四新译，商务印书馆 2006 年版。

[8] ［德］G.拉德布鲁赫：《法哲学》，王朴译，法律出版社 2005 年版。

[9] ［加］威廉·泰特雷：《国际海商法》，张永坚等译，法律出版社 2005 年版。

四、外文论文

[1] Burdick C.K., The origin of the peculiar duties of public service companies. Part I, *Columbia Law Review*, 1911, 11(6): 514—531.

[2] Rosenbaum I.S., The Common Carrier-Public Utility Concept: A

Legal-Industrial View，*J. Land & Pub. Util. Econ.*，1931，7（2）：
155—168.

［3］Rosenbaum I.S. and Lilienthal D.E.，Motor Carrier Regulation：
Federal，State and Municipal，*Colum. L. Rev.*，1926，26(8)：954—987.

［4］Adler E.A.，Business Jurisprudence，*Harv. L. Rev.*，1914，28
（2）：135—162.

［5］Goddard E.C.，Contract Limitations of the Common Carrier's Lia-
bility，*Michigan Law Review*，1910，8(7)：531—554.

［6］Wilcox W.K.，GATT-Based Protectionism and the Definition of a
Subsidy，*BU Int'l L.J.*，1998，16(1)：129—162.

［7］Werth W.H.，Contracts Limiting Carrier's Liability in Virginia，
Virginia Law Register，1903，9(2)：73—85.

［8］Goddard E.C.，The Liability of the Common Carrier as Determined by
Recent Decisions of the United States Supreme Court，*Columbia Law Review*，1915，15(5)：399—416.

［9］Oyedemi W.O.，Cabotage regulations and the challenges of outer
continental shelf development in the United States，Hous. *J. Int'l L.*，
2011，34：607—652.

［10］Lewis J.，Veiled Waters：Examining the Jones Act's Consumer
Welfare Effect，*Issues in Political Economy*，2013，22：77—107.

［11］Hamilton D.，Schwartz P.，A Transatlantic Free Trade Area：A
Boost to Economic Growth，Center for Transatlantic Relations and New
Direction—The Foundation for European Reform，*Washington and Brus-
sels*，January，2012.

［12］Gray W.O.，Performance of major us shipyards in 20th/21st cen-
tury，*Journal of Ship Production*，2008，24(04)：202—213.

［13］R. Pouch，The U.S. Merchant Marine and Maritime Industry in

Review, *Proceedings*, 1998, 124(5).

[14] C. Grabow, U.S. Maritime Sector Among the Jones Act's Biggest victims, *CATO Institute*, Washington, 28 June 2018.

[15] McGeorge R.L., United States coastwise trading restrictions: A comparison of recent customs service rulings with the legislative purpose of the Jones Act and the demands of a global economy, *Nw. J. Int'l L. & Bus.*, 1990, 11(1): 62—86.

[16] R. Joshi, WTO Review Fears Derail Proposed Jones Act Amendment, *Lloyd's List*, London, 28 October 2009.

[17] Galbraith S., Thinking Outside the Box on Coastal Shipping and Cabotage, *Maritime Trade Intelligence*, 2014.

[18] B. Edmonson, Navy Official Calls for a Fleet of Dual-Use Marine Highway Ships, *Journal of Commerce*, 13 July, 2011.

[19] R. O'Rourke, DOD Leases of Foreign-Built Ships: Background for Congress, *Congressional Research Service Report for Congress*, 7-5700-RS22454, Washington, 28 May 2010.

[20] Johnson C.B., Advances in marine spatial planning: Zoning earth's last frontier, *J. Envtl. L. & Litig.*, 2014, 29(1): 191—246.

[21] A. Stoler, The Current State of the WTO', Paper presented at Workshop on the EU, the US and the WTO, *Institute for International Business, Economics and Law*, California, 28 February—1 March 2003.

[22] Kalen S. Cruise Control and Speed Bumps: Energy Policy and Limits for Outer Continental Shelf Leasing. *Envtl. & Energy L. & Pol'y J.*, 2012, 7: 155—189.

[23] J. Chuah, The new German Act on the Reform of Maritime Trade Law, *Journal of International Maritime Law*, 2013, 19(1).

[24] European Commission, Blue Belt: A Single Transport Area for

Shipping，*European Commission COM*（2013）510 final（Brussels，8 July 2013）.

[25] Lopez C.M.，Mexico：the legal treatment of vessels and offshore installations under the Mexican foreign investment and navigation frameworks，Division of the International Bar Association，2013，9(1).

[26] Akpan A.，A Precarious Judicial Interpretation of the Scope of EU Maritime Cabotage Law，*Journal of International Maritime Law*，2015，20(6)：444—446.

[27] Hazledine T.，New Zealand trade patterns and policy，*Australian Economic Review*，1993，26(4)：23—27.

[28] Goldfinch S.，Economic Reform in New Zealand，*The Otemon Journal of Australian Studies*，2004，30：75—98.

[29] May R.，Walsh P.，Thickett G.，et al.，Unions and union members in New Zealand：Annual review for 2000，*New Zealand Journal of Employment Relations*，2001，26(3)：317—328.

[30] N. Prisekina，Cabotage：Frequent Legal Issues for Contractors on Sakhalin Oil and Gas Projects，*Russin & Vecchi*，London，18 November 2003.

[31] Vasuki-Rao N.，India relaxes cabotage law to ease Nehru congestion，*The Journal of Commerce Online*，2005.

[32] P. Ghosh and S. Narayan，Maritime Capacity of India：Strengths and Challenges，*Observer Research Foundation*，2012.

[33] C. Keane，M. Thompson and J. Cockerell，Harper Review Recommends Changes to Australia's Cabotage Regime and Liner Shipping Exemption，*Clyde & Co Newsletter*，Melbourne，2 April 2015.

[34] Berg C.，Lane A.，Coastal Shipping Reform：Industry Saviour or Regulatory Nightmare，*Institute of Public Affairs*，Melbourne，2013(4).

[35] R. Rozas, Shipping and Transport: Chile: Potential Regulatory Changes in the Cabotage Trade, *International Law Office*, London, 22 June 2011.

[36] Nesterowicz M., Freedom to Provide Maritime Transport Services in European Community Law, *J. Mar. L. & Com.*, 2003, 34(4): 629—646.

[37] McConnell Jr. J.W., A Corporate Citizen of the United States for Maritime Law Purposes, *J. Mar. L. & Com.*, 1994, 25(2): 159—220.

[38] Jones C.T., The Practical Effects on Labor of Repealing American Cabotage Laws, *Transp. LJ*, 1994, 22(3): 403—448.

[39] Stevenson D., Costs of Codification, *U. Ill. L. Rev.*, 2014(4): 1129—1174.

[40] McAuley M., Proposal for a Theory and a Method of Recodification, *Loy. L. Rev.*, 2003, 49(2): 261—286.

[41] Benedict R.D., Historical Position of the Rhodian Law, *Yale L.J.*, 1908, 18(4): 223—242.

[42] Okere B.O., The technique of international maritime legislation, *International & Comparative Law Quarterly*, 1981, 30(3): 513—536.

[43] G. H. B. Kenrick, The New Commercial Code of Germany, *Journal of the Society of Comparative Legislation*, 1900, 2(2): 342—347.

[44] Macdonell J., The Codification of the Commercial Law of the Empire, *Journal of the Society of Comparative Legislation*, 1916, 16(2): 265—282.

[45] Perdicas P., On History and Outlines of Greek Maritime Law, *Transactions of the Grotius Society*, 1939, 25: 33—50.

[46] Dobrin S., The Soviet Maritime Code, 1929, *J. Comp. Legis. & Int'l L.* 3d ser., 1934, 16(part 1 and 4): 252—268.

[47] J. Hoffmann, Maritime Cabotage Services: Prospects and Chal-

lenges, *Bulletin on Trade Facilitation and Transport in Latin America and the Caribbean*, 2011, 183.

[48] Oppenheim L., The Meaning of Coasting-Trade in Commercial Treaties, *LQ Rev.*, 1908, 24(3): 328—334.

[49] Preiser W., History of the law of nations: ancient times to 1648, *Encyclopedia of public international law*, 1995, 7(1): 132—159.

[50] Okeke B.V., Aniche E. An evaluation of the effectiveness of the Cabotage Act 2003 on Nigerian maritime administration, *Sacha Journal of policy and strategic studies*, 2012, 2(1): 12—28.

[51] J. Gabriel, Revitalisation of the Shipbuilding Industry, *Petrobas Magazine*, 2009, 58(1), 5—10.

[52] J. Leahy and S. Pearson, Rousseff's Dream of Brazilian Ship-building Titan in Deep Water, *Financial Times*, Rio de Janeiro, 25 January 2015.

[53] Government of Canada, National Shipbuilding and Procurement Strategy, *Results of the National Shipbuilding and Procurement Strategy*, 2011.

[54] U.S. Department of Commerce Bureau of Export Administration (BXA), *National Security Assessment of the U.S. Shipbuilding and Repair Industry*, 2001.

[55] World Maritime News, Chinese Shipyards Vying to Enter LNG Market, *World Maritime News*, Shanghai, 5 August 2014.

[56] Alex Lennane, US Cabotage Protection gets more Expensive, *The Load Star*, Nov.19, 2013.

[57] C. Papavizas and B.Gardner, Coast Guard Rejects Industry Petition to Change Jones Act Vessel Rebuilding Regulations, Winston & Strawn LLP, Mar 20, 2012.

[58] Yost III W.H., Jonesing for a Taste of Competition: Why an Antiquated Maritime Law Needs Reform, *Roger Williams UL Rev.*, 2013, 18 (1): 52—77.

[59] Okeke B.V., Aniche E., An evaluation of the effectiveness of the Cabotage Act 2003 on Nigerian maritime administration, *Sacha Journal of policy and strategic studies*, 2012, 2(1): 12—28.

[60] Sucharitkul S., Liability and responsibility of the State of registration or the Flag State in Respect of Sea-Going Vessels, Aircraft and Space of Registration or the Flag State in Respect of Sea-Going Vessels, Aircraft and Spacecraft Registered by National Registration Authorities, *Am. J. Comp. L.*, 2006, 54: 409—442.

[61] Ajiye S., Nigerian Cabotage: Its policy, prospects and challenges, *Journal of Economics and Sustainable Development*, 2013, 4(14): 11—19.

[62] Li K.X. and Wonham J., New developments in ship registration, *Int'l J. Marine & Coastal L.*, 1999, 14(1): 137—146.

[63] Baker B., Flags of Convenience and the Gulf Oil Spill: Problems and Proposed Solutions, *Houston Journal of International Law*, 2012, 34 (3): 687—715.

[64] Mikelis N., Ship recycling markets and the impact of the Hong Kong convention International Conference on Ship Recycling. World Maritime University Malmo, Sweden, 2013: 7—9.

[65] Koh H.H., Why do nations obey international law, *The Yale Law Journal*, 1996, 106: 2599—2659.

[66] Hodgson J.R.F., Brooks M.R., Towards a North American cabotage regime: A Canadian perspective, *Canadian Journal of Transportation*, 2007, 1(1): 19—35.

[67] Edmond G., The freedom of histories: reassessing Grotius on the

sea, *Law Text Culture*, 1995, 2(9): 179—217.

[68] Desierto D. A., Postcolonial international law discourses on regional developments in South and Southeast Asia, *International Journal of Legal Information*, 2008, 36(3): 387—431.

[69] Oppenheim L., Meaning of Coasting-Trade in Commercial Treaties, *LQ Rev.*, 1908, 24(3): 328—334.

[70] Petrova R., Cabotage and the European Community common maritime policy: moving towards free provision of services in maritime transport, *Fordham Int'l LJ*, 1997, 21(3): 1019—1092.

[71] Sefara A.A., Achieving access to the maritime transport services market in the European Union: A critical discussion of cabotage services, *Australian Journal of Maritime & Ocean Affairs*, 2014, 6(2): 106—110.

[72] Kanuk L., The UNCTAD Code of Conduct for Liner Conferences: Trade Milestone or Millstone—Time WIll Soon Tell, *Nw. J. Int'l L. & Bus.*, 1984, 6: 357—372.

[73] Guidelines towards the Application of the Convention on a Code of Conduct for Liner Conferences, UNCTAD Secretariat, 1986.

[74] Tapia J.A., From the Oil Crisis to the Great Recession: Five crises of the world economy, *Institute for Social Research*, *University of Michigan*, *Ann Arbor*, 2013.

[75] Lekakou M.B. and Vitsounis T.K., Market concentration in coastal shipping and limitations to island's accessibility, *Research in Transportation Business & Management*, 2011, 2: 74—82.

[76] Knowles S., Garces-Ozanne A, Government intervention and economic performance in East Asia, *Economic Development and Cultural Change*, 2003, 51(2): 451—477.

[77] R. Matison, Economic Growths False Paradigm, *The Market*

Oracle, 27 January 2014.

[78] Singer H.W., Dualism revisited: a new approach to the problems of the dual society in developing countries, *The journal of development studies*, 1970, 7(1): 60—75.

[79] Bonefeld W., Freedom and the strong state: On German ordoliberalism, *New political economy*, 2012, 17(5): 633—656.

[80] Taylor L., The revival of the liberal creed—the IMF and the World Bank in a globalized economy, *World Development*, 1997, 25(2): 145—152.

[81] Gurtner B., The financial and economic crisis and developing countries, *International Development Policy*, 2010 (1): 189—213.

[82] Bartik T.J., The market failure approach to regional economic development policy, *Economic development quarterly*, 1990, 4 (4): 361—370.

[83] S. Chester, Grotius, Selden and 400 Years of Controversy, *Slaw Legal Magazine*, 1 November 2009.

[84] Weiss L., Global governance, national strategies: how industrialized states make room to move under the WTO, *Review of international political economy*, 2005, 12(5): 723—749.

[85] Hubner W., Regulatory issues in international maritime transport. Prepared for the Organization for Economic Co-operation and Development (OECD), Directorate for Science, Technology and Industry, Division of Transport, 2003.

[86] M. Igbokwe, "Advocacy Paper for the Promulgation of a Nigerian Maritime Cabotage Law: Present and potential problems of cabotage and recommended solutions" presented on the Public Hearing of the Nigerian cabotage Bill, at the House Committee on Transport, National Assembly

complex，Abuja in April 2001.

［87］Cass R. A.，Competition in Antitrust Regulation：Law Beyond Limits，*Journal of Competition Law and Economics*，2010，6（1）：119—152.

［88］Jackson J. H.，Sovereignty-modern：a new approach to an outdated concept，*American Journal of International Law*，2003，97（4）：782—802.

［89］Stucke M. E.，Is competition always good? *Journal of antitrust Enforcement*，2013，1（1）：162—197.

［90］Phang S. Y.，Competition law and the international transport sectors，*Competition Law Review*，2009，5（2）：193—213.

［91］Podolny J. M.，A status-based model of market competition，*American journal of sociology*，1993，98（4）：829—872.

［92］Lucas Jr. R. E.，On the mechanics of economic development，*Journal of monetary economics*，1988，22（1）：3—42.

［93］Solow R. M.，A contribution to the theory of economic growth，*The quarterly journal of economics*，1956，70（1）：65—94.

［94］Gilbert R. J. and Sunshine S. C.，Incorporating dynamic efficiency concerns in merger analysis：the use of innovation markets，*Antitrust Law Journal*，1995，63（2）：569—602.

［95］Gilbert R. J.，Competition and innovation，*Journal of Industrial Organization Education*，2006，1（1）：1—23.

［96］Goddard E. C.，Limitation of the Amount of the Common Carrier's Liability，*Mich. L. Rev*，1911，9（3）：233—237.

［97］Joseph H. Beale. Jr.，The Carrier's Liability：It's History，*Harvard Law Review*，1897，11（3）：158—168.

［98］Haythe J. G.，Limitation of Carrier's Common Law Liability in Bills of Lading，*The Virginia Law Register*，1903，8（12）：849—857.

五、外文著作

[1] M. Hendrickson, "Trade Liberalisation, Trade Performance and Competitiveness in the Caribbean," in N. Duncan et al. (eds), *Caribbean Development Report*, 2007.

[2] Alan Bollard, "New Zealand," in J. Williamson (ed.), *The Political Economy of Policy Reform*: Institute for International Economics, 1994.

[3] Ganter M., *Australian Coastal Shipping*: *The Vital Link*, Maritime Studies Program, Department of Defence (Navy), 1998.

[4] Alexander von Ziegler, Johan Schelin and Stefano Zunarelli (eds), *The Rotterdam Rules 2008*: *Commentary to the United Nations Convention on Contracts for the International Carriage of Goods Wholly or Partly by Sea*, Kluwer Law International, 2010.

[5] M. J. Shah, "The Revision of the Hague Rules on Bills of Lading within the UN System-Issues," in Samir Mankabady (ed.), *The Hamburg Rules on the Carriage of Goods by Sea*, A. W. Sijthoff International Publishing Company, 2018.

[6] G. Oduntan, "International Laws and the Discontented: Westernisation, the Development and the Underdevelopment of International Laws," in A. Dhanda and A. Parashar (eds), *Decolonisation of Legal Knowledge*, Taylor & Francis. 2009.

[7] M. Brooks, "Maritime Cabotage: International Market Issues in the Liberalisation of Domestic Shipping," in A. Chircop et al. (eds), *The Regulation of International Shipping*: *International and Comparative Perspectives*, Martinus Nijhoff, 2012.

[8] Edward Watt and Richard Coles, *Ship Registration*: *Law and*

Practice, Taylor & Francis, 2013.

[9] John N. K. Mansell, *Flag State Responsibility: Historical Development and Contemporary Issues*, Springer, 2009.

[10] J. Karel, *Consular Reports: Commerce, manufactures, etc*, U.S. Government Printing Office, 1897.

[11] B. Fassbender and A. Peters, "Introduction: Towards A Global History of International Law," in B. Fassbender and A. Peters (eds), *The Oxford Handbook of the History of International Law*, Oxford University Press, 2012.

[12] Immanuel Kant, *Kant's principles of politics: including his essay on Perpetual peace: a contribution to political science*, edited and translated by William Hastie, T. & T. Clark, 1891.

[13] S. Kumar and J. Hoffmann, "Globalization: The Maritime Nexus," in C. Grammenos (ed.), *Handbook of Maritime Economics and Business*, LLP, 2002.

[14] G. Mailer, "Europe, the American Crisis, and Scottish Evangelism: The Primacy of Foreign Policy in the Kirk?" in W. Mulligan and B. Simms (eds), *The Primacy of Foreign Policy in British History, 1660—2000: How Strategic Concerns Shaped Modern Britain*, Palgrave Macmillan, 2010.

[15] C. Staker, "Jurisdiction," in M. Evans (ed.), *International Law*, Oxford University Press, 2014.

[16] Thomas Wemyss Fulton, *The Sovereignty of the Sea: An Historical Account of the Claims to England to the Dominion of the British Seas, And of the Evolution of the Territorial Waters: With Special Reference to the Right of Fishing and The Naval Salute*, William Blackwood, 1911.

［17］Brian Slattery, Bryan Riley and Nicolas D. Loris, *Sink the Jones Act: Restoring America's CompetitiveAdvantage in Maritime-Related Industries*, Heritage Foundation, 2014.

［18］Alan Cafruny, "Flags of Convenience," in R. Jones (ed.), *Routledge Encyclopaedia of International Political Economy*, Routledge, 2002.

［19］Rodney P. Carlisle, *Sovereignty for Sale: The Origins and Evolution of the Panamanian and Liberian Flags of Convenience*, Naval Institute Press, 1981.

［20］Benjamin Parameswaran, *The Liberalization of Maritime Transport Services*, Springer Berlin Heidelberg, 2004.

［21］G. Lee, "Inter-Island Shipping Development in the ASEAN and the Pacific Region," in Korean Maritime Institute (ed.), *Seminaron the Development of an Integrated Transport and Logistics system in ASEAN countries and Pacific sub region*, KMI, 2012.

［22］Rosa Greaves, *EC Transport Law*, Pearson Education, 2010.

［23］Alexandra P. Mikroulea, "Competition and Public Service in Greek Cabotage," in A. Antapassis, L. Athanassiou and E. Rosaeg(eds), *Competition and Regulation in Shipping and Shipping Related Industries*, Martinus Nijhoff, 2009.

［24］D. Coulter, "Globalization of Maritime Commerce: The Rise of Hub Ports," in S. Tangredi (ed.), *Globalization and Maritime Power*, National Defence University, 2002.

［25］Masahiko Aoki & Kevin Murdock & Mashiro Okuno-Fujiwara, "Beyond the East Asian Miracle: Introducing the Market-Enhancing View," in Masahiko Aoki, Hyung-Ki Kim and Masahiro Okuno-Fujiwara, *The Role of Government in East Asian Economic Development: Compara-*

tive Institutional Analysis，Clarendon Press，1997.

[26] J. Powell，"Protectionist Paradise?" in E. Hudgins (ed.)，*Freedom to Trade：Refuting the New Protectionism*，Cato Institute 1997.

[27] M. Syrquin，"Patterns of Structural Change," in H. Chenery and T. Srinivasan (eds)，*Handbook of Development Economics*，Elsevier，1989.

[28] E. Gold，*Maritime Transport：The Evolution of International Marine Policy and Shipping Law*，Lexington Books，1981.

[29] H. Grotius，"Mare Liberum：The Freedom of the Seas or The Right Which Belongs to The Dutch to Take Part in the East Indian Trade," translated by R. Magoffin，in Carnegie Endowment for International Peace. Division of International Law，*The Classics of International Law：Division of International Law，Carnegie Endowment for International Peace*，1916.

[30] David John Harris，*Cases and Materials on International Law*，Sweet & Maxwell，2010.

[31] K. Kennedy，"GATT 1994," in P. Macrory，A. Appleton and M. Plummer (eds)，*The World Trade Organization：Legal，Economic and Political Analysis*，Springer US，2007.

[32] L. Ioannis，A. Mateus and A. Raslan，"Is There Tension between Development Economics and Competition?" in D. Daniel Sokol，Ioannis Lianos and Thomas Cheng(eds)，*Competition Law and Development*，Stanford University Press，2013.

[33] D. Gerber，"Economic Development and Global Competition Law Convergence," in D. Daniel Sokol，Ioannis Lianos and Thomas Cheng (eds)，*Competition Law and Development*，Stanford University Press，2013.

[34] Berend R. Paasman, United Nations. Economic Commission for Latin America and the Caribbean. International Trade Unit, *Multilateral Rules on Competition Policy: An Overview of the Debate*, United Nations Economic Commission for Latin America and the Caribbean, Division of Trade and Development Finance, International Trade Unit, 1999.

[35] T. Arthur, "Competition Law and Development: Lessons from the U.S. Experience," in D. Daniel Sokol, Ioannis Lianos and Thomas Cheng(eds), *Competition Law and Development*, Stanford University Press, 2013.

[36] Bruce Wyman, *The Special Law Governing Public Service Corporations and All Others Engaged in Public Employment; Volume 1*, New York: Baker Voorhis & Co., 1921.

[37] Harleigh H. Hartman, *Fair Value: The Meaning and Application of the Term "Fair Valuation" as Used by Utility Commissions*, Boston and New York: Houghton Mifflin Company, 1920.

[38] Bill Albert, *The Turnpike Road System in England*, Cambridge: Cambridge University Press, 1972.

[39] Brouwer E., van Dalen H., Roelandt T., et al., "Market Structure, Innovation and Productivity: A Marriage with Chemistry" in George Gelauff et al. (eds), *Fostering Productivity: Patterns, Determinants and Policy Implications*, Emerald Group Publishing Limited, 2004.

[40] Sokol D.D., Stephan A., "Prioritizing Cartel Enforcement in Developing World Competition Agencies," in D. Daniel Sokol, Ioannis Lianos and Thomas Cheng(eds), *Competition Law and Development*, Stanford University Press, 2013.

[41] Fels A., Ng W., "Rethinking competition advocacy in developing countries," in D. Daniel Sokol, Ioannis Lianos and Thomas Cheng(eds),

Competition Law and Development, Stanford University Press, 2013.

[42] Mark Furse, *Competition Law of the EC and UK*, Oxford: Oxford University Press, 2008.

[43] Bhattacharjea A., "Who Needs Antitrust? Or, Is Developing-Country Antitrust Different? A Historical-Comparative Analysis," in D. Daniel Sokol, Ioannis Lianos and Thomas Cheng(eds), *Competition Law and Development*, Stanford University Press, 2013.

[44] Martyn D. Taylor, *International Competition Law: A New Dimension for the WTO?* Cambridge: Cambridge University Press, 2006.

[45] Aniekan Akpan, *Maritime Cabotage Law*, New York: Routlege, 2019.

[46] L. Casey, and D. Rivkin, "Making Law: The United Nation's Role in Formulating and Enforcing International Law," in B. Schaefer (eds), *Conundrum: The Limits of the United Nations and the Search for Alternatives*, Rowman & Littlefield, 2009.

[47] G. Underhill, "Global Governance and Political Economy: Public, Private and Political Authority in the Twenty-first Century," in J. Clarke and G. Edwards (eds), *Global Governance in the Twenty-first Century*, Palgrave Macmillan, New York, 2004.

[48] A Lorca, "Eurocentrism in the History of International Law," in B. Fassbender and A. Peters (eds), *The Oxford Handbook of the History of International Law*, Oxford University Press, 2012.

[49] Lincoln Frederick Schaub and Nathan Isaacs, *The Law in Business Problems: Cases and Other Materials for the Study of Legal Aspects of Business*, New York: The Macmillan company, 1921.

[50] Charles Smith and Gareth Rees, *Economic Development*, London: Macmillan Press Ltd., 1998.

［51］David N. Weil and Anisha Sharma，*Economic Growth*，Pearson Education，2013.

［52］Denis Goulet，*The Cruel Choice：A New Concept in the Theory of Development*，New York：Atheneum Press，1971.

［53］Lincoln Frederick Schaub and Nathan Isaacs，*The Law in Business Problems：Cases and Other Materials for the Study of Legal Aspects of Business*，Macmillan，1921.

［54］John Wilson，*Carriage of Goods by Sea*，Pearson Education，2010.

［55］Kerstin Ann-Susann Schäfer，*Application of Mandatory Rules in the Private International Law of Contracts：A Critical Analysis of Approaches in Selected Continental and Common Law Jurisdictions，with a View to the Development of South African Law*，Peter Lang，2010.

［56］Barry J. Rodger and Angus MacCulloch，*Competition Law and Policy in the EC and UK*，Routledge-Cavendish，2009.

［57］Winthrop Lippit Marvin，*The American Merchant Marine：Its History and Romance from 1620 to 1902*，C. Scribner's Sons，1902.

［58］Jean-Paul Rodrigue，Claude Comtois and Brian Slack，*The Geography of Transport Systems*，Routledge，2013.

［59］Benjamin Parameswaran，*The Liberalization of Maritime Transport Services*，Springer Berlin Heidelberg，2004.

［60］Malcolm Alistair Clarke，*Aspects of the Hague Rules：A Comparative Study in English and French Law*，The Hague：Nijhoff，1976.

［61］Thomas Gilbert Carver and Raoul P. Colinvaux，*Carver's Carriage by Sea*，London：Stevens & Sons，1971.

［62］Thomas Edward Scrutton，Bernard Eder and Steven Berry et al.，*Scrutton on Charterparties and Bills of Lading*，London：Sweet & Maxwell, 2011.

[63] Michael G. Bridge, *Personal Property Law*, London: Blackstone, 1996.

[64] G. H. Treitel, Francis Martin Baillie Reynolds and Thomas Gilbert Carver, *Carver on Bills of Lading*, London: Sweet & Maxwell, 2005.

附　录

附录一

---

46 USC App Ch.24：MERCHANT MARINE ACT，1920

From Title 46—Appendix

CHAPTER 24—MERCHANT MARINE ACT，1920

(d)

Prohibition against preference.

(e)

Motion or petition.

(f)

Filing of information.

(g)

Discovery; witnesses; evidence.

(h)

Disclosure to public.

(i)

Finding of unfavorable conditions.

(j)

Refusal of clearance and denial of entry.

(k)

Operation under suspended tariff or service contract.

(l)

Consultation with other agencies.

Chapter Referred to in Other Sections

This chapter is referred to in section 1114 of this Appendix; title 15 section 1014.

§861. Purpose and policy of United States

It is necessary for the national defense and for the proper growth of its foreign and domestic commerce that the United States shall have a merchant marine of the best equipped and most suitable types of vessels sufficient to carry the greater portion of its commerce and serve as a naval or military auxiliary in time of war or national emergency, ultimately to be owned and operated privately by citizens of the United States; and it is declared to be the policy of the United States to do whatever may be necessary to develop and encourage the maintenance of such a merchant marine, and, insofar as may not be inconsistent with the express provisions of this Act, the Secretary of Transportation shall, in the disposition of vessels and shipping property as hereinafter provided, in the making of rules and regulations, and in the administration of the shipping laws keep always in view this purpose and object as the primary end to be attained.

(June 5, 1920, ch. 250, §1, 41 Stat. 988; Ex. Ord. No. 6166, §12, eff. June 10, 1933; June 29, 1936, ch. 858, title II, §204, title IX, §904, 49 Stat. 1987, 2016; Pub. L. 97-31, §12(33), Aug. 6, 1981, 95 Stat. 156.)

REFERENCES IN TEXT

This Act, referred to in text, means act June 5, 1920, ch. 250, 41 Stat. 988, as amended, known as the Merchant Marine Act, 1920, which (except for sections repealed or reenacted in Title 46, Shipping) is classified principally to this chapter. For complete classification of this Act to the Code, see section 889 of this Appendix and Tables.

The shipping laws, referred to in text, are classified generally to Title 46, Shipping, and this Appendix.

AMENDMENTS

1981—Pub. L. 97-31 substituted "Secretary of Transportation" for "United States Maritime Commission". For prior transfer of functions, see Transfer of Functions note below.

TRANSFER OF FUNCTIONS

"United States Maritime Commission" substituted in text for "United States Shipping Board". For dissolution of Board and transfer of functions to Commission, see Ex. Ord. No. 6166 and act June 29, 1936. Ex. Ord. No. 6166 is set out as a note under section 901 of Title 5, Government Organization and Employees. For subsequent transfers of functions, see Reorg. Plan No. 6 of 1949, Reorg. Plan No. 21 of 1950, and Reorg. Plan No. 7 of 1961, set out under section 1111 of this Appendix.

Section Referred to in Other Sections.

This section is referred to in sections 871, 891 of this Appendix.

§864a. Purchase allowance in sale of vessels for cost of putting vessels in class

On and after June 30, 1948, the Secretary of Transportation may make allowances to purchasers of vessels for cost of putting such vessels in class, such allowances to be determined on the basis of competitive bids, without regard to the provisions of the last paragraph of section 1736(d)[1] of the Appendix to title 50.

(June 30, 1948, ch. 775, §101, 62 Stat. 1199; Pub. L. 97-31, §12(35), Aug. 6, 1981, 95 Stat. 156.)

REFERENCES IN TEXT

Section 1736(d) of the Appendix to title 50, referred to in text, was repealed by Pub. L. 101-225, title III, §307(12), Dec. 12, 1989, 103 Stat. 1925.

CODIFICATION

Section was enacted as part of The Supplemental Independent Offices Appropriation Act, 1949, act June 30, 1948, and not as part of the Merchant Marine Act, 1920, which comprises this chapter.

AMENDMENTS

1981—Pub. L. 97-31 substituted "Secretary of Transportation" for "Commission", meaning the United States Maritime Commission.

1 *See References in Text note below.*

§864b. Elements considered in sale of vessels in determination of selling price

On and after June 29, 1949, no sale of a vessel by the Maritime Administration of the Department of Transportation shall be completed until its ballast and equipment shall have been inventoried and their value taken into consideration by the Maritime Administration in determining the selling price.

(June 29, 1949, ch. 281, §1, 63 Stat. 349; Pub. L. 97-31, §12(36), Aug. 6, 1981, 95 Stat. 156.)

CODIFICATION

Section was not enacted as part of the Merchant Marine Act, 1920, which comprises this chapter.

AMENDMENTS

1981—Pub. L. 97-31 substituted "Maritime Administration of the Department of Transportation" for "Maritime Commission" and "Maritime Administration" for "Commission", meaning United States Maritime Commission.

§865. Sale to aliens

The Secretary of Transportation is authorized and empowered to sell to aliens, at such prices and on such terms and conditions as he may determine, not inconsistent with the provisions of section 5$^{\underline{1}}$ (except that completion of the payment of the purchase price and interest shall not be deferred more than ten years after the making of the contract of sale), such vessels as he shall, after careful investigation, deem unnecessary to the promotion and maintenance of an efficient American merchant marine; but no such sale shall be made unless the Secretary of Transportation, after diligent effort, has been unable to sell, in accordance with the terms and conditions of section 5, [1] such vessels to persons citizens of the United States, and has determined to make such sale; and he shall make as a part of his records a full statement of his reasons for making such sale. Deferred payments of purchase price of vessels under this section shall bear interest at the rate of not less than 5½ per centum per annum, payable semiannually.

(June 5, 1920, ch. 250, §6, 41 Stat. 991; Ex. Ord. No. 6166, §12, eff. June 10, 1933; June 29, 1936, ch. 858, title II, §204, title IX, §904, 49 Stat. 1987, 2016; Pub. L. 97-31, §12(37), Aug. 6, 1981, 95 Stat. 156.)

REFERENCES IN TEXT

Section 5, referred to in text, means section 5 of act June 5, 1920, which was classified to section 864 of former Title 46, Shipping, and was repealed by Pub. L. 100-710, title II, §202(4), Nov. 23, 1988, 102 Stat. 4753.

AMENDMENTS

1981—Pub. L. 97-31 substituted "Secretary of Transportation" for "Commission" in two places, "he" for "it" in three places, and "his" for "its" in two places, and struck out "upon an affirmative vote of not less than five of its members, spread upon the minutes of the board," before "determined to make such sale". For prior transfers of functions, see Transfer of Functions note below.

TRANSFER OF FUNCTIONS

"Commission", meaning United States Maritime Commission, substituted in text for "board", meaning United States Shipping Board. For dissolution of Board and transfer of functions to United States Maritime Commission, see Ex. Ord. No. 6166 and act June 29, 1936. Ex. Ord. No. 6166 is set out as a note under section 901 of Title 5, Government Organization and Employees. For subsequent transfers of functions, see Reorg. Plan No. 6 of 1949, Reorg. Plan No. 21 of 1950, and Reorg. Plan No. 7 of 1961, set out under section 1111 of this Appendix.

---

1 *See References in Text note below.*

§865a. Sale of inactive passenger vessels to foreigners; conditions; requisition in emergency; surety bond

Notwithstanding any other provision of law or of prior contract with the United States, any vessel heretofore operated as a passenger vessel, as defined in section 613(a) of the Merchant Marine Act, 1936, as amended [46 App. U.S.C. 1183(a)], under an operating-differential subsidy contract with the United States and now in inactive or layup status, except the steamship Independence and the steamship United States, may be sold and transferred to foreign ownership, registry, and flag, with the prior approval of the Secretary of Transportation. Such approval shall require (1) approval of the purchaser; (2) payment of existing debt and private obligations related to the vessel; (3) approval of the price, including terms of payment, for the sale of the vessel; (4) the seller to enter into an agreement with the Secretary whereby an amount equal to the net proceeds received from such sale in excess of existing obligations and expenses incident to the sale shall within a reasonable period not to exceed twelve months of receipt be committed and thereafter be used as equity capital for the construction of new vessels which the Secretary determines are built to effectuate the purposes and policy of the Merchant Marine Act, 1936, as amended [46 App. U.S.C. 1101 et seq.]; and (5) the purchaser to enter into an agreement with the Secretary, binding upon such purchaser and any later owner of the vessel and running with title to the vessel, that (a) the vessel will not carry passengers or cargo in competition, as determined by the Secretary, with any United States-flag passenger vessel for a period of two years from the date the transferred vessel goes into operation; (b) the vessel will be made available to the United States in time of emergency and just compensation for title or use; as the case may be, shall be paid in accordance with section 902 of the Merchant Marine Act, 1936, as amended (46 App. U.S.C. 1242); (c) the purchaser will comply with such further conditions as the Secretary may impose as authorized by sections 808, 835 and 839 of this Appendix; and (d) the purchaser will furnish a surety bond in an amount and with a surety satisfactory to the Secretary to secure performance of the foregoing agreements.

In addition to any other provision such agreements may contain for enforcement of (4) and (5) above, the agreements therein required may be specifically enforced by decree for specific performance or injunction in any district court of the United States. In the agreement with the Secretary the purchaser shall irrevocably appoint a corporate agent within the United States for service of process upon such purchaser in any action to enforce the agreement.

(Pub. L. 92-296, §1, May 16, 1972, 86 Stat. 140; Pub. L. 97-31, §12(38), Aug. 6, 1981, 95 Stat. 156.)

REFERENCES IN TEXT

The Merchant Marine Act, 1936, referred to in text, is act June 29, 1936, ch. 858, 49 Stat. 1985, as amended, which is classified principally to chapter 27 (§1101 et seq.) of this Appendix. For complete classification of this Act to the Code, see section 1245 of this Appendix and Tables.

CODIFICATION

Section was not enacted as part of the Merchant Marine Act, 1920, which comprises this chapter.

AMENDMENTS

1981—Pub. L. 97-31 substituted "Secretary of Transportation" for "Secretary of Commerce".

§866. Establishment and operation of steamship lines between ports of United States

Investigation and determination by Secretary—The Secretary of Transportation is authorized and directed to investigate and determine as promptly as possible after June 5, 1920, and from time to time thereafter what steamship lines should be established and put in operation from ports in the United States or any Territory, District, or possession thereof to such world and domestic markets as in his judgment are desirable for the promotion, development, expansion, and maintenance of the foreign and coastwise trade of the United States and an adequate postal service, and to determine the type, size, speed, and other requirements of the vessels to be employed upon such lines and the frequency and regularity of their sailings, with a view to furnishing adequate, regular, certain, and permanent service.

Sale or charter of vessels—The Secretary of Transportation is authorized to sell, and if a satisfactory sale cannot be made, to charter such of the vessels referred to in section 863 of this Appendix or otherwise acquired by the Secretary of Transportation, as will meet these requirements to responsible persons who are citizens of the United States who agree to establish and maintain such lines upon such terms of payment and other conditions as the Secretary of Transportation may deem just and necessary to secure and maintain the service desired; and if any such steamship line is deemed desirable and necessary, and if no such citizen can be secured to supply such service by the purchase or charter of vessels on terms satisfactory to the Secretary of Transportation, the Secretary of Transportation shall operate vessels on such line until the business is developed so that such vessels may be sold on satisfactory terms and the service maintained, or unless it shall appear within a reasonable time that such line cannot be made self-sustaining.

Preference in sales or charters—Preference in the sale or assignment of vessels for operation on such steamship lines shall be given to persons who are citizens of the United States who have the support, financial and otherwise, of the domestic communities primarily interested in such lines if the Secretary of Transportation is satisfied of the ability of such persons to maintain the service desired and proposed to be maintained, or to persons who are citizens of the United States who may then be maintaining a service from the port of the United States to or in the general direction of the world-market port to which the Secretary of Transportation has determined that such service should be established.

Lines established by shipping board; continued operation—Where steamship lines and regular service had been established and were being maintained by ships of the United States Shipping Board on June 5, 1920, such lines and service shall be maintained by the Secretary of Commerce until, in the opinion of the Secretary, the maintenance thereof is unbusinesslike and against the public interests.

Additional lines established by Secretary; rates and charges—Whenever the Secretary of Transportation shall determine, as provided in this Act, that trade conditions warrant the establishment of a service or additional service under Government administration where a service is already being given by persons, citizens of the United States, the rates and charges for such Government service shall not be less than the cost thereof, including a proper interest and depreciation charge on the value of Government vessels and equipment employed therein.

(June 5, 1920, ch. 250, §7, 41 Stat. 991; May 22, 1928, ch. 675, §414(b), 45 Stat. 696; Ex. Ord. No. 6166, §12, eff. June 10, 1933; June 29, 1936, ch. 858, title II, §204, title IX, §904, 49 Stat. 1987, 2016; 1950 Reorg. Plan No. 21, §204, eff. May 24, 1950, 15 F.R. 3178, 64 Stat. 1276; Pub. L. 97-31, §12(39), Aug. 6, 1981, 95 Stat. 156.)

References in Text

This Act, referred to in text, means act June 5, 1920, ch. 250, 41 Stat. 988, as amended, known as the Merchant Marine Act, 1920, which (except for sections repealed or reenacted in Title 46, Shipping) is classified principally to this chapter. For complete classification of this Act to the Code, see section 889 of this Appendix and Tables.

Section 863 of this Appendix, referred to in text, was omitted from the Code.

Codification

United States Shipping Board, referred to in fourth undesignated par., dissolved and functions transferred to successive Federal agencies and departments. Secretary of Commerce, referred to in such par., exercised certain functions of Board pursuant to Reorg. Plan No. 21 of 1950, and was not changed to Secretary of Transportation in view of directory language of Pub. L. 97-31. See 1981 Amendment and Transfer of Functions notes below.

Amendments

1981—Pub. L. 97-31 substituted "Secretary of Transportation" for "Commission" wherever appearing except in fourth paragraph and "his" for "its". For prior transfers of functions, see Transfer of Functions note below.

1928—Act May 22, 1928, struck out paragraph which related to contracts for carrying mails.

Transfer of Functions

Functions conferred upon Secretary of Commerce by provisions of Reorg. Plan No. 21 of 1950 to remain vested in Secretary except to extent inconsistent with sections 101(b) and 104(b) of Reorg. Plan No. 7 of 1961. See section 202 of Reorg. Plan No. 7 of 1961, set out under section 1111 of this Appendix.

In fourth undesignated par., "Secretary of Commerce" and "Secretary" substituted for "Commission", meaning United States Maritime Commission, on authority of Reorg. Plan No. 21 of 1950, set out under section 1111 of this Appendix, section 306 of which abolished United States Maritime Commission and section 204 of which transferred to Secretary of Commerce such Commission's functions not transferred to Federal Maritime Board.

Previously, "Commission", meaning United States Maritime Commission, substituted for "board", meaning United States Shipping Board. For dissolution of Board and transfer of functions to United States Maritime Commission, see Ex. Ord. No. 6166 and act June 29, 1936. Ex. Ord. No. 6166 is set out as a note under section 901 of Title 5, Government Organization and Employees. Executive and administrative functions of United States Maritime Commission transferred to Chairman thereof by Reorg. Plan No. 6 of 1949, eff. Aug. 20, 1949, 14 F.R. 5228, 63 Stat. 1069, set out under section 1111 of this Appendix.

Section Referred to in Other Sections.

This section is referred to in sections 891v, 1195 of this Appendix.

§867. Investigation of port, terminal, and warehouse facilities

It shall be the duty of the Secretary of Transportation, in cooperation with the Secretary of the Army, with the object of promoting, encouraging, and developing ports and transportation facilities in connection with water commerce over which he has jurisdiction, to investigate territorial regions and zones tributary to such ports, taking into consideration the economies of transportation by rail, water, and highway and the natural direction of the flow of commerce; to investigate the causes of the congestion of commerce at ports and the remedies applicable thereto; to investigate the subject of water terminals, including the necessary docks, warehouses, apparatus, equipment, and appliances in connection therewith, with a view to devising and suggesting the types most appropriate for different locations and for the most expeditious and economical transfer or interchange of passengers or property between carriers by water and carriers by rail; to advise with communities regarding the appropriate location and plan of construction of wharves, piers, and water terminals; to investigate the practicability and advantages of harbor, river, and port improvements in connection with foreign and coastwise trade; and to investigate any other matter that may tend to promote and encourage the use by vessels of ports adequate to care for the freight which would naturally pass through such ports: *Provided*, That if after such investigation the Secretary of Transportation shall be of the opinion that rates, charges, rules, or regulations of common carriers by rail subject to the jurisdiction of the Surface Transportation Board are detrimental to the declared object of this section, or that new rates, charges, rules, or regulations, new or additional port terminal facilities, or affirmative action on the part of such common carriers by rail is necessary to promote the objects of this section, the Secretary of Transportation may submit his findings to the Surface Transportation Board for such action as such Board may consider proper under existing law.

(June 5, 1920, ch. 250, §8, 41 Stat. 992; Ex. Ord. No. 6166, §12, eff. June 10, 1933; June 29, 1936, ch. 858, title II, §204, title IX, §904, 49 Stat. 1987, 2016; July 26, 1947, ch. 343, title II, §205(a), 61 Stat. 501; Pub. L. 97-31, §12(40), Aug. 6, 1981, 95 Stat. 156; Pub. L. 104-88, title III, §321(1), Dec. 29, 1995, 109 Stat. 949.)

AMENDMENTS

1995—Pub. L. 104-88 substituted "Surface Transportation Board" for "Interstate Commerce Commission" in two places and "Board" for "commission".

1981—Pub. L. 97-31 substituted "Secretary of Transportation" for "Commission" in three places, "his" for "its", and "he" for "it". For prior transfers of functions, see Transfer of Functions note below.

CHANGE OF NAME

Department of War designated Department of the Army and title of Secretary of War changed to Secretary of the Army by section 205(a) of act July 26, 1947, ch. 343, title II, 61 Stat. 501. Section 205(a) of act July 26, 1947, was repealed by section 53 of act Aug. 10, 1956, ch. 1041, 70A Stat. 641. Section 1 of act Aug. 10, 1956, enacted "Title 10, Armed Forces", which in sections 3010 to 3013 continued Department of the Army under administrative supervision of Secretary of the Army.

EFFECTIVE DATE OF 1995 AMENDMENT

Amendment by Pub. L. 104-88 effective Jan. 1, 1996, see section 2 of Pub. L. 104-88, set out as an Effective Date note under section 701 of Title 49, Transportation.

TRANSFER OF FUNCTIONS

"Maritime Commission" and "Commission", meaning United States Maritime Commission, substituted in text for "board", meaning United States Shipping Board. For dissolution of Board and transfer of functions to United States Maritime Commission, see Ex. Ord. No. 6166 and act June 29, 1936. Ex. Ord. No. 6166 is set out as a note under section 901 of Title 5, Government Organization and Employees. For subsequent transfers of functions, see Reorg. Plan No. 6 of 1949, Reorg. Plan No. 21 of 1950, and Reorg. Plan No. 7 of 1961, set out under section 1111 of this Appendix.

§868. Vessels sold under deferred payment plan; insurance

If the terms and conditions of any sale of a vessel made under the provisions of this Act include deferred payments of the purchase price, the Secretary of Transportation shall require, as part of such terms and conditions, that the purchaser of the vessel shall keep the same insured (a) against loss or damage by fire, and against marine risks and disasters, and war and other risks if the Secretary of Transportation so specifies, with such insurance companies, associations or underwriters, and under such forms of policies, and to such an amount, as the Secretary of Transportation may prescribe or approve; and (b) by protection and indemnity insurance with such insurance companies, associations, or underwriters and under such forms of policies, and to such an amount as the Secretary of Transportation may prescribe or approve. The insurance required to be carried under this section shall be made payable to the Secretary of Transportation and/or to the parties as interest may appear. The Secretary of Transportation is authorized to enter into any agreement that he deems wise in respect to the payment and/or the guarantee of premiums of insurance.

(June 5, 1920, ch. 250, §9, 41 Stat. 992; Ex. Ord. No. 6166, §12, eff. June 10, 1933; June 29, 1936, ch. 858, title II, §204, title IX, §904, 49 Stat. 1987, 2016; Pub. L. 97-31, §12(41), Aug. 6, 1981, 95 Stat. 156.)

REFERENCES IN TEXT

This Act, referred to in text, means act June 5, 1920, ch. 250, 41 Stat. 988, as amended, known as the Merchant Marine Act, 1920, which (except for sections repealed or reenacted in Title 46, Shipping) is classified principally to this chapter. For complete classification of this Act to the Code, see section 889 of this Appendix and Tables.

AMENDMENTS

1981—Pub. L. 97-31 substituted "Secretary of Transportation" for "Commission" in six places and "he" for "it". For prior transfers of functions, see Transfer of Functions note below.

TRANSFER OF FUNCTIONS

"Commission", meaning United States Maritime Commission, substituted in text for "board", meaning United States Shipping Board. For dissolution of Board and transfer of functions to United States Maritime Commission, see Ex. Ord. No. 6166 and act June 29, 1936. Ex. Ord. No. 6166 is set out as a note under section 901 of Title 5, Government Organization and Employees. For subsequent transfers of functions, see Reorg. Plan No. 6 of 1949, Reorg. Plan No. 21 of 1950, and Reorg. Plan No. 7 of 1961, set out under section 1111 of this Appendix.

Section Referred to in Other Sections.

This section is referred to in section 1153 of this Appendix.

§869. Creation of fund for insurance of interests of United States

The Secretary of Transportation may create out of insurance premiums, and revenue from operations and sales, and maintain and administer separate insurance funds which he may use to insure in whole or in part against all hazards commonly covered by insurance policies in such cases, any legal or equitable interest of the United States (1) in any vessel constructed or in process of construction; and (2) in any plants or property in the possession or under the authority of the Secretary of Transportation. The United States shall be held to have such an interest in any vessel toward the construction, reconditioning, remodeling, improving, or equipping of which a loan has been made under the authority of this Act, in any vessel upon which he holds a mortgage or lien of any character, or in any vessel which is obligated by contract with the owner to perform any service in behalf of the United States, to the extent of the Government's interest therein.

(June 5, 1920, ch. 250, §10, 41 Stat. 992; May 22, 1928, ch. 675, §501, 45 Stat. 697; Ex. Ord. No. 6166, §12, eff. June 10, 1933; June 29, 1936, ch. 858, title II, §204, title

IX，§904，49 Stat. 1987，2016；Pub. L. 97-31，§12(42)，Aug. 6，1981，95 Stat. 156.)

REFERENCES IN TEXT

This Act, referred to in text, means act June 5, 1920, ch. 250, 41 Stat. 988, as amended, known as the Merchant Marine Act, 1920, which (except for sections repealed or reenacted in Title 46, Shipping) is classified principally to this chapter. For complete classification of this Act to the Code, see section 889 of this Appendix and Tables.

AMENDMENTS

1981—Pub. L. 97-31 substituted "Secretary of Transportation" for "Commission" in two places and "he" for "it" in two places. For prior transfers of functions, see Transfer of Functions note below.

1928—Act May 22, 1928, inserted sentence relating to extent of interest of United States, among other changes.

TRANSFER OF FUNCTIONS

"Commission", meaning United States Maritime Commission, substituted in text for "board", meaning United States Shipping Board. For dissolution of Board and transfer of functions to United States Maritime Commission, see Ex. Ord. No. 6166 and act June 29, 1936. Ex. Ord. No. 6166 is set out as a note under section 901 of Title 5, Government Organization and Employees. For subsequent transfers of functions, see Reorg. Plan No. 6 of 1949, Reorg. Plan No. 21 of 1950, and Reorg. Plan No. 7 of 1961, set out under section 1111 of this Appendix.

§871. Repair and operation of vessels until sale

All vessels may be reconditioned and kept in suitable repair and until sold shall be managed and operated by the Secretary of Transportation or chartered or leased by him on such terms and conditions as the Secretary of Transportation shall deem wise for the promotion and maintenance of an efficient merchant marine, pursuant to the policy and purposes declared in section 861 of this Appendix and section 5 of this Act.[1]

The term "reconditioned" as used in this section includes the substitution of the most modern, most efficient, and most economical types of internal-combustion engines as the main propulsive power of vessels. Should the Secretary of Transportation have any such engines built in the United States and installed, in private shipyards or navy yards of the United States, in one or more merchant vessels owned by the United States, and the cost to the Secretary of Transportation of such installation exceeds the amount of funds otherwise available to him for that use, the Secretary of Transportation may transfer to his funds from which expenditures under this section may be paid, from his construction fund authorized by section 11[1] of the Merchant Marine Act, 1920, so much as in his judgment may be necessary to meet obligations under contracts for such installation; and the Treasurer of the United States shall, at the request of the Secretary of Transportation, make the transfer accordingly: *Provided*, That the total amount expended by the Secretary of Transportation for this purpose shall not in the aggregate exceed $25,000,000. Any such vessel after June 5, 1920, so equipped by the Secretary of Transportation under the provisions of this section shall not be sold for a period of five years from the date the installation thereof is completed, unless it is sold for a price not less than the cost of the installation thereof and of any other work of reconditioning done at the same time plus an amount not less than $10 for each dead-weight ton of the vessel as computed before such reconditioning thereof is commenced. The date of the completion of such installation and the amount of the dead-weight tonnage of the vessel shall be fixed by the Secretary of Transportation: *Provided further*, That in fixing the minimum price at which the vessel may thus be sold the Secretary of Transportation may deduct from the aggregate amount above prescribed 5 per centum thereof per annum from the date of the installation to the date of sale as depreciation: *And provided further*, That no part of such fund shall be expended upon the reconditioning of any vessel unless the Secretary of Transportation shall have first made a binding contract for a satisfactory sale of such vessel in accordance with the provisions of this Act, or for the charter or lease of such vessels for a period of not less than five years by a capable, solvent operator; or unless the Secretary of Transportation is prepared and intends to directly put such vessel in operation immediately upon completion. Such vessel, in any of the enumerated instances, shall be documented under the laws of the United States and shall remain documented under such laws for a period of not less than five years from the date of the completion of the installation, and during such period it shall be operated only on voyages which are not exclusively coastwise.

(June 5, 1920, ch. 250, §12, 41 Stat. 993; June 6, 1924, ch. 273, §2, 43 Stat. 468; Feb. 11, 1927, ch. 104, §1, 44 Stat. 1083; Ex. Ord. No. 6166, §12, eff. June 10, 1933; June 29, 1936, ch. 858, title II, §204, title IX, §904, 49 Stat. 1987, 2016; Pub. L. 97-31, §12(43), Aug. 6, 1981, 95 Stat. 157.)

REFERENCES IN TEXT

Section 5 of this Act, referred to in text, is section 5 of act June 5, 1920, which was classified to section 864 of former Title 46, Shipping, and was repealed by Pub. L. 100-710, title II, §202(4), Nov. 23, 1988, 102 Stat. 4753.

Section 11 of the Merchant Marine Act, 1920, referred to in text, was classified to section 870 of former Title 46, and was repealed by act June 29, 1936, ch. 858, §903 (b), (c), 49 Stat. 2016. See section 1116 of this Appendix.

This Act, referred to in text, means act June 5, 1920, ch. 250, 41 Stat. 988, as amended, known as the Merchant Marine Act, 1920, which (except for sections repealed or reenacted in Title 46) is classified principally to this chapter. For complete classification of this Act to the Code, see section 889 of this Appendix and Tables.

CODIFICATION

The first paragraph of this section originally contained a further provision continuing the United States Shipping Board Merchant Fleet Corporation in existence with authority to operate vessels. The corporation was subsequently dissolved by section 203 of act June 29, 1936.

<h3 style="text-align:center">AMENDMENTS</h3>

1981—Pub. L. 97-31 substituted "Secretary of Transportation" for "Commission" in twelve places, "him" for "it" in two places, and "his" for "its" in three places. For prior transfers of functions, see Transfer of Functions note below.

1927—Act Feb. 11, 1927, substituted " U. S. Shipping Board Merchant Fleet Corporation" for "U.S. Shipping Board Emergency Fleet Corporation" in first par.

1924—Act June 6, 1924, added second par.

<h3 style="text-align:center">TRANSFER OF FUNCTIONS</h3>

"Commission", meaning United States Maritime Commission, substituted in text for "board", meaning United States Shipping Board. For dissolution of Board and transfer of functions to United States Maritime Commission, see Ex. Ord. No. 6166 and act June 29, 1936. Ex. Ord. No. 6166 is set out as a note under section 901 of Title 5, Government Organization and Employees. For subsequent transfers of functions, see Reorg. Plan No. 6 of 1949, Reorg. Plan No. 21 of 1950, and Reorg. Plan No. 7 of 1961, set out under section 1111 of this Appendix.

Section Referred to in Other Sections.

This section is referred to in section 891b of this Appendix.

1 *See References in Text note below.*

§872. Sale of property other than vessels

The Secretary of Transportation is further authorized to sell all property other than vessels transferred to him under section 4$^{\underline{1}}$ upon such terms and conditions as the Secretary of Transportation may determine and prescribe.

(June 5, 1920, ch. 250, §13, 41 Stat. 993; Ex. Ord. No. 6166, §12, eff. June 10, 1933; June 29, 1936, ch. 858, title II, §204, title IX, §904, 49 Stat. 1987, 2016; Pub. L. 97-31, §12(44), Aug. 6, 1981, 95 Stat. 157.)

<h3 style="text-align:center">REFERENCES IN TEXT</h3>

Section 4, referred to in text, means section 4 of act June 5, 1920, which was classified to section 863 of former Title 46, Shipping, and was repealed by Pub. L. 100-710, title II, §202(4), Nov. 23, 1988, 102 Stat. 4753.

<h3 style="text-align:center">AMENDMENTS</h3>

1981—Pub. L. 97-31 substituted "Secretary of Transportation" for "Commission" in two places and "him" for "it". For prior transfers of functions, see Transfer of Functions note below.

<h3 style="text-align:center">TRANSFER OF FUNCTIONS</h3>

"Commission", meaning United States Maritime Commission, substituted in text for "board", meaning United States Shipping Board. For dissolution of Board and transfer of functions to United States Maritime Commission, see Ex. Ord. No. 6166 and act June 29, 1936. Ex. Ord. No. 6166 is set out as a note under section 901 of Title 5, Government Organization and Employees. For subsequent transfers of functions, see Reorg. Plan No. 6 of 1949, Reorg. Plan No. 21 of 1950, and Reorg. Plan No. 7 of 1961, set out under section 1111 of this Appendix.

    1　*See References in Text note below.*

§875. Possession and control of terminal equipment and facilities

The possession and control of such other[1] docks, piers, warehouses, wharves and terminal equipment and facilities or parts thereof, including all leasehold easements, rights of way, riparian rights and other rights, estates or interests therein or appurtenant thereto which were acquired by the War Department[2] or the Navy Department for military or naval purposes during the war emergency may be transferred by the president to the Secretary of Transportation whenever the President deems such transfer to be for the best interests of the United States.

The President may at any time he deems it necessary, by order setting out the need therefor and fixing the period of such need, permit or transfer the possession and control of any part of the property taken over by or transferred to the Secretary of Transportation under this section to the Department of the Army, Department of the Air Force, or Department of the Navy for their needs, and when in the opinion of the President such need therefor ceases the possession and control of such property shall revert to the Secretary of Transportation. None of such property shall be sold except as may be provided by law.

(June 5, 1920, ch. 250, §17, 41 Stat. 994; Ex. Ord. No. 6166, §12, eff. June 10, 1933; June 29, 1936, ch. 858, title II, §204, title IX, §904, 49 Stat. 1987, 2016; July 26, 1947, ch. 343, title II, § §205(a), 207(a), (f), 61 Stat. 501, 502; Pub. L. 97-31, §12(45), Aug. 6, 1981, 95 Stat. 157.)

REFERENCES IN TEXT

Words "such other", referred to in first par., mean other than docks, etc., acquired by President by or under act Mar. 28, 1918, ch. 28, 40 Stat. 459, which was referred to in original first par. prior to repeal by Pub. L. 97-31. See 1981 Amendment note below.

AMENDMENTS

1981—Pub. L. 97-31 struck out first par., directing Commission to take over, on Jan. 1, 1921, possession and control of docks, etc., acquired by President by or under act Mar. 28, 1918, ch. 28, 40 Stat. 459, and substituted "Secretary of Transportation" for "Commission" wherever appearing. For prior transfers of functions, see Transfer of Functions note below.

CHANGE OF NAME

Department of War designated Department of the Army and title of Secretary of War changed to Secretary of the Army by section 205(a) of act July 26, 1947. Section 207(a),

(f) of act July 26, 1947, established Department of the Air Force, headed by a Secretary, and transferred functions (relating to Army Air Forces) of Secretary of the Army and Department of the Army to Secretary of the Air Force and Department of the Air Force. Sections 205(a) and 207(a), (f) of act July 26, 1947, were repealed by section 53 of act Aug. 10, 1956, ch. 1041, 70A Stat. 641. Section 1 of act Aug. 10, 1956, enacted "Title 10, Armed Forces", which in sections 3010 to 3013 and 8010 to 8013 continued Departments of the Army and Air Force under administrative supervision of Secretary of the Army and Secretary of the Air Force, respectively.

TRANSFER OF FUNCTIONS

"Commission", meaning United States Maritime Commission, substituted for "board", meaning United States Shipping Board. For dissolution of Board and transfer of functions to United States Maritime Commission, see Ex. Ord. No. 6166 and act June 29, 1936. Ex. Ord. No. 6166 is set out as a note under section 901 of Title 5, Government Organization and Employees. For subsequent transfers of functions, see Reorg. Plan No. 6 of 1949, Reorg. Plan No. 21 of 1950, and Reorg. Plan No. 7 of 1961, set out under section 1111 of this Appendix.

1 *See References in Text note below.*
2 *See Change of Name note below.*

§876. Power of Secretary and Commission to make rules and regulations

(a) **In general**

The Secretary of Transportation is authorized and directed in aid of the accomplishment of the purposes of this Act—

(1) To make all necessary rules and regulations to carry out the provisions of this Act;

And the Federal Maritime Commission is authorized and directed in aid of the accomplishment of the purposes of this Act:

(2) To make rules and regulations affecting shipping in the foreign trade not in conflict with law in order to adjust or meet general or special conditions unfavorable to shipping in the foreign trade, whether in any particular trade or upon any particular route or in commerce generally, including intermodal movements, terminal operations, cargo solicitation, agency services, ocean transportation intermediary services and operations, and other activities and services integral to transportation systems, and which arise out of or result from foreign laws, rules, or regulations or from competitive methods, pricing practices, or other practices employed by owners, operators, agents, or masters of vessels of a foreign country; and

(3) To request the head of any department, board, bureau, or agency of the Government to suspend, modify, or annul rules or regulations which have been established by such department, board, bureau, or agency, or to make new rules or regulations affecting

shipping in the foreign trade other than such rules or regulations relating to the Public Health Service, the Consular Service, and the steamboat inspection service.

(b) Approval and final action

No rule or regulation shall be established by any department, board, bureau, or agency of the Government which affects shipping in the foreign trade, except rules or regulations affecting the Public Health Service, the Consular Service, and the steamboat inspection service, until such rule or regulation has been submitted to the Federal Maritime Commission for its approval and final action has been taken thereon by the Commission or the President.

(c) Submission of facts to President

Whenever the head of any department, board, bureau, or agency of the Government refuses to suspend, modify, or annul any rule or regulation, or make a new rule or regulation upon request of the Federal Maritime Commission, as provided in subsection (a)(3) of this section, or objects to the decision of the Commission in respect to the approval of any rule or regulation, as provided in subsection (b) of this section, either the Commission or the head of the department, board, bureau, or agency which has established or is attempting to establish the rule or regulation in question may submit the facts to the President, who is authorized to establish or suspend, modify, or annul such rule or regulation.

(d) Prohibition against preference

No rule or regulation shall be established which in any manner gives vessels owned by the United States any preference or favor over those vessels documented under the laws of the United States and owned by persons who are citizens of the United States.

(e) Motion or petition

The Commission may initiate a rule or regulation under subsection (a)(2) of this section either on its own motion or pursuant to a petition. Any person, including a common carrier, tramp operator, bulk operator, shipper, shippers' association, ocean transportation intermediary, marine terminal operator, or any component of the Government of the United States, may file a petition for relief under subsection (a)(2) of this section.

(f) Filing of information

In furtherance of the purposes of subsection (a)(2) of this section—

(1) the Commission may, by order, require any person (including any common carrier, tramp operator, bulk operator, shipper, shippers' association, ocean transportation intermediary, or marine terminal operator, or an officer, receiver, trustee, lessee, agent, or employee thereof) to file with the Commission a report, answers to questions, documentary material, or other information which the Commission considers necessary or appropriate;

(2) the Commission may require a report or answers to questions to be made under oath;

（3）the Commission may prescribe the form and the time for response to a report and answers to questions; and

（4）a person who fails to file a report, answer, documentary material, or other information required under this paragraph shall be liable to the United States Government for a civil penalty of not more than $5,000 for each day that the information is not provided.

(g) Discovery; witnesses; evidence

In proceedings under subsection (a)(2) of this section—

（1）the Commission may authorize a party to use depositions, written interrogatories, and discovery procedures that, to the extent practicable, are in conformity with the rules applicable in civil proceedings in the district courts of the United States;

（2）the Commission may by subpoena compel the attendance of witnesses and the production of books, papers, documents, and other evidence;

（3）subject to funds being provided by appropriations Acts, witnesses are, unless otherwise prohibited by law, entitled to the same fees and mileage as in the courts of the United States;

（4）for failure to supply information ordered to be produced or compelled by subpoena under paragraph (2), the Commission may—

（A）after notice and an opportunity for hearing, suspend tariffs and service contracts of a common carrier or that common carrier's right to use tariffs of conferences and service contracts of agreements of which it is a member, or

（B）assess a civil penalty of not more than $5,000 for each day that the information is not provided; and

（5）when a person violates an order of the Commission or fails to comply with a subpoena, the Commission may seek enforcement by a United States district court having jurisdiction over the parties, and if, after hearing, the court determines that the order was regularly made and duly issued, it shall enforce the order by an appropriate injunction or other process, mandatory or otherwise.

(h) Disclosure to public

Notwithstanding any other law, the Commission may refuse to disclose to the public a response or other information provided under the terms of this section.

(i) Finding of unfavorable conditions

If the Commission finds that conditions that are unfavorable to shipping under subsection (a)(2) of this section exist, the Commission may—

（1）limit sailings to and from United States ports or the amount or type of cargo carried;

（2）suspend, in whole or in part, tariffs and service contracts for carriage to or from United States ports, including a common carrier's right to use tariffs of conferences and service contracts of agreements in United States trades of which it is a member for any period the Commission specifies;

(3) suspend, in whole or in part, an ocean common carrier's right to operate under an agreement filed with the Commission, including any agreement authorizing preferential treatment at terminals, preferential terminal leases, space chartering, or pooling of cargoes or revenue with other ocean common carriers;

(4) impose a fee, not to exceed $1,000,000 per voyage; or

(5) take any other action the Commission finds necessary and appropriate to adjust or meet any condition unfavorable to shipping in the foreign trade of the United States.

(j) Refusal of clearance and denial of entry

Upon request by the Commission—

(1) the collector of customs at the port or place of destination in the United States shall refuse the clearance required by section 91 of this Appendix to a vessel of a country that is named in a rule or regulation issued by the Commission under subsection (a)(2) of this section, and shall collect any fees imposed by the Commission under subsection (i) (4) of this section; and

(2) the Secretary of the department in which the Coast Guard is operating shall deny entry for purpose of oceanborne trade, of a vessel of a country that is named in a rule or regulation issued by the Commission under subsection (a)(2) of this section, to any port or place in the United States or the navigable waters of the United States, or shall detain that vessel at the port or place in the United States from which it is about to depart for another port or place in the United States.

(k) Operation under suspended tariff or service contract

A common carrier that accepts or handles cargo for carriage under a tariff or service contract that has been suspended under subsection (g)(4) or (i)(2) of this section, or after its right to use another tariff or service contract has been suspended under those paragraphs, is subject to a civil penalty of not more than $50,000 for each day that it is found to be operating under a suspended tariff or service contract.

(l) Consultation with other agencies

The Commission may consult with, seek the cooperation of, or make recommendations to other appropriate Government agencies prior to taking any action under this section.

(June 5, 1920, ch. 250, §19, 41 Stat. 995; Ex. Ord. No. 6166, §12, eff. June 10, 1933; June 29, 1936, ch. 858, title II, §204, title IX, §904, 49 Stat. 1987, 2016; Pub. L. 97-31, §12(46), Aug. 6, 1981, 95 Stat. 157; Pub. L. 101-595, title I, §103, Nov. 16, 1990, 104 Stat. 2979; Pub. L. 102-587, title VI, §6205(b), Nov. 4, 1992, 106 Stat. 5094; Pub. L. 105-258, title III, §301, Oct. 14, 1998, 112 Stat. 1915.)

REFERENCES IN TEXT

This Act, referred to in subsec. (a), means act June 5, 1920, ch. 250, 41 Stat. 988, as amended, known as the Merchant Marine Act, 1920, which (except for sections repealed or reenacted in Title 46, Shipping) is classified principally to this chapter. For complete classification of this Act to the Code, see section 889 of this Appendix and Tables.

AMENDMENTS

1998—Subsec. (a). Pub. L. 105-258, §301(a)(1)—(3), (b)(1), (2), redesignated par. (1) as subsec. (a) and former subdivs. (a) to (c) as pars. (1) to (3), respectively, and, in par. (2) as redesignated, struck out "forwarding and" before "agency services" and substituted "ocean transportation intermediary services and operations," for "non-vessel-operating common carrier operations," and "methods, pricing practices, or other practices" for "methods or practices".

Subsec. (b). Pub. L. 105-258, §301(b)(1), redesignated par. (2) as subsec. (b).

Subsec. (c). Pub. L. 105-258, §301(b)(1), (8), (9), redesignated par. (3) as subsec. (c) and substituted "subsection (a)(3)" for "subdivision (c) of paragraph (1)" and "subsection (b)" for "paragraph (2)".

Subsec. (d). Pub. L. 105-258, §301(b)(1), redesignated par. (4) as subsec. (d).

Subsec. (e). Pub. L. 105-258, §301(a)(7), (b)(1), (10), redesignated par. (5) as subsec. (e), substituted "transportation intermediary," for "freight forwarder," and substituted "subsection (a)(2)" for "paragraph (1)(b)" in two places.

Subsec. (f). Pub. L. 105-258, §301(b)(1), (10), redesignated par. (6) as subsec. (f) and substituted "subsection (a)(2)" for "paragraph (1)(b)" in introductory provisions.

Subsec. (f)(1). Pub. L. 105-258, §301(a)(7), (b)(3), redesignated subd. (a) as par. (1) and substituted "transportation intermediary," for "freight forwarder".

Subsec. (f)(2) to (4). Pub. L. 105-258, §301(b)(3), redesignated subds. (b) to (d) as pars. (2) to (4), respectively.

Subsec. (g). Pub. L. 105-258, §301(b)(1), (10), redesignated par. (7) as subsec. (g) and substituted "subsection (a)(2)" for "paragraph (1)(b)" in introductory provisions.

Subsec. (g)(1) to (3). Pub. L. 105-258, §301(b)(4), redesignated subds. (a) to (c) as pars. (1) to (3), respectively.

Subsec. (g)(4). Pub. L. 105-258, §301(b)(4), (11), redesignated subd. (d) as par. (4) and substituted "paragraph (2)," for "subdivision (b)," in introductory provisions.

Subsec. (g)(4)(A). Pub. L. 105-258, §301(a)(4), (5), (b)(5), redesignated cl. (i) as subpar. (A) and substituted "tariffs and service contracts of a common carrier" for "tariffs of a common carrier" and "use tariffs of conferences and service contracts of agreements" for "use the tariffs of conferences".

Subsec. (g)(4)(B). Pub. L. 105-258, §301(b)(5), redesignated cl. (ii) as subpar. (B).

Subsec. (g)(5). Pub. L. 105-258, §301(b)(4), redesignated subd. (e) as par. (5).

Subsec. (h). Pub. L. 105-258, §301(b)(1), redesignated par. (8) as subsec. (h).

Subsec. (i). Pub. L. 105-258, §301(b)(1), (10), redesignated par. (9) as subsec. (i) and substituted "subsection (a)(2)" for "paragraph (1)(b)" in introductory provisions.

Subsec. (i)(1). Pub. L. 105-258, §301(b)(6), redesignated subd. (a) as par. (1).

Subsec. (i)(2). Pub. L. 105-258, §301(a)(6), (b)(6), redesignated subd. (b) as par. (2) and substituted "tariffs and service contracts" for "tariffs filed with the Commission".

Pub. L. 105-258, §301 (a) (5), which directed amendment of par. (2) by substituting "use tariffs of conferences and service contracts of agreements" for "use the tariffs of conferences", was executed by making the substitution for "use tariffs of conferences", to reflect the probable intent of Congress.

Subsec. (i)(3) to (5). Pub. L. 105-258, §301(b)(6), redesignated subds. (c) to (e) as pars. (3) to (5), respectively.

Subsec. (j). Pub. L. 105-258, §301(b)(1), redesignated par. (10) as subsec. (j).

Subsec. (j)(1). Pub. L. 105-258, §301(b)(7), (10), (12), redesignated subd. (a) as par. (1) and substituted "subsection (a)(2)" for "paragraph (1)(b)" and "subsection (i)(4)" for "paragraph (9)(d)".

Subsec. (j)(2). Pub. L. 105-258, §301(b)(7), (10), redesignated subd. (b) as par. (2) and substituted "subsection (a)(2)" for "paragraph (1)(b)".

Subsec. (k). Pub. L. 105-258, §301(a)(8), (b)(1), (13), redesignated par. (11) as subsec. (k), substituted "subsection (g)(4) or (i)(2)" for "paragraph (7)(d) or (9) (b)", and substituted "tariff or service contract" for "tariff" wherever appearing.

Subsec. (l). Pub. L. 105-258, §301(b)(1), redesignated par. (12) as subsec. (l).

1992—Par. (1)(b). Pub. L. 102-587, §6205(b)(1), substituted "systems" for "sysetms" after "integral to transportation".

Par. (7)(d). Pub. L. 102-587, §6205(b)(2), substituted "under subdivision (b)" for "in proceedings under paragraph (1)(b)(7) of this section".

1990—Par. (1)(b). Pub. L. 101-595, §103(1), inserted "including intermodal movements, terminal operations, cargo solicitation, forwarding and agency services, non-vessel-operating common carrier operations, and other activities and services integral to transportation sysetms," after "generally".

Pars. (5) to (12). Pub. L. 101-595, §103(2), added pars. (5) to (12).

1981—Par. (1). Pub. L. 97-31 substituted "Secretary of Transportation" for "Commission", and added after subsec. (a) an undesignated paragraph respecting authority of Federal Maritime Commission. For prior transfers of functions, see Transfer of Functions note below.

Effective Date of 1998 Amendment

Amendments by Pub. L. 105-258 effective May 1, 1999, see section 2 of Pub. L. 105-258, set out as a note under section 1701 of this Appendix.

Transfer of Functions

"Commission", meaning United States Maritime Commission, substituted in text for "board", meaning United States Shipping Board. For dissolution of Board and transfer of functions to United States Maritime Commission, see Ex. Ord. No. 6166 and act June 29,

1936. Ex. Ord. No. 6166 is set out as a note under section 901 of Title 5, Government Organization and Employees. For subsequent transfers of functions, see Reorg. Plan No. 6 of 1949, Reorg. Plan No. 21 of 1950, and Reorg. Plan No. 7 of 1961, set out under section 1111 of this Appendix.

Functions of Public Health Service and of all other officers and employees of Public Health Service, and functions of all agencies of or in Public Health Service transferred to Secretary of Health, Education, and Welfare by Reorg. Plan No. 3 of 1966, eff. June 25, 1966, 31 F.R. 8855, 80 Stat. 1610, set out in the Appendix to Title 5. Secretary of Health, Education, and Welfare redesignated Secretary of Health and Human Services by section 509(b) of Pub. L. 96-88, which is classified to section 3508(b) of Title 20, Education.

All offices of collector of customs, comptroller of customs, surveyor of customs, and appraiser of merchandise in Bureau of Customs of Department of the Treasury to which appointments were required to be made by President with advice and consent of Senate ordered abolished with such offices to be terminated not later than Dec. 31, 1966, by Reorg. Plan No. 1 of 1965, eff. May 25, 1965, 30 F.R. 7035, 79 Stat. 1317, set out in the Appendix to Title 5, Government Organization and Employees. All functions of offices eliminated were already vested in Secretary of the Treasury by Reorg. Plan No. 26 of 1950, eff. July 31, 1950, 15 F.R. 4935, 64 Stat. 1280, set out in the Appendix to Title 5.

Steamboat Inspection Service consolidated in Bureau of Marine Inspection and Navigation which was later abolished. Functions relating to inspection of vessels now vested in Commandant of the Coast Guard. See note preceding section 3 of this Appendix.

Section Referred to in Other Sections.

This section is referred to in sections 1273a, 1710a of this Appendix; title 28 section 2342.

§877. Coastwise laws extended to island Territories and possessions

From and after February 1, 1922, the coastwise laws of the United States shall extend to the island Territories and possessions of the United States not covered thereby on June 5, 1920, and the Secretary of Transportation is directed prior to the expiration of such year to have established adequate steamship service at reasonable rates to accommodate the commerce and the passenger travel of said islands and to maintain and operate such service until it can be taken over and operated and maintained upon satisfactory terms by private capital and enterprise: *Provided*, That if adequate shipping service is not established by February 1, 1922, the President shall extend the period herein allowed for the establishment of such service in the case of any island Territory or possession for such time as may be necessary for the establishment of adequate shipping facilities therefor: *And provided further*, That the coastwise laws of the United States shall not extend to the Virgin Islands of the United States until the President of the

United States shall, by proclamation, declare that such coastwise laws shall extend to the Virgin Islands and fix a date for the going into effect of same.

(June 5, 1920, ch. 250, §21, 41 Stat. 997; Ex. Ord. No. 6166, §12, eff. June 10, 1933; Apr. 16, 1936, ch. 228, 49 Stat. 1207; June 29, 1936, ch. 858, title II, §204, title IX, §904, 49 Stat. 1987, 2016; Proc. No. 2695, eff. July 4, 1946, 11 F.R. 7517, 60 Stat. 1352; Pub. L. 97-31, §12(47), Aug. 6, 1981, 95 Stat. 157.)

CODIFICATION

Provisos of this section authorizing the government of Philippine Islands to regulate transportation between ports or places in Philippine Archipelago until Congress authorized registry of vessels owned in those islands, and providing that this section should not go into effect in Philippine Islands until after investigation and proclamation by President, omitted on authority of Proc. No. 2695 of 1946, set out under section 1394 of Title 22, Foreign Relations and Intercourse, which proclaimed independence of Philippines.

AMENDMENTS

1981—Pub. L. 97-31 substituted "Secretary of Transportation" for "Commission". For prior transfers of functions, see Transfer of Functions note below.

1936—Act Apr. 16, 1936, inserted last proviso.

TRANSFER OF FUNCTIONS

"Commission", meaning United States Maritime Commission, substituted in text for "board", meaning United States Shipping Board. For dissolution of Board and transfer of functions to United States Maritime Commission, see Ex. Ord. No. 6166 and act June 29, 1936. Ex. Ord. No. 6166 is set out as a note under section 901 of Title 5, Government Organization and Employees. For subsequent transfers of functions, see Reorg. Plan No. 6 of 1949, Reorg. Plan No. 21 of 1950, and Reorg. Plan No. 7 of 1961, set out under section 1111 of this Appendix.

CANTON ISLAND

Proc. No. 3215, Dec. 12, 1957, 72 Stat. c19, extended period for establishment of adequate shipping service for, and deferred extension of coastwise laws to, Canton Island.

§883. Transportation of merchandise between points in United States in other than domestic built or rebuilt and documented vessels; incineration of hazardous waste at sea

No merchandise, including merchandise owned by the United States Government, a State (as defined in section 2101 of the$^{\underline{1}}$ title 46), or a subdivision of a State, shall be transported by water, or by land and water, on penalty of forfeiture of the merchandise (or a monetary amount up to the value thereof as determined by the Secretary of the Treasury, or the actual cost of the transportation, whichever is greater, to be recovered from any consignor, seller, owner, importer, consignee, agent, or other person or persons so transporting or causing said merchandise to be transported), between points in the United States, including Districts, Territories, and possessions thereof embraced within the coastwise laws, either directly or via a foreign port, or for any part of the transportation, in any other vessel than a vessel built in and documented under the laws of the United States and owned by persons who are citizens of the United States, or vessels to which the privilege of engaging in the coastwise trade is extended by section 808 of this Appendix or section 22 $\frac{2}{}$ of this Act: *Provided*, That no vessel of more than 200 gross tons(as measured under chapter 143 of title 46) having at any time acquired the lawful right to engage in the coastwise trade, either by virtue of having been built in, or documented under the laws of the United States, and later sold foreign in whole or in part, or placed under foreign registry, shall hereafter acquire the right to engage in the coastwise trade: *Provided further*, That no vessel which has acquired the lawful right to engage in the coastwise trade, by virtue of having been built in or documented under the laws of the United States, and which has later been rebuilt shall have the right thereafter to engage in the coastwise trade, unless the entire rebuilding, including the construction of any major components of the hull or superstructure of the vessel, is effected within the United States, its territories (not including trust territories), or its possessions: *Provided further*, That this section shall not apply to merchandise transported between points within the continental United States, including Alaska, over through routes heretofore or hereafter recognized by the Surface Transportation Board for which routes rate tariffs have been or shall hereafter be filed with the Board when such routes are in part over Canadian rail lines and their own or other connecting water facilities: *Provided further*, That this section shall not become effective upon the Yukon River until the Alaska Railroad shall be completed and the Secretary of Transportation shall find that proper facilities will be furnished for transportation by persons citizens of the United States for properly handling the traffic: *Provided further*, That this section shall not apply to the transportation of merchandise loaded on railroad cars or to motor vehicles with or without trailers, and with their passengers or contents when accompanied by the operator thereof, when such railroad cars or motor vehicles are transported in any railroad car ferry operated between fixed termini on the Great Lakes as a part of a rail route, if such car ferry is owned by a common carrier by water and operated as part of a rail route with the approval of the Surface Transportation Board, and if the stock of such common carrier by water, or its predecessor, was owned or controlled by a common carrier by rail prior to June 5, 1920, and if the stock of the common carrier owning such car ferry is, with the approval of the Board, now owned or controlled by any common carrier by rail and if such car ferry is built in and documented under the laws of the United States: *Provided further*, That upon such terms and conditions as the Secretary of the Treasury by regulation may prescribe, and, if the transporting vessel is of foreign registry, upon a finding by the Secretary of the Treasury, pursuant to information obtained and furnished by the Secretary of State, that the government of the nation of registry extends reciprocal privileges to vessels of the United States, this section shall not apply to the transportation by vessels of the United States not qualified to engage in the coastwise trade, or by vessels of foreign registry, of (a) empty cargo vans, empty lift vans, and empty shipping tanks, (b) equipment for use with cargo vans, lift vans, or shipping tanks, (c) empty barges specifically designed for carriage aboard a vessel and equipment, excluding propulsion equipment, for use with such barges, and (d) any empty instrument for international traffic exempted from application of the customs laws by the Secretary of the Treasury pursuant to the provisions of section 1322(a) of title 19, if the articles described in clauses (a) through (d) are owned or leased by the owner or operator of the transporting vessel and are transported for his use in handling his cargo in foreign trade; and (e) stevedoring equipment and material, if such equipment and material is owned or leased by the owner or operator of the transporting vessel, or is owned or leased by the stevedoring company contracting for the lading or unlading of that vessel, and is transported without charge for use in the handling of cargo in foreign trade: *Provided further*, That upon such terms and conditions as the Secretary of the Treasury by regulation may prescribe, and, if the transporting vessel is of foreign registry, upon his finding, pursuant to information furnished by the Secretary of State, that the government of the nation of registry extends reciprocal privileges to vessels of the United States, the Secretary of the Treasury may suspend the application of this section to the transportation of merchandise between points in the United States (excluding transportation between the continental United States and noncontiguous states, districts, territories, and possessions embraced within the coastwise laws) which, while moving in the foreign trade of the United States, is transferred from a non-self-propelled barge certified by the owner or operator to be specifically designed for carriage aboard a vessel and regularly carried aboard a vessel in foreign trade to another such barge owned or leased by the same owner or operator, without regard to whether any such barge is under foreign registry or qualified to engage in the coastwise trade: *Provided further*, That until April 1, 1984, and notwithstanding any other provisions of this section, any vessel documented under the laws of the United States and owned by persons who are citizens of the United States may, when operated upon a voyage in foreign trade, transport merchandise in cargo vans, lift vans, and shipping-tanks between points embraced within the coastwise laws for transfer to or when transferred from another vessel or vessels, so documented and owned, of the same operator when the merchandise movement has either a foreign origin or a foreign destination; but this proviso (1) shall apply only to vessels which that same operator owned, chartered or contracted for the construction of prior to November 16, 1979, and (2) shall not apply to movements between points in the contiguous United States and points in Hawaii, Alaska, the Commonwealth of Puerto Rico and United States territories and possessions. For the purposes of this section, after December 31, 1983, or after such time as an appropriate vessel has been constructed and documented as a vessel of the United States, the transportation of hazardous waste, as defined in section

6903(5) of title 42, from a point in the United States for the purpose of the incineration at sea of that waste shall be deemed to be transportation by water of merchandise between points in the United States: *Provided*, *however*, That the provisions of this sentence shall not apply to this transportation when performed by a foreign-flag ocean incineration vessel, owned by or under construction on May 1, 1982, for a corporation wholly owned by a citizen of the United States; the term "citizen of the United States", as used in this proviso, means a corporation as defined in section 802(a) and (b) of this Appendix. The incineration equipment on these vessels shall meet all current United States Coast Guard and Environmental Protection Agency standards. These vessels shall, in addition to any other inspections by the flag state, be inspected by the United States Coast Guard, including drydock inspections and internal examinations of tanks and void spaces, as would be required of a vessel of the United States. Satisfactory inspection shall be certified in writing by the Secretary of Transportation. Such inspections may occur concurrently with any inspections required by the flag state or subsequent to but no more than one year after the initial issuance or the next scheduled issuance of the Safety of Life at Sea Safety Construction Certificate. In making such inspections, the Coast Guard shall refer to the conditions established by the initial flag state certification as the basis for evaluating the current condition of the hull and superstructure. The Coast Guard shall allow the substitution of an equivalent fitting, material, appliance, apparatus, or equipment other than that required for vessels of the United States if the Coast Guard has been satisfied that fitting, material, appliance, apparatus, or equipment is at least as effective as that required for vessels of the United States[3]: *Provided further*, That for the purposes of this section, supplies aboard United States documented fish processing vessels, which are necessary and used for the processing or assembling of fishery products aboard such vessels, shall be considered ship's equipment and not merchandise: *Provided further*, That for purposes of this section, the term "merchandise" includes valueless material: *Provided further*, That this section applies to the transportation of valueless material or any dredged material regardless of whether it has commercial value, from a point or place in the United States or a point or place on the high seas within the Exclusive Economic Zone as defined in the Presidential Proclamation of March 10, 1983, to another point or place in the United States or a point or place on the high seas within that Exclusive Economic Zone: *Provided further*, That the transportation of any platform jacket in or on a launch barge between two points in the United States, at one of which there is an installation or other device within the meaning of section 1333(a) of title 43, shall not be deemed transportation subject to this section if the launch barge has a launch capacity of 12,000 long tons or more, was built as of June 7, 1988, and is documented under the laws of the United States, and the platform jacket cannot be transported on and launched from a launch barge of lesser launch capacity that is identified by the Secretary of Transportation and is available for such transportation.

(June 5, 1920, ch. 250, §27, 41 Stat. 999; Ex. Ord. No. 6166, §12, eff. June 10,

1933; Apr. 11, 1935, ch. 58, 49 Stat. 154; July 2, 1935, ch. 355, 49 Stat. 442; June 29, 1936, ch. 858, title II, §204, title IX, §904, 49 Stat. 1987, 2016; 1950 Reorg. Plan No. 21, §204, eff. May 24, 1950, 15 F.R. 3178, 64 Stat. 1276; July 14, 1956, ch. 600, §1, 70 Stat. 544; Pub. L. 85-508, §27(a), July 7, 1958, 72 Stat. 351; Pub. L. 86-583, §1, July 5, 1960, 74 Stat. 321; Pub. L. 89-194, Sept. 21, 1965, 79 Stat. 823; Pub. L. 90-474, Aug. 11, 1968, 82 Stat. 700; Pub. L. 92-163, §1, Nov. 23, 1971, 85 Stat. 486; Pub. L. 95-410, title II, §213, Oct. 3, 1978, 92 Stat. 904; Pub. L. 96-112, §4, Nov. 16, 1979, 93 Stat. 848; Pub. L. 97-31, §12(49), Aug. 6, 1981, 95 Stat. 157; Pub. L. 97-389, title V, §§502, 504, Dec. 29, 1982, 96 Stat. 1954, 1956; Pub. L. 100-239, §6(c) (1), Jan. 11, 1988, 101 Stat. 1782; Pub. L. 101-329, §1(a), June 7, 1988, 102 Stat. 588; Pub. L. 102-587, title V, §5501(b), Nov. 4, 1992, 106 Stat. 5085; Pub. L. 104-324, title VII, §747, title XI, §1120(e), Oct. 19, 1996, 110 Stat. 3943, 3978.)

REFERENCES IN TEXT

Section 22 of this Act, referred to in text, is section 22 of act June 5, 1920, which was classified to section 13 of former Title 46, Shipping, and was repealed by Pub. L. 100-710, title II, §202(4), Nov. 23, 1988, 102 Stat. 4753.

The Presidential Proclamation of March 10, 1983, referred to in text, is Proc. No. 5030, Mar. 10, 1983, 48 F.R. 10605, which is set out as a note under section 1453 of Title 16, Conservation.

PRIOR PROVISIONS

Provisions similar to those in this section were contained in act Feb. 17, 1898, ch. 26, §1, 30 Stat. 248, which was classified to section 290 of this Appendix.

AMENDMENTS

1996—Pub. L. 104-324 in first proviso inserted "of more than 200 gross tons (as measured under chapter 143 of title 46)" after "no vessel", in third proviso substituted "Surface Transportation Board" for "Interstate Commerce Commission" and "the Board" for "said Commission", and in fifth proviso substituted "Surface Transportation Board" for "Interstate Commerce Commission" the first place appearing and "Board" for "Interstate Commerce Commission" the second place appearing.

1992—Pub. L. 102-587, in first sentence, substituted "No merchandise, including merchandise owned by the United States Government, a State (as defined in section 2101 of the title 46), or a subdivision of a State," for "No merchandise".

1988—Pub. L. 100-329 inserted provision relating to alternate determination of penalty as based on actual cost of the transportation, and provisos defining term "merchandise" to include valueless material, making section applicable to valueless or dredged material, and relating to transportation of any platform jacket in or on a launch barge.

Pub. L. 100-239 struck out "of more than five hundred gross tons" after "no vessel" in second proviso.

1982—Pub. L. 97-389，§502，inserted provision relating to the transportation of hazardous waste, the proviso thereto for foreign-flag transport, and further provisions relating to standards for and the inspection of vessels engaged in such transport.

Pub. L. 97-389，§504，inserted proviso defining supplies aboard United States fish processing vessels used for fishery products manufacture as ship's equipment.

1981—Pub. L. 97-31 in fourth proviso substituted "Secretary of Transportation" for "Secretary of Commerce". For prior transfers of functions, see Transfer of Functions note below.

1979—Pub. L. 96-112 inserted proviso that, until April 1, 1984, and notwithstanding any other provisions of this section, any vessel documented under the laws of the United States and owned by citizens of the United States could, when operated upon a voyage in foreign trade, transport merchandise in cargo vans, lift vans, and shipping-tanks between points embraced within the coastwise laws for transfer to or when transferred from another vessel or vessels, so documented and owned, of the same operator when the merchandise movement had either a foreign origin or a foreign destination, but that the proviso would apply only to vessels which that same operator owned, chartered or contracted for the construction of prior to Nov. 16, 1979, and would not apply to movements between points in the contiguous United States and points in Hawaii, Alaska, the Commonwealth of Puerto Rico and United States territories and possessions.

1978—Pub. L. 95-410, in first sentence, substituted "forfeiture of merchandise" for "forfeiture thereof" and inserted parenthetical text for forfeiture of a monetary amount up to the value of the merchandise as determined by the Secretary of the Treasury to be recovered from any consignor, seller, owner, importer, consignee, agent, or other person or persons transporting or causing the merchandise to be transported.

1971—Pub. L. 92-163 inserted "and equipment, excluding propulsion equipment, for use with such barges" after "(c) empty barges specifically designed for carriage aboard a vessel" and inserted reciprocity proviso reciprocally permitting foreign-flag specialty barges, specifically designed and regularly carried aboard a barge carrying ship in foreign trade to carry export or import cargo between United States points which has been transferred from one such barge to another.

1968—Pub. L. 90-474 in final proviso designated existing provisions relating to empty cargo vans, empty lift vans, and empty shipping tanks as cl. (a), added cls. (b) to (d), saved modifying provisions relating to empty cargo vans, empty lift vans, and empty shipping tanks so as to render them applicable to cls. (a) to (d), and added cl. (e).

1965—Pub. L. 89-194 inserted proviso that section should not apply to the transportation of empty cargo vans, lift vans, and shipping tanks by vessels of the United States not qualified to engage in the coastwise trade of by vessels of foreign registry so long as such vans or tanks are owned or leased by the owner or operator of the transporting vessels and are being transported for use in the carriage of goods in foreign trade.

1960—Pub. L. 86-583 prohibits the operation in the coastwise trade of a rebuilt vessel unless the entire rebuilding, including the construction of any major components of the hull and superstructure of the vessel, is accomplished in the United States.

1958—Pub. L. 85-508 substituted "including Alaska" for "excluding Alaska".

1956—Act July 14, 1956, inserted proviso to prohibit the operation in coastwise trade of vessels of more than 500 gross tons which have been rebuilt outside the United States.

1935—Act July 2, 1935, amended section generally.

Act Apr. 11, 1935, inserted fifth proviso.

EFFECTIVE DATE OF 1988 AMENDMENT

Section 6 (c) (2) of Pub. L. 100-239 provided that: "Paragraph (1) of this subsection [amending this section] does not apply to a vessel under contract to be purchased or rebuilt entered into before July 28, 1987, if that vessel is rebuilt before July 28, 1990."

EFFECTIVE DATE OF 1960 AMENDMENT

Section 4 of Pub. L. 86-583 provided that: "This Act [amending this section and section 883a of this Appendix] shall be effective from the time of enactment [July 5, 1960] hereof: *Provided, however*, That no vessel shall be deemed to have lost its coastwise privileges as a result of the amendments made by this Act if it is rebuilt within the United States, its Territories (not including trust territories), or its possessions under a contract executed before such date of enactment and if the work of rebuilding is commenced not later than twenty-four months after such date of enactment."

EFFECTIVE DATE OF 1956 AMENDMENT

Section 4 of act July 14, 1956, provided that: "This Act [amending this section and enacting sections 883a and 883b of this Appendix] shall be effective from the date of enactment [July 14, 1956] hereof: *Provided, however*, That no vessel shall be deemed to have lost its coastwise privileges hereunder if it is rebuilt under a contract entered into before such date of enactment and if the work of rebuilding is commenced not later than six months after such date of enactment."

REGULATIONS

Section 3 of Pub. L. 86-583 provided that: "The Secretary of the Treasury shall prescribe such regulations as may be necessary to carry out the purposes of this Act [amending sections 883 and 883a of this Appendix]."

REPEALS

For effect of subtitle IV (§10101 et seq.) of Title 49, Transportation, see note set out preceding section 801 of this Appendix.

TRANSFER OF FUNCTIONS

Functions conferred upon Secretary of Commerce by provisions of Reorg. Plan No. 21 of 1950 to remain vested in Secretary except to extent inconsistent with sections 101(b) and 104(b) of Reorg. Plan No. 7 of 1961. See section 202 of Reorg. Plan No. 7 of 1961, set out under section 1111 of this Appendix.

"Secretary of Commerce" substituted in text for "United States Maritime Commission" on authority of Reorg. Plan No. 21 of 1950, set out under section 1111 of this Appendix, section 306 of which abolished United States Maritime Commission and section 204 of which transferred to Secretary of Commerce such Commission's functions not transferred to Federal Maritime Board.

Previously, "United States Maritime Commission" substituted for "Shipping Board". For dissolution of Board and transfer of functions to United States Maritime Commission, see Ex. Ord. No. 6166 and act June 29, 1936. Ex. Ord. No. 6166 is set out as a note under section 901 of Title 5, Government Organization and Employees. Executive and administrative functions of United States Maritime Commission transferred to Chairman thereof by Reorg. Plan No. 6 of 1949, eff. Aug. 20, 1949, 14 F.R. 5228, 63 Stat. 1069, set out under section 1111 of this Appendix.

CERTIFICATE OF DOCUMENTATION FOR LIQUIFIED GAS TANKER

Section 1120(f) of Pub. L. 104-324 provided that: "Notwithstanding section 27 of the Merchant Marine Act, 1920 (46 App. U.S.C. 883), section 12106 of title 46, United States Code, section 506 of the Merchant Marine Act, 1936 (46 App. U.S.C. 1156) and any agreement with the United States Government, the Secretary of Transportation may issue a certificate of documentation with a coastwise endorsement for a vessel to transport liquified natural gas or liquified petroleum gas to the Commonwealth of Puerto Rico from other ports in the United States, if the vessel—

"(1) is a foreign built vessel that was built prior to the date of enactment of this Act [Oct. 19, 1996]; or

"(2) is documented under chapter 121 of title 46, United States Code, before the date of enactment of this Act, even if the vessel is placed under a foreign registry and subsequently redocumented under that chapter for operation under this section."

NONAPPLICABILITY OF PUB. L. 100-329 TO CERTAIN VESSELS

Section 5501(c) of Pub. L. 102-587 provided that: "The Act of June 7, 1988 (Public Law 100-329; 102 Stat. 588) [amending this section and section 316 of this Appendix, and enacting provisions set out above and below], including the amendments made by that Act, does not apply to a vessel—

"(1) engaged in the transportation of valueless material or valueless dredged material; and

"(2) owned or chartered by a corporation that had on file with the Secretary of Transportation on August 1, 1989, the certificate specified in section 27A of the Merchant Marine Act, 1920 (46 App. U.S.C. 883-1)."

LAUNCH BARGE INVENTORY; PURPOSE; DEVELOPMENT, MAINTENANCE, AND UPDATING; CONTENTS; PUBLICATION OF INITIAL AND CURRENT INVENTORY

Section 1(b) of Pub. L. 100-329 provided that:

"(1) For purposes of interpreting the proviso pertaining to transportation of any platform jacket by launch barge, as added by subsection (a) of this section to section 27 of the Merchant Marine Act, 1920 (46 App. U. S. C. 883), the Secretary of Transportation shall develop, maintain, and periodically update an inventory of launch barges with less than a launch capacity of 12,000 long tons that are qualified to engage in the coastwise trade. Each launch barge listed on such inventory shall be identified by its name, launch capacity, length, beam, depth, and other distinguishing characteristics. For each such launch barge, the name and address of the person to whom inquiries may be made shall also be included on the inventory. A launch barge not listed on such inventory shall be deemed not to be 'a launch barge of lesser launch capacity identified by the Secretary of Transportation' within the meaning of such proviso to section 27 of the Merchant Marine Act, 1920.

"(2) Not later than 15 days after the date of enactment of this Act [June 7, 1988], the Secretary of Transportation shall publish in the Federal Register an initial inventory of launch barges developed and maintained in accordance with paragraph (1) of this subsection.

"(3) Not later than 60 days after the date of enactment of this Act [June 7, 1988], and periodically thereafter, the Secretary shall publish in the Federal Register a current inventory of launch barges developed, maintained, and updated in accordance with paragraph (1) of this subsection."

TRANSPORTATION OF MUNICIPAL SEWAGE SLUDGE

Section 3 of Pub. L. 100-329 provided that: "Notwithstanding the provisions of section 1 of this Act[amending this section and enacting provisions set out as a note above], a vessel may transport municipal sewage sludge if that vessel, regardless of where it was built, is documented under the laws of the United States and, on the date of enactment of this Act [June 7, 1988], that vessel—

"(1) is in use by a municipality for the transportation of sewage sludge; or

"(2) is under contract with a municipality for the transportation of sewage sludge."

VESSEL UNDER CONTRACT WITH MUNICIPALITY FOR TRANSPORTATION OF SEWAGE SLUDGE: APPLICABILITY OF PROVISIONS

Section 4 of Pub. L. 100-329 provided that: "For purposes of the first paragraph of section 805(a) of the Merchant Marine Act, 1936 (46 App. U.S.C. 1223(a)), a vessel described in section 3(2) of this Act[set out as a note above] is not a vessel engaged in domestic intercoastal or coastwise service, but the prohibitions in the second paragraph apply to that vessel."

CERTIFICATE OF DOCUMENTATION TO VESSEL TRANSPORTING VALUELESS MATERIAL IN COASTWISE TRADE, OR DREDGED MATERIAL, WHETHER OR NOT OF VALUE; ISSUANCE, ENDORSEMENT, ETC.

Section 5 of Pub. L. 100-329 provided that: "Notwithstanding the provisions of section 1 of this Act[amending this section and enacting provisions set out as a note above], the Secretary of the department in which the Coast Guard is operating may issue a certificate of documentation under section 12106 of title 46, United States Code, to a vessel that—

"(1) is engaged in transporting only valueless material in the coastwise trade or transporting dredged material, whether or not of value, (A) from a point or place on the high seas within the Exclusive Economic Zone as defined in the Presidential Proclamation of March 10, 1983 [16 U.S.C. 1453 note], to a point or place in the United States or to another point or place on the high seas within such Exclusive Economic Zone or (B) from a point or place within the United States to a point or place on the high seas within such Exclusive Economic Zone;

"(2) had a certificate of documentation issued under section 12105 of that title on October 1, 1987;

"(3) had been sold foreign or placed under a foreign registry before that certificate was issued; and

"(4) was built in the United States;

except that such certificate of documentation shall be endorsed to restrict the use of such vessel to the transportation of valueless material in the coastwise trade, and to the transportation of dredged material, whether or not of value, (i) from a point or place on the high seas within such Exclusive Economic Zone to a point or place in the United States or to another point or place on the high seas within such Exclusive Economic Zone, or (ii) from a point or place within the United States to a point or place on the high seas within such Exclusive Economic Zone."

TRANSPORTATION OF MERCHANDISE OR PASSENGERS WITHIN ALASKA BY FOREIGN BUILT HOVERCRAFT

Pub. L. 95-599, title I, §146, Nov. 6, 1978, 92 Stat. 2714, provided that:

"(a) Effective during the five-year period beginning on the date of enactment of this Act [Nov. 6, 1978], nothing in section 27 of the Merchant Marine Act, 1920 [this section], or any other provision of law restricting the coastwise trade to vessels of the United States shall prohibit the transportation within the State of Alaska of merchandise or passengers by foreign built hovercraft.

"(b) For the purpose of this section the term 'hovercraft' means a vehicle which travels over land or water in a cushion of air generated by such vehicle."

REPORT TO CONGRESS REGARDING EFFECT OF RECIPROCITY PROVISIONS

Section 2 of Pub. L. 92-163 authorized the Secretary of the Treasury, for a period of five years following Nov. 23, 1971, to make a report at the beginning of each regular session to the Congress regarding activities under Pub. L. 92-163, including but not limited to the extent to which foreign governments are extending reciprocal privileges to the vessels of the United States.

ADMISSION OF ALASKA AS STATE

Effectiveness of amendment of this section by Pub. L. 85-508 was dependent upon the admission of Alaska into the Union under section 8(b) of Pub. L. 85-508. Admission was accomplished Jan. 3, 1959, on issuance of Proc. No. 3269, Jan. 3, 1959, 24 F.R. 81, 73 Stat. c16, as required by sections 1 and 8(c) of Pub. L. 85-508. See notes preceding section 21 of Title 48, Territories and Insular Possessions.

Jurisdiction Over Common Carriers Between Ports in Hawaii and Other Ports

Pub. L. 86-3, §18(a), Mar. 18, 1959, 73 Stat. 12, as amended Pub. L. 86-624, §46, July 12, 1960, 74 Stat. 423, provided that: "Nothing contained in this Act shall be construed as depriving the Federal Maritime Board [now Secretary of Transportation] of the exclusive jurisdiction heretofore conferred on it over common carriers engaged in transportation by water between any port in the State of Hawaii and other ports in the United States, or possessions, or as conferring on the Interstate Commerce Commission jurisdiction over transportation by water between any such ports."

[Interstate Commerce Commission abolished and functions of Commission transferred, except as otherwise provided in Pub. L. 104-88, to Surface Transportation Board effective Jan. 1, 1996, by section 702 of Title 49, Transportation, and section 101 of Pub. L. 104-88, set out as a note under section 701 of Title 49. References to Interstate Commerce Commission deemed to refer to Surface Transportation Board, a member or employee of the Board, or Secretary of Transportation, as appropriate, see section 205 of Pub. L. 104-88, set out as a note under section 701 of Title 49.]

Jurisdiction Over Common Carriers Between Ports in Alaska and Other Ports

Section 27(b) of Pub. L. 85-508 provided that: "Nothing contained in this or any other Act shall be construed as depriving the Federal Maritime Board [now Secretary of Transportation] of the exclusive jurisdiction heretofore conferred on it over common carriers engaged in transportation by water between any port in the State of Alaska and other ports in the United States, its Territories or possessions, or as conferring upon the Interstate Commerce Commission jurisdiction over transportation by water between any such ports."

[Interstate Commerce Commission abolished and functions of Commission transferred, except as otherwise provided in Pub. L. 104-88, to Surface Transportation Board effective Jan. 1, 1996, by section 702 of Title 49, Transportation, and section 101 of Pub. L. 104-88, set out as a note under section 701 of Title 49. References to Interstate Commerce Commission deemed to refer to Surface Transportation Board, a member or employee of the Board, or Secretary of Transportation, as appropriate, see section 205 of Pub. L. 104-88, set out as a note under section 701 of Title 49.]

Transportation of Lumber to Puerto Rico

Pub. L. 87-877, §4, Oct. 24, 1962, 76 Stat. 1201, allowed for suspension of this section during a 1-year period beginning Oct. 24, 1962, with respect to transportation of lumber to Puerto Rico from ports or terminal areas in the United States if Secretary of

Commerce determined that no domestic vessel was reasonably available.

Transportation of Coal Between Points in United States in Canadian Vessels

Act Aug. 7, 1956, ch. 1028, 70 Stat. 1090, permitted Canadian vessels to transport coal to Ogdensburg, N.Y., from other points in the United States, on the Great Lakes, or their connecting or tributary waters for a period ending June 30, 1957.

Transportation of Iron Ore in Vessels of Canadian Registry

Act June 24, 1952, ch. 458, 66 Stat. 156, provided for the transportation of iron ore and terminated on Dec. 31, 1952. Similar provisions were contained in the following acts:

Mar. 29, 1951, ch. 25, 65 Stat. 28.

June 30, 1950, ch. 427, §5, 64 Stat. 309.

Mar. 28, 1949, ch. 36, 63 Stat. 16.

Mar. 24, 1948, ch. 144, 62 Stat. 84.

Jan. 27, 1942, ch. 21, 56 Stat. 19, as amended Aug. 1, 1942, ch. 544, 56 Stat. 735, and repealed July 25, 1947, ch. 327, §2b, 61 Stat. 451, eff. six months after July 25, 1947.

May 31, 1941, ch. 158, 55 Stat. 236.

Transportation of Grain Between United States Ports on Great Lakes by Vessels of Canadian Registry During 1951

Act Oct. 10, 1951, ch. 459, 65 Stat. 371, provided for the transportation of grain and terminated on Dec. 31, 1951.

Transportation of Merchandise Between Hyder, Alaska, and United States

Act July 30, 1947, ch. 387, 61 Stat. 632, as amended June 28, 1948, ch. 693, 62 Stat. 1067, provided for the transportation of merchandise between Hyder, Alaska, and United States and terminated on June 30, 1949.

Section Referred to in Other Sections.

This section is referred to in sections 292, 316, 446b, 883-1 of this Appendix; title 19 section 1554; title 46 sections 3704, 12101, 12106, 14305.

---

1 *So in original. The word "the" probably should not appear.*

2 *See References in Text note below.*

3 *So in original. Probably should be followed by a colon.*

---

§883-1. Corporation as citizen; fisheries and transportation of merchandise or passengers between points in United States; parent and subsidiary corporations; domestic built vessels; certificate; surrender of documents on change in status

Notwithstanding any other provision of law, a corporation incorporated under the laws of the United States or any State, Territory, District, or possession thereof, shall be deemed to be a citizen of the United States for the purposes of and within the meaning of that term as used in sections 316, 808, 835, and 883 of this Appendix, and the laws relating to the documentation of vessels, if it is established by a certificate filed with the Secretary of the Treasury as hereinafter provided, that—

(a) a majority of the officers and directors of such corporation are citizens of the United States;

(b) not less than 90 per centum of the employees of such corporation are residents of the United States;

(c) such corporation is engaged primarily in a manufacturing or mineral industry in the United States or any Territory, District, or possession thereof;

(d) the aggregate book value of the vessels owned by such corporation does not exceed 10 per centum of the aggregate book value of the assets of such corporation; and

(e) such corporation purchases or produces in the United States, its Territories, or possessions not less than 75 per centum of the raw materials used or sold in its operations

but no vessel owned by any such corporation shall engage in the fisheries or in the transportation of merchandise or passengers for hire between points in the United States, including Territories, Districts, and possessions thereof, embraced within the coastwise laws, except as a service for a parent or subsidiary corporation and except when such vessel is under demise or bareboat charter at prevailing rates for use otherwise than in the domestic noncontiguous trades from any such corporation to a carrier subject to jurisdiction under subchapter II of chapter 135 of title 49, which otherwise qualifies as a citizen under sections 802 and 803 of this Appendix, and which is not connected, directly or indirectly, by way of ownership or control with such corporation.

As used herein (1), the term "parent" means a corporation which controls, directly or indirectly, at least 50 per centum of the voting stock of such corporation, and (2), the term "subsidiary" means a corporation not less than 50 per centum of the voting stock of which is controlled, directly or indirectly, by such corporation or its parent, but no corporation shall be deemed to be a "parent" or "subsidiary" hereunder unless it is incorporated under the laws of the United States, or any State, Territory, District, or possession thereof, and there has been filed with the Secretary of the Treasury a certificate as hereinafter provided.

Vessels built in the United States and owned by a corporation meeting the conditions hereof which are non-self-propelled or which, if self-propelled, are of less than five hundred gross tons as measured under section 14502 of title 46, or an alternate tonnage measured under section 14302 of that title as prescribed by the Secretary under section 14104 of that title, shall be entitled to documentation under the laws of the United States, and except as restricted by this section, shall be entitled to engage in the coastwise trade and, together with their owners or masters, shall be entitled to all the other benefits and privileges and shall be subject to the same requirements, penalties, and forfeitures as may be applicable in the case of vessels built in the United States and otherwise documented or exempt from documentation under the laws of the United States.

A corporation seeking hereunder to document a vessel under the laws of the United States or to operate a vessel exempt from documentation under the laws of the United States shall file with the Secretary of the Treasury of the United States a certificate under oath, in such form and at such times as may be prescribed by him, executed by its duly authorized of ficer or agent, establishing that such corporation complies with the conditions of this section above set forth. A "parent" or "subsidiary" of such corporation shall likewise file with the Secretary of the Treasury a certificate under oath, in such form and at such time as may be prescribed by him, executed by its duly authorized officer or agent, establishing that such "parent" or "subsidiary" complies with the conditions of this section above set forth, before such corporation may transport any merchandise or passengers for such parent or subsidiary. If any material matter of fact alleged in any such certificate which, within the knowledge of the party so swearing is not true, there shall be a forfeiture of the vessel (or the value thereof) documented or operated hereunder in respect to which the oath shall have been made. If any vessel shall transport merchandise for hire in violation of this section, such merchandise shall be forfeited to the United States. If any vessel shall transport passengers for hire in violation of this section, such vessel shall be subject to a penalty of $200 for each passenger so transported. Any penalty or forfeiture incurred under this section may be remitted or mitigated by the Secretary of the Treasury under the provisions of section 2107(b) of title 46.

Any corporation which has filed a certificate with the Secretary of the Treasury as provided for herein shall cease to be qualified under this section if there is any change in its status whereby it no longer meets the conditions above set forth, and any documents theretofore issued to it, pursuant to the provisions of this section, shall be forthwith surrendered by it to the Secretary of the Treasury.

(June 5, 1920, ch. 250, §27A, as added Pub. L. 85-902, Sept. 2, 1958, 72 Stat. 1736; amended Pub. L. 104-88, title III, §321(2), Dec. 29, 1995, 109 Stat. 950; Pub. L. 104-324, title VII, §706, Oct. 19, 1996, 110 Stat. 3934.)

CODIFICATION

In fourth par., "section 2107(b) of title 46" substituted for "section 7 of title 46, United States Code" on authority of Pub. L. 98-89, §2(b), Aug. 26, 1983, 97 Stat. 598, section 1 of which enacted Title 46, Shipping.

AMENDMENTS

1996—Pub. L. 104-324, in third par., inserted "as measured under section 14502 of title 46, or an alternate tonnage measured under section 14302 of that title as prescribed by the Secretary under section 14104 of that title," after "five hundred gross tons".

1995—Pub. L. 104-88, in first par., substituted "carrier subject to jurisdiction under subchapter II of chapter 135 of title 49, which otherwise" for "common or contract carrier subject to part 3 of the Interstate Commerce Act, as amended, which otherwise".

EFFECTIVE DATE OF 1995 AMENDMENT

Amendment by Pub. L. 104-88 effective Jan. 1, 1996, see section 2 of Pub. L. 104-88, set out as an Effective Date note under section 701 of Title 49, Transportation.

Section Referred to in Other Sections.

This section is referred to in title 30 section 1522; title 46 section 14305.

§883a. Reports required of United States vessels rebuilt abroad; penalty for failure to report; mitigation of penalty

If any vessel of more than five hundred gross tons as measured under section 14502 of title 46, or an alternate tonnage measured under section 14302 of that title as prescribed by the Secretary under section 14104 of that title documented under the laws of the United States, or last documented under such laws, is rebuilt, and any part of the rebuilding, including the construction of major components of the hull and superstructure of the vessel, is not effected within the United States, its Territories (not including trust territories) or its possessions, a report of the circumstances of such rebuilding shall be made to the Secretary of the Treasury, upon the first arrival of the vessel thereafter at a port within the customs territory of the United States, if rebuilt outside the United States, its Territories (not including trust territories), or its possessions, or, in any other case, upon completion of the rebuilding, in accordance with such regulations as the Secretary may prescribe. If the required report is not made, the vessel, together with its tackle, apparel, equipment, and furniture, shall be forfeited, and the master and owner shall each be liable to a penalty of $ 200. Any penalty or forfeiture incurred under this Act may be remitted or mitigated by the Secretary under the provisions of section 2107(b) of title 46.

(July 14, 1956, ch. 600, §2, 70 Stat. 544; Pub. L. 86-583, §2, July 5, 1960, 74 Stat. 321; Pub. L. 104-324, title VII, §707, Oct. 19, 1996, 110 Stat. 3934.)

REFERENCES IN TEXT

This Act, referred to in text, means act July 14, 1956, ch. 600, 70 Stat. 544, as amended, which enacted sections 883a, and 883b of this Appendix, amended section 883 of this Appendix, and enacted provisions set out as a note under section 883 of this Appendix. For complete classification of this Act to the Code, see Tables.

CODIFICATION

"Section 2107 (b) of title 46" substituted in text for "section 5294 of the Revised Statutes of the United States, as amended (U.S.C., title 46, sec. 7)" on authority of Pub. L. 98-89, §2(b), Aug. 26, 1983, 97 Stat. 598, section 1 of which enacted Title 46, Shipping.

Section was enacted as part of act July 14, 1956, and not as part of act June 5, 1920, ch. 250, 41 Stat. 988, known as the Merchant Marine Act, 1920, which comprises this chapter.

AMENDMENTS

1996—Pub. L. 104-324 inserted "as measured under section 14502 of title 46, or an alternate tonnage measured under section 14302 of that title as prescribed by the Secretary under section 14104 of that title" after "five hundred gross tons".

1960—Pub. L. 86-583 provided for a report of the rebuilding of any part of the vessel, including the construction of major components of the hull and superstructure of the vessel, and for a report upon completion of the rebuilding in certain cases.

EFFECTIVE DATE OF 1960 AMENDMENT

Amendment by Pub. L. 86-583 effective July 5, 1960, and effect on rebuilding contracts executed before such date, see section 4 of Pub. L. 86-583, set out as a note under section 883 of this Appendix.

EFFECTIVE DATE

Section effective July 14, 1956, see section 4 of act July 14, 1956, set out as an Effective Date of 1956 Amendment note under section 883 of this Appendix.

REGULATIONS

Secretary of the Treasury to prescribe regulations to carry out the purposes of this section, see section 3 of Pub. L. 86-583, set out as a note under section 883 of this Appendix.

Section Referred to in Other Sections.

This section is referred to in title 46 section 14305.

§883b. Regulations

The Secretary of the Treasury shall prescribe such regulations as may be necessary to carry out the purposes of this Act.

(July 14, 1956, ch. 600, §3, 70 Stat. 544.)

REFERENCES IN TEXT

This Act, referred to in text, means act July 14, 1956, ch. 600, 70 Stat. 544, as amended, which enacted sections 883a, and 883b of this Appendix, amended section 883 of this Appendix, and enacted provisions set out as a note under section 883 of this Appendix. For complete classification of this Act to the Code, see Tables.

CODIFICATION

Section was enacted as part of act July 14, 1956, and not as part of act June 5, 1920, ch. 250, 41 Stat. 988, known as the Merchant Marine Act, 1920, which comprises this chapter.

EFFECTIVE DATE

Section effective July 14, 1956, see section 4 of act July 14, 1956, set out as an Effective Date of 1956 Amendment note under section 883 of this Appendix.

§884. Charges for transportation subject to interstate transportation provisions

No carrier shall charge, collect, or receive for transportation subject to subtitle IV of title 49 of persons or property, under any joint rate, fare, or charge, or under any export, import, or other proportional rate, fare, or charge, which is based in whole or in part on the fact that the persons or property affected thereby is to be transported to, or has been transported from, any port in a possession or dependency of the United States, or in a foreign country, by a carrier by water in foreign commerce, any lower rate, fare, or charge than that charged, collected, or received by it for the transportation of persons, or of a like kind of property, for the same distance, in the same direction, and over the same route, in connection with commerce wholly within the United States, unless the vessel so transporting such persons or property is, or unless it was at the time of such transportation by water, documented under the laws of the United States. Whenever the Secretary of Transportation is of the opinion, however, that adequate shipping facilities to or from any port in a possession or dependency of the United States or a foreign country are not afforded by vessels so documented he shall certify this fact to the Surface Transportation Board, and the Board may, by order, suspend the operation of the provisions of this section with respect to the rates, fares, and charges for the transportation by rail of persons and property transported from, or to be transported to such ports, for such length of time and under such terms and conditions as he may prescribe in such order, or in any order supplemental thereto. Such suspension of operation of the provisions of this section may be terminated by order of the Board whenever the Secretary of Transportation is of the opinion that adequate shipping facilities by such vessels to such ports are afforded and shall so certify to the Board.

(June 5, 1920, ch. 250, §28, 41 Stat. 999; Ex. Ord. No. 6166, §12, eff. June 10, 1933; June 29, 1936, ch. 858, § §204, 904, 49 Stat. 1987, 2016; Pub. L. 97-31, §12 (50), Aug. 6, 1981, 95 Stat. 157; Pub. L. 104-88, title III, §321(3), Dec. 29, 1995, 109 Stat. 950.)

CODIFICATION

"Subtitle IV of title 49" substituted in text for "the Interstate Commerce Act [49 U.S.C. 1 et seq.]" on authority of Pub. L. 95-473, §3(b), Oct. 17, 1978, 92 Stat. 1466, the first section of which enacted subtitle IV of Title 49, Transportation.

AMENDMENTS

1995—Pub. L. 104-88 struck out "common" after first reference to "carrier", substituted "Surface Transportation Board" for "Interstate Commerce Commission", and substituted "Board" for "commission" wherever appearing.

1981—Pub. L. 97-31 substituted "Secretary of Transportation" for "Commission" in two places and "he" for "it". For prior transfers of functions, see Transfer of Functions note below.

EFFECTIVE DATE OF 1995 AMENDMENT

Amendment by Pub. L. 104-88 effective Jan. 1, 1996, see section 2 of Pub. L. 104-

88，set out as an Effective Date note under section 701 of Title 49，Transportation.

REPEALS

For effect of subtitle IV（§10101 et seq.）of Title 49，Transportation，see note set out preceding section 801 of this Appendix.

TRANSFER OF FUNCTIONS

"Maritime Commission"，meaning United States Maritime Commission，substituted in text for "board"，meaning United States Shipping Board. For dissolution of Board and transfer of functions to United States Maritime Commission，see Ex. Ord. No. 6166 and act June 29，1936. Ex. Ord. No. 6166 is set out as a note under section 901 of Title 5，Government Organization and Employees. For subsequent transfers of functions，see Reorg. Plan No. 6 of 1949，Reorg. Plan No. 21 of 1950，and Reorg. Plan No. 7 of 1961，set out under section 1111 of this Appendix.

§885. Association of marine insurance companies; application of antitrust laws

（a）Whenever used in this section—

（1）The term "association" means any association，exchange，pool，combination，or other arrangement for concerted action; and

（2）The term "marine insurance companies" means any persons，companies，or associations，authorized to write marine insurance or reinsurance under the laws of the United States or of a State，Territory，District，or possession thereof.

（b）Nothing contained in the "antitrust laws" as designated in section 12 of title 15，shall be construed as declaring illegal an association entered into by marine insurance companies for the following purposes: To transact a marine insurance and reinsurance business in the United States and in foreign countries and to reinsure or otherwise apportion among its membership the risks undertaken by such association or any of the component members.

（June 5，1920，ch. 250，§29，41 Stat. 1000.）

§887. Partial invalidity

If any provision of this Act is declared unconstitutional or the application of any provision to certain circumstances be held invalid，the remainder of such Act and the application of such provisions to circumstances other than those as to which it is held invalid shall not be affected thereby.

（June 5，1920，ch. 250，§36，41 Stat. 1007.）

REFERENCES IN TEXT

This Act，referred to in text，means act June 5，1920，ch. 250，41 Stat. 988，as amended，known as the Merchant Marine Act，1920，which（except for sections repealed or reenacted in Title 46，Shipping）is classified principally to this chapter. For complete classification of this Act to the Code, see section 889 of this Appendix and Tables.

§888. Definitions

When used in this Act, unless the context otherwise requires, the terms "person", "vessel", "documented under the laws of the United States", and "citizen of the United States" shall have the meaning assigned to them by sections 801, 802, and 803 of this Appendix; and the term "alien" means any person not a citizen of the United States.

(June 5, 1920, ch. 250, §37, 41 Stat. 1008; Pub. L. 86-327, §2, Sept. 21, 1959, 73 Stat. 597.)

REFERENCES IN TEXT

This Act, referred to in text, means act June 5, 1920, ch. 250, 41 Stat. 988, as amended, known as the Merchant Marine Act, 1920, which (except for sections repealed or reenacted in Title 46, Shipping) is classified principally to this chapter. For complete classification of this Act to the Code, see section 889 of this Appendix and Tables.

CODIFICATION

The words "the term 'commission' means the United States Maritime Commission;" were omitted preceding the definition of "alien" in view of Reorg. Plan No. 21 of 1950, §§204, 306, eff. May 24, 1950, 15 F.R. 3178, 64 Stat. 1276, 1277, set out under section 1111 of this Appendix, which abolished United States Maritime Commission and transferred its functions to Federal Maritime Board and to Secretary of Commerce.

AMENDMENTS

1959—Pub. L. 86-327 substituted "sections 1 and 2 of the 'Shipping Act, 1916,' as amended" for "sections 1 and 2 of the 'Shipping Act, 1916,' as amended by this Act", which sections are referred to in the text as "sections 801, 802, and 803 of this Appendix" for purposes of codification.

TRANSFER OF FUNCTIONS

"Commission", meaning United States Maritime Commission, and "United States Maritime Commission" substituted in text for "board" and "Shipping Board", meaning United States Shipping Board, respectively. For dissolution of Board and transfer of functions to United States Maritime Commission, see Ex. Ord. No. 6166 and act June 29, 1936. Ex. Ord. No. 6166 is set out as a note under section 901 of Title 5, Government Organization and Employees. Executive and administrative functions of United States Maritime Commission transferred to Chairman thereof by Reorg. Plan No. 6 of 1949, eff. Aug. 20, 1949, 14 F.R. 5228, 63 Stat. 1069 set out under section 1111 of this Appendix.

Section Referred to in Other Sections.

This section is referred to in title 46 section 31329.

§889. Short title

This Act may be cited as the Merchant Marine Act, 1920.

(June 5, 1920, ch. 250, §39, 41 Stat. 1008.)

REFERENCES IN TEXT

This Act, referred to in text, means act June 5, 1920, ch. 250, 41 Stat. 988, as amended, known as the Merchant Marine Act, 1920, which (except for sections repealed or reenacted in Title 46, Shipping) is classified principally to this chapter. For complete classification of this Act to the Code, see Tables.

附录二

COUNCIL REGULATION (EEC) No 3577/92

of 7 December 1992

applying the principle of freedom to provide services to maritime

transport within Member States (maritime cabotage)

THE COUNCIL OF THE EUROPEAN COMMUNITIES,

Having regard to the Treaty establishing the European Economic Community, and in particular Article 84 (2) thereof,

Having regard to the amended proposal of the Commission[1],

Having regard to the opinions of the European Parliament[2],

Having regard to the opinion of the Economic and Social Committee[3],

Whereas on 12 June 1992, the European Parliament adopted its Resolution on the liberalization of maritime cabotage and its economic and social consequences;

Whereas in accordance with Article 61 of the Treaty freedom to provide services in the field of maritime transport is to be governed by the provisions of the Title relating to transport;

Whereas the abolition of restrictions on the provision of maritime transport services within Member States is necessary for the establishment of the internal market; whereas the internal market will comprise an area in which the free movement of goods, persons, services and capital is ensured;

Whereas therefore freedom to provide services should be applied to maritime transport within Member States;

Whereas the beneficiaries of this freedom should be Community shipowners operating vessels registered in and flying the flag of a Member State whether or not it has a coastline;

Whereas this freedom will be extended to vessels also registered in Euros once that register is approved;

Whereas in order to avoid distortion of competition, Community shipowners exercising the freedom to provide cabotage services should comply with all the conditions for carrying out cabotage in the Member State in which their vessels are registered; whereas Community shipowners operating ships registered in a Member State who do not have the right to carry out cabotage in that State should nevertheless be beneficiaries of this Regulation during a transitional period;

---

[1]　OJ No C 73, 19. 3. 1991, p. 27.

[2]　OJ No C 295, 26. 11. 1990, p. 687, and opinion delivered on 20 November 1992 (not yet published in the Official Journal)

[3]　OJ No C 56, 7. 3. 1990, p. 70.

Whereas the implementation of this freedom should be gradual and not necessarily provided for in a uniform way for all services concerned, taking into account the nature of certain specific services and the extent of the effort that certain economies in the Community showing differences in development will have to sustain;

Whereas the introduction of public services entailing certain rights and obligations for the shipowners concerned may be justified in order to ensure the adequacy of regular transport services to, from and between islands, provided that there is no distinction on the grounds of nationality or residence;

Whereas provisions should be adopted so that safeguard measures can be taken as regards maritime transport markets affected by a serious disturbance or in the event of an emergency; whereas, for this purpose, suitable decision-making procedures should be introduced;

Whereas, in view of the need to ensure the proper functioning of the internal market and of possible adaptations in the light of experience, the Commission should report on the implementation of this Regulation and if necessary submit additional proposals,

HAS ADOPTED THIS REGULATION:

Article 1

1. As from 1 January 1993, freedom to provide maritime transport services within a Member State (maritime cabotage) shall apply to Community shipowners who have their ships registered in, and flying the flag of a Member State, provided that these ships comply with all conditions for carrying out cabotage in that Member State, including ships registered in Euros, once that Register is approved by the Council.

2. By way of derogation, the application of the provision of paragraph 1 requiring that ships fulfil all conditions for carrying out cabotage in the Member State in which they are registered at that time shall be temporarily suspended until 31 December 1996.

Article 2

For the purposes of this Regulation:

1. "maritime transport services within a Member State (maritime cabotage)" shall mean services normally provided for remuneration and shall in particular include:

(a) mainland cabotage: the carriage of passengers or goods by sea between ports situated on the mainland or the main territory of one and the same Member State without calls at islands;

(b) off-shore supply services: the carriage of passengers or goods by sea between any port in a Member State and installations or structures situated on the continental shelf of that Member State;

(c) island cabotage: the carriage of passengers or goods by sea between:

— ports situated on the mainland and on one or more of the islands of one and the same Member State,

— ports situated on the islands of one and the same Member State;

Ceuta and Melilla shall be treated in the same way as island ports.

2. "Community shipowner" shall mean:

(a) nationals of a Member State established in a Member State in accordance with the legislation of that Member State and pursuing shipping activities;

(b) shipping companies established in accordance with the legislation of a Member State and whose principal place of business is situated, and effective control exercised, in a Member State;

or

(c) nationals of a Member State established outside the Community or shipping companies established outside the Community and controlled by nationals of a Member State, if their ships are registered in and fly the flag of a Member State in accordance with its legislation;

3. "a public service contract" shall mean a contract concluded between the competent authorities of a Member State and a Community shipowner in order to provide the public with adequate transport services.

A public service contract may cover notably:

— transport services satisfying fixed standards of continuity, regularity, capacity and quality,

— additional transport services,

— transport services at specified rates and subject to specified conditions, in particular for certain categories of passengers or on certain routes,

— adjustments of services to actual requirements;

4. "public service obligations" shall mean obligations which the Community shipowner in question, if he were considering his own commercial interest, would not assume or would not assume to the same extent or under the same conditions;

5. "a serious disturbance of the internal transport market" shall mean the appearance on the market of problems specific to that market and which:

— are likely to lead to a serious and potentially lasting excess of supply over demand,

— are due to, or aggravated by, maritime cabotage operations, and

— pose a serious threat to the financial stability and survival of a significant number of Community shipowners,

provided that the short-term and medium-term forecasts for the market in question do not indicate any substantial and lasting improvements.

Article 3

1. For vessels carrying out mainland cabotage and for cruise liners, all matters relating to manning shall be the responsibility of the State in which the vessel is registered (flag state), except for ships smaller than 650 gt, where host State conditions may be applied.

2. For vessels carrying out island cabotage, all matters relating to manning shall be

the responsibility of the State in which the vessel is performing a maritime transport service (host State).

3. However, from 1 January 1999, for cargo vessels over 650 gt carrying out island cabotage, when the voyage concerned follows or precedes a voyage to or from another State, all matters relating to manning shall be the responsibility of the State in which the vessel is registered (flag State).

4. The Commission shall make an in-depth examination of the economic and social impact of the liberalization of island cabotage and shall submit a report to the Council before 1 January 1997 at the latest.

On the basis of this report, the Commission shall submit a proposal to the Council which may include adjustments to the manning nationality provisions laid down in paragraphs 2 and 3 so that the definitive system shall be approved by the Council in due time and before 1 January 1999.

Article 4

1. A Member State may conclude public service contracts with or impose public service obligations as a condition for the provision of cabotage services, on shipping companies participating in regular services to, from and between islands.

Whenever a Member State concludes public service contracts or imposes public service obligations, it shall do so on a non-discriminatory basis in respect of all Community shipowners.

2. In imposing public service obligations, Member States shall be limited to requirements concerning ports to be served, regularity, continuity, frequency, capacity to provide the service, rates to be charged and manning of the vessel.

Where applicable, any compensation for public service obligations must be available to all Community shipowners.

3. Existing public service contracts may remain in force up to the expiry date of the relevant contract.

Article 5

1. In the event of a serious disturbance of the internal transport market due to cabotage liberalization, a Member State may request the Commission to adopt safeguard measures.

After consulting the other Member States, the Commission shall decide where appropriate on the necessary safeguard measures, within 30 working days of receipt of the relevant request from a Member State. Such measures may involve the temporary exclusion, not exceeding 12 months, of the area concerned from the scope of this Regulation.

The Commission shall communicate to the Council and the Member States any decision on its safeguard measures.

If after the period of 30 working days the Commission has taken no decision on the subject, the Member State concerned shall be entitled to apply the measures requested until the Commission has taken its decision.

However, in the event of an emergency, Member States may unilaterally adopt the appropriate provisional measures which may remain in force for no more than three months. In such an event, Member States must immediately inform the Commission of the adoption of such measures. The Commission may abrogate the measures or confirm them with or without modification until it takes its final decision in accordance with the second subparagraph.

2. The Commission may also adopt safeguard measures on its own initiative, after consulting the Member States.

Article 6

1. By way of derogation, the following maritime transport services carried out in the Mediterranean and along the coast of Spain, Portugal and France shall be temporarily exempted from the implementation of this Regulation:
— cruise services, until 1 January 1995,
— transport of strategic goods (oil, oil products and drinking water), until 1 January 1997,
— services by ships smaller than 650 gt, until 1 January 1998,
— regular passenger and ferry services, until 1 January 1999.

2. By way of derogation, island cabotage in the Mediterranean and cabotage with regard to the Canary, Azores and Madeira archipelagoes, Ceuta and Melilla, the French islands along the Atlantic coast and the French overseas departments shall be temporarily exempted from the implementation of this Regulation until 1 January 1999.

3. For reasons of socio-economic cohesion, the derogation provided for in paragraph 2 shall be extended for Greece until 1 January 2004 for regular passenger and ferry services and services provided by vessels less than 650 gt.

4. By way of derogation from the second subparagraph of Article 4(1), public service contracts concluded before the date of Croatia's accession may continue to be applied until 31 December 2016.

5. By way of derogation from Article 1(1), until 31 December 2014, cruise services carried out between Croatian ports by ships smaller than 650 gross tonnes shall be reserved to ships registered in, and flying the flag of, Croatia, which are operated by shipping companies, established in accordance with Croatian law, and whose principal place of business is situated, and effective control exercised, in Croatia.

6. By way of derogation from Article 1(1), and for the transitional period until 31 December 2014, the Commission may, upon a substantiated request by a Member State, decide, within 30 working days of receipt of the relevant request, that ships benefiting from the derogation set out in paragraph 5 of this Article shall not carry out cruise services between ports of certain areas of a Member State other than Croatia where it is

demonstrated that the operation of these services seriously disturbs or threatens to seriously disturb the internal transport market in the areas concerned. If after the period of 30 working days the Commission has taken no decision, the Member State concerned shall be entitled to apply safeguard measures until the Commission has taken its decision. In the event of an emergency, the Member State may unilaterally adopt appropriate provisional measures which may remain in force for no more than three months. That Member State shall immediately inform the Commission thereof. The Commission may abrogate the measures or confirm them until it takes its final decision. Member States shall be kept informed.

Article 7

Article 62 of the Treaty shall apply to the matters covered by this Regulation.

Article 8

Without prejudice to the provisions of the Treaty relating to the right of establishment and to this Regulation, a person providing a maritime transport service may, in order to do so, temporarily pursue his activity in the Member States where the service is provided, under the same conditions as are imposed by that State on its own nationals.

Article 9

Before adopting laws, regulations or administrative provisions in implementation of this Regulation, Member States shall consult the Commission. They shall inform the latter of any measures thus adopted.

Article 10

The Commission shall submit to the Council, before 1 January 1995, and thereafter every two years, a report on the implementation of this Regulation and, if appropriate, shall also put forward any necessary proposals.

Article 11

This Regulation shall enter into force on 1 January 1993.

This Regulation shall be binding in its entirety and directly applicable in all Member States.

附录三

COASTAL AND INLAND SHIPPING(CABOTAGE) ACT, 2003

ARRANGEMENT OF SECTIONS

COASTAL AND INLAND SHIPPING
(CABOTAGE) ACT, 2003
2003 ACT No.5

AN ACT TO RESTRICT THE USE OF FOREIGN VESSELS IN DOMESTIC COASTAL TRADE TO PROMOTE THE DEVELOPMENT OF INDIGENOUS TONNAGE AND TO ESTABLISH A CABOTAGE VESSEL FINANCING FUND; AND FOR RELATED MATTERS

Commencement.

[30TH APRIL, 2003]

ENACTED by the National Assembly of the Federal Republic of Nigeria—

PART I.—SHORT TITLE AND INTERPRETATION

Short Title.

1. This Act may be cited as the Costal and Inland Shipping (Cabotage) Act, 2003.

Interpretation.

2. In this Act—

"Cargo" means goods carried in or on a vessel whether or not of commercial value and includes livestock;

"Coastal Trade" or "cabotage" means—

(a) the carriage of goods by vessel, or by vessel and any other mode of transport, from one place in Nigeria or above Nigeria waters to any other place in Nigeria or above Nigeria waters, either directly or via a place outside Nigeria and includes the carriage of goods in relation to the exploration, exploitation or transportation of the mineral or non-living natural resources of Nigeria whether in or under Nigerian waters;

(b) the carriage of passengers by vessel from any place in Nigeria situated on a lake of river to the same place, or to any other place in Nigeria, either directly or via a place outside Nigeria to the same place without any call at any port outside Nigeria or to any other place in Nigeria, other than as an in-transit or emergency call, either directly or via a place outside Nigeria;

(c) the carriage of passengers by vessel from any place in Nigeria to any place above or under Nigerian waters to any place in Nigeria, or from any place above Nigerian waters to the same place or to any other place above or under Nigerian waters where the carriage of the passengers is in relation to the exploration, exploitation or transportation of the mineral or non-living natural resources in or under Nigerian waters; and

(d) the engaging, by vessel, in any other marine *transportation* activity of a commercial nature in Nigerian waters and, the carriage of any goods or substances whether or not of commercial value within the waters of Nigeria;

"enforcement officer" means a person so designated to be an

267

enforcement officer for the purposes of this Act;

"enforcement unit" means the department within the National Maritime Authority charged with the reponsibility of enforcing the provisions of this Act;

"Exclusive Economic Zone" has the meaning given to it under the Exclusive Economic Zone Act Cap 116, Laws of the Federation of Nigeria 1990;

"foreign vessel" means a vessel other than a Nigerian vessel;

"hull" means the shell, or outer casting, and internal structure below the main deck which provide both the floatation envelope and structural integrity to the vessel in its normal operation;

"in-transit call" means any call, other than an emergency or technical call, by a vessel at any place where passenger go ashore temporarily but re-board the vessel before the vessel leaves that place or are transported by land to another location to re-board the same vessel and include cargo not discharged at the transit call;

"inland waters" has the meaning given to it under the National Inland Waters ways Authority Act, 1997;

"licence" means a document issued pursuant to the Act, authorizing a foreign ship or vessel to be registered for participation in the coastal trade while in Nigerian Waters;

"master" in relation to a vessel has the same meaning as in the Merchant Shipping Act Cap. 224, Laws of the Federation of Nigeria 1990;

"Minister" means the head of the Ministry for the time being charged with the responsibility for matters relating to shipping and Ministry has the corresponding meaning;

"Nigerian citizen" means a citizen of Nigeria as defined in the Nigerian Constitution;

"Nigerian Vessel" means a vessel which is registered in Nigeria and has the meaning given to it in Section 23(1) or (2);

"Nigerian waters" shall include inland waters, territorial waters or waters of the Exclusive Economic Zone(respectively, together or any combination thereof) and the meaning given to them by the National Inland;

"owner", in relation to a vessel, includes the person having for the time being, either by law or by contract, the rights of the owner of the ship as regards the possession and use thereof;

"place above Nigerian waters" in the context of "coastal trade" includes any vessel, offshore drilling unit, production platform, artificial island, subsea installation, pumping station, living accommodation, storage structure, loading or landing platform, dredge, floating crane, pipe laying or other barge or pipeline and any anchor cable or rig pad used in connection therewith;

"superstructure" means the main deck and any other structural part above the main deck;

"Territorial waters" has the meaning given to it under the Territorial Waters(Amendment) Act 1998;

"vessel" includes any description of vessel, ship, boat, hovercraft or craft, including air cushion vehicles and dynamically supported craft, designed, used or capable of being used solely or partly for marine navigation and used for the carriage on, through or under water of persons or property without regard to method or lack of propulsion;

"vessel built in Nigeria" means where all the major component of its hull and superstructure are fabricated in Nigeria or assembled entirely in Nigeria;

"vessel wholly manned by Nigerians" means where all the shipboard officers and crew employed aboard the vessel are exclusively of Nigerian citizenship;

"wholly owned Nigerian vessel" means a vessel which is owned and registered in Nigeria whose 64 shares are beneficially owned by Nigerian citizens or a company registered in Nigeria with 100 per centum of its share capital beneficially owned by Nigerian citizens and the share in the vessel and the ship owning company shall be held by Nigerian citizens free from any trust or obligation in favour of non-Nigerians.

PART II.—RESTRICTION OF VESSELS IN DOMESTIC COASTAL TRADE

Prohibition.

3. A vessel other than a vessel wholly owned and manned by a Nigerian citizen, built and registered in Nigeria shall not engage in the domestic coastal carriage or cargo and passengers within the Coastal, Territorial, Inland Waters, Island or any point within the waters of the Exclusive Economic Zone of Nigeria.

Restriction on Towage.

4.—(1) A tug or vessel not wholly owned by a person who is a Nigerian citizen shall not tow any vessel from or to any port or point in Nigerian Waters, or tow any vessel carrying any substance whatsoever whether of value or not or any dredge material whether or not it has commercial value from a port or point within Nigerian waters.

(2) Nothing in this Section shall preclude a foreign vessel from rendering assistance to persons, vessels or aircraft in danger or distress in Nigerian waters.

Carriage of Petroleum Products and ancillary services.

5. A vessel, tug or barge of whatever type other than a vessel, tug

and barge whose beneficial ownership resides wholly in a Nigeria citizen shall not engage in the carriage or materials or supply services to and from oil rigs, platforms and installations or the carriage of petroleum products between oil rigs, platforms and installations whether offshore or onshore or within any ports or points in Nigerian waters.

6. A vessel of whatever type or size shall not engage in domestic trading in the inland waters of Nigeria except a vessel that is wholly owned by Nigerian citizens.

Navigation in inland waters.

7. —(1) In the case of rebuilding a vessel, such vessel, shall be eligible for cabotage services if the entire rebuilding including the construction of any major components of the hull or superstructure of the vessels is effected in Nigeria.

Rebuilt vessels.

(2) Vessels built in a foreign yard but forfeited to any Nigerian Governmental authority for breach of any laws of Nigeria or captured as war prizes are exempted from the Nigerian built requirement.

8. —(1) Sections 3-6 apply to every foreign vessel except any foreign vessel that is—

Application to foreign vessels.

(a) engaged in salvage operations provided such salvage operation is determined by the Minister to be beyond the capacity of Nigerian owned and operated salvage vessels and companies;

(b) engaged with the approval of the Minister *or any other relevant government agency* in activities related to a marine pollution emergency or to any threatened risk thereof;

(c) engaged in any ocean research activity commissioned by the Department of Fisheries or any other department of the government responsible for such research; or

(d) operated or sponsored by a foreign government that has sought and received the consent of the Minister of Foreign Affairs to conduct Marine Scientific Research.

(2) *Notwithstanding the provisions of subsection (1), the requirement for ministerial determination shall not apply to any vessel engaged in salvage operations for the purpose of rendering assistance to person, vessels or aircraft in danger or distress in Nigerian waters;*

PART III.—WAIVERS

9. The Minister may on the receipt of an application grant a waiver *to a duly registered vessel* on the requirement for a vessel under this Act to be wholly owned by Nigerian citizens where he is satisfied that there is no *wholly* Nigerian owned vessel that is suitable and available to provide the services or perform the activity described in the application.

Waiver on wholly Nigerian ownership.

10. The Minister may on the receipt of an application grant a

Waiver on manning requirement.

waiver *to a duly registered vessel* on the requirement for a vessel under this Act to be wholly manned by Nigerian citizens where he is satisifed that there is no qualified Nigerian officer or crew for the position specified in the application.

Waiver on Nigerian built vessels.

11. —(1) The Minister may on the receipt of an application grant a waiver *to a duly registered vessel* on the requirement for a vessel under this Act to be built in Nigerian where he is satisifed that no Nigerian shipbuilding Company has the capacity to construct the particular type size of vessel specified in the application.

(2) *The Ministry shall immediately after the commencement of this Act compile and publish information on the type, size and characteristic of vessels and craft which are built in Nigeria.*

Order for granting of waivers.

12. Where the circumstances described in Sections 9-11 apply, *and the Minister has determined that a waiver be granted, the order for granting the waiver shall be—*

(*a*) in the first instance, to a shipping company and vessels owned by a joint venture arrangement between Nigerians citizens and non-Nigerians—

(*i*) the equity shareholding of the Nigerian(s) joint venture partner in the vessel and the shipping company shall not be less than 60 *per centum; and*

(*ii*) *the percentage so determined to be held by Nigerian joint venture partner is held by Nigerian citizen(s) free from any trust or obligation in favour of non-Nigerians; and*

(*b*) in the *second instance, to* any vessel registered in Nigeria and owned by a shipping company registered in Nigeria provided that the applicant shall comply with all the relevant provisions of this Act.

Duration of a waiver.

13. A waiver granted under this Act shall *specify* the period of time for which it shall be valid, which period shall not in any circumstance exceed one (1) year.

Minister to issue guidelines on waivers.

14. —(1) The Minister shall immediately after the commencement of this Act, establish *and publish the* criteria and guidelines for the issuance of waivers under this Act.

(2) *The waiver system provided for under this Act may be reviewed after five (5) years from the commencement of this Act by the National Assembly.*

PART IV.—LICENCE TO FOREIGN VESSEL

Grant of licence to foreign vessels and conditions.

15. —(1) Upon application for a licence by a person resident in Nigeria acting on behalf of a foreign owned vessels; the Minister may issue a restricted licence *for* the foreign owned vessel *to be registered* for participation in the Coastal Trade, where the Minister is satisfied that—

(*a*) any of the circumstances in sections 9-12 is applicable;

(*b*) the foreign owned vessel is eligible to be registered in Nigeria;

(*c*) the owning company of the foreign vessel has a representative office in Nigeria;

(*d*) all applicable duties, levies and tariffs imposed by the relevant authorities applicable to foreign vessels with respect to its participation in the Costal Trade have been paid;

(*e*) the foreign vessel possess all certificates and documents in compliance with international and regional maritime conventions whether or not Nigeria is a party to the conventions and that such certificates and documents are current and valid; and

(*f*) the foreign vessel meets all safety and pollution requirements imposed by Nigerian law and any international conventions in force.

(2) In making a determination referred to in subsection (1), the Minister may request from the applicant for the licence to which the determination relates, and from the owner of any Nigerian vessel to which the determination relates, such information and documentation as the Minister may deem necessary.

(3) The issuance of a licence pursuant to subsection (7) does not affect the application to such foreign vessel of any Nigerian law that imposes safety or pollution prevention requirements in respect of vessels.

(4) The licence issued under subsection (1) shall be carried on board the vessel at all times.

16. —(1) The Minister may issue a licence under section 15 subject to any terms and conditions that the Minister considers appropriate including without restricting the generality of the foregoing terms and conditions respecting— *Terms and conditions of licence.*

(*a*) the service or foregoing that is to be performed by the foreign vessel to which the licence relates; and

(*b*) the place or places where the foreign vessel may perform that service or activity.

(2) Any licence granted under section 15 shall be for a fee and the Minister shall, by a notice in the Gazette, specify the amount of the licence fee and the terms thereof.

17. A licence issued pursuant to section 15 to a foreign vessel shall set out the period of time for which it is valid, which period shall not exceed one (1) year or the term of any certificate or document referred *Duration of licence.*

to in section 15(1)(e) provided that the licence term shall not in any circumstance exceed one year.

Suspension cancellation and variation of licence.

18. The Minister may by order, suspend or cancel a licence or vary the terms and conditions of a licence where—

(a) the owner or master of the licencsed vessel is convicted of an offence under this or any other Act of the National Assembly relating to navigation or shipping;

(b) there has been a contravention of or failure to comply with any term or condition to which the licence is subject to; or

(c) it is expedient to cancel, suspend or vary the licence or permit for reasons of national or public interest.

Tariff on licence.

19. Where it is deemed expedient to grant a licence in conformity with the provision of this Act, the Minister shall impose a tariff on the vessel as a condition for granting the waiver.

Minister to issue guidelines on licence.

20. The Minister shall immediately after the commencement of this Act, establish *and publish the criteria and guidelines for the issuance of licences under this Act.*

Operating without licence.

21. A foreign owned and foreign crewed vessel shall not participate in the domestic coastal trade without the licence and authorization required by the provisions of this Act.

PART V.—REGISTRATION

Registration.

22. —(1) Notwithstanding the provisions of any other laws and subject to section 47 every vessel intended for use under this Act shall be duly registered by the Registrar of Ships in the Special Register for Vessels and Ship Owning Companies engaged in Cabotage and shall meet all the requirements for eligibility as set forth under this Act and the Merchant Shipping Act and its amendments to the extent that the said Merchant Shipping Act is not inconsistent with the provisions of this Act.

Cap. 224 LFN.

(2) A vessel intended for use in the domestic trade whether for coastal or inland waters shall obtain all the applicable licences and permits as shall from time to time be determined by the Minister and the relevant Agencies of the Government.

(3) In order to carry out its functions under this Act, the Minister shall on a continuous basis collect information and keep records in the Special Register concerning the *availability*, characteristics and uses of Nigerian vessels.

(4) The Minister shall immediately after the commencement of this Act issue appropriate guidelines and criteria for the registration of bareboat chartered vessel in the Cabotage Register.

(5) Vessels eligible for registration under this Act include:

(*a*) passenger vessels;

(*b*) crew boats;

(*c*) bunkering vessels;

(*d*) fishing trawlers;

(*e*) barges;

(*f*) off-shore service vessels;

(*g*) tugs;

(*h*) anchor handling tugs and supply vessels;

(*i*) floating Petroleum storage;

(*j*) dredgers;

(*k*) tankers;

(*l*) carriers; and

(*m*) any other craft or vessel used for carriage on, through or underwater of persons, property or any substance whatsoever.

23. —(1) Subject to sections 9-12 a vessel shall not be registered for use in the domestic trade unless the Minister is satisfied that— Ownership requirements.

(*a*) the vessel is wholly and beneficially owned by Nigerian citizens or *by a company wholly and beneficially owned by Nigeria citizens and a vessel or company is wholly and beneficially owned by Nigerian citizens where all the shares in the vessel and the company are held by Nigerian citizens free from any trust or obligation in favour of any person not a citizen of Nigeria*;

(*b*) the vessel is on *bareboat* charter to Nigerian citizens and is under this full control and management of Nigerian citizens or *a company* wholly and beneficially owned by Nigerian citizens in terms of subsection (1)(*a*);

(*c*) *the vessel is owned by a company registered in Nigeria and the percentage of shares in the company owned by Nigerian citizens is not less than 60 per centum*;

(*d*) *any foreign vessel is licenced in compliance with Part II of this Act*;

(*e*) the vessel is exclusively manned by officers and crew of Nigerian citizenship *except where Section 10 applies*; and

(*f*) the vessel possesses all certificates and documents in compliance with international and regional maritime conventions to which Nigeria is a party including all safety and pollution requirements imposed by a Nigerian law and any international convention in force.

(2) A vessel shall not be registered for use in the domestic trade unless the controlling interest in the company is owned by Nigerian

Citizens.

(3) The *controlling interest shall not be deemed to be vested in Nigerian Citizens*—

  (*i*) if the title to a majority of the shares thereof or 60 per centum are not held by such citizens free from any trust or fiduciary obligation in favour of any person not a citizen of Nigerian; or

  (*ii*) if the majority of the voting power in such company is not held by citizens of Nigeria; or

  (*iii*) if through any contract or understanding it is so arranged that more than 40 per centum of the voting power may be exercised, directly or indirectly on behalf of any person who is not a citizen of Nigeria; or

  (*iv*) if by any other means whatsoever control of any interest in the company in excess of 40 per centum is conferred upon or permitted to be exercised by any person who is not a citizen of Nigeria.

Proof of ownership.

24. In the performance of his duties under this Part, the Minister shall take due care and carry out adequate investigation to ascertain the true ownership of vessels and ship owning companies and shall issue guidelines for determination thereof which shall include—

(*a*) the last certificate of registration of the vessel;

(*b*) the bill of sale;

(*c*) the ownership of shares in the company applying to be registered;

(*d*) the apportionment of shares in the vessel;

(*e*) a certificate under oath sworn to in a court of superior records by the owner, its duly authorized officer or agent establishing that such applicant has complied with the condition of this Act; and

(*f*) affidavit or statutory declaration by the owners of the owning company sworn to in a court of superior records stating their shares and the capacity in which the shares are held; and

(*g*) such further requirements as the Minister may specify.

Deletion from Registry.

25. Any vessel registered, granted a licence or permit in accordance with the provisions of this Act shall be deleted from the registry where it is determined that—

(*a*) a subsequent change in the ownership structure of the vessel or the owning company as the case may be has contravened the provisions of this Act under which the vessel was registered and the relevant provisions of the Merchant Shipping Act; or

(*b*) the required certification and documentation has expired or it is no longer eligible for registration under the Merchant Shipping Act or under this Act.

26. —(1) In the case of ship mortgage or ship financing by financial institutions a vessel would be eligible for registration under this Act where the following requirements are satisifed—

(*a*) the vessel shall be under charter for a term hot less than three years; and

(*b*) the charterer or mortgagee shall meet the citizenship requirement for operating vessels in the domestic coastal trade under Parts II and IV of this Act;

(2) In addition to the requirements under subsection (1), the charterer or mortgagee shall before registration produce an affidavit sworn to by the financial institutions in a court of superior *records* certifying that the financial institution's interest is solely and primarly a financial investment without the ability and intent to contract the vessel's operation to a non-citizen and that it does not derive a majority of its aggregate revenue from the operation or management of the vessel.

Citizenship requirement for ship financing.

27. The Minister shall immediately after the commencement of this Act issue regulations and guidelines which shall permit foreign owned vessels engaged in the domestic trade, a temporary registration in the Nigerian Registry, which registration shall cover the duration of the contract for which the vessels are employed.

Temporary registration.

28. Any vessel registered under this Nigerian Registry at the date of coming into force of this Act and who is over 15 years old shall continue to be eligible for participation in the coastal trade for a period of five years after the commencement of this Act provided the vessel possesses a certificate of registry and a certificate of seaworthiness from a recognized classification authority.

Age of vessels.

PART VI.—ENFORCEMENT

29. —(1) For the purpose of enforcing this Act, the Minister shall maintain in the office of the Registrar of Ships a separate Register for vessels intended for use in the domestic coastal and inland waters trade under this Act to be called Special Register for Vessels.

Special Register.

(2) Notwithstanding the provisions of any other laws, the Register for vessels involved in the coastal and inland waters trade under subsection (1) of this section shall be for both large and small vessels.

30. —(1) The Minister shall immediately after the commencement of this Act create an enforcement unit within the National Maritime Authority with appropriate operational guidelines and shall designate the officers in that unit as enforcement officers.

Enforcement unit and officers.

(2) The National Maritime Authority shall issue every enforcement

officer with an identity card of that designation which specifies the officer's name and office, and on which appears a recent photograph of the enforcement officer.

(3) In carrying out the duties and functions of an enforcement officer under this Act, an enforcement officer shall, if so requested, produce the identity card referred to in subsection (2) of this section to the person appearing to be in charge of any ship in respect of which the enforcement officer is acting.

Powers of enforcement officers.

31. —(1) Where an enforcement officer believes on reasonable grounds that a vessel has contravened the provisions of this Act, the enforcement officer may stop and board the vessel, *detain* the vessel or its officers or both and, with a warrant, search the vessel and seize anything found in or on both vessel that the enforcement officer, believes on reasonable grounds shall afford evidence with respect to any contravention of this Act.

(2) Notwithstanding the provisions of any existing Act, an enforcement officer may carry out the powers under subsection (1) of this section without a warrant if by reason of exigencies it would not be practicable to obtain a warrant.

(3) While carrying out any of the powers under this section, an enforcement officer may—

(a) require the owner, master or any other person who may have possession of the official log book of the ship, or any other document or paper that may provide evidence of the contravention, to produce, for inspection or for the purposes of obtaining copies thereof or extracts therefrom, the log book or other document or paper;

(b) require the master of such ship to give such information relating to the ship, cargo, stores, crew, passengers or voyage as he may consider necessary;

(c) require the master or any person found on board the ship to give all reasonable assistance in the power of the master or other person, as the case may be, to enable the enforcement officer to carry out the enforcement officer's duties and functions under this Act; and

(d) where necessary enlist the assistance of the Nigerian Customs Service, the Nigerian Navy, the Nigerian Police and any other law enforcement agencies as he may deem necessary.

Detention order.

32. —(1) Where an enforcement officer believes on reasonable grounds that an offence under this Act has been committed by or in respect of a vessel, the enforcement officer may without a court order by reasons of exigent circumstance make a detention order in respect of the ship.

(2) A detention order made under subsection (1) shall as soon as it is practicable be registered in court.

33. Notwithstanding the provisions of any other laws, no port clearance shall be granted to a vessel engaged in domestic coastal shipping unless the owner, charterer, master or agent satisfies the proper customs or such other authority authorized to issue port clearance that the vessel is licensed to engage in domestic shipping or has the prescribed waiver.

Port clearance to vessels.

34. Any person engaged in the business of employing vessels for the domestic coastal trade shall specify and publish all the requirements to be satisfied with respect to the employment of vessels.

Publishing requirements for employment of vessels.

PART VII.—OFFENCES

35. —(1) A vessel commits an offence if the vessel contravenes;

Offences against this Act.

(*a*) sections 3-6 and is liable on conviction to a fine of not less than ₦ 10,000,000.00 and or forfeiture of the vessel involved in the offence or such higher sum as the Court may deem fit.

(*b*) section 21 and is *liable* on conviction to a fine of not less than ₦ 15,000,000.00 and or forfeiture of the vessel or such higher sum as the Court may deem fit and.

(*c*) section 22 and is liable on conviction to a fine of not less than ₦ 5,000,000.00.

36. Any person who without reasonable excuse; fails to comply with a requirement made, or direction given, by an enforcement officer under this Act commits an offence and shall on conviction if it is an individual, be liable to a fine not less than ₦ 100,000.00 and if the offence is committed by a body corporate, be liable to a fine of not less than ₦ 5,000,000.00.

Failure to comply with a requirement etc., of an enforcement officer.

37. —(1) A person shall not, in purported compliance with a requirement under this Act or for any other reason, provide to the relevant governmental authorities or an enforcement officer—

False or misleading statements.

(*a*) information that is, to the person's knowledge false or misleading in a material particular; or

(*b*) any document containing information that is, to the person's knowledge false or misleading in a material particular.

(2) Any person who contravenes subsection (1) shall be guilty of an offence and on conviction, if it is an individual be liable to a fine not less than ₦ 500,000.00 and if it is a body corporate to a fine not less than ₦ 15,000,000.00 and or forfeiture of the vessel involved with the offence.

Deemed separate offence.

38. When an offence is committed by a vessel under sections 3, 4, 5, 6 and 21 on more than one day or is continued by the vessel for more than one day, it shall be deemed to be a separate offence for each day on which the offence is committed or continued.

Liability of ship owners, companies and officers.

39. —(1) Where an offence is committed under this Act or regulations made under it by a vessel, a ship owning company or a body of persons—

(*a*) in the case of a vessel, the shipping company responsible for the vessel or the captain of the vessel shall be deemed to have committed the offence.

(*b*) in the case of a ship owning company or a body corporate other than a partnership, every director or an officer of the company or body shall also be deemed to have committed the offence;

(*c*) in the case of a partnership every partner or officer of that body shall also be deemed to have committed that offence.

(2) Any activity engaged in on behalf of a body corporate or a natural person by a director, officer or agent of the body, or an officer or agent of the person, within the scope of his or her actual or apparent authority is to be taken, for the purposes of a prosecution for an offence under this Act, to have been engaged in also by the body or person.

(3) An officer may be prosecuted and convicted of an offence under subsection (1) whether or not the body corporate has been prosecuted for or convicted of the offence.

(4) In this section an officer in relation to an offence committed by a body corporate, means—

(*a*) a director of the body corporate or other person however described, responsible for the direction, management and control of the body corporate; or

(*b*) any other person who is concerned in, or takes part in the management of the body corporate and whose responsibilities include duties with respect to the matters giving rise to the offence.

(5) A reference in this section to director of a body corporate is to be read as including a reference to a member of a body corporate incorporated under the laws of the Federal Republic of Nigeria.

(6) A reference in this section to engage in an activity is to be read as including a reference to failing or refusing to engage in the activity.

Strict liability and general penalty.

40. Any person who contravenes any provision of this Act or any regulations made there under commits an offence and shall on conviction, where no specific penalty is prescribed thereof, be liable to a fine not less than ₦ 500,000,00.

41. Jurisdiction over the matters and offence referred to in this Act lie with the Federal High Court.

Jurisdiction.

PART VIII.—CABOTAGE VESSEL FINANCING FUND

42. —(1) There is established a fund to be known as the Cabotage Vessel Financing Fund(herein in this Act referred to as "the Fund")

Cabotage Vessel Financing Fund.

(2) The purposes of the Fund shall be to promote the development of indigenous ship acquisition capacity by providing financial assistance to Nigerian operators in the domestic coastal shipping.

43. There shall be paid into the Fund—

Funding.

(*a*) *a surcharge of 2 per centum of the contract sum performed by any vessel engaged in the coastal trade*;

(*b*) a sum as shall from time to time be determined and approved by the National Assembly;

(*c*) *monies generated under this Act including the tariffs, fines and fees for licences and waivers*;

(*d*) such further sums accruable to the Fund by way of interests paid on and repayment of the principal sums of any loan granted from the Fund.

44. *The fund shall be collected by the National Maritime Authority and deposited in commercial banks and administered under guideline that shall be proposed by the Minister and approved by the National Assembly.*

Collection etc, fund.

45. *The beneficiaries of the fund shall be Nigerian citizens and shipping companies wholly owned by Nigerians.*

Beneficiaries.

PART IX.—MISCELLANEOUS

46. —(1) The Minister shall, in accordance with this Act and as practicable after the commencement of this Act make regulations for the purposes of this Act, and, in particular, may make regulations prescribing the criteria to be applied by the Minister for the making of the determinations referred to in sections 9-16.

Regulations.

(2) The Minister may from time to time make regulations for all or any of the following purposes:

(*a*) prescribing the manner or content of applications notice, or any other documentation or informations as may be required under this Act;

(*b*) prescribing the fees payable or the methods for calculating fees and recovering costs in respect of applications for permits, licences, loans and guarantees or other matters under this Act;

(*c*) prescribing the amount, methods for calculating the amount, and circumstances and manner in which holders of licences and permits shall be able to pay for participation in the domestic coastal trade under this Act;

(*d*) requiring the holders of permits and licences granted for any activity under this Act to keep records for any purpose under this Act and prescribing the nature of records, information, and returns, and the form, manner, and times in or at which they shall be kept or furnished;

(*e*) requiring any person engaged in the employment of vessels for the domestic coastal trade to publish their pre-tender qualifications with respect to the desired vessels within a prescribed period; and

(*f*) providing for any other such matters as are contemplated by, or necessary for giving full effect to this Act and for its due administration.

Licence waivers on board.

47. Licences, waivers, approvals or permits referred to in this Act shall be carried on board the vessel at all times.

Requisition of vessels by Minister.

48. The Minister may in times of economic crisis or national emergency, by order, compel vessels registered under this Act, to provide essential services to sustain basic needs of people or to fulfil existing multi-lateral agreements.

Powers of delegation.

49. —(1) The Minister may by instrument delegate his powers, duty or function under this Act to any person to be exercised or performed by such person, as the case may be, and, if so exercised or performed, shall be deemed to have been exercised by the Minister.

(2) Any delegation by the Minister under this section may be revoked by instrument.

Units of accounts.

50. —(1) Where any sum of money is mentioned in this Act, it shall be the value of such sum of money at the date of the coming into force of this Act.

(2) The value of such money shall be determined by the Central Bank of Nigeria from time to time and may be made public as and when required by the courts.

Transitional Provisions.

51. The provisions under this Act shall be enforced from the first anniversary of the day on which this Act comes into force, that is to say, 1(one) year after the commencement date of this Act.

Vessels valid licence on Cap. 224 LFN. 1990. Cap. 404 LFN 1990.

52. In the case of any vessel that, immediately prior to the coming into force of this Act, is operating pursuant to a valid coastal trade licence under the Merchant Shipping Act or Sea Fisheries Act, the provisions of this Act shall apply to that vessel in respect of any activity authorized to be performed by the licence from the day that licence would otherwise have expired had this Act not come into force.

53. —Any provision of any existing laws with respect to the registration of vessels, ownership, size and type of vessels, participation in Nigerian domestic coastal and inland waters trade in whatever form that is inconsistent with the provisions of this Act is repealed in so far as it affects matters under this Act and in particular as set out in the Schedule to this Act.

Repeals and amendments.

Schedule.

54. All of the provisions of the Merchant Shipping Act and other relevant legislation and regulations that are in force immediately before the commencement of this Act shall, so far as they are consistent with this Act continue to be in force.

Savings Cap. 224 LFN 1990.

55. Except as expressly provided in this Act, nothing in this Act shall effect the rights of any party to any proceedings commenced in any court on or before the commencement of this Act.

Savings as to court proceeding.

SCHEDULE

Section 53

Short title of the Act	*Repeal or Amendment*
Merchant Shipping Act, Cap. 224, Laws of the Federation of Nigeria, 1990	Section 5 is repealed
Merchant Shipping (Manning) Regulations Cap. 224, Laws of the Federation of Nigeria 1990.	Regulations 1(2) is repealed.
Merchant Shipping(Licenced Ships) Regulations Cap. 224, Laws of the Federation of Nigeria 1990.	Regulation 1 is repealed.
The Finance(Control and Management) Act, Cap. 144, Laws of the Federation of Nigeria 1990. The Coastal and Inland Shipping(Cabotage) Act 2003.	In First Schedule, Part II, insert after paragraph 8, paragraph 9- "9 Cabotage Vessel Financing Fund: The Fund established by section 45 of the Coastal and Inland Shipping (Cabotage) Act, 2003"

I certify, in accordance with Section 2(1) of the Acts Authentication Act, Cap. 4, Laws of the Federation of Nigeria 1990, that this is a true copy of the Act passed by both Houses of the National Assembly.

IBRAHIM SALIM, CON.
Clerk to the National Assembly
23rd April, 2003

EXPLANATORY MEMORANDUM

This Act restricts the use of foreign vessels in domestic Coastal Trade, promotes the development of indigenous tonnage and establishes a Cabotage Vessel financing Fund.

SCHEDULE TO THE COASTAL AND INLAND SHIPPING(CABOTAGE) BILL, 2003

(1) Short Title of the Bill	(2) Long Title of the Bill	(3) Summary of Contents of the Bill	(4) Date passed by Senate	(5) Date passed by House of Representatives
The Coastal and Inland Shipping(Cabotage) Bill, 2003.	An Act to restrict the use of foreign vessels in domestic Coastal Trade, to promote the development of indigenous tonnage and to establish a cabotage vessel financing fund; and for related matters.	This Bill seeks to restrict the use of foreign vessels in domestic Coastal Trade, to promote the development of indigenous tonnage and to establish a cabotage vessel financing fund.	6-3-2003	12-3-2003

I certify that this Bill has been carefully compared by me with the decision reached by the National Assembly and found by me to be true and correct decision of the Houses and is in accordance with the provisions of the Acts Authentication Act Cap. 4, Laws of the Federation of Nigeria 1990.

IBRAHIM SALIM, CON
Clerk to the National Assembly
23rd April, 2003

CHIEF OLUSEGUN OBASANJO, GCFR
President of the Federal Republic of Nigeria
30th April, 2003

I ASSENT.

图书在版编目(CIP)数据

沿海运输权法律问题研究/马得懿著.—上海:
上海人民出版社,2023
(国际法与涉外法治文库)
ISBN 978-7-208-18436-7

Ⅰ.①沿… Ⅱ.①马… Ⅲ.①海上运输-货物运输-
海商法-中国 Ⅳ.①D922.294

中国国家版本馆 CIP 数据核字(2023)第 140570 号

责任编辑　罗俊华
封面设计　谢定莹

国际法与涉外法治文库

沿海运输权法律问题研究
马得懿　著

出　　版　上海人民出版社
　　　　　　(201101　上海市闵行区号景路 159 弄 C 座)
发　　行　上海人民出版社发行中心
印　　刷　上海商务联西印刷有限公司
开　　本　720×1000　1/16
印　　张　18
插　　页　2
字　　数　246,000
版　　次　2023 年 8 月第 1 版
印　　次　2023 年 8 月第 1 次印刷
ISBN 978-7-208-18436-7/D·4169
定　　价　88.00 元

国际法与涉外法治文库

中国参与的"区域"环境治理:以国际法为视角   王 勇 著

涉外法治前沿问题研究   李伟芳 主编

沿海运输权法律问题研究   马得懿 著